Joey Adams'

# COMPLETE ENCYCLOPEDIA OF LAUGHTER

# Joey Adams'
# COMPLETE ENCYCLOPEDIA OF LAUGHTER

Written by
JOEY ADAMS

Compiled by
Robert W. Cabell

DOVE
BOOKS

ISBN 0-7871-0562-7

Printed in the United States of America

Dove Books
8955 Beverly Boulevard
West Hollywood, CA 90048

Distributed by Penguin USA

Text design and layout by Bret Perry
Cover design and layout by Rick Penn-Kraus

# Contents

# Contents

# Contents

# Contents

# Preface

This book is dedicated to three of the greatest men in my life: President John F. Kennedy, Rev. Dr. Martin Luther King, Jr., and Mayor Fiorello La Guardia, who have brought love, laughs, and joy to a troubled world.

It was John F. Kennedy who sent me around the world as his goodwill ambassador for the United States in 1964. Instead of sending troops or bombs to Vietnam, China, Indonesia, and points east, he suggested, "Use a joke instead of a stick."

It was Martin Luther King, Jr., who passed the integration law in my name. At the time, I was president of the American Guild of Variety Artists and I fought against the idea of having designated organizations for black dancers, Jewish singers, or Italian musicians. I believed that they were dancers, singers, or musicians, period, without any other titles. Dr. King and I marched arm in arm down Fifth Avenue in support of the law. People were shouting obscenities and racial slurs at us. After I was hit by an egg, I said to the Reverend, "How do you handle your enemies?" He replied,

"Love the hell out of them." And that became our slogan: "Use a laugh instead of a bomb."

It was former New York mayor Fiorello H. La Guardia who took me in as a little boy and always preached love and laughs. When the newspapers went on strike, he read the funnies to the children over the radio. "Who cares if we don't get the news?" he said. "I want the children to get the laughs and the joy—and the love."

The people of show business like to show their love by roasting their fellow performers. The idea is, if you can't think of anything nice to say about the guy . . . I went to the Friars Club one day and saw Milton Berle sitting with Henny Youngman at the front table. I said, "Hello, Henny. Hello, Milton. Glad to see you," and continued walking to my appointment. I heard Milton say to Henny, "Is Joey mad at me?" Henny answered, "No, why?" Milton said, "He passed me by and didn't louse me up once."

That's the whole idea of this book: Use a joke instead of a stick. Laugh yourself well.

# Joey Adams—America's Goodwill Ambassador

Joey Adams, world-renowned comedian, toastmaster, and star of nightclubs, television, radio, motion pictures, and theater, holds doctorate of comedy degrees from his alma mater, City College of New York, Columbia University, and New York University. He has also received doctorates from Chung Ang University of Korea and Fu-Jen Catholic University of Taiwan. He has established the Joey Adams American Libraries in Korea, Taiwan, Thailand, and points east, and the Joey Adams Toy Libraries in the United States and throughout Asia.

Honored in Israel and by His Holiness the Pope in Rome, Joey Adams has toured the world for the armed forces and has been goodwill ambassador to the troubled areas of the world for three presidents of the United States and represented the State Department in a cultural siege of Southeast Asia, India, and Africa.

He has been distinguished as Man of the Year by the March of Dimes, the police of the city of New York, and the Friars; Trouper of the Year by *Show Business*; and Scout of the Year by the Boy Scouts of America. Mr. Adams has received awards from thousands of charities and philanthropic organizations for his great humanitarian efforts.

He has appeared in the theatrical productions *Guys and Dolls* and *The Gazebo* and has produced and starred in the films *Ringside* and *Singing in the Dark*. He has recorded several Coral Comedy records and two albums, *Cindy and I* with his wife, Cindy Adams, and *Jewish Folk Songs* with Molly Picon and Sholum Secunda for Roulette Records.

He has a daily radio show on WEVD radio and is the author of twenty-five books. His syndicated column, "Strictly for Laughs," appears in dozens of papers coast to coast and abroad, including the *New York Post*.

Among the many bestsellers Mr. Adams has authored are:

*From Gags to Riches*
*It Takes One to Know One*
*Joey Adams' Joke Book*
*Around the World Joke Book*
*Cindy and I*
*On the Road for Uncle Sam*
*The Curtain Never Falls*
*Joey Adams' Joke Dictionary*
*LBJ's Texas Laffs*
*The Swingers*
*Strictly for Laughs*
*Here's to the Friars*
*The Borscht Belt*
*Speaker's Bible of Humor*
*Laugh Your Calories Away*
*The God Bit*
*You Could Die Laughing*
*Joey Adams' Ethnic Humor*

Joey Adams was born in New York and is the protégé and "adopted son" of the late mayor of New York, Fiorello H. La Guardia.

# Forewarned

Anybody can make a speech if he or she is prepared for battle. To attack a roomful of rich men, poor men, beggar men, or even friends, Romans, or countrymen, you've got to be ready. And in this arena words are your weapons.

That's the idea of this book: to arm you with words, jokes, gags, anecdotes, stories, insults, and roasts for when you meet the butcher, the baker, or the candlestick maker, or for a family gathering, a dais of murderers, or an audience of fans. The important thing is that the word fits, and fits you. When Will Rogers was criticized for using the word "ain't," he quipped: "Maybe ain't ain't correct, but I notice a lot of folks who ain't usin' ain't, ain't eatin'."

I'll give you the gems to fit every occasion and I'll pick out the right setting. I'll tell you how and where to tell that joke and how to tailor it to your particular needs. At a Catholic gathering for Paul Cardinal Yu Pin, I said: "I never refuse to do a Catholic benefit. I did once, and it snowed in my living room for five days." And, conversely, when I was master of ceremonies at Greenhaven State Prison, I opened my routine by saying to the inmates: "I really don't care if I'm a hit here. If I do good, you'll want to hold me over."

I'll tell you how to accept the cheers, and I'll set you up with savers when you feel the flop sweat. I'll even give you your own portable gag file. When you're called on to "say a few words" at the roast for the governor, the stag for the star, the lodge meeting, the convention, or the dinner in your honor, I'll have you ready for anything but failure.

This book does not distinguish between amateur and professional. When you are on your feet and the spotlight is on your face, you are the star, whether you're Bob Hope or Irving Schwartz. It doesn't matter if the audience is 20 million on TV or two Jews in a kibbutz. To be the life of the party—for fun or for profit—you've got to be prepared for battle.

A plumber can't work without his tools. Liberace could never go on without his neon jackets. "The only thing that looks good in a brown jacket," said Liberace, "is a baked potato." Sophia Loren never shows up without her props; she doesn't need words. And what would Guy Lombardo do with that stick if his band didn't show up? Now take Engelbert Humperdinck —please. His trousers are so tight they wear out from the inside, but if he wore loose ones they would hide his talent. Even old Hump is ready with words when he faces those female piranhas. One old broad actually threw her bra on stage. "If you'll fill that, lady," he said, "I'll take it home."

When a pro says he is speaking off the cuff, it only means he's got his notes written on his shirt sleeve. Bob Hope uses idiot cards and reads every line prepared for him by his army of writers. Me, I use index cards. I used to write my notes on my cuff but I stopped when I saw my laundry man go on "The Tonight Show" and get laughs, too.

Hope once told me he comes prepared with gags even if he is just going to dinner with friends or on a golf date with one of the presidents. Bob's writers work overtime when he is golfing with presidents. He has golfed with almost every U.S. president in the past fifty years. One of his favorite stories is about golfing with Nixon and Agnew. He got his biggest laugh during one game when he told Nixon, "You should send Agnew into Vietnam with a number three wood." Hope's audience of one howled when he noted that Palm Springs, California, where Agnew hit three tournament fans with wild drives, is now known as Agnew's Fault.

He told Nixon that on one of the vice president's drives, Agnew got a birdie, an elk, a moose, and a mason. Then Bob added, "It's hard to concentrate when the entire gallery is saying the Lord's Prayer." Of course, Hope was already armed with these "ad libs" even though he acted like he was talking without a cuff.

You need to learn how to pause while talking to an audience so as to make them believe that you were thinking of something important, or that some great line had just come to mind, when all along it is something tried and true that you knew would get a laugh. Every speaker has his own way of pausing before the punchline. Sam Levinson laughed before he dropped his funny. Groucho Marx flicked his cigar. The wit glares before he fires his shot; the humorist scratches his head.

Everybody needs practice. Thomas Edison wasn't born with a lightbulb in his mouth. I'm sure Genghis Khan and his bunch didn't win every battle. Even Milton Berle didn't have great delivery when he was born, no matter what his mother told us. My wife, Cindy, is the exception to the rule. She was a great cook when we first got married. She made me toast every morning until she lost the recipe.

In this book I'll supply the material and the examples, but you'll have to practice on your own. Choose a joke that fits and that fits you, and then repeat it to any friend who will listen.

If you don't have a friend, buy a dog. Most men try out their material on their wives. In some cases that's helped them win an audience but lose a wife—which could have been the idea in the first place. George Bernard Shaw was admittedly one of the great storytellers of all time—and he was the first to admit it. Mr. Shaw always used his wife to rehearse his ad libs. A friend who was visiting the famous wit noticed Mrs. Shaw was knitting while her famous husband kept spinning his yarns. The friend asked her, "What are you knitting?" To which Mrs. Shaw replied, "Nothing in particular—it's just that I've heard these stories of his a thousand times, and if I didn't keep my hands busy, I'd strangle him."

I'm not saying it's easy to be a good storyteller. A comedian's job is the toughest of all. His option comes up after every joke. But if you practice over and over again with the taxi driver, the doorman, or your friendly bookie, your option is bound to be picked up, at least for the next gag. Naturally, you can't be a Joey Adams the first time out, but then, neither can I.

I try out all my gags on Cindy, and you know something? Now she tells them better than I do, and I have to fight her for the spotlight. The human brain is a wonderful machine. It starts working the moment you are born and never stops until you stand up to speak in public. That's why you need the notes to tell you where to go—or the audience will.

Of course, you've got to make sure that the material fits the occasion, but more important, it must be tailored to fit you. I remember one big-shot manufacturer who had to make a speech at his company dinner. He hired the best writers to get him ready. When he was introduced that night, he pulled his prepared speech from his pocket and put it on the lectern. "Now before I start my speech," he announced, "I would like to say something."

I recall one candidate who was called on to make a speech. "I was so surprised in getting the nomination," he blurted out, "I almost dropped my acceptance speech." Speeches are like babies: easy to conceive, but hard to deliver unless you've done your homework.

# Prepare for Battle

Laughter has eased the tensions of a troubled world from the days of the court jesters to the age of the wandering minstrels, from the burlesque bananas to the sick comedians and the sicker audiences who laugh at them. That's why I am writing this book: to give you the tools to sustain that laughter, and to show you how, when, and where to use them, for fun and for profit. I'll give you jokes to fit every occasion and every setting. I'll tell you how to tell the jokes and how to tailor them to fit each setting. I'll rehearse you and give you your own portable gag file. I'll show you how to adapt the humor to suit you, and how to personalize your stories. I'll even set you up with "savers" in case the joke dies. In other words, I'll get you ready for everything but failure.

Below, I show you in ten easy steps—or twenty hard ones—how to be the life of the party when you're asked to "say a few words":

1. Be funny. Leave the preaching to the rabbi, priest, or minister. Win your argument with a funny story instead of a sad one.

2. Be prepared. Don't get caught with your gags down and your mouth open without anything to say.

3. Use the joke or the gag that fits and fits you.

4. Practice. Every day on the butcher, the baker, or the candlestick maker's wife.

5. Personalize your stories. Name the characters and the place.

6. Be brief. The mind cannot accept what the seat cannot endure.

7. Laugh at yourself. Use yourself or your family as the butt.

8. to 10. Come in installments.

What's your style? Are you a satirist by instinct? Are you angry? A little peeved maybe? Or are you a natural clown? Don't pick your style off a rack. Be custom-made. Select the material and niche in comedy that suits *you*. Don't pattern yourself after Bob Hope when you're a natural clown. Don't make with the one-liners if you have the flair to do dialect stories.

Whatever you decide to do, don't rush it. Study the comedians on television, and then do plenty of research using the portable gag file I have in this book. If you think you have the talent of a wit, look under Adlai Stevenson or Will Rogers or John F. Kennedy. If it's a gag man you're suited for, look under Bishop or Youngman or Berle and dozens of other comics. Your gag file has jokes, stories, anecdotes, routines, and monologues on every subject and every style. Choose your ammunition and enjoy!

# Choose Your Weapons
## Wit, Humorist, Satirist, or Clown?

In life, no matter what you are trying to peddle, the first thing you must do is sell yourself. It's the same thing in comedy. But in order to sell yourself, you must make sure you know just what it is you are. You must decide what kind of comic you want to be. Are you a wit, humorist, satirist, or clown? These are the basic types. But there are other categories, such as Joan Rivers, who is a great wit. Rodney Dangerfield is a "shrugger;" he doesn't do anything except "shrug" to get a laugh. Johnny Carson is a "personality" who gets a good laugh. And if we were to cross Jay Leno with, say, Roseanne, the result would be . . . David Letterman?

In this era of specialists, you must choose your specialty carefully if you want to be a hit with the public. Nowadays they have doctors who specialize only in right-handed thumbs or palmists who read only knuckles. The parlor or table comic who wears his wife's hat could find himself in enemy territory if he tries to use the same old wheezes in the outside world. You can't always depend on the reaction of your family. But even with them you should know your subject as well as your subjects. Tell Mama a sexy joke and she may throw you out of the house, but tell the same fireball at a stag party and you may bring down the house.

The guys at the office may scream when you deliberately take that pratfall or the pie in the face, even if your maiden aunt doesn't find it amusing. On the other hand, the gang at the house may howl at your family barbs even if the boys at the club don't get it. In other words, you've got to find out first what is funny, and second, what is funny for you. They do not necessarily go together.

Here's a classic example from one of the all-time greats, Ed Wynn. In his funniest sketch, his straight man, wearing a brand-new straw hat, came out to the middle of the stage and told three of Ed's favorite stories while Ed watched from the proscenium. All the man got were polite snickers. He turned to Ed and asked, "What's wrong? When you tell these same stories they get big laughs." "Oh," Ed said, "maybe the audience doesn't think you're funny or the joke is funny." "Well," the straight man asked, "what is funny?" "Damned if I know," Ed replied. Then he walked over, took the straw hat off the man's head, admired it, and asked him if he liked it. "Sure," the man said, "it's expensive . . ." And as he was talking, Ed took out a huge knife and cut the hat to pieces, leaving only the crown, which he gravely put back on the man's head.

Then Ed asked him, "Do you think that's funny?" The reply could be heard in the next town: "No!" Ed pointed to the audience, which had greeted each slice of the hat with a roar, and said, "Look, *they* think it's funny." And while the poor man was still protesting, Ed cut off his tie and dropped it onto the stage. Then he cut off all his coat buttons, and as the unhappy soul grabbed his coat, Ed cut his suspenders. While the man was trying to hold up his pants and the audience was falling out of their seats laughing,

Ed asked: "Do you think *that's* funny?" "No! No!" howled the man. Then Ed pointed to the audience as he walked off and said, "Look, *they do!*"

The point of all this is, first, what's funny for one may not be funny for another, and second, maybe you should stick to being a straight man or a storyteller instead of a clown, or vice versa. Choose your style and choose it well if you want to be the hit of the party. Like the man who went to the Turkish baths, this book will help you find yourself.

Let's define two different styles of comedy.

# The Wit

Wit is the most respected form of comedy. A brilliant wit has always been regarded by his less endowed fellows as an uncrowned king. He is quoted even by his rivals, and his sayings are repeated through the generations like the proverbs from the Bible.

The influence of such men has been great for both good and evil. To be able to seize the words of friend or foe and twist them around to turn the laugh in one's own favor—that's wit. Any character, given time and topic, can, through hard work and research, come up with something that can pass for humor. But only the most brilliant minds can come up against an opponent, one who has undergone basic training in the joke files and is ready to kill, and eliminate him with one cutting line.

Of course, it's very easy to be witty tomorrow after you get a chance to do some research and rehearse your ad libs. If only the attacker could be induced to wait a day or two!

The wit thinks while he's talking, or, even worse, while you're talking. At one party for Elizabeth Taylor, the toastmaster opened the ceremonies by toasting, "Tonight we present the lives and loves of Elizabeth Taylor." Jack E. Leonard interrupted, "Relax, folks—we're gonna be here a long time."

Groucho Marx was sitting in a hotel lobby when an attractive woman approached and asked, "Are you Harpo Marx?" Groucho sizzled, "No, are you?" At one point, a young Winston Churchill was growing a mustache. The young lady who was to be his dinner companion didn't seem to appreciate the future prime minister. "Mr. Churchill," she remarked, "I care for neither your politics nor your mustache." "Don't distress yourself," Churchill replied. "You are not likely to come in contact with either."

A true wit transforms experience into humor. He doesn't tell jokes; he just spins a humorous web of life and expression. But when he catches someone in this web, the laugh is at the other's expense. Some people call Oscar Levant a "sick wit." He spares nobody, including himself. "They asked me to be on 'This Is Your Life,' " he remarked, "but they couldn't find one friend." Levant had a typical Oscar for the sweet singer Dinah Shore. "I can't watch her," he said. "I have diabetes."

Henry (acid wouldn't melt in his mouth) Morgan explains Levant away by saying, "People who watch Oscar are like people who stand on street corners waiting for an accident to happen."

A wit's bite can be far worse than a snake's, but he must have people around to watch him needle. Without an audience he is like a bandmaster whose band didn't show up. What's he going to do with the baton?

Fred Allen waited until everybody turned on his radio before he got angry: "If the United States can get along with one vice president, I don't know why NBC needs twenty-six." Will Rogers turned his wit on the entire government: "We are a nation that runs in spite of and not on account of our government. Yep, the U.S. never lost a war or won a conference." President John F. Kennedy used his great wit on all, including his family, friends, foes, the press, and himself. Barry Goldwater is an excellent photographer. The former presidential candidate took a nice picture of Kennedy and sent it to him for an autograph. Kennedy inscribed it: "For Barry Goldwater, whom I urge to follow the career for which he has shown so much talent—photography. From his friend, John Kennedy." At one point, when Kennedy was asked to comment on the press treatment of his administration, he replied: "Well, I'm reading more and enjoying it less." Like the true wit he was, nobody escaped his bite, not even his family: "I see nothing wrong with giving Bobby some legal experience as attorney general before he goes out to practice law."

There is no weapon more feared by man than ridicule, and no wounds take longer to heal than those caused by the tongue. With nothing more than his caustic wit, Will Rogers single-handedly scared more people in Washington than all the house detectives put together. Voltaire was feared more than any other man in Europe because of his cutting tongue. Fred Allen has made many an opponent quake when he was on the attack: "Jack Benny is the only fiddler who makes you feel that the strings would sound better back in the cat."

You don't have to be a college graduate to be a wit. It doesn't matter if you're a prince or a pauper, a straight man or a comic. If you are capable of throwing that one-punch knockout under attack, you have a brilliant mind and, naturally, a brilliant wit. Would you call yourself a wit? Are you the type who gets bugged when the headwaiter sees you standing with just your girlfriend and asks, "How many?" Do you get the urge to purr, "Seventy-eight, please"? If you are sitting in a theater and a friend approaches and asks, "What are you doing here?" do you answer, "I'm hunting tigers"? Or when the switchboard operator sings, "May I ask who is calling?" do you jab back with, "No, you may not!"

Well, if you get a kick out of things like that, you have the makings of a wit.

# The Humorist

The humorist is a storyteller who doesn't let you take yourself too seriously. The world is a better place because these fellows laugh at it on every front. While the wit is more aggressive and destructive, the humorist just pokes fun at the daily happenings as they unfold. The wit wields a sword, but the humorist uses a pen, caricaturing the world as he sees it, for fun rather than abuse. Humorist Herb Shriner comments about his Indiana hometown: "Well, usually it's pretty slow weekdays, but on Saturday we go down and watch 'em give haircuts." Herb likes to talk about his travels. "Of course I've been to Europe. I was there during the war; you know about World War II, don't you? It was in all the papers."

. One of the great humorists of all time was the legendary Mark Twain. He was able to put the world on just by writing the story as he saw it, and we have been laughing ever since. Of course, like all stars, he was never a hero in his own neighborhood. One old crony discounted the glory and fame of his erstwhile school chum: "Shucks," he said, "I knew as many stories as Sam Clemens; he just rit 'em down." In his reporting days, Mark Twain was instructed by an editor never to state anything as a fact that he could not verify from personal knowledge. Sent out to cover an important social event some time later, he turned in this story: "A woman giving the name of Mrs. James Jones, who is reported to be one of the society leaders of the city, is said to have given what is purported to be a party yesterday to a number of alleged ladies. The hostess claims to be the wife of a reputed attorney."

Twain could be as biting as the sharpest wit. About an alleged friend he said: "I admire him, I frankly confess it; and when his time comes I shall buy a piece of the rope for a keepsake." The humorist doesn't care too much if he doesn't get big laughs—just big money. He'll settle for a smile or a chuckle or even a pat on the head, depending on what's in your fist when you're patting him. He is not as bitchy as the wit, and he makes use of longer comments rather than the short, hardhitting stabs. The humorist comes prepared with categories of jokes or stories, whereas the wit relies on quick thinking to capitalize on the immediate situation. You might be able to spot the humorist as the guy who leaves the room to dig up remarks he can ad-lib later. Then again, he might just be going to the john—or both.

Let me make this clear: A good wit *should* have his material or routines ready when he is called on. His extemporaneous wit will then be the plus factor that makes him stand out from the others. The humorist must also be prepared. Of course, like Mark Twain and Will Rogers, the wit and the humorist are often entwined. Nobody was faster than Rogers as a wit, but he could also paint with words a picture that was always an amusing and often a hysterical caricature of life. "I must tell you about Venice," he said after a trip to Europe. "Say, what a fine swamp that Venice, Italy, turned out to be. I stepped out of the wrong side of a Venice taxicab, and they were three minutes fishing me out. . . . I got seasick crossing an alley."

## Abortion

DOCTOR: This is the fourth time you have been here for an abortion. Is it the same man? PATIENT: Yes, Doctor. Why do you ask? DOCTOR: Well, I know it's none of my business, but why don't you marry him? PATIENT: He doesn't appeal to me.

———

DOCTOR: What do you think of the Abortion Bill? PATIENT: I think we ought to pay it.

———

SHE: How many times have you had to worry about raising money for an abortion? HE: Many more times than you, madam.

## Absent-minded People

"What's Dick's last name?" "Dick who?"

———

The professor mislaid his umbrella and went from store to store looking for it. When he finally found it, he was jubilant. "You are the only honest shopkeeper in town," he told the owner. "All the others denied having it."

———

I was taking a course to improve my memory, but I've forgotten where the school is.

———

He was so absent-minded, he parked his car in front of the loan company.

———

The executive was so absent-minded, he took his wife to dinner instead of his secretary.

———

SECRETARY: Your husband is so absent-minded that last night I had to keep reminding him that he's married to you and not to me.

———

How absent-minded can you get? The waitress kissed her boyfriend good night and then said, "Is that all, sir?"

———

An elephant never forgets—but then, what has he got to remember?

———

He threw his cigar out the window and forgot to let go.

———

He cut his finger and forgot to bleed.

———

A man was lying in the gutter in his pajamas. He explained to the cop, "As far as I can remember it, my wife and I were sleeping in bed when there was a knock on the door. My wife said, 'Good heavens—it's my husband,' and the first thing you know, I jumped out the window."

———

The absent-minded auto mechanic was out on a motorboat when the engine stalled, and he got out to get under the boat and fix it.

———

I once suffered from senility, but I've forgotten about it.

———

The executive was so absent-minded, he had his mail sent to the golf course and played with his secretary all day.

———

A man I know was traveling by train. The conductor came and asked for his ticket. The man searched his pockets but couldn't find it. The conductor, who knew him, saw that he was upset and said, "Don't worry, please. You send it to me when you find it." The man replied, "Oh, that's not the problem. I want to know where I'm going!"

———

The TV star did all his shows by using TelePrompTers. Even at his own wedding ceremony he had to use cue cards.

———

"What's that string tied to your finger for?" "To remind me to mail a letter." "Did you mail it?" "I forgot to write it."

———

I used to be very absent-minded. So I hit on an idea by which I could cure myself. One night, before I went to bed, I took a piece of paper and a pencil and wrote, "Coat in the closet, hat on the rack, tie in the bureau, pants on the chair, and shoes and stockings on the floor." Then I went to sleep. The next morning when I got up, I checked each item on the paper and, sure enough, everything was just where I had put it: my shoes and socks on the floor, my pants on the chair, my tie on the bureau, my hat on the rack, and my coat in the closet. Then I looked in the bed and whatta ya know? I'm not there.

A man in a restaurant absent-mindedly started off with someone else's umbrella, and when the owner, a matronly lady, jumped up to make a scene, the man apologized profusely and returned it. Later that day he stopped at a repair shop to pick up three umbrellas he had left there. Walking out of the store with his three umbrellas, he ran smack into the lady from the restaurant. She eyed him coldly and sneered, "I see you've done pretty good for yourself today."

---

MAN ON THE STREET: Why did you put your hand in my pocket? PICK-POCKET: Beg your pardon, sir, I am so absent-minded. I used to have a pair of pants just like those you are wearing.

---

And how about the professor who kissed his students good-bye and then went home and gave his wife an examination?

---

Everyone in town knew Grandpa was getting a little forgetful, so Grandma wasn't surprised when he came home announcing that he had lost his umbrella. "When did you first miss it?" she asked. "Just this minute," he replied. "The rain stopped and when I reached up to close it, it was gone!"

---

AL: My wife has the worst memory in the world. JACK: Forgets everything? AL: No, she remembers everything.

---

HUSBAND: I saw the doctor today about my loss of memory. WIFE: What did he do? HUSBAND: He made me pay him in advance.

---

HE: I know I proposed to you last night, but I can't remember whether you accepted or not. SHE: Well, that explains it. I know I said no to somebody last night, but I couldn't remember to whom.

---

"That Charlie is really getting absent-minded. Last night he kissed a woman by mistake." "You mean he thought it was his wife?" "I mean it *was* his wife."

---

He was so absent-minded that he poured ketchup on his shoelaces and tied knots in his spaghetti.

---

NURSE: The doctor's here. PATIENT: Tell him I can't see him, I'm sick.

---

The absent-minded professor dictated to his dog—then tried to give his stenographer a bath.

---

An absent-minded girl fiddler kissed her violin good night and took her beau to bed with her.

_____

He's so absent-minded, he complained to his wife that his secretary doesn't understand him.

_____

An absent-minded idiot stopped his girl and went too far with his car.

_____

In the middle of the movie the wife let out a shriek and said, "Geez! I forgot to turn off the iron."

"Pipe down," the husband calmed her. "It won't burn too long. I forgot to turn off the faucet in the bathtub."

## Accidents

_(see also Automobiles, Cars, Driving, Traffic)_

He fell out of the window feet first. His widow collected the insurance, as well as the federal, state, and Social Security benefits. But then came the lawyers, relatives, government deductions, bills, inheritance tax, and so forth. When the doctor came to see her, she was a wreck. "Sometimes," she cried, "I almost wish my husband hadn't fallen out of the window."

_____

The woman driver hit the little man. He was knocked twelve feet in the air— then the cop arrested him for leaving the scene of the crime.

_____

They say that 97 percent of accidents are in the kitchen. I figure my wife cooked quite a few of them.

_____

Comedian Pat Cooper says his wife worries about accidents. The other day she put a safety mat in the birdbath.

_____

The Seventh Avenue manufacturer was hit by a car while crossing the street. As he lay on the ground in pain, a little old lady put his head in her lap and asked, "Are you comfortable?" He answered through his agony, "I make a living."

_____

My father had a slight accident, but he won't be back at work for a long time—compensation set in.

_____

My brother-in-law was in a bad accident. He threw a cigarette in a manhole and then stepped on it.

_____

"It's a lucky thing for you that your accident happened in front of a doctor's house." "Yeah, but I'm the doctor."

The Scotsman was in a bad accident. He lit a bomb and hated to throw it away.

————

The two assassins were lying in wait for their "hit," who came that way every day at the same time. When he didn't show after two hours, one said to the other, gun in hand: "I can't understand what happened to him. I hope he didn't have an accident."

————

"Ma'am, your husband has just been run over by a steamroller!" "I'm in the tub. Slide him under the door."

————

DOCTOR: What's your name so we can notify your family? ACCIDENT VICTIM: My family knows my name.

————

WIFE: How did you happen to hit that telephone pole? DRUNK: I only hit it in self-defense.

————

"In New York there's a man run over every five minutes." "Somebody ought to tell him—he'll get killed."

————

I don't believe that stuff about breaking mirrors and having seven years of bad luck. My uncle broke a mirror last week, and he was killed in an accident that very same day.

"What happened to you?" "I threw a horseshoe over my shoulder." "So?" "There was a horse nailed to it!"

————

My brother fell down the stairs with two pints of gin and didn't spill a drop—he kept his mouth closed.

————

A woman was hit by a car, but the driver kept going. A hundred yards away the driver stopped and looked back. "Watch out!" he shouted. The woman raised herself up on her elbows and screamed, "What's the matter— are you coming back?"

————

I had a bad accident. I tried to turn the corner—only I was in the middle of the block.

————

He was injured in the football game. He fell off the bench.

————

The policeman rang the doorbell, not knowing how he was going to break the news. The door opened and a woman stood there, gazing anxiously into the officer's eyes.

"I'm sorry to tell you this, Mrs. Murphy," he said, "but your husband's new watch is broken." "All broken?" she exclaimed. "How did it happen?" "A piano fell on him."

————

"My uncle died in the spring and fall." "How could he die in the spring and in the fall?" "Warden pulled the spring, and he died in the fall."

———

I guess the reason why there are less train accidents than auto accidents is because you never hear about the engineer driving with his arm around the fireman.

# Actors

*(see also Critics, Egotists)*

You can always tell an actor by the faraway look that comes into his eyes when the conversation gets away from him.

———

Lionel Barrymore was asked by a reporter if he still found acting as much fun as it used to be. "Look, son," said Barrymore, "I'm seventy-five years old. Nothing is as much fun as it used to be."

———

Two old-time actors met at the Lambs in the early days of TV. "What do you think of the new medium?" one asked. "Great," the other responded, "just great. I can see a whole new field of unemployment opening up."

The great thespian Sir Ralph Richardson once said, "The art of acting consists of keeping people from coughing."

Author George Bernard Shaw once said of an actor: "His trouble is that he is in love with his wife—and an actor can only afford to be in love with himself."

———

Somebody asked a famous actress what it had been like acting with her latest leading man. She answered, "Like acting with a ton of condemned veal."

———

Actor Lou Jacobi happened into a run-down restaurant and spotted a fellow actor sweeping the floor. "I can't understand," Lou cried. "Someone with your talent, working in a joint like this?" "At least," snapped the man, "I don't eat here!"

———

Groucho Marx said, "I have no advice to young struggling actors. To young struggling actresses, my advice is to keep struggling. If you struggle long enough, you will never get in trouble, and if you never get in trouble, you will never be much of an actress."

———

The difference between an actor and a civilian: When a civilian's house burns down, he calls his insurance agent; when an actor's house burns down, he calls his press agent.

"How could you stand up in court and say you're the greatest living actor of all time?" the agent asked his client. The ham pulled himself up to his full five-foot-two height. "I was under oath. I didn't want to commit perjury."

***

The famous Jewish star entertained many young ladies in his dressing room. One day the star handed a girl a pass for his performance that night. "But," she pleaded, "I'm hungry. I need bread!" "If you want bread," he emoted, "make love to a baker. I'm an actor. I give passes."

***

The first film made by Alfred Lunt and Lynn Fontanne, entitled *The Guardsman,* was good, but being perfectionists, they were unsatisfied. Miss Fontanne was the first to view the film's rushes, and she sped back to their suite, where her husband was waiting. She burst into tears.

"Alfred, Alfred!" she cried. "We're ruined! I've seen the rushes. You photograph without lips and I come out old and haggard and ugly and my tongue is thick and I lisp and I stumble around ungratefully. I look like I forgot my lines and my feet are big and my clothes look like a sack on me!" She stopped, overwhelmed by sobs. In the silence that ensued, Mr. Lunt muttered, "No lips, eh?"

***

"An actor has three salaries: the one he thinks he ought to get, the one he really gets, and the one he tells the income tax collector he gets."—Morey Amsterdam

***

Entertainer Emil Cohen swears a lady came up to him at the end of a performance and asked if she could get a script of his act. "Is it printed anywhere? Can I buy a copy?" He said, "I'm not that well known. Mine will probably be published posthumously." She said, "Oh, that's wonderful. I hope it'll be soon."

***

Comic Stanley Myron Handelman says, "I once did a magic act. One night there was only one guy in the audience, and I needed a volunteer. He wouldn't come up because he wanted to see the show."

***

Alfred Hitchcock once quipped, "I never said actors are cattle. I said they should be treated like cattle."

***

Somebody said about the big-headed star, "I hear he's changing his faith." "You mean," asked somebody else, "he no longer believes he's God?"

***

An actress explained her bit part in an off-Broadway play: "I have even less to say than I have to wear."

Lou Jacobi defined an actor as a guy who takes a girl in his arms, looks tenderly into her eyes, and tells her how great he is.

---

She sued him for divorce and named his mirror as co-respondent.

---

John Barrymore said, "One of my chief regrets during my years in the theater is that I couldn't sit in the audience and watch me."

---

Mrs. Patrick Campbell said of actor Basil Rathbone, who played Sherlock Holmes: "He's got a face like two profiles stuck together." And another time she said, "He looks like a folded umbrella taking elocution lessons."

---

A fan club is a group of people who tell an actor he's not alone in the way he feels about himself.

---

I was crazy about this girl, but her father said, "I'll never let my daughter marry an actor." I countered, "At least come and see my show." After the performance I ran to see her old man. "You can marry my daughter," he announced. "You're not an actor."

---

One small-time producer was interviewing girls for the lead in an off-Broadway extravanonsense! This gorgeous fugitive from Hollywood caught his eye. "You're just right," he told her. "Right face, right voice, right coloring—just what the script calls for. By the way, what's your salary?" The girl replied, "Twelve hundred a week!" He said, "Sorry, you're too tall!"

---

Actors aren't people, although there are plenty of people who are actors. I love them for their illusions just as much as I love them for their talents, their exaggerations, their persistency, their guts, and their faith in God and themselves. And I know in this case they'll forgive me for giving God top billing.

---

An actor is a man who tries to be everything but himself.

---

A true actor will never find anyone who can give him the love and devotion that he gives himself. That's why we have fan clubs.

---

Actors never give up. Two old thespians in their mid-eighties were sitting at the Actor's Retirement Home, bragging about their next starring roles. During a pause in their boasting, one turned to the other and said, "Hey, I forgot. Was it you or your brother who died last year?"

Ed Wynn decided to leave home at the age of fifteen and join a theater company. His father was furious. "A son of mine on the stage?" he boomed. "It's a disgrace. What if the neighbors find out?" The comic-to-be said, "I'll change my name." The old man yelled, "Change your name? What if you're a success? How will the neighbors know you're my son?"

———

This ham was bragging that all his fan mail kept five secretaries busy. "It sure does," said his press pal. "They're busy writing it."

———

The only thing an actor fears more than losing his mind is regaining it.

———

A celebrity works all his life to become famous, then goes around in dark glasses so nobody will know who he is.

———

She was the wife of a third-rate actor. When she announced she was going to have his baby, his agent said, "I hope you have a better delivery than your husband."

———

"I can't leave the theater," he told his wife. "I'm married to it." She snapped, "Then why not sue it for nonsupport?"

———

A reporter once asked the aging actor-lothario, who was playing Hamlet at the Barrymore Theater, "In your opinion, did Shakespeare intend that Hamlet was making it with Ophelia?" The actor answered, "I'm not sure, but I frequently do."

———

An actor was sitting with a playwright on the opening night of the playwright's show. "What's with all the booing?" the actor asked the writer. "There's some clapping," the author noted. "Don't fool yourself," the actor said. "That's for the booing."

———

The best actors at the Tony Awards ceremonies are the good losers.

———

The overweight actress claimed all her weight was just water. One critic wrote, "It's true. On the right side she's got the Atlantic Ocean, on the left, the Pacific, and in the rear, the Dead Sea."

———

I'm going to watch the Academy Awards whether I need the sleep or not. It's what they call escapist entertainment: Before it's over, you want to escape.

———

I don't know why they hold the Academy Awards ceremonies in Los Angeles. The best acting is done in Washington.

I know one actor who has such an ego, he brings his makeup man when he goes for his passport photos.

———————

One star had an alias, an unlisted phone number, a cable address, and a Swiss bank account. When his agent finally got a job for him, he couldn't find him.

———————

Scientists have just constructed a new clock that will lose only one second per five million years—but the Academy Awards ceremonies will still run two hours overtime.

———————

"The actor's style would have been great in 1923. Unfortunately he wasn't able to get a 1923 audience."—Garson Kanin.

———————

The bum approached the Shakespearean actor and begged for a quarter for something to eat. The disciple of the bard looked down at him and in his full Shakespearean manner said, "Young man, 'neither a lender nor a borrower be'—William Shakespeare." The bum looked up and said, "'Screw you'—Tennessee Williams."

———————

The actor complained that his home was filled with his wife's relatives: "My house looks so much like a hotel, last night I caught myself stealing my own towels."

"Please, doctor," the ham actor pleaded to the psychiatrist, "I'm developing a terrible inferiority complex. I'm beginning to think that there are other people as good as me."

———————

He's always me-deep in conversation.

———————

The great actor was known for his many romances coast to coast. He was faced with many claimants to his paternity through the years. One day in his dressing room, a young man entered and introduced himself. "I'm your son," he said. The Great One looked intently at the youth for a moment. "So you are!" he exclaimed. Then he turned to his valet and said, "Give the boy a pass."

———————

Did you hear about the ham actor who died and was buried in a curved casket so it would look like he was taking a bow?

———————

An unemployed actor applied for a Santa Claus job at a large midtown department store. He told the interviewer that he had experience working two winters in the largest department store in Brooklyn. The interviewer said, "Well, that would be fine for an off-Broadway store, but we're looking for Broadway experience."

"What's with the ten bouquets of flowers?" the actress shouted on her opening night. "That's wonderful!" the manager said gleefully. "What's wonderful?" she snapped back. "I paid for fifteen!"

———

"I'm not conceited," insisted the actor, "although God knows I have every reason to be."

———

An actor is a guy who if you ain't talking about him, ain't listening.

———

Actors don't like to get up in the morning. But they'll stay up all night and all day if they can help some person they've never met to live an extra day by their devoted deeds.

———

Actors like to laugh a lot and cry a lot and sleep a lot and make a lot of money so they can pay a lot of taxes and brag about it.

———

Actors were the originators of the credo of blood, sweat, and tears. They give blood to the Red Cross. They sweat to make the Big Time. They shed tears when one performance out of a thousand dies a dud.

———

Actors wear toupees but not spectacles, elevated heels under flat feet, dress suits with torn shorts and holey socks.

———

Actors love to play death scenes. At funerals they try to upstage the corpse and steal the final bow.

———

Actors would rather have a front chaise longue at Danny's or Toots Shor's than a seat on the Stock Exchange.

———

An actor would rather have his caricature hanging above the pantry wagon at Sardi's than his portrait hanging in the Metropolitan Museum of Art.

———

An actor prefers his name in electric lights rather than on bank books.

———

His scrapbook is a dramatic demonstration of the power of a free press. To bulk it up, he even pastes in the sour notices.

———

The actor had a miracle drug long before miracle drugs ever existed—he called it flattery.

———

An actor is always on the go. He likes to sign up for a Broadway play, hoping it's a hit so he can complain he's weary of working in the city.

An actor likes to go on the road so he can complain he misses Broadway.

———

An actor likes to make a movie so he can complain about Hollywood.

———

An actor likes any job where he can make a buck or make a pass at a pretty lass.

———

An actor falls in love at first sight, marries at second sight, and then falls out of sight forever. An actor is a motor gypsy. He can be led and bled, used and abused, kicked and caressed and always comes up smiling.

———

An actor is the first to sign a loyalty oath—to himself.

———

I love actors. Most of all, I love the kind of humor that runs in their funny bones. An odd kind, a philosophical kind, a wonderful kind, an exclusive kind of humor that proves with every studied ad lib that there's no business like show business, no people like show people . . . It's a tradition that will survive A-bombs, H-bombs, and Z-bombs. The only bomb an actor worries about is the one he may drop at the theater.

Did you hear about the nearsighted Hollywood actor? He bought the Pacific Ocean thinking it was a swimming pool.

———

For years the no-talent actor had been trying to get into a Broadway play, and he was becoming a pest. Finally a kind-hearted producer told him, "Look, I'll give you a one-line part in my next play, but promise me you won't hang around. I don't want you hanging around the theater either. Don't come to rehearsal, just come here the night of the play." Thrilled, the actor went home and rehearsed his part over and over again. In his sleep he was saying, "Hark, I hear the cannons roar." Finally, on the night of the show, he went to the theater and, with great anticipation, got ready to go on. Finally, the stage manager pushed him on stage. He stood there and suddenly the shot of a cannon was heard. The actor turned and said, "What the hell was that?"

———

There was the actor who was so vain that when he opened his refrigerator and the little light went on, he took a bow.

———

At a Hollywood dinner a star actor was given a long, drawn-out introduction telling how great he was. When the actor came out, he said, "After that introduction, I can hardly wait to hear what I have to say."

# Adolescents

*(see also Children, Kids, Babies, Dating)*

MOTHER: Now, Willie, I want you to go in and kiss the new nurse. WILLIE: And get my face slapped like Papa did?

---

TEACHER: Forgotten your pen? What would you call a soldier who went to battle without a gun? PUPIL: I would call him a general.

---

PLUMBER: I've come to fix the old tub in the kitchen. YOUNG SON: Mama, the doctor's here to see the cook.

---

ANNIE: Come in and see our baby. TEACHER: Thank you, but I will wait until your mother is better. ANNIE: You needn't be afraid. It's not catching, teacher.

---

DOG CATCHER: Do your dogs have licenses? SMALL BOY: Yes, sir, they're just covered with them.

---

ANXIOUS MOTHER: But sir, don't you think my boy is trying? MASTER: Yes, madam, your son is the most trying boy in school.

---

TEACHER: Johnny, would you like to go to heaven? JOHNNY: Yes, but Mother told me to come home right after school.

# Advertising

*(see also Business, Signs)*

The ad in the theater paper read: "Wanted: Human Cannonball. Must be able to travel."

---

The stenographer put an ad in the classified section of the paper: "Secretary wants job—no bad habits—willing to learn."

---

Dick Jacobs of the Joseph Jacobs Organization has a great way to convince you of the importance of advertising. "Doing business without advertising," says Dick, "is like winking in the dark at a pretty girl: You know what you are doing but nobody else does."

---

Did you ever notice that the man who writes the bank ads is never the man who makes the loans?

---

You do know that sometimes advertising can give you the wrong idea. One girl I know swears that her living bra bit her.

---

The inventor of Sweet 'n Low tells me he got the idea for his sugar substitute when he asked a neighbor's little girl, "And what will you do, my dear, when you are as big as your mother?" And the kid answered, "Diet!"

The Sweet 'n Low people now have a tonic for fat heads and a pill for fat mouths.

———

American Airlines advertises that they care about you. And they do. They are the cleanest and neatest airline—under each wing they have a deodorant pad.

———

While flying from L.A. to New York on a 747, I was sitting around the piano singing songs and swapping stories with some of the big guys in advertising at American Airlines, Bernal Quiros, Brian Dwyer, and Paul Gold. Naturally, they all came up with flying stories. Bernal Quiros said, "In China, the space program was dealt a terrible blow when, with only minutes to go before take-off, the astronaut ate the fortune cookie that held the flight plan."

———

Brian Dwyer reminded us of the pilot who said, "I have good news and bad news. First the bad news: We're doing 750 miles an hour, 32,000 feet, but we're lost. Now for the good news: We're making very good time."

———

Naturally, I came up with some other good news, bad news bits. The agent called the actor and told him, "I have good news and bad news. First

the good news. We can buy that beautiful estate in Beverly Hills that you like so much for only $380,000. Now the bad news. They want $2,000 in cash as a down payment."

———

Did you hear about the husband and wife who went to see the doctor? After examining the wife the doc told the husband, "I have good news and bad news. First the bad news. Your wife has VD. And now the good news. You didn't give it to her."

———

Paul Gold told us the story of the reporter who went to see one of the big generals at Cape Kennedy to find out how accurate their missiles are. "Well," said the general, "from Cape Kennedy we can hit targets in Miami, Fort Lauderdale, and Tampa." "Can you hit Russian targets?" the reporter wanted to know. "Sure," the general answered. "If they're located in Miami, Fort Lauderdale, or Tampa."

———

Talk about honest advertising. I saw this sign in the window of an antique shop: COME IN AND BUY WHAT YOUR GRANDMOTHER THREW AWAY.

———

Yuban has a reverse-advertising story. They say it costs about a quarter cent more for each cup of coffee. But think of the rich executive who has two secretaries, one for each knee. Imagine the cost of his coffee breaks.

---

Oscar Rose, who sells Yuban on WEVD radio, swears that a bum approached him and asked for twenty and one-fourth cents for a cup of coffee, "because I only drink Yuban," he said.

---

Dick Rettig of Whitehall Laboratories knows the meaning of good public relations. He sells Anacin but he gives you good advice to go with it. "The best way to avoid a cold," he explains, "is to drink water—lots and lots of water. Did you ever see a fish with a cold?"

Dick tells a story that has some kind of moral to it—figure it out for yourself. The lady walked over to the man standing on the corner and asked, "How many cigars do you smoke a day, sir?" "Oh, about twenty, I would say." "Twenty? How much do you spend on them?" "Oh, about fifty or sixty cents apiece." "That's more than ten dollars a day. How long have you been smoking?" "At least twenty-five years." "Ten dollars a day for twenty-five years. You realize how much money that is?" "I guess I do." "Well, do you see that big office building across the street?" "Yes." "Well, if you never smoked a cigar in your life, you might now own that fantastic building." "Do you smoke, madam?" "No, and I never have." "Do you own that building?" "No." "Well, I do."

Harry Riley is the president of Sunshine Biscuits and is proud of the fact that his product is stacked as well as Anna Nicole Smith. Being a brilliant, intelligent, and discerning executive, he hired me to advertise Sunshine on my radio show. Would you say I was sort of a wisecracker for Sunshine Biscuits? Okay, I'll go quietly.

Mr. Riley has always felt that any good product needs a goodwill ambassador. And Harry himself is a master of diplomacy. A widow asked Mr. Sunshine to guess her age, to which he said, "I hesitate to answer, only because I don't know whether to make you ten years younger because of your looks, or ten years older because of your intelligence."

---

One TV station went on the air to say, "Quit smoking and you'll really be able to taste food." I know one man who took the advice. He quit smoking completely. "Now," he said, "I can really taste food—and I find I've been eating a lot of things I don't like."

---

The big business man was complaining, "Advertising costs me a lot of money."

"But," his friend said, "I never see your merchandise advertised." "They aren't—but my wife reads other people's ads."

---

There's one thing in this country I can't figure out: Streets aren't safe, parks aren't safe, and subways aren't safe, but under our arms we have complete protection.

———

"Advertising is 85 percent confusion and 15 percent commission."—Fred Allen

———

Talk about progressive advertising: A department store ad in a local New York paper said, "Maternity dresses—for the modern miss."

———

Advertising sure brings quick results. One day last week I advertised for a night watchman, and that same night my safe was robbed.

———

The manufacturer decided to stop advertising to save money. "You might as well stop your watch to save time," his salesman advised.

———

Wire your Congressman now! Demand they stop defacing our billboards with highways.

———

"Girl needs job—is willing to struggle if given opportunity."

———

An ad in a local paper read: "We do not tear your laundry with machinery—we do it carefully by hand."

———

Here's an amusing ad: "Small boat for sale by widow—with a wide bottom."

———

Sign in the window of a health food store: CLOSED ON ACCOUNT OF SICKNESS.

———

WANTED: a salesgirl—must be respectable—until after Xmas.

———

FOR SALE: Large crystal vase by lady slightly cracked.

———

I saw an ad for a loan company. It said: "Don't borrow from your friends, borrow from us. You'll lose your friends. You'll never lose us."

———

Before there was advertising, a virus used to be known as the flu.

———

Classified ad in newspaper: "For sale: complete set of encyclopedias. Never used. Wife knows everything."

———

"Didn't you advertise for a wife the other day?" "Yes. I got hundreds of replies, and they all said the same thing."

A serious ad in *Mines Magazine:* "Wanted: Man to work on Nuclear Fissionable Isotope Molecular Reactive Counters and Three-Phase Cyclotronic Uranium Photosynthesizers. *No experience necessary.*"

A man was walking down Madison Avenue wearing a blank sandwich board. When I asked him what he was advertising, he said, "Shhh. I'm on a secret mission."

Samson had the right idea about advertising. He took two columns and brought down the house.

The owner of a fish store advertised, "We sell anything that swims." A man came in the next day and demanded Esther Williams.

An advertisement appeared in the paper: "Wanted: Young man with ambition. Must like to travel. Chance for rapid advancement. Write to Cape Canaveral."

## Advice

We would all be more willing to accept good advice if it didn't always interfere with our plans.

Listen, if you can't tell the difference between good and bad advice, then you sure don't need advice.

It's always more blessed to give than to receive—especially if you're a professional boxer.

Never buy an evening gown from a vending machine.

There's an old proverb that goes something like this: If one man calleth thee a donkey, pay him no mind. If more than one man calleth thee a donkey, get thee a saddle.

A woman phoned the Legal Aid Society for some advice. "I want to know if I can get a divorce because of my husband's flat feet," she asked. "Hmm," answered the lawyer cautiously, "I don't think so, unless you can prove his feet are in the wrong flat."

"The only thing to do with good advice is to pass it on. It is never of any use to oneself."—*Oscar Wilde*

An out-of-towner asked a native New Yorker, "How can I get to Carnegie Hall?" The New Yorker replied, "Practice."

One reader wrote me, "I was on Eighth Avenue and a girl asked me, 'Do you want to have some fun?' I said yes. So she sold me a joke book."

———

Be kind to your mother-in-law. Babysitters are expensive.

———

I'd like to help you out. Which way did you come in?

———

Next time you pass my house, pass my house.

———

If you're driving, make sure you have a car.

———

The average bride gets enough advice to last several husbands.

———

The widow told a group of bachelors, "Take it from me: don't get married."

———

Never let a fool kiss you—or a kiss fool you.

———

MAN: I'm in love with a beautiful girl, but she's poor. There's an ugly girl with lots of loot who's in love with me. Shall I marry the rich girl or the poor girl? LONELYHEARTS ADVISER: Marry the rich girl and be good to the poor.

———

Don't marry for money—you can borrow it cheaper.

———

People aren't going to take your advice unless you are a lawyer or a doctor and charge them for it.

———

My niece cried, "I set out to reform my fiancée. I got him to give up smoking, drinking, swearing, and gambling. When I finished with him, he decided I wasn't good enough for him, so he got rid of me."

———

Don't play in the street—you may get that run-down feeling.

———

Don't drop out of school, especially if you're on the third floor.

———

Don't kiss a girl under the mistletoe—it's more fun under the nose.

———

The difference between virtue and vice is that the former is usually learned on Mother's knee, while the latter is learned at some other joint.

## Africa

I was rather disappointed with the pictures I took in Africa of the native women—they weren't very well developed.

They've educated the Ubangis in Africa to work. Some of them now work for the post office sealing envelopes after they're dropped in the mailbox.

———

In Africa the savage tribes pay no taxes. So what makes them savage?

———

A man in Africa had a frightening experience. He lost his guide, wandered into the jungle, and suddenly found himself surrounded by hostile natives. Then he remembered a trick he'd seen in an old movie. He fumbled in his pocket for his cigarette lighter, pulled it out, and flicked it once. A big flame popped up. Then the chief of the natives spoke. "It's a miracle," he said. "I've never seen a lighter that worked the first time."

———

"I once came across a tribe of wild women who had no tongues," the lecturer was saying. "Fascinating," squealed the lady in the first row. "How could they talk?" "They couldn't, ma'am. That's what made them wild."

———

"We all must love each other," the missionary was preaching to the African tribe.
"Moola goola," hollered the natives. "We all must live like brothers," the white man continued. "Moola goola,"
the natives cried out. The missionary told the chief of the tribe that he was pleased with the response. "Thank you for coming," said the chief, "but be careful as you pass my cattle that you don't step in the moola goola."

# Age
*(see also Anniversaries, Birthdays, Children, Juvenile Delinquents, Kids, Old Maids)*

What is 10, 9, 8, 7, 6, 5, 4, 3, 2, 1? Bo Derek getting older.

———

Humorist Dave Barry tells this story: My mother-in-law is a widow. She is eighty-two years old. One night, just to get her out of the house, I arranged a date for her with a man who is eighty-five years old. She returned home from the date very late that evening, more than a little upset. "What happened?" I asked. "Are you kidding?" she snapped. "I had to slap his face three times!" "You mean," I said, "he got fresh?" "No," she replied, "I thought he was dead!"

———

The great actress Marlene Dietrich once said: "I've been asked if a man pushing sixty should continue to exercise in order to maintain his physique. I've always felt that pushing sixty is exercise enough."

Maybe it's true that life begins at forty. But everything else starts to wear out, fall out, or spread out.

---

There are three signs of old age. The first is your loss of memory, the other two I forget.

---

You're getting old when you don't care where your wife goes, just as long as you don't have to go along.

---

I'm at the age now that when I go out with a girl, I can't take yes for an answer.

---

He's so old he doesn't learn history—he remembers it.

---

From birth to age eighteen, a girl needs good parents. From eighteen to thirty-five, she needs a good personality. From fifty-five on, she needs good cash.

---

The ninety-year-old man married the nineteen-year-old girl. They were very happy for three months and then he passed on. It took three days just to wipe the smile off his face. The bride was disconsolate in spite of the fact that he left her $35 million. Her friends tried to make her understand: "You are so young. You have a great life ahead and $35 million to boot. He had to go sooner or later." "You don't understand," she sobbed. "He was the greatest lover. We lived next door to a church, and he used to make love to me by the sound of the church bells— ding . . . dong . . . ding . . . dong. If it wasn't for that damn fire truck, he'd be alive today."

---

Middle age is when work is a lot less fun and fun a lot more work.

---

Statistics show that at the age of seventy there are five women to every man. Isn't that the damnedest time for a guy to get those odds?

---

I must be getting old. I threw out a *Playboy* calendar merely because it was last year's.

---

Did you hear about the beautiful young gal who married an elderly gent worth $85 million and got "Get Will" cards from her friends?

---

She says she just turned thirty, but she must have made a U-turn someplace.

---

You know you're getting on in years when the girls at the office start confiding in you.

———

That Jackie-Ari marriage was something else. Apparently some of those old Greek ruins still work.

———

Middle age is when it takes longer to rest than to get tired.

———

By the time a man is wise enough to watch his step, he's too old to go anywhere.

———

Zsa Zsa Gabor tells about the time her daughter, Francesca Hilton, then fifteen, asked, "Mommy, how old are you?" Replied Zsa Zsa, "I'm twenty-one, darling." Thoughtful pause, then, "Mommy, I have a feeling that someday I may be older than you."

———

Middle age is when you have stopped growing at both ends—and have begun to grow in the middle.

———

Comedian Flip Wilson tells the story of a traveling salesman who was passing through a small hick town in the West when he saw a little old man sitting in a rocking chair on the stoop of his house. The old man looked so contented that the salesman couldn't resist going over and talking to him. "You look as if you don't have a care in the world," the salesman told him. "Is that your formula for a long and happy life?" "Well," replied the little old man, "I smoke six packs of cigarettes a day, and I drink a quart of bourbon every four hours and six cases of beer a week. I never wash and I go out every night." "My goodness," exclaimed the salesman, "that's just great. How old are you?" "Twenty-five," was the reply.

———

He was eighty and she was twenty when they got married. He explained his marriage simply: "I decided it would be better to smell perfume for the remainder of my life than to smell liniment."

———

The film star Marie Dressler said, "It's not how old you are, but how you are old."

———

Of course I'm against sin—I'm against anything that I'm too old to enjoy.

———

A woman never forgets her age—once she decides what it is.

———

Dean Martin left a party in Hollywood explaining, "I have to go home now and burp my girlfriend."

The octogenarian went to the psychiatrist to complain about her husband's impotence.

"And how old is your husband?" the doc asked. "He's ninety," she replied. "When did you first notice his disinterest in you physically?" the doc continued. "Well," she said, "the first time was last night—and again this morning."

———

Did you ever stop to think that even back in the Stone Age, when women wrote down their ages, they were chiseling?

———

WIFE: I don't think I look forty. Do you, darling? HUSBAND: Not now, dear, but you used to.

———

You can stay young forever if you live modestly, get lots of sleep, work hard, pray daily, and lie about your age.

———

When a girl starts calling you sir, about the only thing you have to look forward to is your Social Security.

———

I wouldn't say she's old, but the last time she lit the candles on her birthday cake, it turned into a three-alarm fire.

———

Humorist Harry Hershfield made his first trip to Paris when he was past the Social Security age. He confided to his traveling companion, Max Asnas, that he wished he'd seen it forty years ago. "You mean," Max asked, "when Paris was really Paris?" "No," said Harry, "when Hershfield was really Hershfield."

———

The old man was letting his hands roam over the pretty young thing's body. "What are you doing," the girl asked, "taking a memory course?"

———

The two old gentlemen were sitting in their Fifth Avenue club. "Well," said the younger of the two, "what will we talk about tonight?" "One thing," answered the older one. "Let's not discuss sex. What was, was. I'm at the age now where I only chase girls if it's downhill."

———

A woman has reached middle age when her girdle pinches and the men don't.

———

When a pretty girl smiles at a man of twenty, he looks himself over to see what makes him so attractive. When a pretty young thing smiles at a man of forty, he looks around to see who the handsome fellow behind him is. But when a lady of any age smiles at a man of sixty, he looks down to see what's unzipped.

You've reached the point of no return when you would rather have a banker say yes than a beautiful girl.

---

Now that I have money to burn, my pilot light went out.

---

When a woman is twenty-one she believes in long engagements. When she's forty-one she doesn't even believe in long introductions.

---

He's got young blood, but he keeps it in an old container.

---

He's at the age now when he gets winded playing chess.

---

You know you have reached middle age when you are sitting at home relaxing, the phone rings, and you hope it isn't for you.

---

You know you have reached middle age when weightlifting consists of just standing up.

---

I won't say he's old, but his Social Security number is "z."

---

A man went to see his doctor on his eighty-second birthday and announced he wanted to get married.

"Will I be able to sire an heir?" he asked. The doctor, after examining him, explained, "You're heir-minded but not heir-conditioned."

---

Two octogenarians were sitting in their club. One cracked, "Do you think there's as much lovemaking going on as there used to be?" "Yes, but there's a new bunch doing it," wheezed the other.

---

Kids say everybody has their own bag. Of course, I'm getting to the age when my bag is a hot-water bottle.

---

I realized I had passed the point of no return when my wife told me to pull in my stomach, and I already had.

---

An eighty-two-year-old man married a teenager. For a wedding present, he gave her a do-it-yourself kit.

---

I asked one eighty-nine-year-old gentleman the secret of his long and healthy life. His answer was direct: "I never smoked, drank liquor, or ran around with girls until I was twelve years old."

---

"My grandfather is ninety-five years old and every day he goes horseback riding except during the month of

July." "Why not during July?" "'Cause that's when the man who puts him on is on his vacation."

———◦○◦———

He's been smoking since he was fourteen. Now at ninety he's giving it up. He doesn't want to get the habit.

———◦○◦———

An eighty-five-year-old man was complaining to his friend, "My stenographer is suing me for breach of promise." His friend answered, "At eighty-five, what could you promise her?"

———◦○◦———

He's so old, he gets winded playing chess.

———◦○◦———

The ninety-three-year-old man married the ninety-one-year-old lady. They spent the first three days of their honeymoon just trying to get out of the car.

———◦○◦———

Don't let age bother you—it's all in the mind. Now I'm past fifty, but every morning when I get up I feel like a twenty-year-old, and just my luck, there is never one around.

———◦○◦———

The aging actress was so pleased with the huge birthday cake they wheeled on stage. "The cake is just lovely," she gushed. "Forty candles— forty brilliant candles—one for each year of my exciting life." After a moment of silence, one "friend" spoke up. "Forty? You must have been burning them at both ends."

———◦○◦———

When Charlie got married at the age of eighty-one, his friends were aghast, and when they learned his bride was only nineteen, they exploded. One pal warned him: "Do you realize that sex with a young girl like that at your age could be fatal?" "Well," Charlie answered, "if she dies, she dies. I'll get another one."

———◦○◦———

"There are four ways you can tell when you're getting old," said Harry Hershfield. "First is when you forget names. Second is when you forget places. Third is when you forget to zip up. Fourth is when you forget to zip down."

———◦○◦———

Some women are very loyal. When they reach an age they like, they stick to it.

———◦○◦———

The three stages of man are: Youth, Middle Age, and "You're Looking Fine."

———◦○◦———

Two women were meowing over lunch. "Time separates the best of friends," purred one. "How true," clawed the other. "Twenty-five years ago we were both fourteen. Now I'm thirty-nine and you're twenty-three."

Every woman knows that if she wants to keep her youth, she shouldn't let him go out at night.

———

Middle age is when the narrow waist and the broad mind begin to change places.

———

Most every woman's age is like the speedometer on a used car. You know it's set back, but you don't know how far.

———

The father was reprimanding his son, who didn't want to do his homework: "When Abraham Lincoln was your age, he walked ten miles to school every day and studied by the light of the fire in his log cabin." "So what?" the kid retorted. "When John F. Kennedy was your age, he was president."

———

Nowadays they have respect for old age only if it is bottled.

———

It's easy to find out how old a woman is—just ask her sister-in-law.

———

The best way to tell a woman's age is not to.

———

"How long have you known her?" "Why, I've known her ever since we were the same age."

———

"I hope I look as good as you do when I'm your age." "You did."

———

Her family didn't approve of her marrying me, mostly because of the difference in our ages. She was nineteen and I was poor.

———

Even though Mr. Goldberg was sixty-five, he still loved to chase after young girls. A neighbor brought this to Mrs. Goldberg's attention and asked her what she was doing about it. "Who cares? Let him chase girls," she said. "Dogs chase cars, but when they catch them, they can't drive them."

———

Middle age is that time of life when you can feel bad in the morning without having had fun the night before.

———

"I don't intend to be married until I'm thirty." "Oh, really? I don't intend to be thirty until I'm married!"

———

He had been reading about Frank Sinatra, Xavier Cugat, Cary Grant, and Justice William O. Douglas marrying all the pretty young girls, so the seventy-five-year-old bachelor married a girl of twenty. After the third day of his honeymoon he collapsed, and the doctor was called. "Overweight?" the man asked the doc. "No, overmatched," said the doctor.

A trim-looking octogenarian was asked how he maintained his slim figure. "I get my exercise," he boasted, "acting as a pallbearer for all my friends who exercise."

———

An elderly couple appeared before the judge in divorce court. The judge said to the woman, "How old are you?" "Eighty-six," replied the woman. "And you, sir?" the judge asked the man. "Ninety-two years old," replied the husband. The judge said, "How long have you been married?" "Sixty-six years," said the woman. "And now you want a divorce?" the judge exclaimed. The wife looked at him and said, "Look, Judge, enough is enough."

———

A lonely man was lamenting to his bartender, "It's terrible growing old alone." "But you have your wife," said the bartender. "You don't understand," the man said. "My wife hasn't celebrated a birthday in eight years."

———

He's still a gentleman, but at his age the most he can do is pick up her handkerchief, not the woman.

———

You're only as old as the girls you feel.

———

The best way to cure your wife of anything is to tell her it's caused by advancing age.

———

If you want to get a youthful figure, ask a woman her age.

———

She was born in the year of our Lord only knows.

———

She claims she just turned twenty-three—before she turned it she was thirty-two.

———

She's at the age where any man who looks back, looks good.

———

He doesn't have an enemy in the world—he's outlived them all.

———

He just got a letter from an old-age home and it was marked URGENT.

———

Nothing makes a woman feel older than seeing a bald-headed man who was two grades back of her in school.

———

Getting older? Enjoy it. You know you're getting older when your wife gives up sex for Lent and you don't notice it till Labor Day . . . when you take off your stockings and go to a costume party as a road map . . . when you sink your teeth into a thick, juicy steak—and they stay there . . . when Peter, Paul and Mary sing at your wedding . . . when you have lots of gorgeous antiques—but you got them when they were new.

———

Middle age is when the girl you smile at thinks you are one of her father's friends.

———

The best thing about getting old is that all the things you couldn't have when you were young, you no longer want.

———

Comedienne Phyllis Diller says, "The younger men have better concentration than older men—they don't lose their place during sex."

———

Stop beefing about getting old—just be glad you made it. And enjoy the signs: You know all the answers but nobody asks you the questions, you look forward to a dull evening, and after painting the town red, you have to take a long rest before applying a second coat.

———

The best part of the day is over when the alarm clock goes off.

———

Bob Hope says, "I'm at the age where I'm beginning to wonder if my sex drive was taken over by the Post Office. It sometimes takes me five days to deliver. Bob explains, "Being ninety-two is getting up in the middle of the night as often as Burt Reynolds—but not for the same reason."

———

This Social Security dude got on a very crowded bus on Madison Avenue. A pretty young thing got up and offered him her seat. He was pleased but embarrassed. "How about getting on my lap?" he suggested. She took him up on his offer. After five minutes he said, "Miss, I'm sorry, but you'll have to get off my lap. I'm not as old as I thought I was!"

———

David Brown's advice on dating much younger women: "Don't try too hard, or her kisses may turn into mouth-to-mouth resuscitation."

———

David Brown was at a party, staring at a pretty young lady. She saw him and said, "Why are you undressing me with your eyes?" He answered, "Because I have arthritis in my hands."

———

Girls, you know you're over thirty when you ask him to shave first.

———

A girl's age is her own business. But in her case, she's practically out of business—even her hot flashes are lukewarm.

She's proud of the fact that when she was a child, the Statue of Liberty was a little girl.

————

My neighbor's wife told me, "I've reached the most disappointing period of my life: My husband now trusts me."

————

I won't call her old, but her birthday cake has been declared a fire hazard.

————

She could add years to her life by simply telling the truth.

————

She doesn't object to men who kiss and tell—in fact, at her age she needs all the publicity she can get.

————

Her driver's license is good for covered wagons.

————

Her little black book doesn't have a name in it that doesn't end in M.D.

————

What a lovely couple. They married late in life but they keep trying. She takes vitamins and he takes iron. The trouble is, when she's ready, he's rusty.

————

My friend Milton Berle said to me. "If you want to live to be a hundred, first you've got to make it to ninety-nine, and then for the last year, take it easy." . . . "By the time you learn to read girls like a book, your library card has expired." . . . "Sixty-five is when our sex drive goes into park."

————

These two octogenarians checked into the Plaza on their honeymoon. As soon as they got into bed, he reached out and held her hand. In a little while they fell asleep. The next night he reached for her hand and again they fell asleep. The third night as he reached for her hand, she hollered, "Three nights in a row! What are you, a sex maniac?"

————

So this older guy asks this younger girl, "How about coming up to my hotel suite so we can have a little fun?" Said the girl to this older guy: "Mister, I wouldn't be interested in you for a million dollars." Said the guy to this younger girl: "Well, thank God, at least now we're talking price."

————

You know you're getting older when you are 17 around the neck, 42 around the waist, and 128 around the golf course.

————

The great George Burns bragged, "At my age, my vital juices are prunes. At my age, I'm grateful if a girl says no." I once asked my friend George, "If you had your life to live over again, do you think you would make the same mistakes again?" He smiled and said, "Certainly, but I'd start a lot sooner." George says, "I now read *Playboy* for the same reason I read *National Geographic:* to see places I'll never get to visit." "Middle age," says George, "is when you can't turn the TV set off—or your wife on." One day George was staring at the pretty girl who was auditioning for his play. "Wow," he said, "I'd like to kiss her and hug her and . . . what's that other thing I used to do?"

Actor Anthony Quinn was telling us, "I won't say how old I am, but last week I was in an antique shop and three people tried to buy me."

Actor Ernest Borgnine says, "I knew I was getting older when I took my dog out for a walk and I couldn't keep up with him—so I swapped him for a turtle."

I asked Bob Hope, "You look good. How do you stay so young?" He said, "I have a great makeup crew. They're the same people who restored the Statue of Liberty." Bob explains, "The thing that worries me about temptation at my age is that if I resist it, it may never come again."

Phyllis Diller reports, "Age creeps up on a woman, especially when she marries an older man."

Age is a matter of mind: If you don't mind, it really doesn't matter.

Believe it or not, sex with a younger man is not all a bed of roses. There are some drawbacks. For example, he may expect you to respond.

You know you're getting old when you pay for sex and get a refund.

My cousin claims: "Your whole life turns around when you hit middle age. You start to eat and you feel sexy; you go to bed and you feel hungry. By the time a man is able to read a woman like a book, his eyes go bad."

You know you getting old when:
Your wife wakes up feeling amorous, and you have a headache.
Your sex drive is in park.
You bend down to tie your shoe and you try to think of other things to do while you're down there.
Heartburn is more frequent than heartache.

Your friends who accuse you of robbing the cradle are more jealous than shocked.

Whether you're desired for your money or your looks becomes less of an issue.

There's less of a mad scramble to arrange your face when you wake up next to someone.

———

I know a guy who married an old gal for her money. "Drink makes you look young and gorgeous," he told her. "But I haven't been drinking," she said. "No," he agreed, "but I have."

———

I'm at the age now where I look at *Playboy* through an interpreter.

———

You're so old, even your hairpiece is turning gray.

———

The old guy was boasting at the party: "I'm as good now as I ever was. I can do everything now I could do at thirty." He turned to his wife and said, "Isn't that right, Mildred?" She said, "That's right—which gives you an idea of how pitiful you were at thirty."

———

The big trouble with us is that when we're old enough to know better, we don't want to.

———

Nine out of ten doctors will tell you that sexual activity can lengthen your life. It can also shorten your life. I know one young fellow who was very active physically with this older lady—until her husband shot him.

———

Having sex at eighty-eight isn't the problem. The problem is getting the girl.

———

I'm fortunate to be alive at age ninety. Somebody up there must like me—or somebody up there does *not* want me. Many of my contemporaries who have retired say that without something to do their lives became boring. They say the only time they actually *have* to do anything is when they get up during the night.

———

I won't say he's old, but the picture on his driver's license is by Van Gogh.

———

He looks the same as he did twenty years ago, but so does a dollar bill.

———

He's found the secret of eternal youth: He won't go with girls over twenty even if the price is much higher.

———

He brought his young bride to his Park Avenue home. "Isn't she gorgeous?" he asked his valet. "Could be," the valet answered. "But I do hate to see a man begin a full day's work so very late in the afternoon."

———

I nicknamed my waterbed Lake Placid. Our song was taps.

———

An eighty-year-old man was reading in his hotel room when he heard a knock on the door. He opened the door and a gorgeous girl was standing there. "Did you send for room service?" she inquired. He said, "I don't think so." She said, "I must have the wrong room." The old guy said, "You got the right room—but you're twenty years too late."

———

Middle age is the period of life when one look at a man's checkbook and his waistline reveals the same thing: He's overextended again.

———

You know you're getting old when you go to a drive-in movie and keep the seat belt fastened.

———

Grandpa told me, "I'm at the age where sex is a four-letter word:—H-E-L-P!"

———

"I must be growing old," a man grumbled to his friend. "I can tell by the way people talk to me." "You don't look old," the friend told him. "What do people say?" The man muttered, "They used to ask me, 'Why don't you marry?' Now they ask, 'Why didn't you marry?'"

———

For a man, the most disturbing part of being a grandfather is that he's now sleeping with a grandmother.

———

I don't mind being a senior citizen. I just don't look forward to graduation.

———

The one good thing about old age is that you go through it only once.

———

You know you're old when you have to put tenderizer in your Cream of Wheat.

———

You know you're old when you sit in a rocking chair and you can't get it started.

———

You know you've reached the golden years when:
What you want for your birthday is a hot-water bottle.
You use the stairs to get in and out of a swimming pool.
You believe it is okay for other women to wear a bikini, but not your wife or daughter.

You take a little nap before going to bed at night

On a romantic evening you hope the stars come out and your teeth don't.

You celebrate your fortieth anniversary with hors d'oeuvres, champagne, and oxygen.

———

I'm in favor of senior citizen sex. I'm in favor of anything that's a spectator sport.

———

I asked my grandmother, "Is there as much sex among senior citizens today?" She said, "Probably, because it takes twice as long."

———

I'm at the age now where I find farina spicy.

———

My big nighttime cocktail is prune juice on the rocks.

———

This widow and her elderly boyfriend were alone in her apartment but were having no success in making love. She said, "You can't think of anyone either?"

———

A widow in her late seventies was sitting on a park bench sobbing her heart out. Her friend asked, "What's wrong?" She said, "I have a beautiful house, I just married a young man who loves me and can't do enough for me, and I get love day and night."

"Then why are you crying?" her friend asked. "I forgot where I live."

———

My aunt tells about the widow who moved to Florida and was sitting on the beach when she saw this handsome young man sunning himself. She rushed over to introduce herself: "Are you new here? You look so pale." He replied, "Yes, I've been in prison." She said, "My dear, really? What for?" He said, "I bludgeoned my wife to death." "Oh," she cried joyfully. "You're single!"

———

It's not your age that matters, it's how your matter ages. An old maid is a yes-girl who didn't have a chance to talk. A spinster is a woman who knows all the answers but nobody asks her the questions.

———

The sweet old lady went to the post office to mail a package. She was afraid she didn't put enough stamps on it, so she asked the clerk to weigh it. He told her she used too many stamps. She said, "Oh, dear, I hope it won't go too far."

———

One resident at a senior citizens center recalled: "A lady asked me if I play bridge. I replied no, but I play post office." She said, "Good. Now you go and become a letter that just got lost."

The Social Security agent told the applicant: "Feeling sixty-five isn't good enough. You have to be sixty-five."

---

An elderly man was driving way below the minimum speed limit when a policeman pulled him over to the side of the road. "Do you know why I stopped you?" the cop asked. "Sure do, sonny," the old man said. "I'm the only one you could catch."

---

A little old lady crossed the street against the light and was promptly stopped by a policeman. "Didn't you see that sign up there? It says DON'T WALK!" "Oh, *that* sign," she said. "I thought the bus company had put those up."

---

Old age is in. An archaeologist is the best husband any woman can have: The older she gets, the more interested he is in her.

---

What is age? My first girlfriend was Cleopatra. I'm still interested in romance, although now it's a memory course. I remember when a union man was a supporter of Abraham Lincoln. I'm at the age now where every time I see a girl I used to know—it's her daughter.

---

My brother complained about his loss of physical desire. I explained, "It's not to worry—it's natural at your age." My brother said, "But my neighbor is past ninety and he says he makes love every night." "So," I advised, "why don't you say the same thing?"

---

There are two ways to keep from getting old: Lie about your age and drink while you're driving.

---

A friend was telling me: "It's no fun getting old. Nearly all my friends are gone now. Of course, Andy Marshall is the one I miss most." I asked, "Why is that?" He said, "Because I married his widow."

---

The ten best years of a woman's life come between twenty-eight and thirty.

---

My older sister says she doesn't have wrinkles, she has laugh lines. She must do a lot more laughing at her age.

---

My older sister tells me she has discovered a wonderful way to eliminate wrinkles: When you look in the mirror, take off your glasses.

---

You know you're growing old when a pregnant woman offers you her seat on the bus.

She has a twin brother who is identical except for one minor detail: He's forty-five and she's thirty-five.

———

At last she admitted she was forty, but she didn't say when.

———

You know you're old when:

You don't mind when someone else drives.

You produce a heretofore unheard sound when kneeling or bending.

Your biological urge dwindles into an occasional nudge.

You have an insurance policy actually signed by John Hancock.

Your favorite night spot is a seat in front of the television.

———

How to have a young mind and a healthy body at age ninety: Have a young mind and take a healthy body out to a disco tonight.

———

I once asked Betsy Ross to go dancing with me, but she couldn't. She was busy sewing something at the time.

———

My friend's doctor told him to slow down, so he took a job with the post office.

———

The definition of a dirty old man: A guy who has three daughters and only one bathroom.

A man who correctly guesses a woman's age may be smart, but he's not very bright.

———

A woman starts lying about her age when her face begins telling the truth about it.

———

If you can't afford to touch up your face, touch up the date of birth on your driver's license.

———

You can usually tell when you hit middle age: It starts hitting back.

———

My brother was telling me about his two friends, Irving and Irene, who finally got married after all these years. "Why, how old are they?" I asked. "Well, he's at the age when the only thing he can sink his teeth into is water. She doesn't show her age, but if you look under her makeup it's there." "So what's the problem?" "Well, I'm not sure, but if they waited this long, you'd think they would have held out for a couple of more months. They could have charged the wedding to Medicare."

———

Have you ever noticed that you have to get old before anybody will say you look young?

———

The first hint I got that I was getting older was when I played the slot machine and it came up three prunes.

———

Old age is when a man wakes up tired and lustless.

———

I love it when people say, "You're not getting older, you're getting better." But I have one problem with that: The only thing I seem to be getting better at is getting older.

———

Whatever Mother Nature gave me, Father Time is taking away.

———

My aunt never reveals her age. I told her, "That hat makes you look ten years younger. How old are you?" She said, "Thirty-nine." I said, "I mean without your hat." She admitted she was touching forty. "Touching it?" I squealed. "You're beating the hell out of it." Auntie wouldn't even tell the judge her real age. She told him she was thirty. He said, "You may have trouble proving that." She explained, "You will find it difficult to prove the contrary. The church that had the record of my birth burned down in 1920." My aunt even lies about her dog's age.

———

The ninety-one-year-old tycoon married the eighteen-year-old doll.

She told him he looked like a million and she meant every penny of it. Everybody laughed but the groom. He went to see his doctor and said, "I'm in trouble." The doc said, "Sure, you're ninety-one and she's eighteen." He said, "No, it's not that. My romance is great, but after I make love to her, I can't remember her name."

———

My neighbor admits, "I'm at the time of life when a woman buys herself a see-through nightgown and then can't find anybody who can still see through one."

———

I see nothing wrong with an older woman marrying a younger doctor. Lots of women put their men through medical school, but a teething ring instead of a stethoscope? And operating with surgical mittens?

———

Woman, forty-six, married designer, twenty. She wore formal clothes and he wore Pampers. The wedding was held in the afternoon because his mother wouldn't let him stay up late. Young? This fellow signed his marriage certificate in crayon.

———

As people become older they tend to become quieter. They have more to keep quiet about.

Childhood is the time when you make funny faces in the mirror. Middle age is the time when the mirror gets even.

———

The eighty-five-year-old man was crying to his friend, "My secretary is suing me for breach of promise." His friend said, "At eighty-five, what could you promise her?"

———

Most of the things I liked to do as a kid are now being done by batteries.

———

The secret to living longer is to fall in love with what you're doing. That way, you can't wait to get out of bed in the morning and get to work—unless you've got someone in bed with you.

———

Growing old means never having to walk into a maternity ward and say you're sorry.

———

He's at the age now that when a girl flirts with him at the movies, she's really after his popcorn.

———

One thing about getting older: All the people you could have married now look like the one you did.

There's a bright side to getting older: You get fewer calls from insurance salesmen.

———

My mother-in-law reports, "Cosmetics are nice, but old Mother Nature always has the last laugh. Careful grooming may make you look twenty years younger, but it still won't fool a flight of stairs."

———

Being nearsighted has its advantages and disadvantages. An advantage is that there seem to be more pretty girls on the street. A disadvantage is that they are usually on the other side of the street.

———

Middle age is when women stop worrying about getting pregnant and men start worrying about looking like they are.

———

Retirement is that part of life when you have twice as much husband and half as much money.

# Agents
*(see also Actors, Hollywood and Beverly Hills)*

An agent watched an act where a guy was shot out of a cannon and was propelled a hundred feet in the air. As he came down, he played a violin solo in midair. After he landed, he approached the agent. "Well?" he said proudly. "Well," the agent commented, "a Jascha Heifetz you're not."

———

When the agent died, all the people in show business were approached to contribute to his funeral. One actor approached comic Jack Zero who hated all 10 percenters. "Will you give me five dollars to bury this agent?" the actor asked. Jack scowled, "Here's ten dollars. Bury two agents."

———

A tired-looking actor marched into a vaudeville house with a kangaroo and asked for a job. "A job?" the booker asked. "What does the kangaroo do? Can he sing, dance, tell funny stories?" "He doesn't do anything," the actor replied. "Then why did you bring him here?" queried the booker. To which the actor said, "I had to. He's my agent."

———

A small-time nightclub act was in a plane crash and found himself in a strange place. "Where am I?" he asked a man standing near him. "You're in hell!" the man said. "That's my agent for you," sighed the comic, "still booking me in these crappy joints."

———

I give my agent 10 percent of my unemployment checks: After all, this is one situation he is responsible for.

I got a great agent. He books me in Miami during the summer, Boston during Holy Week, Alaska during the winter, and Vegas during the atom bomb tests.

———

PRODUCER: The girl we're looking for must be five-foot-one. Your client is at least five-foot-nine. AGENT: Have you seen her lately?

———

The agency is only hiring young agents now. Mine is so young, he can't come and see me in nightclubs. His mother won't let him out after dark.

———

The actor pleaded with the agent to at least see his act. "My act is different. Look, I fly." He lifted his arms and flew around the room before landing on the desk. "Okay," said the agent, "so you can imitate birds. What else can you do?"

———

AGENT: If you carry out my instructions to the letter, I'll make a big star out of you. ACTOR: What's the first thing I have to do? AGENT: The first thing is to get an extra cot put in your room so I can move in with you.

———

An actor showed up at a party with a deep tan. "What a wonderful sunburn," the hostess said. "Such a bronze color. How did you get it?" "I have a lousy agent," the actor growled.

———

"Kid," the agent said, "I want to book you when the time is right, not before." "When is that?" "When I get an offer for you."

———

AGENT: Some actor called me a pig—and with the price of pork today, that's a compliment.

———

When the small-time actor came home, his wife grabbed him hysterically and cried, "Darling, your agent was here and he tried to make love to me and forced me to kiss him and ripped off my clothes and beat me." "Hmmmm," mused the actor. "My agent was here, huh? I wonder what he wanted."

———

Her agent went along on her honeymoon. He insisted on 10 percent of everything.

———

The agent listened to the talking dog recite scene after scene from Shakespeare, Truman Capote, and Arthur Miller. Finally the dog's manager asked the agent, "Well, what do you say?"

"Oh," said the agent, "I'm not sure. Let's see her legs."

An agent was discussing an act with a stubborn club owner. "I have an act," said the agent, "who'd be great in your club. He specializes in putting his right arm into a lion's mouth." "That sounds interesting," said the owner. "What's he call himself?" "Lefty," said the agent.

———

Two actors were discussing their agent. One said, "He's so mean, if you kicked him in his heart you'd break your toe."

———

An act walks into the office of an agent who books the jobs in the classy country clubs of Scarsdale. The guy takes his suitcase, opens it, and fifty mice in tuxedos jump out and set up their instruments on top of the suitcase. Guy snaps his fingers, and the little mice play music that sounded like the New York Philharmonic. He snaps his fingers again, and the little mice play a great Lawrence Welk arrangement. Snaps again, and the mice play better than Stan Kenton's jazz band. Then the mice all go back in the suitcase. Guy says to agent, "Well?" Agent says, "I'll see." Guy says, "Whatta ya mean? What's the matter with this act?" Agent says, "Well, they play all right, but the drummer looks too Jewish."

———

# Air Force
*(see also Airplanes, Army)*

My brother was in the Air Force. He brought down five planes. All his own.

———

A sweet young thing gushed to the young captain: "How many successful parachute jumps have you made?" "Oh," said the captain, "they all must be successful."

———

The pretty little doll was quite impressed with the major: "It must be wonderful to be a parachute jumper. I imagine you have had some terrible experiences." "Yes, Miss," the major agreed. "Why, once I came down where there was a sign, KEEP OFF THE GRASS."

———

Congressman flying an Air Force plane: "How will I know if anything goes wrong?" "Oh," said the Captain, "you'll know immediately; our co-pilot will become hysterical."

———

An Air Force major had just been promoted to colonel and gotten a new office. An airman knocked on the door to speak to him. The colonel, wanting to impress the airman, quickly picked up his phone and said, "Yes, General. I thank you, sir. Yes, I'll see you soon," as the man entered. Then, hanging up the phone, he asked, "And what can I do for you, airman?" The airman replied, "I came to install your phone, sir."

Young lady parachutist to Air Force captain making a jump: "This is frightfully slow. Isn't there some way of speeding things up?"

———

A government inspector visiting an airfield inquired about a former student of the corps who had been transferred. "Why did he go into the air service?" he asked. "He was no earthly good," replied a ground crew member.

———

The pilot was flying home after a mission in his plane, which was pretty banged up. He radioed to the air tower and said both his engines were gone and his one wing was falling off. He ended by saying, "Awaiting further orders." The tower voice came back and said, "Repeat after me . . . Our Father, who art in Heaven . . ."

# Airplanes
*(see also Air Force, Hijacking)*

The passengers heard this over the intercom system after their plane had taken off: "Sit back and relax. This plane is entirely automatic. Automatic pilot, automatic food servers, and automatic landing devices. You are perfectly safe. Enjoy your ride. Nothing can go wrong . . . nothing can go wrong . . . nothing can go wrong. . . ."

———

During my plane trip, we lost one engine. Everyone got excited and scared. The man next to me said, "Everybody's panicking. Quick, do something religious." So I took up a collection.

———

Jet planes can already travel faster than sound—and so does a secret if you tell it to my neighbor.

———

"Does anyone on this plane know how to pray?" "I do." "Good. Start praying. The rest of us will use parachutes—we're short one."

———

Those plane schedules are very important—otherwise, how would we know how late we are?

———

The passenger list on one flight across the Atlantic included people of many different nationalities. During the course of the flight, a storm blew up and forced the pilot to lighten the weight of the plane. He asked for volunteers to bail out. A Frenchman arose and yelled, "Vive la France," and jumped out the door. Then an Englishman got up and said, "Long live the Queen," and leaped out. Finally, a Texan arose and shouted, "Remember the Alamo," and pushed a Mexican out the door.

———

Before her first plane ride a little old lady was told that chewing gum would keep her ears from popping during the flight. After landing, she turned to her seat companion and said, "The chewing gum worked fine, but how do I get it out of my ear?"

———

One major trouble with jet planes is that they've put us all in an awful spot. We no longer have any distant relatives.

———

The French airline doesn't show movies, just postcards.

———

PEPPER DAVIS: I'm going to California by train. TONY REESE: Why don't you fly? DAVIS: I think planes are unsafe. REESE: Statistics prove planes are the safest way to travel. DAVIS: I still prefer the train. REESE: Did you hear about the train wreck yesterday? DAVIS: What train wreck? REESE: A train was going down the track at eighty miles an hour when all of a sudden—*CRASH!* DAVIS: What happened? REESE: A plane fell on it!

———

I'm fascinated with those no-frills airlines. On one flight the stewardess announced, "In case of emergency, your oxygen mask will drop down. If not, open the window." On no-frills they charge you for everything. It's the first time I ever saw an oxygen mask with a meter.

Comfort, safety, relaxation? Fly no-frills and get away from all that.

---

I like to watch the searching parties at the airlines. You ought to see this old maid. She's been out at the airport three days, getting frisked. What's amazing is that she doesn't even have a ticket.

---

I'll tell you how intimate the airline search is: One airline got five complaints: two from passengers and three from massage parlors.

---

Where might you find atheists at prayer? In an airport baggage claim area.

---

One airline received this letter: "Gentlemen: May I please suggest that your pilots do not turn on the little light that says 'Fasten Seat Belts,' because every time they do, the ride gets bumpy."

---

One of the commercial airlines recently had a bit of trouble, and the pilot had the chance to show his great courage. When both engines caught fire, he strapped on his parachute and yelled to the passengers, "Don't anybody panic. I'm going for help!"

---

I wasn't surprised at Castro's interest in the 747 in the 1970s. No wonder—it has three more bathrooms than Cuba.

---

El Al is the only airline where you don't have to worry about overweight. You're only in trouble if you're underweight.

---

The airlines sent out letters to all the wives of businessmen who used the special half-fare rates asking how they enjoyed the trip. Thousands of wives replied, "What trip?"

---

With the new jets you can have breakfast in Honolulu, lunch in Tokyo, dinner in Hong Kong, and heartburn in India. The trouble with jet lag is that your timing is always off. Sit down to dinner, you're sexy. Go to bed, you're hungry.

---

Does all lost baggage go to Columbus, Ohio? Columbus is Central Losing. Your misplaced luggage will go there unless Columbus is where you are going. What if you're traveling on an airline that doesn't have any flights to Columbus? Don't worry— your bags will get there anyway.

---

What is the best way to avoid having your baggage lost when traveling by air? Go by bus.

---

Last week the airline luggage handlers were going to go on strike but decided against it—somebody lost the picket signs.

---

Why do they tell you to check in at the gate an hour before departure time? It's for your own good: The sooner you check in, the sooner you will find out about the delay.

---

When can you be reasonably certain of a delay in departure time? When you make your reservations.

---

How can you tell a plane is about to hit turbulence? The stewardess is serving coffee.

---

The last time I flew on one of those no-frills airlines I didn't feel too safe. During the middle of the flight, our pilot came back to the tourist section and proudly showed everybody his new learner's permit.

---

Some airlines are real nasty: They're slashing their fares but figure to get even with passengers by serving larger portions of food!

Boy, talk about a small airline. During an emergency, a little compartment over my seat popped open and a rabbit's foot came out. The stewardess was a midget, and she was serving condensed milk. During a flight to Europe, they handed out fishing poles at dinnertime and flew real low.

---

My brother walked up to the ticket counter and said, "I'd like two chances on your three o'clock flight to Miami."

---

"Ladies and gentlemen," the pilot announced, "the cabin attendants will now begin our food service. Since this is a low-cost, no-frills flight, you are to take only one bite before passing the sandwich along."

## Alaska
*(see also Cold Weather)*

Nobody was happier than I was when Alaska become our forty-ninth state, but I don't intend to go there until it melts.

---

I love God's frozen people, but I get a chill when I open the refrigerator.

---

It was so freezing, I was cold in places I didn't even know I had.

---

In Alaska the penguins were delivering babies instead of the stork.

One Eskimo advertised in the local snowsheet that she was looking for a man with a high fever for a roommate.

---

I worked in a nightclub in Anchorage and I must admit I was a big hit. The only trouble was the audience was a little cold. I talked to one guy for an hour before I realized he was a snowman. Everybody came formal, sporting tuxedos with built-in parkas and patent leather snowshoes. The ringside was reserved for eight: the mayor, his missus, and six huskies.

---

Many young couples are shoving off to Alaska on their honeymoons. They want to have a long first night—and six months is a long night.

---

Just a word or two of warning if you move to Alaska: Make sure there's Prestone in your waterbed. And remember, it's a little tough to start your car in the morning and your wife at night, but you can make a little extra money renting out your bedroom as a meat locker.

---

In Alaska everybody talks about the weather, which isn't easy when your teeth are chattering.

It was so cold I sneezed and broke my Kleenex.

---

It was so cold Superman froze his S off.

---

The man in Alaska was arrested for bigamy. He had a wife in Nome, another in Fairbanks, and still another in Anchorage. The judge screamed at the culprit, "How could you do such a thing?" The guy shrugged. "Fast dog team."

---

She was hollering "Mush," I was hollering "Mush," and while we were mushing, somebody stole our sled.

---

Even the rich still ride sleds. They're not pulled by dogs, though, but by six Corvettes.

---

Alaska is so cold, even the janitors are complaining.

---

So what if I didn't go to Florida this winter? I came back from Alaska with a color—blue.

---

As the bop musician put it: "This country is cool."

---

I couldn't buy a thing in Alaska. My assets were frozen.

———

If there's one thing tougher than selling a Ford to a Texan, it's selling a refrigerator to an Alaskan.

———

If they don't have blankets in Alaska, they cover themselves with ice to keep warm. Four picnickers found themselves away from home with only enough ice for three. The fourth one froze to death.

———

Alaskan women aren't frigid. They're just *cold*.

———

TEXAN: Just tell me one thing that Alaska has that Texas doesn't have more of. ALASKAN: Modesty.

———

It's not that the bus system in Fairbanks is old-fashioned, but it's the first time I ever heard a cross-town bus bark.

———

A snowman was stationed in front of my hotel, and all night long he kept knocking on the door and asking for a hot-water bottle.

———

It is so cold in Alaska that the flashers just hand out 8 x 10 glossies.

# Alcohol
*(see also Booze, Drinking)*

CUSTOMER: I'll take a Dr. Jekyll and Mr. Hyde cocktail. BARTENDER: A Dr. Jekyll and Mr. Hyde cocktail? CUSTOMER: Yeah, one drink and you're another man.

———

He was so drunk that when he came out of the hotel and saw a man with gold braid and medals on his chest, he said, "Will you call me a cab?" The man was offended and said, "How dare you insult me? I'm no doorman, I'm an admiral in the Navy." "All right," corrected the drunk, "call me a boat. I'm in a hurry."

———

"How did you get arrested?" asked a man who had come to bail his pal out of jail. His buddy explained, "Well, my friend told me that if I got home late, I should take off my clothes and shoes and sneak up the stairs quietly." "Well, how could you get arrested doing that?" "When I got upstairs I found it was the elevated station."

———

DRUNK: Has Mike been here? MAN: Oh, yes, he was here about an hour ago. DRUNK: Was I with him?

He was so drunk, he spent all night throwing pennies in the sewer and looking up at the clock on City Hall to see how much he weighed.

---

SHE: Why is it that you're much more affectionate after a few drinks? HE: All I can get to drink is rubbing alcohol.

---

I have an uncle who's such a heavy drinker, at Christmastime we put him by the window because he's more lit up than the Christmas tree.

---

"Your uncle is always drunk. I think he'd get run over crossing the street." "He'll never get run over. He always carries a box marked DYNAMITE and no one ever hits him."

---

They are hard drinkers. In fact, they had their water cut off on Monday and didn't discover it until the following Saturday.

---

"Have a scotch and soda." "No." "Why not?" "Never had one in my life." "Try this and see how it tastes." "Hey, you bum. This is rye."

---

"I fell downstairs with two pints of rye." "Did you spill any?" "No, I kept my mouth closed."

---

"I wish I had my wife back." "Where is she?" "I sold her for a bottle of whiskey." "So you found out that you really love her?" "No, I'm thirsty again."

---

"I found a ten-dollar bill today." "I knew that." "How?" "I smelled it on your breath."

# Alimony
*(see also Divorce)*

Alimony is like pumping gas into another man's car.

---

Alimony is taxation without representation.

---

Alimony has one advantage: A husband no longer has to bring his paycheck home to his wife. He can mail it to her.

---

Marriage is the only business that pays money to one of its partners—after it fails.

---

Alimony is something that enables a woman to profit by her mistakes.

---

When a woman sues for divorce, there's only one thing she wants: everything.

You never realize how short a month is until you pay alimony.

———

Alimony: When two people make a mistake, one of them continues to pay for it.

———

My first husband wants to marry me again, but I suspect he's after the money I married him for.

———

Alimony is like paying off the installments on the car *after* the wreck.

———

Alimony is a man's cash surrender value.

———

I don't believe it either, but one Texan was so rich, he was *ahead* in his alimony payments.

———

He got custody of the kids, she got custody of the money.

———

She's been married five times and gets richer by decrees.

———

There are only two ways to avoid alimony: Stay single or stay married.

———

# America

"The thing that impresses me most about America is the way parents obey their children."—*the Duke of Windsor*

———

In America we produce more food than any other country in the world, and more diets to keep us from eating it.

———

America is still the land of opportunity: Everybody can become a taxpayer.

———

Most Americans I know drive last year's car, wear this year's clothes, and live on next year's earnings.

# Allen, Fred
*(see also Comedians)*

Advertising is 85 percent confusion and 15 percent commission.

———

A vice-president in an advertising agency is a Molehill Man—that's an executive who comes to work at 9 A.M. and finds a molehill on his desk. By 5 P.M. he makes it into a mountain.

———

California is great—if you happen to be an orange.

———

Our great country has one vice president. I can't understand why NBC needs twenty-six.

⁂

He's so anemic, when a mosquito lands on him, all it gets is practice.

⁂

On his fun feud with Jack Benny: Jack Benny ought to pluck the horsehairs out of his bow and return them to the tail of the stallions from which they were taken. He has a ramrod in the back of his vest to keep his spine from drooping. He has to starch his legs so they won't wobble. Muscles? His arm looks like a buggy whip—with fingers. I've seen better looking legs on a bridge table.

⁂

The first time I saw Jack Benny he was doing a monologue on stage at a vaudeville theater in Ohio. He had a pig on stage with him. The pig was there to eat up the stuff the audience threw at him.

## Allen, Woody
*(see also Comedians)*

I went to a psychoanalyst for years and it helped. Now I get rejected by a much better class of girls.

⁂

I don't dig ballet. The last time I went with friends, there was a lot of money bet on the swan to live.

My parents didn't want me. They put a live teddy bear in my crib.

⁂

A woman ran into the drugstore screaming, "My husband took poison by mistake! He's turning blue at home! An antidote—hurry!" But the druggist was Allen Funt, and he kept her there half an hour.

⁂

I was kidnapped as a kid. As soon as my father got the ransom note, he sprang into action. He rented out my room.

⁂

My education was dismal. I went to a series of schools for mentally disturbed teachers.

⁂

I have a lovely gold watch—a family heirloom. My grandfather, on his deathbed, sold it to me.

⁂

My apartment has been robbed so many times that finally, in desperation, I pasted a blue-and-white sticker on the door that said: WE GAVE.

⁂

I was married once, but my wife was very immature. Whenever I was in the bathtub taking a bath, she would come in and sink all my boats.

I made a big mistake the first year of my marriage. I kept trying to put my wife underneath the pedestal.

———

The only reason I wear glasses is for little things, like driving my car—or finding it.

———

I seldom drink. Once I sipped a martini, and I tried to hijack an elevator and fly it to Cuba.

———

My luck is getting worse and worse. The other night, for instance, I was mugged by a Quaker.

## Ambition
*(see also Business)*

Smith, who was out of work, met Jones on the street. "I heard you refused a job as president of the Apex Company!" Jones said. "Yeah," said Smith, "there was no chance for advancement!"

———

"How old are you?" asked the office manager of the job applicant. "Twenty-seven," answered the young man. "Well, what do you expect to be in three years?" "Thirty," the young man replied without hesitation.

———

SON: Dad, what was your ambition when you were a kid? FATHER: To wear long pants. And I got my wish. If there's anybody in this country who wears his pants longer than I do, I'd like to see him.

———

Two college presidents were discussing what they'd like to do when they retired. The first said, "I'd like to be superintendent of an orphan asylum, so I'd never get any letters from parents." The second said, "Well, I've a much better ambition. I want to be warden of a penitentiary. The alumni never come back to visit."

## Amsterdam, Morey
*(see also Comedians)*

An actor has three salaries: the one he thinks he ought to get, the one he really gets, and the one he tells the income tax collector he gets.

———

The reason some chorus boys wear flowers in their lapels is because they can't wear them in their hair.

———

Song title: "I Walked Her Down to the Meadow and She Listened to My Bull."

———

If Noah had forgotten to put two herrings in the ark, half of Far Rockaway would have starved to death years ago.

Things are so tough in Chicago that at Eastertime, instead of bunnies, the little kids use porcupines.

———

I was so sick, the insurance companies wanted me to give back their free blotters.

———

MAN: I love you. GIRL: Hold me in your arms. Not so tight. I haven't eaten in three days. MAN: Then put your arms around me. I ate yesterday.

———

"Did you have a reputation for being a great lover?" "Man, every time I kissed a girl in the cornfield, the corn started popping."

———

"Show me one lovesick man and I'll show you fifty lovesick women." "Say, how long is that offer good?"

———

A chestnut is a guy who's crazy about chests.

———

"Honey, wake up! There are burglars in the kitchen! I think they're eating the biscuits I baked this morning!" "What do we care, as long as they don't die in the house!"

———

A man was having sex with a beautiful young woman. She said, "Kiss me, kiss me." He said, "What are you, crazy? I'm a married man."

———

I was a Boy Scout till I was sixteen. Then I became a Girl Scout.

———

Nothing is entirely wrong. Even a clock that stops is right twice a day.

———

People who live in glass houses might as well answer the doorbell.

———

You wanna lose ten pounds of ugly fat? Cut off your head.

———

Guy went in a drugstore and said, "Gimme some roach powder." Clerk said, "Should I wrap it up?" Guy said, "No, I'll send the roaches down here to eat it."

## Analysis
*(see also Psychology and Psychiatry)*

"Yes," she explained to the analyst, "I'm a virgin, but I'm not a fanatic about it."

———

I realized after four years and $10,000 worth of analysis that if I'd had the $10,000 in the first place, I wouldn't have needed the analysis.

"I went to a psychoanalyst for years and it helped. Now I get rejected by a much better class of girls."—Woody Allen

———

Sam Levinson says his first visit to an analyst was a big letdown. "I was paying him fifty dollars for a ten-minute visit, and all he did was ask me the same question my father used to ask: 'Who do you think you are, anyway?' "

———

The analyst was annoyed with her patient, who said she didn't dream the night before. "Look," she warned her, "if you don't do your homework, I can't help you."

———

I've just learned my husband wants a divorce. I don't know what to think— my analyst is out of town.

———

FIRST ANALYST: A man came to see me last week who thinks he's a taxi-cab. SECOND ANALYST: Are you helping him? FIRST ANALYST: Why should I? He drives me home every night.

## Ancestry
*(see also Age)*

OLD FRIEND: I understand you had your family tree looked up. MR. NEW-LYRICH: Yes, and it cost me five thousand dollars. OLD FRIEND: Quite expensive, wasn't it? MR. NEW-LYRICH: Yes, but it cost only two thousand to have it looked up. The other three thousand was what I paid to have it hushed up.

———

We all spring from animals, but some of us didn't spring far.

———

A kind old lady stopped to speak to a park caretaker who was jabbing scraps of paper with a stick. "Don't you find that work very tiring?" she asked. "Not so very, Mum," the caretaker replied. "You see, I was born to it. My father used to harpoon whales."

## Animals
*(see also Circus, Dogs, Hunting, Zoo)*

"That's a beautiful stuffed lion you've got there. Where did you get him?" "In Africa, when I was on a hunting expedition with my uncle." "What's he stuffed with?" "My uncle."

———

How do porcupines make love? Very carefully.

———

The male porcupine said to the female porcupine, "Of course I want to make love to you again. But I don't think I can take the pain."

———

They crossed a parrot with a boa constrictor. They don't know what they've got, but believe me, when it talks, *they listen.*

How to tell the difference between male and female worms: The female doesn't signal when she turns.

---

The mother turkey was reprimanding her children. "You bad kids," said the gobbler. "If your father could see you now, he'd turn over in his gravy."

---

An impresario was interested in a dancing fly for his new show. A carnival man promised to deliver one. Later he apologized: "I couldn't train that fly to dance. He's got two left wings."

---

When the bottle of scotch broke on the floor, the three little mice lapped it all up. Now they were really blind: "I'm going to find Mike Tyson and knock his brains out," said the first one. The second said, "Just let me at that Arnold Schwarzenegger. I'll annihilate him." The third mouse had his own plans: "You boys do what you want. I'm going upstairs to make love to the cat."

---

The rooster passed by the kitchen window and saw a basket of brightly colored Easter eggs. Then he ran out and beat up the peacock.

---

Two camels were taking a stroll in Cairo. One said to the other, "I don't care what people say. I'm thirsty."

A woman complained that she was having trouble with her prize boxer Chester, who liked to chase automobiles. "Every boxer chases cars," the vet explained. "I know," she said, "but Chester catches them."

---

Did you hear about the whale who fell in love with a submarine? The whale followed the submarine all around the ocean, and every time the submarine shot off a torpedo, the whale passed out cigars.

---

FIRST SHARK: What's that funny two-legged thing that just fell in the water?
SECOND SHARK: I dunno, but I'll bite.

---

Three dogs—an English bulldog, a French poodle, and a Russian wolfhound—were talking. The English bulldog and the French poodle agreed that they loved their respective countries and were content to stay there. The Russian wolfhound said, "I have the best of everything to eat and drink in Russia, but I sure would like to go to America." "How come?" the other two dogs asked. "Well," said the wolfhound, "I'd like to bark once in a while."

---

A very rich lady had an English bulldog who had his own little doghouse complete with little furniture. A neighbor was looking at it one day and asked, "How does he keep it so clean?"

The owner said haughtily, "Oh, he has a French poodle come in once a week."

---

A tiger walked into the bar and the bartender gave him a funny look. "It's okay," said the tiger, "I'm over twenty-one."

---

The goat was at the dump and picked up a can of film. After he ate it all up, his friend asked him, "How was it?" "To tell the truth," he answered, "the book was better."

---

Two monkeys were arguing, and one was putting the other down pretty good. "Don't fool with him," said the third monkey, "he'll make a man out of you."

---

The gambler rode into the dusty little Western town. His poker chums were standing in front of the saloon. One of them asked, "Care for a little stud?" The horse looked at him and said, "Don't mind if I *do*!"

---

One cow said to the other: "Here comes that louse with the icy fingers again."

---

Two fleas were talking. One said, "I'm saving up to buy my own dog."

---

Mama cat was scolding one of her kittens for coming home late, and the kitten said, "Can't I lead one of my own lives?"

---

Two leopards were having dinner. One sat back and sighed contentedly, "Mmmmmm, just hit the right spots."

---

The mother mouse said to her daughter, "Go ahead and marry that rat if you wanna live in a hole the rest of your life."

---

A trout stopped a herring one day and asked pleasantly, "Where's your brother?" To which the herring responded rudely, "What am I? My brother's kipper?"

---

The elephant and the lion were talking. "I fill my trunk with peanuts," the elephant bragged. "Really?" the lion said. "Where do you keep your clothes?"

---

One worm proposed to the other and the answer was, "Are you kidding? I'm your other end!"

---

Two elephants were talking. "I don't care what people say," said one of them. "I can't remember a thing."

Guy went to his psychiatrist and said, "Look, just answer me two questions." Doctor said, "Certainly." Guy said, "One, can I possibly be in love with an elephant?" Doctor said, "Of course not. Now what's the other question?" Guy said, "Where can I sell a rather large engagement ring?"

---

Why do elephants have spots on the bottom of their feet? Because the natives didn't run fast enough.

---

A tiger was prowling through the jungle when he happened to run into a gorgeous hunk of female tigress. "How about a little kiss, baby?" he purred. "Scram," she answered, "you smell from gasoline."

---

One firefly to another: "Give me a push—my battery is dead."

---

So the girl octopus married the boy octopus and they walked down the aisle hand-in-hand, hand-in-hand, hand-in-hand, hand-in-hand, hand-in-hand . . .

---

A skunk family was cornered by a pack of wolves. The mama skunk said to her babies, "Let us spray."

---

A woman called the vet to administer to her sick cat. The animal doctor examined the cat and told the woman the cat was expecting. "That's impossible," said the woman. "She hasn't been near a male cat." Just then a big tomcat walked into the room. "How about him?" asked the doctor. "Don't be silly," said the woman. "That's her brother."

---

The mother scolded her son for pulling the cat's tail. The young boy protested, "I'm not pulling the cat's tail. I'm standing on it, and he's doing the pulling."

---

I wouldn't say it rained hard, but some nut at the zoo was loading the animals onto an ark.

---

Comedian Phil Brito says his wife bought a parrot, but as soon as she brought it home it started to spout a streak of vile language. She took the bird back to the shop. "I don't want this bird. He keeps screaming for whiskey and uses the foulest language." Said the man, "Don't be too critical, lady, just be happy he doesn't gamble."

---

As the caterpillar said to the butterfly, "You'll never get me up in one of those things."

Did you hear about the widowed alligator? His wife is an old bag.

———

Said the male elephant as he watched a female elephant wiggle by: "Wow! A perfect 250 by 250 by 400."

———

This is funnyman Jack Carter's favorite horse story: A man went to a ranch to buy a horse. He pointed at one and said, "My, that's a beautiful pony right there. What kind is it?" "That's a palomino," said the rancher. "Well, I'd like to buy that pony," said the man. The rancher replied, "I gotta tell you, sir, it was owned by a preacher man. If you want the horse to move, you say, 'Good Lord.' If you want the horse to stop, you gotta say 'Amen.'" "Let me try that horse," said the buyer. He mounted and said, "Good Lord." The horse promptly moved out and was soon galloping up into the mountains. The man was yelling, "Good Lord, Good Lord!" and the horse was really moving. Suddenly he was coming up to the edge of a cliff and, panic-stricken, he yelled, "Whoa, whoa!" That didn't work. Then he remembered and said, "Amen." The horse stopped right at the edge of the cliff. Wiping his brow with relief, the man said, "Good Lord."

———

Humorist Ken Friedman says, "I have bad luck with pets. I just bought a centipede and it turns out that it has one hundred cases of athlete's foot."

———

Then there's my parrot. It comes from a tough neighborhood and refuses to talk without an attorney.

———

Actor Lou Jacobi told of the football game in which elephants were playing bugs. In the first half, the elephants beat the bugs 40–0; in the second half, the bugs came back and beat the elephants 85–40. The elephant captain asked the bug captain, "What happened? We were beating you 40–0 and you came back to beat us 85–40?" The bug captain said, "We put a centipede in the second half." The elephant captain asked, "Why didn't you put him in the first half?" The reply was, "Well, he was putting on his shoes."

———

The dog walked into the agent's office and asked for a job. "My God," said the agent, "a talking dog. I'll get rich." His secretary said, "Don't be an idiot. Dogs can't talk." "But I just heard him. He talked." "I told you, dogs can't talk. It's that wiseguy cat of mine. He's a ventriloquist."

———

After retiring, a middle-aged man decided he wanted to be a big game hunter. He bought himself an outfit and went off to Africa. He was not in the jungle fifteen minutes when he saw a man-eating lion. The man got so excited he dropped the gun and ran. The lion gave chase and just as it got ready to pounce, the man fell to his knees and started praying. The lion saw this and fell to its knees also. The man looked up and said, "Are you praying, too?" "Not me," replied the lion contemptuously. "I'm just saying grace before dinner."

———

Two explorers were going through the jungle when a ferocious-looking lion appeared on the path in front of them. "Keep calm," said the first explorer. "Remember what we read in that book on wild animals? If you stand absolutely still and look a lion straight in the eye, he will turn tail and run away." "Fine," said the second explorer. "You've read the book. I've read the book. But has *he* read the book?"

———

The vicar was taking tea with the old lady and was very impressed with her talking parrot.

"But tell me, dear lady," he said, "why does the parrot have a piece of string tied to each leg?" "If you pull the string on the right leg," said the old lady, "he sings 'Onward Christian Soldiers.' And if you pull the other string he sings 'Nearer My God to Thee.'" "What happens," said the vicar, "if you pull both strings at once?" "I fall on my ass, you old fool," said the parrot.

———

The sweet young female oyster had just returned from her first date and was telling several of her oyster girl-friends about it. As she was recounting how striking her oyster date was and how soulfully he looked into her eyes, she suddenly clutched her throat and screamed, "My God—my pearls!"

———

We no longer believe that people can change themselves into animals, yet the world is full of men who make hogs and asses of themselves.

———

A theatrical agent wouldn't listen to the actor who claimed he could do any kind of bird imitation. "At least listen to my act," he begged. The agent said, "Haven't got time for bird imitators. They died with vaudeville." "Okay," the artist said. "If that's how you feel, nuts to you!" And he flew out the window.

———

A lobster strolled into a restaurant and sat down at a table by the window. "What would you like, sir?" the waiter asked. The lobster answered, "A little mayonnaise."

An elephant lumbered into a saloon. "We're not allowed to serve alcohol or fruit to pachyderms," the bartender said. "Who wants intoxicating liquids?" the elephant said. "I just came in for the peanuts!"

---

I had a long talk with the elephant at the circus and cleared up a lot of things:

Why do elephants have trunks? Because they don't have glove compartments.

Why do elephants live in the jungle? Because it's out of the high-rent district.

Why don't many elephants go to college? Few finish high school.

Why aren't elephants allowed on beaches? Because they can't keep their trunks up.

---

The actor walked into the restaurant with his pet terrier. The maitre d' gave them a corner table for two and handed the actor the menu. "Does it look like I'm eating alone?" the star yelled. "Service for two." After coffee and brandy, the waiter brought the check and placed it in front of the actor. "Are you nuts?" he yelled again, throwing the check in front of the dog. "Don't you understand *anything*? I'm his guest."

---

I was in the card room at the club and was surprised to see three men and a dog playing bridge. I stopped to watch and then remarked on the extraordinary performance of the dog. "He's not so smart," the dog's partner said. "Every time he gets a good hand he wags his tail and gives it away."

---

If any animal tells you he can talk, he's lying.

---

I found a donkey with an IQ of 138. He hasn't got a friend in the world because nobody likes a smart ass.

---

My neighbor has a dog and says, "In some ways he's better than a wife. The license is cheaper, he doesn't have in-laws, and he already comes with a fur coat."

---

The rock-'n-roller's dog got loose and ran away from the jam session. He noticed a parking meter by the curb and was about to approach it when a motorist slipped a quarter into the slot. "Man," said the dog. "Dig that crazy pay toilet!"

---

Why does the hummingbird hum? Because he can't remember the words.

---

My cousin and his dog entered the talent agency. Before my cousin could finish his sales pitch, the agent cut him short. "Dog acts are out!" he shouted as he slammed the door on the pair. A moment later the dog burst back in and said indignantly, "At least you gotta admit, you couldn't see my lips move."

———

I used to have a turtle but it passed away. It fell in love with a motorcycle helmet and died of a broken heart.

———

How can you tell when an elephant is about to charge? He takes out his American Express card.

———

Animals are very valuable, especially in a woman's life. She needs four animals: a Jaguar in her garage, a tiger in her bed, a mink in her closet, and a jackass to pay for it all.

———

A father mosquito who supervised a trial flight of his two young sons over the beach in Atlantic City was lecturing: "What a wonderful age we live in. When I was young, the only places you could bite those girls was on the hands and face."

———

My nephew told me, "I don't think animals are so smart. I took my dog to obedience school and I learned to sit and speak two hours before he did."

———

My neighbor rushed into the hospital emergency room: "A dog took a bite out of my leg!" he cried. The nurse said, "Did you put anything on it?" He said, "No, he liked it just the way it was."

———

Two mosquitoes were cruising down the street one day when one said to the other, "Look down there—that drunk's an easy target." The other answered, "You bite him. I'm driving."

———

A dog has so many friends because he wags his tail instead of his tongue.

———

A dog is the only friend you can buy for money.

———

You never realize a dog is man's best friend until you start betting on the horses.

———

Don't misunderstand, animals can talk to each other—you just have to learn their language.

———

Some buffalo were grazing on the open range when a cowboy rode up. He stared at them for a few minutes and then screamed out, "You are such ugly creatures! Your hind legs are longer than your front ones, you have humps on your backs, shaggy hair, beady eyes, and tails with bushes. Ugly! Disgusting!" Then he rode away. "Gee," one buffalo remarked to the others, "I think we just heard a discouraging word!"

---

How much did the psychiatrist charge the elephant? Thirty-five dollars for the visit and $350 for the couch.

---

What do you get when you cross an elephant and a prostitute? A three-quarter-ton pickup.

---

Do animals talk? All I know is, I bought a parrot that was guaranteed to talk. My phone bill tripled.

---

I wanted to teach my parrot to talk. I stood in front of the cage and said, "Hello, pretty boy." But he just looked at me and said, "*No hablo inglés.*" So now he's teaching me Spanish.

---

Animals are not as dumb as people think. For instance, they have no lawyers.

---

A well-known actor comes into a bar with a gorilla and orders two martinis. The bartender says to the actor, "Okay, what can he do, sing? Tell jokes? Dance? Act? What?" The actor replied, "Nothing." The bartender said, "Then why did you bring him into this bar?" The actor said, "He's my agent."

---

The salesman dropped in to see a customer. No one was in the office except a big dog emptying wastebaskets. The salesman thought he was imagining it until the dog looked up and said, "Don't be surprised, Buddy, this is part of my job." The man muttered, "Incredible. I can't believe it. I'm gonna tell that guy what a prize he has in you—an animal that can talk." The dog pleaded, "Please don't. If that bum finds out I can talk, he'll make me answer the phones!"

---

Way out on the prairie, a cowboy fell off his horse and broke his leg. The faithful animal grabbed his master's belt in his teeth and carried him to a safe place under a tree. Then he went for the doctor. A friend later praised the horse's intelligence. The cowboy said, "Hell, what's so smart about him? He came back with the veterinarian."

---

The cowboy asked the vet, "My horse walks normally sometimes, and sometimes he limps. What shall I do?" Said the vet, "The next time he walks normally, sell him."

---

The sheriff of a small town upstate also happened to be the veterinarian. One night the telephone rang and his wife picked up the phone. A hysterical voice pleaded, "Is Doctor Dixie there?" She asked, "Do you want my husband as a veterinarian or a sheriff?" The nervous reply came, "Both. We can't get our bulldog to open his mouth, and there's a burglar in it."

---

I walked by a pet shop the other day, and a sign in the window read, 100 RABBITS FOR SALE. A few days later I walked by the same pet shop, and the sign read, 1,500 RABBITS FOR SALE.

---

If you're thinking of having an animal over for dinner, a cow eats seven times as much as a sheep.

---

My friend brought his sick parrot to the ASPCA. The doctor asked him, "What seems to be wrong?" My friend started to tell him when the parrot interrupted, saying, "Hold on, Buster, I'm not like your stupid cat. I can speak for myself!"

---

A woman went to a pet store to buy a dog. The manager showed her a dachshund. "He's cute," she said, "but his legs are too short." "What do you mean, too short?" exclaimed the manager. "All four of them touch the floor!"

Two dogs met on the street and struck up a conversation. "I'm a mess," said one. "I think I'm headed for a nervous breakdown." "Why don't you see a psychiatrist?" said the other. "I can't. I'm not allowed on the couch."

---

A baby mouse and his mother were walking through a cave. A bat flew by, and the baby looked up and said, "Look Mama, an angel!"

## Anniversaries
*(see also Marriage)*

He was very sentimental. "Today is a very important anniversary," he mused. "William Tell was born nine hundred years ago. When I was a kid, William Tell was my idol. I remember I used to go in the backyard with my best friend. He would put an apple on his head and I would shoot it off. He would have been thirty-four years old tomorrow."

---

Last week my wife and I celebrated our tin anniversary—ten years eating out of cans.

---

She's celebrating the tenth anniversary of her thirty-second birthday.

---

Every anniversary her husband takes a day off—and she takes a year off.

Wedding anniversaries are the rest periods between rounds.

———◦○◦———

Henry Ford, when asked on his fiftieth wedding anniversary to give his formula for a successful married life, replied that it was the same formula he had used to make his automobile so successful: "Stick to one model."

———◦○◦———

Comedian Myron Cohen kills people with the story of the happy couple celebrating their twenty-fifth wedding anniversary at their sumptuous home on Long Island. Everybody was happy—that is, everybody but the husband. He was glum. When his lawyer came in to congratulate him on his silver anniversary, the husband screamed, "You louze! You doidy dug! You bum! Remember when I waz married five years to dot doidy skunk, end I esked you waht would happen if I stick a knife in her, and you said I would get twenty years in jail? Vell, tonight I would have been a free man!"

## Answering Machines

If I call somebody and hear, "This is Charlie. I'm not home now. Please leave a message when you hear the beep," I say, "I know you're not home— I prefer it. I'd rather talk to your machine than to you!" *CLICK!*

———◦○◦———

One woman left this message: "This is Sylvia. I'm not home. If it's important leave your name and a short message when you hear the beep." I said, "Just tell *your* machine to talk to my machine."

———◦○◦———

The man on the phone cried hysterically: "What do you mean this is a recording? *You* phoned *me!*"

———◦○◦———

One secretary answered the phone: "Hello, this is 444-5555. Our answering machine is out of order. This is a real person talking."

———◦○◦———

"Hi! You've reached Fred and Ruth. We're gonna be out of town for a few days. We found that getting away once in a while helps our relationship, so I went to Acapulco and she went to Miami."

———◦○◦———

"Hello, this is Marvin. You won't be able to reach me all weekend because I have a tremendous sex drive—my girl lives a hundred miles away."

———◦○◦———

"Hi! This is Charlie. I'm busy. . . . This is tax time and I'm one of those unlucky guys who got audited. I don't know when I'll be able to return your call. I asked the judge. He said, 'Ten-to-twenty.'"

"Hello! I've gone to visit a friend. I feel sorry for her. She's homely and lonely and has trouble getting dates. The last time I went to see her, she was playing strip solitaire!"

———

"This is your lawyer's office. Sorry I can't come to the phone, I've got a tough case going. This couple had a big fight. When she threatened to leave him, he brought up their wedding vow, 'Until death do us part'—so she shot him."

———

"Hi! The Constitution guarantees free speech, but it doesn't guarantee listeners, so keep it short!"

———

"This is Doctor Dick. I'm out now. Go get an apple."

———

"Sorry I can't talk now—I'm going for a beauty treatment. If I were a building I'd be condemned!"

———

"I'm as forlorn and neglected as Whistler's father. Call me when you hear the . . ." *Beep.*

———

"It's nice to hear from friends, even if you're not mine."

———

"Excuse me if I sound depressed, but I haven't been able to score with any women lately. Even my inflatable doll has a headache."

———

"This is Cliff. If you're calling about the money I owe you, you've got the wrong number."

———

"Hello. You've reached Dial-a-Prayer. Leave your name and number and pray I call you back."

———

"Hello. This is John. I don't know about you, but I'm concerned about the fast-rising traffic statistics. My neighbors are calling me paranoid, but I say you can't be too careful! Anyway, I'm out installing seat belts on my bicycle."

———

"Hello. This is Jane, the girl you met at that wild surprise party eight months ago. Well, in about a month, I'll have another surprise for you."

———

"This is the city zoo. We know where you're hiding out. Are you going to come quietly, or do we bring a net?"

———

"This is the National Charities Advertising Division. Congratulations! You've been named the poster boy for athlete's foot."

"Hello, and congratulations! You've been selected as a member of the city beautification committee. Your job is to keep out of sight!"

―――――

"Hello! This is the Darwin Foundation. We're currently running tests to prove conclusively that man evolved from apes. Several people volunteered your name as a research subject!"

# Antiques

One man's luck is another man's antique.

―――――

An antique is anything that's too old for the poor, but not too old for the rich.

―――――

When the wife came home with her arms loaded with antiques, the husband commented: "I'm amazed to see all the things you would rather have than money."

―――――

One way to get rich is to be able to determine when a piece of junk becomes an antique.

―――――

If you really want trouble, walk into an antique shop and ask, "What's new?"

―――――

To make sure the stuff is authentic, the man in the antique business makes it all himself.

―――――

Two people were in a museum ogling a mummy. On the bottom was marked: 1268 B.C. "What does that number mean?" asked the first. The second, all-knowing, said, "That must be the number of the car that hit him."

―――――

In an antique shop on Third Avenue, the owner was "selling" the pair of early American portraits. "They're really old," he enthused, "they're ancestors." "Whose?" "Be my guest," he answered.

―――――

The witty Pat Henry bought a statue of the Venus de Milo. "I got it cheap," Pat said, "because it was an irregular. It had both arms."

―――――

My friend bought an antique on credit. After three months he received a letter: "I sold you a genuine French desk that goes back to Louis the Fourteenth. If you don't send me the final payment immediately, it goes back to Shapiro's Antique Shop on the Fifteenth."

―――――

If George Washington slept in as many beds as the antique shops claim, no wonder they call him the Father of Our Country.

# Apartments and Landlords

She asked me for the rent three times last week. If she asks me again, I'm going to move.

———

I have a swell room with northern exposure. There's no roof.

———

She's so flat-headed that when she wants to ask me for rent, she just sticks her head under the door.

———

"Of course, Van Buren is a nice place, and my aunt's boarding house is okay for those who like to rough it. She has a roller towel there, and for ten years she's used the same towel.

Why, that towel's had a longer run than *Uncle Tom's Cabin*."

———

It was so cold in my apartment house, even the janitor was complaining. In fact, he came up and banged on the radiator with me.

———

Myron tells me, "I told the manager of my building that the apartment had roaches. He raised my rent for keeping pets."

———

This apartment house was so particular when I was looking for an apartment, they quizzed me longer than the CIA. "Do you have any children? Do you have any dogs?" When I said no to both he continued, "We insist on quiet here. Do you have any canaries or any other pets?" "No," I said, "but I do have a fountain pen that scratches a little."

———

"How much are they asking for your apartment right now?" "About twice a day."

———

TENANT: My roof is leaking and the rain keeps coming in through the broken window, and my floors are flooded. How long is this going to continue? LANDLORD: What the hell are you asking me for? What am I, a weatherman?

———

The landlord insisted he could not carry him any longer. He was six months behind in his rent. "I'll give you just three more days and out you go." "Good," said the tenant. "I'll take the Fourth of July, Labor Day, and Christmas."

———

"I wish I were living back in the Stone Age. Ask me why." "Okay, why?" "Because they used rocks for money, and boy, would I like to pay off my landlord."

———

"Darling," he announced to his wife excitedly, "now we don't have to move to a more expensive apartment. The landlord just raised our rent."

———

Most of the new swank apartment houses don't allow children, and they're very strict, too. In one apartment building on Third Avenue, there's a woman who's so afraid of being evicted, she's in her fifteenth month.

———

The best way to make the landlord paint the apartment is to move out.

———

The landlord ignored all the restrictions, rent laws, and frozen rents and tried to evict the tenant illegally anyway. But the tenant knew the law and answered in writing, short and to the point: "Sir, I remain. Yours truly."

———

The only time we'll get enough heat is when the house burns down.

———

Apartment house: Where the tenant and the landlord are both trying to raise the rent.

———

I tried to get into one of those low-priced housing projects, but the rent was too much.

———

Actress Molly Picon says, "My grandmother raised eleven children in four rooms."

"How did she manage?" she was asked. "Easy. She took in boarders."

The walls of our apartment are so thin, I asked my wife a question and got four different answers. The walls are so thin, when my wife peeled onions the guy next door cried.

———

My landlord bought his niece a doll house and it has two mortgages on it.

———

"Why don't you take your complaint to the landlord?" "That landlord of ours? Why, if we told him the roof leaked he'd charge us extra for shower baths."

———

"That landlady's having plenty of trouble between her husband and the furnace." "What do you mean?" "Every time she watches one the other goes out!"

———

I remember my first apartment. I had just gotten married and carried my wife over the threshold. She saw the apartment. She said, "Don't put me down."

———

Co-operative apartments are the greatest. Where else in the winter can you find the janitor banging on the pipes?

———

Rodney Dangerfield says, "In my apartment building all the tenants have the same pets—cockroaches."

It's a lifetime job in New York to get a decent place to live. I ran into this landlord. "I was passing the building," I told him, "and I saw a guy jump out the window. I figured maybe I could rent his apartment." "No, that's already taken by the guy who pushed him out. What do you do for a living? Oh, you're a writer. Remember, we don't allow loud banging on the typewriter." "I write very softly on a feather cushion." "Gonna have any furniture? Any friends?" "No furniture. I'll live in the closet. No friends, either." "Okay. It's a forty-eight-hour lease. Raise your right hand. Do you take this apartment, 4B, for better and for worse, in sickness and in health . . ."

———

When I moved into my apartment the renting agent told me there was a seven-mile view. I found out there's a seven—mile view . . . if I look up.

———

I was reading about Michelangelo, the Italian painter who spent seven years painting the ceiling of the Sistine Chapel. Seven years to get a ceiling painted? They must have the same landlord I do!

## Arabia
*(see also Egypt)*

In Arabia, I understand that a girl is proposed to by at least a dozen men, who get down on their knees all at one time. Then she chooses one and the rest stay on their knees and wind up the occasion with the damnedest crap game you ever saw.

## Arithmetic

"Here are four apples. Now tell me: How would you divide the four apples among five children?" "I'd make applesauce."

———

"One time I won a prize in arithmetic. The teacher asked us what was 2 x 20 and I said 34." "You know that was wrong; 2 x 20 is 40." "I was closer to it than anyone in the class."

———

"Take thirteen from twenty. What's the difference?" "That's what I say. What's the difference?"

———

"Johnny, if your father earned forty dollars a week and gave your mother half, what would she have?" "Heart failure."

———

"Put two and two together and the result is always what?" "Bridge."

———

"Mum, do you know how to get the cubic contents of a barrel?" "No, ask your father."

———

"If you had five apples and now you have only two apples, what would I have taken?" "An awful chance of getting your eye blacked."

"Find the greatest common denominator." "Great heavens, is that thing lost again?"

# Army

*(see also Air Force)*

I don't know why they call them privates. They eat with five hundred other guys, they sleep with five hundred other guys, and they can't even go to the canteen alone.

———

The Declaration of Independence says, "All men are created equal." Those guys who made that up never saw a bunch of draftees taking their physical.

———

Harvey Stone was the Will Rogers of World War II. He received the Bronze Star, the Purple Heart, and, adds Harvey, "the Purple Head for scheming how to get out."

———

I loved the Army. Where else can you lie around in bed until four o'clock in the morning? The sergeant used to come around every morning, pat us on the head, and say, "Good morning, little man from Armyland. Time to get up, up, up!" Everyone got up, too. Why not? He had a bayonet in his hand! I had the largest vaccination in the Army.

———

The food was great in the Army. My favorite dish was Filet of Sand. Another is Borscht and Alka-Seltzer. You eat it, then you belch in Technicolor.

———

They had signs all over the mess hall that read: FOOD IS AMMUNITION. Why shoot 'em? Get 'em to eat it! Invite 'em to dinner and get 'em all.

———

One of the best things I liked about the Army were the sex films that showed you what *not* to do while on pass. So why go?

———

She had a lot of private affairs until she married the colonel.

———

The general was wounded during a battle. His barber cut him.

———

I wonder what Private Adams did before he joined the Army. Every time he fires a shot, he wipes his fingerprints off the gun.

———

The soldier was asked what kind of cook his wife was. "Figure it out for yourself," he answered. "I'm the only soldier on the base who packs a lunch to go home."

———

That French broad has been contributing to the delinquency of a major.

———

"My uncle has twelve medals. He won them during the war." "He must have been a great sharpshooter." "No, a great crapshooter!"

———

When I was in the Army they used to wake us at four o'clock in the morning. The first thing I used to do is run out and shake a tree. I figured if I'm awake, why should the birds sleep?

———

I was the only guy in the Army who was awarded the Yellow Heart.

———

The chef noticed that the soldier wasn't eating his food. "You shouldn't waste food like that," he scolded. "Don't you know the old saying, 'Food will win the war'?" "It sure would," the private agreed. "Now how do we get the enemy to eat here?"

———

If you believe the saying that old soldiers fade away, try getting into your old Army uniform.

———

The private told his buddies: "This has got to be love at first sight. I've only got an eight-hour pass."

The troop train was passing through the private's hometown. He hadn't seen his wife in six months and the train was making a fifteen-minute stop. He figured he'd run home and say hello. He did, and returned to the train just in time. A buddy saw that he was dripping wet and asked, "What happened?" "My wife was in the tub," he replied.

———

When I was in the Army my outfit was so chicken the chaplain went AWOL.

———

The Army now has a reserve plan which is referred to as the Army Installment Plan. Six months down and you pay for the rest of your life.

———

A private was rushing into the Army PX when he bumped into the colonel and almost knocked him down. "Ooops," said the private, and went on in. The colonel stopped him and said, "Hold it, soldier, don't you see these two eagles on my shoulder?" "No," said the private, "and you wouldn't either if you laid off that PX beer."

———

SHE: What's your rank? HE: Pfc. SHE: What's that? HE: Praying for civilian.

———

SOLDIER: Do you know that ugly sap of an officer standing over there? He's the meanest egg I have ever seen. GIRL: Do you know who I am? I am that officer's daughter. SOLDIER: Do you know who I am? GIRL: No. SOL-DIER: Thank God.

---

Two soldiers went out one night and got well tanked-up on the famed Blacksburg corn. About two hours later, the following conversation ensued: "Has the moon come up yet?" "Naw, but it feels like it's on its way."

---

COMMANDER: Now suppose you are on your post one dark night. Suddenly a person appears from behind and wraps two strong arms around you so that you can't use your rifle. What will you say then? SOLDIER: Let's go, honey.

---

FIRST SOLDIER: I've been a soldier in every part of the world and have never received a scratch. SECOND SOL-DIER: What is this power you have over women?

---

Mose and Sam are digging a trench in France. A shell flies over and bursts. More shells follow. Between the fifth and sixth Mose asks: "Don't you think it's about time we done got religion?" "You suttin'ly is a shiftless boy, Mose," said Sam. "I done got religion when dat fust shell bust."

---

CADET: Look me over, little girl. I'm a big West Pointer. GIRL: I don't care if you're an Irish Setter.

PRIVATE SMITH: Do you like it at this base? PRIVATE BROWN: Yes, it's great. PRIVATE SMITH: You must have a lousy home life.

## Art and Artists

Picasso said it: "The world today doesn't make sense, so why should I paint pictures that do?"

---

There's only one way you can tell when a modern painting is completed: If the paint is dry, it's finished.

---

Trying to figure out abstract art is like trying to follow the plot in a Bowl of alphabet soup.

---

Two five-year-old kids were looking at an abstract painting in the Guggenheim Museum. "Let's get out of here," one said, "before they say we did it."

---

Modern art is what you buy to cover a hole in the wall, and then you find out the hole looks better.

---

I hung the picture because I couldn't locate the artist.

---

People are still buying fake oil paintings. You have to be so careful these days. I saw one guy trying to sell an original Rembrandt. He said it was the only picture Rembrandt ever did in ballpoint.

———

It's very obvious what Picasso is trying to say: He needs cash.

———

He who claims things aren't as bad as they are painted has never seen pop art.

———

All I know about art is if it's on the wall, it's a painting, and if you have to walk around it, it's a sculpture.

———

An art collector spotted an ad in the paper for a Van Gogh for $250. Although he was positive it was a misprint, he rushed over to the address listed in the ad. "It's no mistake," said the lady who had placed the ad. "It's a genuine Van Gogh." The collector quickly made out a check and bought the painting. "I don't get it, lady," he questioned after the sale. "You could get at least a hundred times as much for this picture." "Well," explained the woman, "my husband died two weeks ago and stipulated in his will that the picture was to be sold and the money given to his secretary. And I," she added triumphantly, "am the executor of his will!"

———

"She's as pretty as a picture." "She is?" "Yeah, she's always got the same expression."

ART CRITIC: Are you doing anything in the nude now? ARTIST: Only bathing, sir.

———

As the artist heard his wife coming up the stairs, he quickly said to his model, "Quick, take your clothes off."

———

Art: a collaboration between God and the artists, and the less the artist does, the better.

———

A woman in Greenwich Village looked at a sidewalk painter's wild modern painting and said, "It's frightful." The artist said, "I only paint what I see." The woman replied, "You shouldn't paint when you're in that condition."

———

There's an artist who paints a picture in five days and thinks nothing of it, and neither does anyone else.

———

Most famous artists die in poverty, and the rest live in it.

———

ARTIST: Shall I paint you in a fur coat? MODEL: No, that's okay, just wear your smock.

———

MAN: Do you think you can paint a good portrait of my wife? ARTIST:

Sure, you'll jump every time you look at it.

---

"Honey, I just bought a Rembrandt!" "Oh, you know I don't like sports cars."

---

CRITIC: How do you get such a modernistic, wild effect? ARTIST: I use a model with hiccups.

---

Abstract art gives beautiful meaning to the word *ugly*.

---

I bought a painting in Europe and showed it to a dealer on Madison Avenue. He said, "First the good news: Your painting is a genuine Palagrini, finished during the Renaissance. Now for the bad news: Palagrini was a plumber."

---

The most complete museum I ever visited was the one in Italy where they had two skulls of Christopher Columbus, one when he was a boy and one when he was a man.

---

Michelangelo spent seven years painting the ceiling of the Sistine Chapel, and they couldn't say anything because he was union. He didn't mind the seven years so much; what bugged him was when they asked for a second coat.

A visitor to the modern artist's studio found the great painter staring dejectedly at his latest creation and muttering, "It's a failure." "How can you say that?" protested the visitor. "I think it's a masterpiece." "No," said the artist, "the nose is wrong. It throws the picture out of perspective." "Then why not fix the nose?" asked the visitor. "That's not possible," said the artist. "I can't find it."

---

In Greenwich Village, a couple stopped in front of a shop window of abstract sculpture that was labeled "Art Objects." The man turned to his wife and said, "I can't say I blame art for objecting."

---

No woman is ever satisfied with the way she looks in a painting. "I don't like this at all," the society lady said to the artist. "The last time you painted me, I was gorgeous." He said, "Forgive me, but when I painted that picture I was ten years younger."

---

One lady screamed at an artist: "I look plump in this picture! I expected you to give me a slender appearance." He said, "Madam, I paint, I don't do liposuction."

---

The artist whose Expressionistic paintings sell for $10,000 or more admits, "I need a lot of light to paint.

It's so hard to see those little numbers." When I told the artist his stuff was great but a little too expensive, he told me about his brother: "He's also a painter, but much cheaper—two rooms for $300."

———

After posing all day, she asked the artist, "Well, does it look like me?"

"Hours ago, lady. I'm now improving it."

———

At the art museum, the kid said to his mother, "Look, Mama, this painting—they copied it from the calendar we have in our kitchen."

———

While touring France, a couple from Texas decided to send some gifts to three friends at home. Sauntering into an art gallery, they picked out a Van Gogh, a Rembrandt, and a Picasso. "That'll be $600,000 in American money," the dealer told them. The husband paid him in cash and then turned to his wife. "Now that we've got the cards, let's go get the presents."

———

Mrs. Newlyrich was told to get some culture. She walked into a famous Madison Avenue art gallery. The first painting she saw was by one of the masters. It was a beautiful oil of a bum in ragged clothes sitting on a park bench. "Well," she remarked, "I'll never give those beggars a cent again. He's too broke to buy a decent suit, but he's

got enough money to get his picture painted."

———

As soon as the pretty model comes in, the first thing he draws is the venetian blinds.

———

"Do you draw pictures in the nude?"
"No, I always wear a smock."

———

It's easy to recognize a modern painting. It's the one you can't recognize.

———

Many a time he had to paint on an empty stomach. He couldn't afford a canvas.

———

A modern artist is one who throws paint at the canvas, wipes it off with a cloth, and sells the cloth.

———

A pop artist fell in love with one of his models: a can of soup.

———

I won't have any of those abstract paintings around my house. I have a teenage daughter and you never know for sure whether or not those paintings are decent.

———

A holdup man robbed Picasso and stole some of his paintings. When the police questioned the famous artist, he drew a picture of the thief. "Now," Picasso said, "you'll have no trouble capturing him." With the picture the gendarmes went out and arrested a one-eyed ballet dancer, the Eiffel Tower, and a wheelbarrow.

# Astronauts

There are some people who ask if an astronaut has the qualifications to run for Congress. I don't know why not. After all, he's already been around the world three times at government expense!

———

The astronaut is the second highest Man has been. Dean Martin holds the record.

———

In Russia they let me visit a launching site. I met the astronaut. Through an interpreter I said, "He looks worried. What's he concerned about?" The interpreter said, "The landing. If he makes a mistake, he might come back here."

———

"Did the astronaut come down yet?" "I don't know. I didn't see him go up. I live in the back."

———

Did you hear about the sporty astronaut? When the weather is nice he wants to ride with the top down.

We'll really be in trouble if the astronauts form a union, like the taxi drivers. Imagine having to pay them by the mile.

———

Our astronauts have the latest equipment. Inside the space capsule, they have oxygen masks, pressurized space suits, automatic controls, a safety ejector button, and, in front of the seat, a little paper bag.

———

One astronaut's space suit costs $30,000. And it only comes with one pair of pants.

———

When our first astronaut returned safely from his trip, the other astronauts asked him if he could give them any advice. He said, "The whole secret is, don't look down."

———

Trouble with being an astronaut is it's too seasonal.

———

We send the first girl astronaut to Mars and she returns a year later, pregnant.

———

What's so new about the way astronauts count down—10, 9, 8, 7 . . .? My wife has been counting her birthdays like that for years.

When the astronaut told his wife he was going to the moon, she retorted, "Sure. You'll do anything to avoid going to dinner at my mother's!"

———

HE: Isn't that great the way the two astronauts went around the world sixty-two times? SHE: Big deal. You got money, you can travel.

———

Our astronaut went to space and back in fifteen minutes. So what? I'd like to see him go across town in that time.

———

Many of our astronauts are so handsome, they've been offered Hollywood movie contracts with 25th Century Fox.

———

The American space plan is to send three astronauts to the moon in the first rocket. Then in the second rocket, they'll send Bob Hope to entertain them.

———

The American space plan is to send three astronauts in one rocket, but there's still a little disagreement as to who should sit by the window.

———

We'll never have women astronauts. They would never all agree to wear the same style suit.

You think you got trouble? I know one astronaut who got on a scale and his fortune said: "Beware of long trips."

———

Two Polish astronauts were talking. One said, "Forget the moon. Everybody is going to the moon. We go direct to the sun." "But we can't go to the sun. If we get within thirteen million miles of the sun, we'll melt." "Not if we land at night."

———

When the astronauts found out they were allowed 110 pounds of recreational equipment, they requested Cindy Crawford.

## Atheists

An atheist is a man who has no invisible means of support.

———

The atheist says, "There ain't no such thing as hell." The Christian says, "The hell there ain't."

———

I am really sorry for the poor atheist who is doing good and feels grateful— he has no one to thank.

———

There is no such thing as an atheist at a tax audit.

## Athletes

*(see also Baseball, Sports)*

"Did you have many athletes in your college?" "Oh, no, we wouldn't have any athletes around our college." "Why not?" "Well, haven't you heard about their feet?"

"Did you ever notice that during the Gay Nineties there were very few girl athletes? I wonder why?" "Because they were all bustle-bound."

"What race did you run in?" "The human race." "Ha ha, I got you then." "What are you laughing at? You weren't in it."

## Atomic Energy

With all the atom bombs, H-bombs, and ballistic missiles, I'm moving into the Harmon Theater. It hasn't had a hit in years.

With all these newfangled bombs that can destroy worlds, my mother-in-law's only worry is: "Wherever they send you, I'm going with you."

Don't worry about the bombs. You want to be safe, just go to your friend at Chase Manhattan. He'll give you a $10,000 loan. Then forget about it. He'll see to it that nothing happens to you.

"Our planes now travel faster than sound." "Yeah? Try telling a secret to my mother-in-law."

A couple of scientists were watching their colleagues at the crap tables in Vegas between experiments. "Say," said one of them, "that Anderson is gambling like there's no tomorrow." "Maybe," said the other, "he knows something."

With all the new bombs that people claim they have and threaten to use, it doesn't pay to save green stamps or Raleigh coupons.

## Auctions

The scene is an auction. Bidding for the various objects is going furiously when the auctioneer suddenly slams down his hammer and announces, "A gentleman in this room has lost a wallet containing $1,000. If it's returned, he will pay a reward of $200." There's a moment of silence and then, from the back of the room, comes the cry, "$210."

## Automation

*(see also Computers, Office)*

Automation could never replace my brother-in-law. They still haven't found a machine that does absolutely nothing.

I'll be for automation when they can find a machine to replace my mother-in-law.

———

"I know, it's supposed to replace twelve men," the secretary said, "but I'd rather have the men."

———

I really loused up the machine—I stepped on my card with my golf shoes. Do you know I'm now worth a million? If only my machine will tell it to my bank.

———

"Replacing you with automation," the boss said, "is going to be a tough job. I've never been able to figure out just what it is you do."

———

Automation has taken over. The only thing people do with their hands anymore is scratch themselves.

———

I had a tough day at the office. The electronic brain broke down and I had to think all afternoon.

———

Automation is a $75-a-week clerk replaced by a $250,000 machine.

## Automobiles
*(see also Cars, Driving, Traffic, Accidents)*

Automobile manufacturers have a new safety test. They crash new cars with dummies in them to study accidents and injuries. The truth is, they have made cars safer—for dummies. But that's great, considering all the dummies that are driving cars these days.

———

Talk about treacherous driving! Did you ever own one of those really low sports cars and find yourself surrounded by a dozen tall dogs?

———

It's not so easy to get parking tickets these days. First, you got to find a place to park.

———

I got a friend that figured out a way to beat parking tickets. He removed his windshield wipers.

———

A woman driver wouldn't have as much trouble squeezing into a parking space if she would imagine it was a girdle or a pair of shoes.

———

A friend of mine who was out driving one day was hit by another automobile. He wound up with eight holes in his hood and the top down, and it wasn't even a convertible! My friend looked like he had just finished ten rounds with Mike Tyson. From out of nowhere, a lawyer approached and said, "Look here, man, I can get you some damages!" The fellow said,

"Nothing doing. I've got plenty of damages already. What I need are some repairs!"

———

He had to push his automobile two miles to a garage. And the way those garages take advantage of you, they made him push it back again two miles so they could send out a tow truck for it!

———

One word of advice: If you're out driving, just make sure you have a car.

———

The English make a sports car so small, it has a monocle instead of a windshield.

———

The best way to stop that noise in your car is to let her drive.

## Babies

*(see also Children, Jokes for Children, Kids)*

I was a war baby. My parents took one look at me and started fighting.

———

I was such a big baby, when I was born the doctor was afraid to slap me.

———

I was offered a job as a babysitter. But who wants to sit on babies?

———

They said the baby looked like me— then they turned him right side up.

———

The neighbors think the baby is spoiled, but I told them all babies smell like that.

———

We feed our baby onions so we can find it in the dark.

———

Getting the baby to sleep is hardest—when she's about eighteen years old.

We spent three weeks poking a broom in the baby's face to get him used to kissing Grandpa.

———

The best way to keep this baby quiet is to let him suck on a bottle of glue.

———

Many a woman's mistakes are covered by a baby blanket.

———

I was a premature baby. My father wasn't expecting me.

———

I read somewhere that in the world today a woman gives birth to a child every tenth of a second. Somebody better stop this lady before she falls down altogether.

———

"Doctor," screamed the young woman over the phone, "my baby just swallowed a bullet. What should I do?" "The first thing is, don't point him at anybody."

———

A woman in London gave birth to twins, one at 2 P.M. and the other at 8 P.M. You know the English—everything stops for tea.

———

I was born at home, but when my mother saw me she went to the hospital.

———

The six-year-old looked at the new wrinkled baby and remarked, "So that's why Mother hid him under her coat for so long."

———

Entertainer Joan Rivers says she was an ugly baby: "When my parents left me on a doorstep they were arrested. Not for abandonment—for littering."

———

Babies haven't any hair;
Old men's heads are just as bare;
Between the cradle and the grave
Lies a haircut and a shave.

## Bachelors

As the widow said to the bachelor, "Take it from me—don't get married."

———

A bachelor is a guy who goes to work every morning from a different direction.

———

Never trust a husband too far—or a bachelor too near.

———

A bachelor past fifty is a remnant. There is no good material left in him.

———

A bachelor is a guy who doesn't have to leave a party when he starts having a good time.

———

MARRIED MAN: How in the world have you managed to stay single so long? BACHELOR: It's easy. Every time I look at television commercials I learn that women are anemic, have stringy hair and large pores, are overweight, and have rough hands.

———

A bachelor wouldn't make the same mistake once.

———

A bachelor has nobody to share his troubles with—but then, why should a bachelor have troubles?

———

BACHELOR: Come up to my apartment. We'll toast the New Year with some beautiful imported champagne. GIRL: But the New Year is three months away. BACHELOR: What's our hurry?

———

The only thing worse than being a bachelor is being a bachelor's son.

———

A bachelor is a man who is lucky in love.

———

A bachelor would rather have a woman on his mind than one on his neck.

———

A man calls himself a bachelor until he gets married, then you should hear what he calls himself.

———

A man who refuses to fight used to be called a coward. Today they call him a bachelor.

———

Not all men are fools; some are bachelors.

———

Bachelor's Day on Leap Year is when women propose to men—and you should hear what they propose.

———

My unmarried brother tells me, "It's wonderful to be a bachelor. You eat home-cooked meals, but you have your choice of cooks."

———

Show me a man who does what he wants, and I'll show you a bachelor.

———

A bachelor is someone who occasionally wonders who would make the best wife—a blonde, brunette, or redhead—but who comes to his senses in the end and remembers that it really doesn't matter what color the truck is if it's going to run him over anyway.

———

A bachelor is a careful man who does not get married until he has saved enough money, and then he doesn't get married so he can keep what he's saved.

———

This guy knows more about women than married men do. Why else would he stay single?

———

"My girlfriend wants to creep into my gut," my friend told me. "She said, 'I want to be part of you.' I said, 'Thanks, but who wants to have another kidney?'"

———

A bachelor is a guy who likes to love as long as it's not followed by honor and obey.

———

Two women met and one said to the other, "Say, I haven't seen you around here for months. Are you still engaged to that sensible, thrifty young man you were telling me so much about?" Her friend replied, "No, I married the cheap bum."

Steve Masters, of the Masters Discount House, defined the word *bachelor* for me: A bachelor is a guy who wants to have a girl in his arms without having her on his hands.

---

The employer explained why he would hire a married man instead of a bachelor: "The married men don't get so upset if I yell at them."

---

"Gee, Harry's been lucky in love." "You mean he always gets his woman?" "No, he's still a bachelor."

---

A bachelor is a guy who thinks before he acts and then doesn't act.

---

Bachelors like girls who avoid being called flirts by giving in easily.

---

A bitter bachelor once said: "I wish Adam had kept his ribs to himself!"

---

Bachelor's theme song: "I Plucked a Lemon in the Garden of Love."

## Baldness

Bald actor Patrick Stewart is envious of men with hair: "To people like me, dandruff is a thrill."

---

This is a great way to defend your bald spot, or to introduce somebody with a bald head: "God made a lot of heads. Those he was ashamed of he covered with a lot of hair."

---

One thing about being bald—it's very neat.

---

Bald is great for a guy romancing a girl on the couch. When her parents come in, all he has to do is straighten his tie.

---

He's either bald, or that's the longest face I ever saw.

---

He looks like something I shot into the side pocket this afternoon.

---

He has a beautiful head of skin.

---

His head looks like a landing field.

---

I wouldn't say he was bald, but he has the widest part I have ever seen.

---

He looks like his neck is blowing bubble gum.

---

I could look into his head to tell the future.

My mother told me I would come out on top someday. She's right—I'm getting bald.

———

He was so bald, he looked like a part with ears.

———

A bald-headed man is one who came out on top and still lost.

———

What a woman said about a bald-headed man: "I love to run my fingers through his hair because I can make better time on the open road."

———

FATHER: No, you can't wear your hair like Elvis Presley. SON: But, Dad, you wear yours like Yul Brynner.

———

The suspicious wife went over her husband's suit for traces of red or blond hair but found none. Finally, she said to her husband, "Aha, so you're going out with bald-headed women!"

———

"My hair's falling out. What can I get to keep it in?" "A paper bag."

———

He isn't bald; he just has a tall face.

———

I asked my uncle, "Is it true that you wear a toupee?" He answered, "No, the hair is real. It's the head that's fake."

# Ballet
*(see also Opera)*

"I don't dig ballet. The last time I went with friends, there was a lot of money bet on the swan to live."— Woody Allen

———

Why do ballet dancers have to dance on their toes? Why don't they just get taller dancers?

———

Frankly, I don't think the ballet has anything on the Broadway musical. I have yet to go to one of those things where any dancer remembered one single line. And what is it with these tutus? Those ladies work awfully hard. You'd think they could make enough money to afford a real dress.

# Bands
*(see also Orchestra)*

"I have twenty men in my band." "You ought to go to Canada. The police wouldn't follow you there." "I didn't do anything." "You must have done something, or all those men wouldn't be following you."

———

"Isn't he rather young to be leading an orchestra?" "Not the way he leads it."

———

"What are you going to play next, maestro?" "I like it when you call me maestro. It gives me that international flavor." "Garlic will do the same."

"I can't find my baton." "Can't you lead without it?" "It isn't that—I've got something between my teeth."

———

"That's a hot band you have there." "They're going to be much cooler this summer. I'm adding three wind instruments."

———

"He knows everything about music." "Oh, not everything." "What is there about music that he doesn't know?" "That I just dropped his violin down the elevator shaft."

———

"You are three bars ahead of the rest of us." "Yes. But didn't I tell you that I could play to beat the band?"

———

"Say, let me have five dollars." "What for?" "For five dollars I could get a band that is better than this one." "What would you do with the change?"

———

"How much does he get for playing the fiddle?" "Seven hundred and fifty dollars a week." "What? For running a horse's tail over a cat's gut and making it screech?"

———

"I want it played the way I told you. Forget the way it was written. All I can say is that you're a lousy musician."

———

"Listen, if I was a musician I'd be sitting in the band playing the clarinet instead of leading the band."

———

"Anyone want any brains? You want some brains?" "No, I don't need any brains." "Oh, I forgot; you're an orchestra leader."

———

"What's wrong with my arrangement?" "You wrote in a part for a shoe horn." "That was to give the music a little sole." "That's good. Soul music from a heel."

———

"His cousin has one of the biggest orchestra leaders in New York after him." "Who's he playing with now?" "The leader's wife."

———

They were a three-piece band. They only knew three pieces.

———

The piano player wasn't part of the regular band, but he had the car.

———

He was the leader of the band. He always finished four bars ahead of everyone else.

———

Introduction: You've heard of the sweetest band this side of heaven? Well, this is what was on the other side.

The drummer has three sets of drums: one to play on, one to practice on, and one to eat off of.

---

This band has played many a champagne hour—without instruments.

---

The new pupil listened to the band for a few minutes. Then the teacher asked, "Where is the trumpet section?" The pupil pointed to the oboe section. In disgust, the teacher turned to the conductor and said, "This guy doesn't know his brass from his oboe."

# Bankruptcy
*(see also Business)*

Many a going business is going the wrong way.

---

Business was so bad that even people who didn't pay had stopped buying.

---

Things got so bad I asked the boss, "What goes?" and he said, "You!"

---

Business is so quiet you can hear the overhead piling up.

---

This guy had been going bankrupt for twenty-two years and always had a sign in his window: GOING OUT OF BUSINESS. Now he's opening another store for his son, so his son can go out of business for himself.

---

This year business has gone directly from the summer slump to the fall recessional.

---

Business is really slow right now. A fellow walked into a place to change a twenty-dollar bill and they made him a partner.

---

A store that went bankrupt after only a few weeks displayed this sign: OPENED BY MISTAKE.

# Banks
*(see also Money)*

In the typical neighborhood bank there are always four people standing behind the counter. One is called Sylvia Potkin, the rest are called "Next Window."

---

Nowadays you can always tell when a bank is in trouble by the little things—like when they come and repossess your toaster and take back their calendar.

---

I always wanted to work in a bank. Banks have everything I love: money and holidays.

There's one bank in my neighborhood that's so anxious to do business they'll give you a gift even when you make a withdrawal. This bank is so classy, instead of a camera that takes pictures of bank robbers, they have a guy who does charcoal sketches.

———

My bank is offering premiums for new deposits. For $500 you get a blanket. For $1,000 you get a digital clock. And for $10,000 you get an audit by the IRS.

———

This woman said to the manager of the bank, "I'd like to open a joint account with someone who has a lot of money."

———

I told my neighbor I couldn't loan him any money because everything I have is in a joint account. He said, "But you can withdraw money from a joint account." "Not this one," I replied. "Our joint account is in the name of my wife and her mother."

———

If it's as easy to borrow money from a bank as the advertising claims, why should anyone want to rob it?

———

My neighbor went to the bank and applied for a loan, and to his surprise he got it immediately. The next day he went to the bank and withdrew all the money he had on deposit there. He explained, "I don't trust a bank that would lend money to such a poor risk."

———

The man shouted at the loan arranger: "Of course I don't have any security—that's why I want the money!"

———

President Franklin Delano Roosevelt ordered our banks closed on March 6, 1933, to save our economy. Today the banks are open, but only to save our money for the IRS.

———

The finance company is for the man who has everything but can't afford to pay for it.

———

If interest rates go any higher, pretty soon the loan sharks will be suing the banks for unfair competition.

———

When a poor man has too much money, he lends it to the bank. When a rich man doesn't have enough money, the bank lends it to *him*.

———

Show me a man with a gold tooth, and I'll show you someone who puts his money where his mouth is.

———

What is a banker? A pawnbroker with a manicure.

———

Money is so tight, some banks may have to diversify. But how will it sound? First National Savings and Pizza.

———

The vice president of the bank said to the businessman, "Eighty thousand dollars? That's a lot of money you want. I'll have to ask you for a statement." The man said, "And you can quote me: *I'm optimistic.*"

———

My neighbor told me, "I have two brothers. One is a banker, and the other was executed in the electric chair. Recently I met a wonderful girl who was just released from the reformatory. I want to marry her. My problem is: If I marry this girl, should I tell her about my brother who is a banker?"

———

I liked it better when we had folding money instead of folding banks.

———

Personally, I always like to put aside a little something for a rainy day. Yesterday, I stopped by the savings and loan and deposited my galoshes.

———

Interest rates are murder. I walked into a bank yesterday and the loan officer was wearing a stocking mask.

———

A holdup guy became slightly confused when he shoved a note at a bank teller that read: "I've got you covered; hand over all the dough in the cage," and the teller handed him a note back: "Kindly go to the next window. I'm on my lunch hour."

———

A new bank teller was told to count a bundle of singles and make sure he had $100. The teller counted fifty-eight, then threw the bundle down. "Why did you stop counting?" asked the bank manager. "If it's all right this far, it's probably right all the way," said the teller.

———

Remember the good old days when bank robbers didn't work in the bank?

———

At my bank they always try to interest me in an IRA. What I'm interested in is an IOU.

———

I have a friend who borrowed $10,000 and spent one year opening new bank accounts. He got free radios, TV sets, luggage, clocks, pots, pans, dishes. At the end of the year he gave the ten grand back and opened his own discount house.

Some fellow held up a bank and shoved a note at the teller that said, "This is a stickup! Hand over your cash." She shoved a note back at him that read, "Straighten your tie, stupid, we're taking your picture."

---

The holdup man goes into the bank and whispers to the cashier, "Give me all that money in a bag." The cashier says, "Here, take the books, too. I'm $50,000 short."

---

Jim Farley, the president of Central State Bank, swears one depositor asked for him personally. The depositor wanted a one-cent check cashed. "How do you want it?" asked the patient president. "Heads or tails?"

---

One woman to another: "Funny thing with checkbooks. Once I've started one I can't put it down till I've finished."

---

Getting a loan from a bank is tough these days because of the tight-money situation. A senior loan officer was standing by the desk of a junior loan officer when the telephone rang. The junior officer answered it. He said, "No. No . . . no . . . no . . . yes . . . no," and hung up. The senior officer questioned him immediately: What had he said yes to? "Don't worry," said the junior officer reassuringly. "I said yes only when he asked me if I was still listening."

---

HUSBAND: The bank has returned your check. WIFE: Splendid! What can we buy with it this time?

---

A woman went into the bank and noticed there was a new face behind the window. "Has the cashier gone away to take a rest?" she inquired. "No," replied the new man, "he's gone away to avoid it."

---

A banker is a man who lends you an umbrella when the sun is shining and wants it back when the rains come.

---

A bank is a place where you keep the government's money until the tax man asks for it.

---

A bank robber opened the safe with his toes just so he could drive the fingerprint experts crazy.

---

The captured bank robber was told that the bank's hidden camera had taken pictures of him, and that was what led to his capture. The bank robber replied, "Gee, do you think I could get some wallet-size for my wife?"

---

MISS GOTROCKS: You! You want to marry me? YOUNG MAN: Yes! MISS GOTROCKS: But my dear boy, you've only known me three days. YOUNG MAN: Oh, much longer than that, really! I've been two years in the bank where your father has his account.

———————

A: Where are you going to get your check cashed? B: I don't know. I can't think of a single place where I'm unknown.

———————

The Texan received his check back from the bank marked "insufficient funds." Added to it was "ours, not yours."

———————

The bank is so big, they have a special window for holdups.

———————

My wife had an accident at the bank. She got in the wrong line and made a deposit.

———————

A wife to her husband: "I can't be overdrawn. I still have five checks left."

———————

"Why this bank?" the efficiency expert asked the new depositor. "I'm in love with your teller," he answered.

———————

The local bank teller is worried, reports comedian Pat Cooper. The bank examiner's due tomorrow, and he's short two toasters and a set of dishes.

———————

Two retired bank thieves were talking about all the new branches that were opening, and one said that the stickup business sure has changed. "If we were to try to heist a bank now," he explained, "we'd need two shopping bags, one for the money and the other for the gifts."

———————

I don't trust banks with counting money. If bankers can count, why do they always have eight windows and two tellers?

———————

"This is to inform you that this is the last time we will spend forty cents to let you know you have two cents!"

———————

MAN: Can you direct me to the Fifth National Bank? KID: If you give me a dollar I will! MAN: A dollar! Don't you think that's too much money? KID: No, sir! Not for a bank director!

———————

The bravest man I ever knew once took a taxi to the bankruptcy court and invited the driver in as a creditor.

# Barbers
*(see also Baldness)*

A customer just back from London said to his barber, "Over there I was able to get a haircut for only $6.50!" The barber replied, "Yeah, but look at the fare."

———

A Times Square barber advertises: SIX BARBERS—CONTINUOUS DISCUSSION.

———

After a haircut, when the barber says, "Is that the way you want it, sir?" drive him crazy and say, "Not quite, a little longer in back."

———

He spent twenty minutes combing his hair, then forgot to bring it with him.

———

The barber was cutting me with every stroke of the razor. After half a dozen nicks, I sat up. "Will you give me a razor?" I asked. "Why, do you want to shave yourself?" the barber asked. "No, defend myself!" I said.

———

BARBER: Did you have ketchup for lunch? CUSTOMER: No. BARBER: Then I've cut your throat.

———

The way hairstyles are today, you can't tell from the back if it's a man who needs a haircut or a woman who just had one.

"Just a shave, please. I haven't time to listen to a haircut."

———

"Do you want your hair cut? Or just change the oil?"

———

Advice: When you go into a barbershop, always pick the barber with the lousiest haircut. Remember, they cut each other's hair."

———

Comedian Jack Carter had survived a pretty close shave. When the barber was through, Jack asked for a drink of water: "I want to see if my neck leaks," he explained.

———

BARBER: How would you like your hair cut? CUSTOMER: In silence.

———

The man told the barber he wanted the kind of haircut Tony Curtis has. "Can you give me exactly the same haircut?" "Sure," the barber assured him. With that the customer sat back in the chair and dozed off. Fifteen minutes later he woke up and looked in the mirror. Much to his horror, his head was completely shaved. He jumped out of the chair and screamed at the barber. "Tony Curtis! I told you I wanted a haircut like Tony Curtis!" "Sure," said the barber, "and that's what I gave you. I know what Tony Curtis's haircut looks like. Why, only last week I saw him on TV in *The King and I.*

# Bars
*(see also Drinking)*

"I hate to see young girls like you hanging around in bars. Why don't you come up to my apartment?"

———————

"Do you serve women at the bar?" "No, you have to bring your own."

———————

Sign in bar: "We don't have TV, but we have fights every night."

———————

I asked the bartender for something tall and cold with plenty of gin in it, and he called his wife over.

———————

The bartender put two cherries in my Manhattan—my doctor told me I should eat more fruit.

———————

When men drink at bars, it means that they have no wife to go home to— or that they do have one.

———————

I'm for safety belts on bar stools.

———————

A man walked into a bar, had a beer, and left fifty cents on the counter, which the bartender put in his pocket. The owner saw what happened and said, "What do you think you're doing?" The bartender calmly replied,

"How do you like that? A guy comes in, has a beer, doesn't pay the check, and leaves me a fifty-cent tip."

———————

A drunk ran into a bar and asked the bartender how high a penguin was. The bartender told him about waist high. The drunk then asked if there were any penguins that were taller, and the bartender told him there weren't. The drunk said, "Oh, my gosh, then I just ran down two nuns."

———————

The bartender redecorated his bar. He put new drunks around it.

———————

SON: Daddy, what is the person called who brings you in contact with the spirit world? DAD: A bartender, my boy.

———————

A man came into a bar, drank half his beer, and threw the rest of it on the bartender. He then apologized profusely and explained it was a nervous compulsion and he was very embarrassed. The bartender suggested he see a psychiatrist. Six months later the man returned to the same bar and did the exact same thing. This time the bartender was indignant. "I thought you went to see a psychiatrist," he said. "I did," the man said. "Well," said the bartender, "it certainly didn't do much good." "Oh, yes," the man said, "I'm not embarrassed about it anymore."

# Baseball

*(see also Athletes, Sports)*

Watching baseball games on TV is very educational. It used to take me ten minutes to shave. Now I can do it between innings.

———

I remember back when Marilyn Monroe and Joe DiMaggio were married and she would come to the games at Yankee Stadium. Every time she sat in the stands, the seventh inning stretch lasted three hours.

———

A couple of Yogi Berra's waggish teammates on the New York Yankee ball club swear that one night the stocky catcher was horrified to see a baby toppling off the roof of a cottage across the way from him. He dashed over and made a miraculous catch, but then force of habit proved too much for him. He straightened up and threw the baby to second base.

———

The conceited new rookie was pitching his first game. He walked the first five men he faced and the manager took him out of the game. The rookie threw his glove to the ground as he walked off and yelled, "Dammit, the jerk takes me out when I have a no-hitter going."

———

Mickey Mantle, the great Yankee star, was walking in civilian clothes outside the stadium and was obviously favoring his bad leg. A woman passing by asked a friend, "What's wrong with him?" The friend replied, "He got hurt playing baseball." "Won't they ever grow up?" the woman replied.

# Beach

Someone once described Coney Island as a place where the beer cans come to spawn.

———

Two lobsters got lost on the Sahara Desert, and, after three hours walking, one turned to the other and said, "Man, what a beach!"

———

If you ever get hungry on the beach, you can always eat the sand-wiches there.

# Beauty

When I worked in the Catskills, I was the social director at a hotel where the girls were so ugly, we had a beauty contest and nobody won.

———

A raving beauty is a girl who comes out last in a beauty contest.

A beauty contest is like a candy store. Everything looks good, but you can't touch.

She won a beauty contest in England. It was a very foggy day in London town.

When she was twenty-one she was chosen Miss America. In those days there were very few Americans.

Comedienne Phyllis Diller was told she is beautiful on the inside. "Leave it to me," she complained, "to be born inside out."

A thing of beauty is a great expense.

Show me a man who doesn't turn around and look at a beautiful woman, and I'll show you a man who is walking with his wife.

Every time I meet a beautiful girl, either she is married or I am.

## Beggars and Bums

He's not afraid of work. He's fought it for years—and won.

He doesn't drink coffee in the morning because it keeps him awake all day.

He's the idol of the family. He's been idle for years.

A guy tossed a nickel in the beggar's cup but didn't take a pencil. The beggar advised him, "Whether you take one or not, pencils cost ten cents each now."

The beggar approached the lady and pleaded, "Please, lady, can you give me five dollars?"
"That's a nerve," the lady said, "five dollars?" "Yah, I want to quit early tonight."

A panhandler walked up to a man and asked, "May I borrow ten dollars till payday?" "When's payday?" "How do I know? You're the one that's working."

The woman lectured the beggar. "How come I always see you around here half drunk?" He answered, "Because I run out of money, lady."

These days there is more begging done through the mail than with tin cups.

---

Let's not forget the bums on the street. If you help a bum he'll never forget you—especially the next time he is looking for a handout.

---

Not only is it more blessed to give than to receive, it is a lot more expensive.

---

To enjoy a good reputation, give publicly and steal privately.

---

A true philanthropist is one who gives away what he should give back.

---

One well-dressed man in Atlantic City was approached by a seedy-looking character, who asked, "Can you lend me twenty-five dollars? I've got no place to sleep and I haven't eaten in two days." The well-dressed man said, "How do I know you're not going to take the money and gamble with it?" The bum said, "No way. Gambling money I've got."

---

The street character told the overweight dowager, "Lady, please help. I haven't eaten in three days." She said, "I wish I had your willpower."

An elegant society matron was stopped by a bum just as she was leaving one of the season's biggest charity balls. "Lady," said the beggar, "can you spare a poor man a dollar?" The matron screamed, "You must be out of your mind! I spent $250 for a ticket to the ball, $1,500 for my gown, and on top of that, I'm completely exhausted from all that dancing! How dare you ask me for money when I did all that for you?"

---

"Unless you give me some aid," the bum said to Mrs. Vanderschwartz, "I'm afraid I will have to resort to something it shocks me to contemplate doing." Mrs. Vanderschwartz handed him a five-dollar bill and asked lovingly, "What is it, my poor man, that I saved you from?" He said, "Work, madam."

---

The lady asked the beggar, "Can't you find work?" He said, "Yes, but they want a reference from my last employer." "So can't you get one?" "No, madam. He's been dead twenty-eight years."

---

One bum approached me and said, "Mister, can I have a hundred and twenty-five dollars for a cup of coffee?" I said, "A hundred and twenty-five dollars?" He said, "Well, I can't go into a nice restaurant dressed like this!"

---

One tramp knocked on the door and asked the lady of the house for something to eat. She replied, "Yes, I'll feed you, if you'll chop a load of wood first." The bum said, "Madam, I asked for a donation, not a transaction."

―――――

I was in a hurry and told the beggar, "I'll take care of you on my way back." He cried, "Oh, no, you don't. Already this year I've lost too much on charge accounts."

―――――

A bum knocked on the door of an inn called George and the Dragon. A woman opened it and he asked for some money. She screamed "No!" and slammed the door. He knocked again and the woman opened the door. He said, "Now could I have a few words with George?"

―――――

Have you heard about that new welfare doll? You wind it up and it doesn't work.

―――――

A bum approached a man and asked for a dime. The man told him he didn't have a dime, but he'd be glad to buy him breakfast. "Man," the bum said, "I've had three breakfasts now, trying to get a dime."

―――――

"Actually, I'm an author," one bum told me. "I once wrote a book entitled *One Hundred Ways to Make Money*." I asked, "Then why are you begging?" He said, "It's one of the ways."

―――――

The bum asked for twenty dollars and twenty-five cents for a cup of coffee. I protested, "But coffee only costs twenty-five cents." He said, "I know, but coffee always makes me sexy."

―――――

A ragged stranger came to see my uncle. "You did me a favor ten years ago," the bum said, "and I've never forgotten it." My uncle remarked, "Ah, and you've come back to repay me?" The stranger said, "Not exactly. I just got into town and I need another favor, and I thought of you right away."

―――――

I asked the beggar if he had ever been offered work. He said, "Only once. Apart from that, sir, I've met with nothing but kindness."

―――――

My brother-in-law said, "Remember last year when I was broke, and you helped me out and I said I would never forget you?" I said, "Yes." He said, "Well, I'm broke again."

―――――

"Do you think it's right for you to go begging from door to door?" the lady asked. The panhandler said, "No, I don't. But they refuse to bring it to me."

# Benchley, Robert
*(see also Comedians)*

Benchley was quietly drinking his martini in the corner when a lady approached him. "Don't you know," she said, "that stuff you're drinking is slow poison?" "That's all right—I'm in no hurry," Benchley replied.

———

It took me fifteen years to discover I had no talent for writing, but I couldn't give it up because by that time I was too famous.

———

Benchley once sent a foreign check to his bank in New York with this legend on the back: "Having a wonderful time—wish you would cover!"

———

Benchley told a new listener about the clown in the circus who got himself shot out of a cannon—it was a great new act. When the new listener asked how the clown had withstood the shock, Benchley answered, "I really don't know. We haven't found him yet."

———

In America there are two classes of travel: first class and with children.

———

Benchley was spending the weekend at the estate of a very boring elderly maiden aunt. She had planned to go walking with him one morning, but he excused himself because of bad weather. Later on she saw him sneaking out of the house alone and said, "Oh, Robert, has it cleared up?" "Just partly. Enough for me, but not enough for two," he said.

———

Benchley was annoyed at all the hands out when he was leaving the fashionable hotel. When the doorman stuck his hand out and said, "I hope you won't forget me, sir!" Benchley grasped his hand and said warmly, "I should say not. I'll write you every week."

# Benny, Jack
*(see also Comedians)*

Give me my golf clubs, the fresh air, and a beautiful woman as a partner, and you can have the golf clubs and the fresh air.

———

All through the years Jack Benny and Fred Allen shared a phony feud. Once, after Allen had massacred Benny with gags, Benny cried, "You wouldn't call me that if I had my writers with me."

———

Bob Hope says he remembers that during World War II Jack Benny was a dollar-a-year man. "You mean that's all he got?" he was asked. "Oh, no," Hope replied. "That was all he spent."

The honeymoon is really over when he phones to say he'll be late for dinner—and she's already left a note saying his TV dinner is in the freezer.

———

I like the one about the Englishman who says to the waiter, "Didn't you hear me say, 'Well done'?" The waiter, ignoring the rare steak, absent-mindedly answers, "Yes, sir. Thank you, sir. It's seldom we get any thanks."

———

The captain of the cruise ship invited the rich couple to sit at the table with him. "We spent a fortune to get the best of everything on this ship," the husband shouted, "and now they want us to sit with the help."

———

Fred Allen, in his fun feud with Jack Benny, said, "There is a saying that you can't take it with you. But if you see a funeral procession with a Brink's armored car behind the hearse, you'll know Jack is having a try at it."

———

Remember the total eclipse of the sun? Jack Benny ran over to the Western Union office to send a night letter.

## Berle, Milton
*(see also Comedians)*

What is this, an audience or an oil painting?

I was an old newspaperman, but then I found out there was no money in old newspapers.

———

I never file my nails. I just cut them off and throw them away.

———

My girl was so skinny, she swallowed an olive and four men left town.

———

I lost my TV show. I knew I was in trouble when I found 50 percent of the studio audience wasn't listening.

———

My room is so small, I closed the door and the doorknob got in bed with me. I put the key in the keyhole and broke the window.

———

I learned dancing with Arthur Murray. Later I found out it was more fun with a girl.

———

There's something about him, but he won't spend it.

———

The way she's built, it takes her twenty minutes to get her feet wet under a shower.

My brother is very superstitious. He won't work any week that has a Friday in it.

———

Guy called the doctor and said, "My kid just swallowed my pen. What should I do?" Doc said, "Use a pencil."

———

I said to my mother-in-law, "Make like this is your home." So she sold it.

———

I gave my wife a new watch for her birthday—waterproof, shockproof, unbreakable, and antimagnetic. Absolutely nothing could happen to it. She lost it.

# Berman, Shelley
*(see also Comedians)*

I had a hotel room that was so small, the mice ran around hunchback.

———

I'm so nervous, I keep coffee awake.

———

I know a three-fingered pickpocket. He steals bowling balls.

———

I know there's an audience out there, I can hear you breathing. What is this, an audience or a jury?

I was so drunk last night, I picked up a snake and hit a stick.

———

I call my kid Webster. Words can't describe him.

———

Phone conversation of the world's greatest theatrical agent: "Hello, Eleanor? Did you put my call through to Africa yet? Fine, I'll take it here. How are you, Al, kiddo, kiddo? This is Artie. Yeah, fine. Fine, I'm glad to hear it. Tell me, how is Mrs. Schweitzer? Good. Good. Listen, Dockie, I got some very good news for you, Dockie boy. Your American tour is all set—you're all booked up. You open in Chicago at the Chez Paree. Yeah, the Chez in Chi. Listen, Al baby, I had to do a little maneuvering. I'm afraid they wouldn't take you as a straight organ player, so what I did, see, I sold you as a combination organist-comedian, see, so I tell you what to do. You dress up your act with a little patter—you know, a few of those funny little anecdotes you pick up around the leper colonies. . . . Okay, Al. Fine, baby, give my regards to the missus, fine, good-bye. . . . Eleanor, you got Picasso? . . . Where, on six? Okay, I got it. Hello, Pablo baby, how are you? Fine. Yeah, it's all set. She wants you to start painting on Thursday. Yeah, this Thursday? Right. Now remember, Pab baby, go over it once more. Yeah, she wants the kitchen in green and the bathroom in baby blue. Fine, Pab. Okay, bye."

# Bible Humor

*(see also Church, Religion)*

"What's another name for God?" the little boy was asked. "Harold," the child answered. "How do you get that?" "Well, when I say my prayers at night I say, 'Our Father, who art in heaven, Harold be thy name.'"

———

The man hoeing in the field asked the farmer if he could stop to get a drink of water. "No," said the farmer. "Remember, it says in the Bible: 'Ho! Everyone that thirsteth'!"

———

Peter the fisherman was stopped by a bunch of hoodlums on the corner. "Is it true that your Master tells you to turn the other cheek? Is that in the Bible?" the head of the riffraff asked. "Yes," said Peter quietly. "Well, here's a slap on the kisser," the hoodlum said, striking Peter on the cheek. "Now, how about the other cheek?" Then he slapped Peter a second time, on the other cheek. The hoodlum smirked, "And here's another." But as he lifted his hand for the third time, Peter picked him up and threw him over the fence. "It also says in the Bible," Peter reminded them, "'Thou shalt not tempt the Lord.'"

———

As the waters of the Red Sea were parted, Moses remarked, "Why do I always have to go first?"

"I'll be glad to turn the water into wine, but the first one that gets drunk is out of the game."

———

This song was first written by Cain for his brother, Abel: "I'm Walking Behind You."

———

The young gay men said to Noah, "You said two of every kind."

———

The zebras started getting very nervous when they heard a rumor that Noah was boarding the ark alphabetically.

———

The youngster listened attentively as the rabbi read the Bible. "May I ask a question?" the boy said. "Sure." "The Bible says the children of Israel built the Temple, the children of Israel crossed the Red Sea, and the children of Israel did this and that. Didn't the grown-ups ever do anything?"

———

The Three Wise Men were on their way to Bethlehem. All of a sudden, one of them ground his camel to a halt. "Now listen, fellows," he said to the other two, "remember, no mentioning how much we paid for the gifts."

———

Two refugees were working on the Negev. They were tired and weary trying to make the desert bloom. "Who needs it?" said one, perspiration running down his body. "So we were persecuted a little in Russia, but who worked so hard?" "You jerk," said the other, "don't you realize Moses walked forty years, day and night, just to get here? This is the Promised Land." "You know something?" the first refugee said. "If Moses walked one more day and night, we'd be on the river right now."

———

As one of the boys said after the Last Supper, "Talk about miracles. Judas says he's buying tonight."

———

The kid said to his father, "The rabbi told us a fantastic story about the Jews who were chased out of Israel and came to the Red Sea. The Jews are so smart, they saw the Egyptians following them, so they built a bridge over the Red Sea and went over in safety. But when the Egyptians kept coming, the Jews are so smart, they put dynamite under the bridge. When all the Egyptians were on top of the bridge, the Jews blew up the bridge and the Egyptians fell into the Red Sea and were drowned." "The rabbi told you this story?" the father wanted to know. "No," said the boy, "but if I told you what the rabbi told me, you'd never believe it."

———

Moses was addressing his audience after his chat on Mount Sinai. Pointing to his tablet, he said, "And now, a word from my sponsor."

———

As Pontius Pilate said to his prisoner, "This has nothing to do with the fact that you happen to be Jewish."

———

"Father, weren't the Apostles Jews?" "Yes." "So how come the Jews let go of a good thing like the Catholic church and let the Italians grab it?"

———

"Why did you hit your sister?" "We were playing Adam and Eve, and instead of tempting me with the apple, she ate it herself."

———

It happened in the Garden of Eden. "Do you really and truly love me?" Eve asked Adam.

"Who else?" he answered. Eve was still suspicious. That night she sneaked over to where Adam was sleeping and quietly started counting his ribs.

———

This lady wanted to mail a Bible to her son at college. The post office clerk wanted to know if the package contained anything breakable. "Only the Ten Commandments," the woman said.

———

I sometimes wish I were Adam in the garden of Eden. At least then, when I told a joke, no one else could say he or she told it first.

Do you think the Three Wise Men are the guys who got out of the stock market at the right time?

———

All the trouble started in the Garden of Eden when Eve bit into a piece of fruit. It was nothing compared to the trouble I had when I did the same thing in Mexico.

———

On their first night together Adam said to Eve: "Stand back, I don't know how big this thing gets."

———

There are so many headaches in the world today, if Moses came down from Mount Sinai now, the only tablets he would be carrying would be aspirin.

———

The hardest thing for me to believe about the Bible is that there were only two asses in the Ark.

———

Eve was created from Adam's rib. Sometimes I wish he had kept his big side shut.

———

The eternal feminine problem is always, "What will I wear?" It probably began the day after the initial rebellion, when Eve looked up at the leaves of the fig tree and said, "I wonder which one I will wear today?"

———

This traveling salesman opened the Gideon Bible in his motel room. On the front page he read this inscription: "If you are sick, read Psalm 18; if you are troubled about your family, read Psalm 45; if you are lonely, read Psalm 92." He was lonely, so he opened to Psalm 92 and read it. When he was through, he noticed on the bottom of the page the handwritten words: "If you are still lonely, call 888-3468 and ask for Myrtle."

———

Joseph the carpenter hit his thumb with a hammer and cursed out loud. His son ran in from the other room and asked, "Did you call me, Dad?"

———

The kid said to the little girl next door, "Let's play Adam and Eve. You tempt me to eat the apple, and I'll give in."

## Bigamy

The penalty for bigamy is two mothers-in-law.

———

The man in Alaska was arrested for bigamy. He had a wife in Nome, another in Fairbanks, and still another in Anchorage. The judge growled at the culprit, "How could you do such a thing?"
The guy shrugged. "Fast dog team."

———

He was an odd bigamist. He married his wife's sister so he wouldn't have to break in a new mother-in-law.

# Bills

*(see also Business)*

She couldn't pay the grocer—she had given all she had to the butcher.

———

"Mama, the bill collector is here. Have you got the money, or do you want me to go out and play for a while?"

———

"Daddy, I saw Mommy kissing the TV repairman this morning." "My God! She wastes time with him and we owe the furniture man $300!"

———

WIFE: I bought this dress for a song. HUSBAND: Okay. Then send the bill collector in when he comes and I'll sing to him.

———

My wife should run for Congress. Nobody else brings so many bills to the house.

———

We were at an elegant dinner party when a friend looked at Cindy and said, "Joey, that dress your wife is wearing is a poem." "A poem?" I said. "No, that dress is two short stories and a novel!"

———

"You owe me this bill for a year. I tell you what I'll do. I'll meet you halfway. I'm ready to forget half of what you owe me." "Great. I'll meet you halfway. I'll forget the other half."

———

There's something much bigger than money: bills.

———

I don't have any trouble meeting my obligations. My trouble is ducking them.

———

He got a bill from his dentist with this notation in red: "This bill is one year old." His answer came quickly: "Happy Birthday."

———

Running into debt isn't so bad—it's running into creditors that hurts.

———

"Madam," the butcher said, "I can't give you any more credit. Your bill is bigger now than it should be." The customer said, "I know that. If you make it out for what it should be, I'll pay it."

———

"If you didn't intend to pay the bill anyway, why the hell did you haggle on price with your tailor?" "I wanted to help him cut his losses."

———

"Please pay these bills immediately. After all, we've done more for you than your mother. We've carried you for twelve months."

---

"How come you haven't hounded me to pay my bill?" "I never ask a gentleman for money." "But suppose he doesn't pay?" "After a certain time, if he doesn't pay, I know he's not a gentleman, and then I ask him."

## Birth Control

The Italians have no problem with birth control. They have been practicing it for five hundred years: garlic.

---

My uncle Harry is furious about America sending $3 million to India just to buy contraceptives: "Couldn't they just do what my wife does? Pretend she's asleep."

---

They now have a birth-control pill for men. They've been testing it for two years and after two years they found that not one man became pregnant.

---

A woman mixed her birth-control pills with saccharin. She now has the sweetest baby in the world.

---

An eighty-year-old woman went to the doctor for a complete physical examination. The doctor announced,

"You're in perfect health." "Thank you, Doctor, but I also take birth-control pills," she explained. "What do you take them for?" he asked. "I take them to get rid of my headache." The doctor asked her to please explain. "I live with my granddaughter, a lovely twenty-three-year-old girl. Every morning we get up and have breakfast together. When she's not looking I take the birth-control pill and put it in her coffee. It gets rid of my headache."

## Birthdays
*(see also Age)*

My wife said she wanted some pearls for her birthday, so I gave her an oyster and a rabbit's foot.

---

If you want to know what your wife wants for her birthday, take a peek at what she bought.

---

Never forget your wife's birthday—just forget which one it is.

---

Here's a great excuse to give when you have forgotten your wife's birthday: "How do you expect me to remember your birthday, darling, when you never look any older?"

---

There's the story about the fellow who walked to work each day and passed a window through which he saw a lady hitting a boy over the head with a loaf of bread. The fellow decided it was none of his business and walked on. He saw this same thing happen every morning for five months—each day the lady hitting the boy with a loaf of bread. Then one morning he saw the woman toss an entire chocolate cake into the boy's face. Astounded, he peered into the open window and asked why. "Oh," the lady said, "it's his birthday."

————

He was so old that instead of candles they built a bonfire in the center of the cake.

————

WIFE: Happy birthday, darling, I have a surprise for you. HUSBAND: Really? What is it? WIFE: Wait a minute, darling, I'll put it on.

————

"I'm looking forward to my twenty-third birthday." "You're facing the wrong direction."

————

"Today is my wife's birthday." "What are you getting for her?" "Make me an offer!"

————

Her thirtieth birthday isn't far away—it was only eight years ago.

————

My wife is so economical, she had only twenty-six candles on her fortieth birthday cake.

At her birthday party, I tried to count the candles on the cake, but the heat drove me back.

————

WIFE: For weeks I've been telling you not to buy me anything for my birthday and still you forgot to bring me something.

————

He always remembers your age but forgets your birthday.

————

She's celebrating the twenty-fifth anniversary of her thirty-fifth birthday.

————

She could add years to her life—just by telling the truth.

————

A well-adjusted woman is one who not only knows now what she wants for her birthday, but what she's going to exchange it for.

## Birthstones

For Maids: The Soapstone
For Builders: The Cornerstone
For Politicians: The Blarney Stone
For Executives: The Grindstone
For Stockbrokers: The Curbstone
For Motorists: The Milestone
For Pedestrians: The Tombstone
For Borrowers: The Touchstone

For Policemen: The Paving Stone
For Burglars: The Keystone
For Wits: The Headstone

———

Dean Martin and Phil Harris don't need any special birthstones; they're stoned all year round. One day I gave Dean Martin a cigarette lighter. He finished it in one gulp.

## Bishop, Joey
*(see also Comedians)*

Dean Martin and Frank Sinatra will now tell you about some of the good work the Mafia does.

———

Dennis the Menace has a great TV show but a terrible barber.

———

Art Linkletter has interviewed so many children he can't talk to you unless he bends down.

———

How do you do, William Bendix! Don't act up or I won't buy your washing machine.

———

When I performed in Washington for the president, I didn't stay at the White House. My mother wasn't too crazy about the neighborhood.

———

The traffic was so heavy yesterday I drove fifteen miles in neutral.

## Boats

"Do boats like this sink often?" "Only once."

———

I was so seasick, I looked like my passport photo.

———

He is so rich, he bought a new yacht. The old one got wet.

———

Message to deep-sea diver: "Come up quick—the boat's sinking."

———

And you think you have trouble? What about the deep-sea diver coming up, who passed his ship going down?

———

SAILOR: They've just dropped their anchor. LADY: I was afraid they would. It's been dangling outside all day.

———

Her family is so exclusive, they didn't come over on the *Mayflower*. they had their own boat.

## Bloopers and Typographical Errors
*(see also Leno, Jay, Signs)*

An Italian restaurant featured this item on its menu: melon and prostitute ham.

This sign in a laundry on Staten Island: "Ladies: Leave your clothes here and spend the afternoon having a good time."

Sign in the window of a restaurant: "Wanted: Man to wash dishes and two waitresses."

Notice at an exclusive club: "A sports jacket may be worn to dinner—but no trousers."

The California paper put this story on the front page: "Her pretty face and slim figure were to be found at the best parties and on the floors of the smartest nightclubs."

In a cemetery, there's a sign that says, "Persons are prohibited from picking flowers from any but their own graves."

Headline on a Philadelphia paper: "Woman Kicked by Her Husband Said to Be Greatly Improved."

Front-page story in a newspaper: "Officer Convicted of Accepting Bride."

On a church bulletin board: "Greater love hath no man than this, that a man lay down his wife for his friends" (John 15:13). From the church magazine: "Sorry about that story on the bulletin board. That should have been *life*, not *wife*, but Mr. Myron, who wrote it, has been quite unwell owing to his recent death, and he is taking a short holiday to convalesce."

I'm still not sure if this was a blooper: After my speech at the YMHA, one woman said to me, "You're a blessing. For forty years I've been suffering from insomnia. Went to doctor after doctor who couldn't help. As soon as you opened your mouth I was cured." Another woman told me, "I loved your talk. I woke up from it refreshed." Then a man said, "Your speech was like water to a drowning person." One guy started to walk out on me. "Sorry," he explained, "I'm going for a haircut." I said, "Why didn't you get it before my speech?" He said, "I didn't need it then!"

The fashionable lady stepped into the elevator at Saks and asked the operator: "Where can I find silk covering for my settee?" The young man said, "Third floor, lingerie department."

A local coach ran this classified ad in a show business magazine: "Girls who have ambitions to sing with a band should take vice lessons."

I loved this story in the paper: "Doctor Is Eulogized" was the headline. The story began, "The New York obstetrician practiced more than sixty years and is responsible for most of the babies born in this community." (Practiced, hell—the doc was perfect.)

---

The sign in the window of the jewelry store said, "Why go elsewhere to be cheated when you can come here?"

---

The store poster declared: "We exchange everything. Bicycles, washing machines, etc. Bring your wife and get the deal of your life."

---

This notice was displayed in bold letters on the photocopier in an advertising office: "The typist's reproduction equipment is not to be interfered with without prior permission."

---

In a large park there is a small bandstand, around which are many seats. A sign states: "The seats in this vicinity of the bandstand are for the use of ladies. Gentlemen should make use of them only after the former are seated."

---

The story declared: "Owing to the fuel crisis, officials are advised to take advantage of their secretaries between the hours of 12 and 2."

There was an accident on Wall Street today: A streetwalker was hit by a car. She was hurt in the business section.

---

"The members of Congress," read the editorial, "meet in Washington to disgust the nation and its problems."

---

"Myron Dunleavy of this station is going to be married next Saturday, so I'm dedicating the next number to Myron and his expectant bride."

---

"The operator of the other car, charged with drunken driving, crashed into Mrs. Field's rear end, which was sticking out into the road."

---

I told the waiter at the restaurant, "My soup tastes funny." He said, "Well, go ahead and laugh."

---

I asked the waiter, "Will the spaghetti I ordered be long?" He said, "I don't know, sir, we never measure it!"

---

The evangelist introduced a choral group and said, "Okay, now sin, you singers."

---

# Bookmakers

Definition of a bookmaker: That's a pickpocket who lets you use your own hands.

———◆◆◆———

I don't bet with bookmakers any more. I give my money directly to the cops.

———◆◆◆———

I bet fifty dollars on the horse to win. The next day I found out they sold her for twenty-five.

———◆◆◆———

As one cop said to another, "My life is an open bookie."

———◆◆◆———

The cops are really going after the bookies now. The bookies claim race prejudice.

# Books and Authors
*(see also Critics)*

"Have you read all of Shakespeare's plays?" "Yes, unless he's written something new lately."

———◆◆◆———

Speak no evil, see no evil, and hear no evil—and you'll never get a publisher to publish your book.

———◆◆◆———

The writer admitted that his greatest work of fiction was "filling out my income tax return."

———◆◆◆———

Erich Maria Remarque once said, "An author never finishes a book. He abandons it."

———◆◆◆———

Men who can read girls like a book usually like to read in bed.

———◆◆◆———

Funnyman Shecky Greene says he was asked to let his biography be written, but he insists that it be authentic: "Something like, 'As told to his bookmaker.'"

———◆◆◆———

Dedication: "To my wife—without whom I never would have been able to spend the money I made on my last book."

———◆◆◆———

My book is in its fifth printing. The first four were blurred.

———◆◆◆———

My book is a Book-of-the-Month selection, but you can't make money selling one book a month.

———◆◆◆———

There's a new book out called *How to Be Happy Without Money*, but it costs fifteen dollars.

———◆◆◆———

Your book is going like wildfire. Everybody is burning it.

———◆◆◆———

I'm a comparative unknown as a writer, and when you compare me to other writers, you'll know why I'm unknown.

———

My first book was so funny, one fellow fell out of his chair laughing. But Dad's all right now.

———

A book is like TV. It can reach millions of people who fortunately can't reach you.

———

Your book is selling like mad. Whoever reads it goes away mad.

———

Your book is attracting big crowds—to television.

———

Your book is fine. The only trouble is the covers are too far apart.

———

Your book packs a wallop. As soon as I started it, I fell asleep.

———

"Have you read my last book?" "I sure hope so."

———

Your book has a happy ending—I was so glad when it was over.

———

My latest book has sold 500,000 copies. If you can't get a copy, call me. I got 500,000 copies.

———

Who needs a dictionary? If you read one, you've read them all.

———

It's a little silly to spend six months writing a novel when you can buy one for $3.98.

———

"There are so few books in my house," said Myron, "when the TV set is busted, we have to talk to each other."

———

The dedication in one book I wrote was to my wife, Cindy, "who spent her days writing this book with me—and spent the royalties before I received them."

———

Earl Wilson's dedication was, "To the wonderful little woman who cooks my meals, darns my socks, and rears my son: my mother-in-law."

———

Copy from a dust jacket: "Can a girl from a small mining town out west find love and happiness in a small mining town out east?"

———

And now our story asks the question, "Can a nice run-of-the-mill girl find happiness running a mill?"

"All the historical books that contain no lies are extremely tedious."—Anatole France

———

"If you want to get rich from writing, write the sort of thing that's read by persons who move their lips when they're reading to themselves."—Don Marquis

———

"When I want to read a book, I write one."—Disraeli

———

HE: I'm reading a sad book. FRIEND: What book? HE: *Lady Chatterley's Lover.* FRIEND: That's not a sad book. HE: It is at my age.

———

Another warm dedication: "To my wife, without whose constant companionship on my trips I'd have met a hell of a lot more girls."

———

I gladly dedicate this book to the one I shall always owe a great deal as long as I live: the Collector of Internal Revenue.

———

My book is in its twentieth printing. We printed them one at a time.

———

Shakespeare's plays are nothing but famous quotations strung together.

———

I read the dictionary but I don't care for it. It changes the subject too often.

Oh, I don't like the telephone book—a lot of names but no plot.

———

Larry Gore dedicates his book *Blintzkrieg '67,* about the Israeli—Arab war, "to my wife, Selma, who always puts up a better fight than the Egyptians!"

———

And now, here are some classic book titles:

*Brain Surgery—Self-Taught.*

———

*How to Build a Swamp.*

———

*How to Retire at the Age of Eight.*

———

*Love Letters From King Faisal to Phyllis Diller.*

———

*Musical Favorites of Dr. Sam Sheppard.*

———

*Will the Pressure Cooker Replace the Atomic Bomb?*

———

*How to Cheat at Badminton*

———

*How to Stop Raising Rabbits*

# Booze

*(see also Alcohol, Bars, Drinking)*

"I went to a dozen different bars this afternoon, but I couldn't get what I wanted." "What did you want?" "Credit."

———

He was a drinking man. He took his liquor where he found it, and they usually found him where he took his liquor.

———

Weekend liquor: You drink it on Monday and the week ends right there.

———

The only new fiction he reads is the liquor labels.

———

Leave the gin on the table. I may think of something I wanna forget.

———

"Have a drink of elephant whiskey?" "What's that?" "Take one drink and you throw your trunk out the window."

———

"Here's a message from the people upstairs." "Put it under the door." "I can't. I might spill it."

———

"What're ya drinkin'?" "Northwest Mounted." "What do you mean?" "It always gets its man."

———

"Lips that touch liquor shall never touch mine." "Your lips?" "My liquor."

———

He drank so much beer that when he ate a pretzel you could hear it splash.

———

People who carry glass bottles shouldn't sit on stone benches.

———

The girl who drinks like a fish shouldn't be surprised if her head swims.

# Bores

A bore never runs out of conversation, just listeners. The biggest bore in town:

You ask him how he feels and he tells you.

———

I interrupted one dull fellow with, "Excuse me, my leg has gone to sleep. Do you mind if I join it?"

———

One dullard said to my brother, "I passed by your place yesterday." My brother responded, "Thank you so much."

———

A bore is a person who talks when you want him to listen.

———

This speaker, running for office, was really waxing dull. The restive audience began to argue among themselves. "There's so much interruption," the orator complained, "that I can hardly hear myself speak." A voice in the rear yelled out: "Cheer up, Gov, you ain't missing much."

————

A bore is a man who never seems to have any previous engagements.

————

Bores are people who talk of themselves when you are thinking of yourself.

————

He lights up a room—when he leaves it.

————

They have parties—just not to have him.

————

He never opens his mouth unless he has nothing to say.

————

He's very cultured—he can bore you on any subject.

————

I know a guy who has nothing to say, but you have to listen to him a long time to find out.

————

This lady's life was so dull that she looked forward to dental appointments. Even her dog got bored and left her.

————

This actor was so dull, he was upstaged by the scenery.

————

He's so dull, he could go on color TV and come out in black and white.

————

His life is so dull, he looks forward to dentist appointments.

————

He died at twenty but he was buried at seventy.

————

You take him with you when you want to be alone.

————

## Borscht Belt Laughs

My father received this letter in answer to a request for accommodations at a hotel in Monticello:

"Dear Sir: We regret to inform you that all the worthwhile accommodations are already taken. We have nothing left but the Luxury Lodge."

————

Today the Borscht Belt is so big, one hotel is thinking of air-conditioning the forest. Another is planning an indoor mountain. A third will have tiger hunting under glass.

———⋄———

At one luxury hotel a rich manufacturer fell in the pool and would have drowned if the lifeguard hadn't pulled him out. He asked a friend: "What do you tip for a thing like that?"

———⋄———

The lifeguards were working over a young lady they had just fished out of the water. "What are you doing?" her father asked. "We're giving her artificial respiration," one answered. "I can afford it," he said, "give her the real thing."

———⋄———

I regret that I have but one wife to send to the country.

———⋄———

Vacations are easy to plan. Your boss tells you when, and your wife tells you where.

———⋄———

A resort in the Catskills is going to make a fortune. No more actors; they're going to book only unmarried doctors and lawyers.

———⋄———

The hotel had so many "dogs" that one Fourth of July they had a beauty contest, and nobody won.

"Will I get a sin for playing golf on the Sabbath?" "The way you play, it's a sin to play any day."

———⋄———

This fellow was crazy about the chambermaid, but she kept running away from him. One day he finally grabbed her and whispered his dishonorable intentions in her ear. To his amazement, she readily consented. "If that's the way you felt, Olga," he panted, "why have you been running away from me all this time?" "Well," she said, "all time I tink ya vant extra towel!"

———⋄———

Grossinger's, the Catskill Mountains resort, observes dietary laws adhered to by the Jewish people, and accordingly has two kitchens: one where milk or dairy products are prepared, and one for meats. Strictly separate. One night I drove up to emcee an all-star show and found that due to alterations the theater was closed, and the performance was scheduled to go on in the dining room. A stage, spotlights, and so forth had been set up, and a thousand persons jammed the huge hall. After the overture, I took over with greetings and opening jokes. As I began to introduce the first act, Tip, Tap, and Toe, two of the hoofing trio hissed from the side near the kitchen door: "Stall, stall! Toe just got here and he's changing clothes." So I announced, "The boys need another minute. One of them is changing clothes." Paul Grossinger, sitting up front, yelled, "Where?" I pointed and said, "Right through that door." "Oh, my God," he wailed, "in the dairy kitchen?"

———

Lyndon Baines Johnson was in the Catskills last summer for the first time. They have a sign at the Nevele in Ellenville where the president spent his time: "LBJ shlept here."

———

The people on the Borscht Belt have their own way of speaking. They answer a question with a question: "How do you feel?" "How should I feel?" "What's new?" "What could be new?" After the president's visit to the Borscht Belt, I asked him: "Did you enjoy it?" "Why not?" he answered.

———

My room has a beautiful view—if you look straight up.

———

My room is so small, when a girl comes in, she *must* lie down.

———

Sign in bathroom: "Watch your children—don't throw anything in the bowl."

———

Max was standing in front of the hotel in Fallsburgh when a farmer passed by. "Good morning," the city man greeted him. "Mornin'," answered the farmer. "Where are you going?" "T' town." "What have you in the wagon?" "Manure." "What do you do with the manure?" "Spread it over the strawberries." "Why don't you come over to our place? We get sour cream!"

## Bosses
*(see also Bankruptcy, Business, Cheating, Labor, Secretaries)*

My nephew told me, "I told the boss he's got to pay me what I'm worth, but he says he refuses to pay below the minimum wage."

———

The boss explained, "We pay every two weeks because you can't buy anything with one week's pay."

———

The young lady looking for a job in a Madison Avenue advertising firm was asked by the boss, "What are your aims and ambitions?" She said, "I want to go as far as my education and sex will allow."

———

When secretaries work late, they won't go home by themselves anymore. They wait for their bosses to take them. At least then, if they get attacked, it could mean a raise.

———

My neighbors were talking about their bosses. "I think he's great," the bookkeeper said. "You can't help liking him. If you don't, he fires you." My neighbor's wife said, "My boss gave me a big raise." Her husband said, "Really? How did you get it?" She said, "I can tell you, but I don't think it will help you much."

———

"Our company is just one big happy family," my neighbor told me. "The main reason for this is because I hire all my relatives."

———

My boss told me, "There are hundreds of ways of making a fortune, but only one honest way." I asked, "What's that?" He said, "How should I know?"

———

One of the models at a Seventh Avenue dress house spent a weekend in an Atlantic City hotel with her boss. When she got back to the showroom on Monday morning, her friend was waiting with questions. "Tell me," she asked, "how did the boss register at the hotel?" The model squealed, "Terrific."

———

My cousin's secretary resigned when she caught him being a little too friendly with his wife. He immediately hired three gorgeous stenographers, each more sexy than the other. His buyer asked as he eyed the new beauties, "How the hell do you expect to accomplish anything?" My cousin replied, "Easy. I'll give two of them the day off!"

A very handsome young lady walked into a sporting goods store and ordered all the equipment necessary for a baseball game, including a baseball bat, a catcher's mitt, and a catcher's mask. The salesman asked, "Are you sure you want all these?" She said, "Yes. My boss said if I'd play ball with him we'd get along fine."

———

The pretty little baby-faced secretary phoned her mother to inform her, "I'll be late again for dinner tonight, Mom. I made a mistake last night and the boss wants me to do it over again."

———

The secretary said to the nontypist, "You'll love working for the boss. Lots of opportunity for advances."

———

I asked my secretary, "How long did your sister work for her last boss?" She said, "Until she got him."

———

One secretary got her job when the boss saw her résumé. It was very impressive, especially the centerfold.

———

The boss dictated a very difficult letter to his curvy secretary. When she brought it back for his signature, he read a garbled version of his carefully thought-out remarks. "Didn't you read this letter before you put it on my desk?" he yelled. She answered, "Oh, no, I thought it was confidential."

The salesman took his boss out for dinner on his birthday and presented him with a stereo and solid gold cuff-links. The boss was overwhelmed that an employee would spend so much money on him, until he found out the salesman had put it on his expense account.

The new maid was the slowest thing on two feet. It took her at least three times as long as anyone else to do something. One day, the boss of the house reached her boiling point. "You're worse than a snail," she screamed. "Tell me, Alice, is there anything you can do fast?" Alice thought for a moment and then replied, "Get fired."

The boss introduced the newcomer to the office staff: "This is my son. He's going to start at the bottom for a few days."

The boss approached one of his most ambitious and competent men and told him: "I've had my eye on you for a long time. You're a very hard worker and you've put in long hours. You're very ambitious." Before the employee could say thanks, the boss continued: "So, consequently, I'm going to fire you before you learn too much. It's men like you who start up competing companies."

A big garment manufacturer became extremely fond of one of his models, a gorgeous blonde. One day, he gave her a peck on the cheek and suggested that they visit his beach house for the weekend. "We'll have lots of fun," he added. "Okay," she agreed. "And I'll bring my fiancé." He asked, "What for?" She said, "In case your wife wants to have some fun, too!"

The boss was telling his son, "I'm retiring. The business is all yours. I've made a good living because of two principles: honesty and wisdom. Honesty is important. If you promise the goods by the first of the month, no matter what happens, you must deliver by the first." The kid said: "Sure, Pop, but what about wisdom?" The boss said, "Wisdom means: Dummy, who said you should promise?"

# Boxing

BOXER: Have I done him any damage? DISTRUSTED SECOND: No, but keep swinging. The draft might give him a cold.

"What are you putting in your glove?" "My good-luck piece—my horseshoe."

"Don't be frightened. I'll not hit you with both hands." "You won't?" "No, I'll only hit you with one hand. I'll need the other to hold you up."

## Boy Scouts

He was so in love with her that he offered her everything. "I'll build a home for you atop the George Washington Bridge. I'll get you sable linings for your mink coats. I'll buy you a platinum Cadillac. Just say the word." "All I want," cooed the beautiful one, "is a solid gold Boy Scout knife." "But," said the stunned suitor, "you can have anything in the world." "That's all I want," purred the doll. When he brought her the solid gold Boy Scout knife, she expressed her thanks. "Is this all you want to make you happy?" he asked. "What are you going to do with it?" She then opened up a huge hope chest, revealing hundreds of similar solid gold Boy Scout knives. "Why?" asked the bewildered lover. "Well," she explained, "right now I'm very young and beautiful and everybody wants me, but when I get old and not so attractive, can you imagine what a Boy Scout will do for one of these?"

A group of Cub Scouts visited the local FBI office and viewed pictures of the ten most wanted men in the United States. One kid pointed to a picture and asked if that really was the photo-graph of the wanted person. The agent said yes. "Then why," asked the boy, "didn't you keep him when you took his picture?"

I actually caught a Boy Scout doing his good deed. He was helping a little old lady across the street, and she wasn't even a lady—it was a hippie.

"I was a Boy Scout till I was sixteen. Then I became a Girl Scout."—Morey Amsterdam

## Brides and Grooms
*(see also Marriage)*

The bride didn't look happy, she looked triumphant.

Telling a bride what she should know on her wedding night is like giving a fish a bath.

The only time you see a blushing bride these days is when the groom doesn't show up.

BRIDE'S FATHER TO GROOM: My boy, you are the second happiest man in the world.

Did you hear about the sleepy bride who couldn't stay awake for a second?

———

The bride was so ugly, everybody kissed the bridesmaid.

———

The bride was so ugly, everybody kissed the groom.

———

A newlywed shouldn't expect his first few meals to be perfect. After all, it takes time to find the right restaurant.

———

Like the bride said on her honeymoon, "So that's what I've been saving myself for, all these years?"

———

The sign on the back of the car read, "Just married! Today she got him— tonight he gets her!"

———

Bride to groom as they walked down the aisle: "Well, it won't be wrong now!"

———

Modern brides are wearing their wedding dresses shorter and oftener.

———

The bridegroom tried to fool everybody in the hotel lobby by letting his bride carry the luggage.

USHER: Are you a friend of the groom? LADY: Indeed no! I'm the bride's mother.

———

The groom didn't get his pants back in time for the wedding, so he sued the tailor for promise of breeches.

## British Humor
*(see also England)*

A woman in a London court was charged with shoplifting. The magistrate asked if she had anything to say in her own behalf. "Yes, your honor," she said proudly, "I only take British goods."

———

"I think it's disgusting that some of our comedians earn more than Cabinet ministers." "Well, it's only fair: On the whole, they're funnier."

———

PEDDLER: Any pens, pencils, plates, pots, teapots, or baskets today? LADY OF THE HOUSE: If you don't go 'way, I'll call the police. PEDDLER: 'Ere you are, mum—whistles, sixpence each.

———

DOCTOR: Now what about this ear? COCKNEY PATIENT: This 'ere wot?

———

I was visiting an English friend and his wife for the weekend. One morning I accidentally walked in on the wife in her bath. I immediately rushed to the husband and apologized. He looked up and said nonchalantly, "Skinny old thing, isn't she?"

---

"I'll give you fifty shillings for that pup." "Oh, sir, that's impossible. That pup belongs to me wife, and she'd sob 'er 'art out. But I tell yer wat. Give me another twenty bob an' we'll let 'er sob a little!"

BUTLER: The post, m'lady. THE LADY: Oh, Christmas cards, I imagine. Well, Jeeves, examine them carefully, and if you consider any of them too familiar, just destroy them!

---

"What's all the commotion at Percy's house?" "Nothin' much—they're takin' 'im away in the ambulance for beatin' 'is missus."

---

POLICEMAN: Beg pardon, sir, if you're the dog-faced gentleman with the bald head, the green teeth, the vegetable nose, and ears like taxi doors, I am to tell you that your wife couldn't wait for you any longer and she'll see you at home."

---

Jenkins and Diggs had a big fight, and the bartender insisted they make up. "I hold no anger in me," Diggs said, "and to prove it I'll drink to yer. 'Ere's lookin' at yer—and 'eaven knows that's a real heffort!"

## Brooklyn

If we didn't have Brooklyn, where would the other end of the bridge rest?

---

"How could a guy almost blind himself drinking coffee?" "He left the spoon in the cup."

---

How about the tough neighborhood he hailed from? It was so tough that a cat with a tail was considered a tourist, and we used to play games like Spin the Cop.

## Burlesque

Men always claim they go to burlesque to see the comics. They then bring binoculars to see the comics better.

---

The stripper was so ugly they were hollering, "Up in front."

---

She does a very unusual dance—the only thing on her is the spotlight.

---

My father always warned me not to go to burlesque, because there are things I wouldn't expect to see. He was right. The first time I went I saw my father in the first row.

---

She was barefoot—up to her chin.

# Burns, George
*(see also Comedians)*

You know, today it costs a young fellow ten dollars to take a girl to lunch. When I was a boy, if you asked your father for ten dollars, it meant you were going to get married and have enough money left over to open a business. . . . In those days money went a long way. For a dollar you could take a girl to dinner and to a movie and have sodas afterward. My only problem was to find a girl who had a dollar. . . . I remember when I was seventeen I had a real big date, and my father gave me a dollar. I told him I'd be home at twelve, but I didn't get in till four in the morning. There was my father, sitting up. He wasn't worried about me, he was waiting for his change. . . . My father didn't believe in spoiling his sons. He made us work for our money. And he started us out pretty early. Once at dinner he suddenly pointed at me and said, "Look at that big boy, sits around and does nothing but eat!" I really wasn't that big, it was the high chair I was sitting in. It made me look that way.

When I was a kid, it wasn't always girls. If I had a few nickels saved, I'd go to a ball game. They let you in for fifty cents if you wore long pants, and twenty-five cents if you wore short pants. One day I figured out a way to get in for nothing, but I caught cold before I even left the house.

I remember some of the tricks I used to save money. When a girl suggested dinner, I always said, "Fine," and then I'd go to her house and have it. And I'd sit around her parlor and eat some fruit and candy and smoke a good cigar. I wouldn't go out with a girl unless her father smoked good cigars.

If a girl said, "How about going to a movie?" I'd give her a kiss, and ask her if any boy had ever given her a better one. By the time she'd named all the boys, it was too late for the movie. But if she insisted on going out somewhere anyway, I was a good sport about it. And when she came home, I was still there, smoking her father's good cigars. After a while my reputation got around. You know how fathers sit in the parlor and watch their daughters? The fathers I knew used to sit in theirs to watch their cigars.

# Business
*(see also Bankruptcy, Bills, Bosses, Clerks, Labor)*

A businessman can't win nowadays: If he does something wrong, he's fined; if he does something right, he's taxed.

If you want to know how to run a business, ask a man who hasn't any.

Sign on closed Broadway store: "We undersold everybody."

I wanted my son to share in the business, but the government beat me to it.

---

MAX IN MIAMI: Sam, this is Max. How's everything in New York? SAM IN NEW YORK: Very good. MAX: How's the weather up there? SAM: The weather's how it should be. MAX: How's business in the shop? SAM: Very good, but I got bad news for you. MAX: What's the matter? SAM: We've been robbed. MAX: Don't be silly. Put it back!

---

Two partners decided to take a trip to Florida. Just as they got on the train and were seated comfortably, one of them jumped up and screamed, "My God! I left the safe open!" The other partner shrugged his shoulders and replied, "What are you worried about? We're both here, ain't we?"

---

FIRST SALESMAN: I'd like to learn the secret of your success as a house-to-house salesman. SECOND SALESMAN: Oh, it's easy. The minute a woman opens the door I say, "Miss, is your mother in?"

---

Whenever the American businessman comes up with a new idea, a month later the Russians invent it, and two months later the Japanese copy it and sell it to us cheaper.

---

"Business is so bad, this last year I've been losing at least $500 a week, week after week." "Why don't you give up the business?" "Then how am I going to make a living?"

---

"I can't understand it," he cried to his partner, "here we are bankrupt, through, *kaput*, and only yesterday the President said business was booming." "Maybe the President has a better location."

---

The preacher was lecturing to his flock: "Remember, my good friends, there will be no buying and selling in heaven." "That's not where business has gone," a salesman in the rear mumbled.

---

The young business executive gave an interview to the *Wall Street Journal* and bragged: "Those early days were tough, but I put my shoulder to the wheel, rolled up my sleeves, gritted my teeth, and borrowed another $100,000 from my father."

---

We're a nonprofit organization. We don't mean to be, but we are.

---

An efficiency expert died and was being carried to his grave by six pallbearers. As they approached their destination the lid popped open and the efficiency expert sat up and shouted, "If you'd put this thing on wheels, you could lay off four men."

A big-business tycoon died and went to his eternal resting place. When he arrived in the other world, he was greeted by a salesman who used to visit him on Earth. "Max, old boy, I'm here for the appointment," said the salesman. "What appointment?" asked the businessman. "Don't you remember?" asked the salesman. "Every time I used to try to see you at your office, you'd tell me you'd see me here."

---

"How can you make money selling watches so cheap?" "Easy. We make our profit repairing them."

---

If at first you do succeed, it's probably your father's business.

---

A businessman talks golf at the office and business on the golf course.

---

Then there's the absent-minded businessman who took his wife to dinner instead of his secretary.

---

The big executive told his new secretary he wanted some old-fashioned loving, so she introduced him to her grandmother.

---

The little old man asked the boss for Monday off to celebrate his golden wedding anniversary. The boss growled, "My God, will I have to put up with this chutzpah every fifty years?"

---

The secretary said to her boss: "Me marry you? Are you kidding? You'll do anything to get out of paying overtime, won't you?"

---

When your wife goes along to a convention, you have twice the expenses and half the fun.

---

Women in business present a problem: If you treat them like men, they start complaining; if you treat them like women, your wife may find out.

---

The high-priced call girl cried, "If my business were legitimate, I would deduct a substantial percentage for depreciation of my body."

---

A firm advertising its product stated: "Money returned if not satisfactory." When someone requested the return of his money, the reply he received was, "Your money is quite satisfactory and therefore we decline to return it."

---

The clerk asked the paymaster in the big plant, "Where's my paycheck?" The cashier explained, "Well, after deducting withholding tax, state income tax, city tax, Social Security, retirement fund, unemployment insurance, hospitalization, dental insurance, group life insurance, and your donation to the company welfare fund, you owe us $14.25."

---

The guy said to his boss, "On the salary you pay me, I can't afford to get married." "That's true," the boss admitted, "and in twenty years, you'll thank me!"

---

The secretary said to the young man, "How did you get this big executive job? You've only been here three months!" He explained, "I ran into my father and he took a liking to me."

---

The owner of one garment manufacturing company was asked, "How's business?" He replied, "Not too good. I've had to lay off my son-in-law and two of my wife's nephews."

---

The contractor wanted to give the government official a sports car. The official objected, saying, "Sir, common decency and my basic sense of honor would never permit me to accept a gift like that." The contractor said, "I quite understand. Suppose we do this: I'll sell you the car for ten dollars." The official thought for a moment, then said, "In that case, I'll take two."

---

Everybody is complaining about their businesses. My neighbor told me, "It's so bad, even my bills come postage due."

---

One young man applied for the job of bookkeeper. "Can you do double entry?" he was asked. "Yes," he said, "and I can do triple entry." The boss asked, "Triple entry?" "Sure. One for the working partner, showing the true profits, another for the sleeping partner, showing small profits, and a third for the income tax authorities, showing a loss."

---

It's great to take out a loan. At least you know somebody is going to call you.

---

One Queens shoe store ordered a large consignment of shoes from a manufacturer in Buffalo. A week later the store manager received a letter saying, "Sorry, we cannot fill your order until full payment is made on the last one." The manager wrote back, "Please cancel the new order. I can't wait that long."

---

A manufacturer said to a storekeeper, "Thank you, Mr. Schwartz, for your patronage. I wish I had twenty customers like you." Schwartz said, "Gee, it's good to hear you talk like that. I'm surprised. You know that I protest every bill and I'm late in paying." The manufacturer said, "I still would like twenty customers like you;

but the trouble is, I have two hundred."

———

My neighbor went to see his best friend and told him, "I badly need some extra money in my business, and they told me at the bank that if you endorse the note they will be glad to advance it." His pal said, "I'm surprised at you. Why bother strangers for money when you can get it from a friend? You go to the bank and let them endorse the note and I'll give you all the money you need."

———

Two clothing manufacturers are discussing their business problems. In the middle of the conversation, one bolts to the window and says, "I'm going to end it all and jump out this window." And he does. The other is very depressed, but five minutes later his partner comes walking in. The first partner says, "What happened? I saw you jump out the window." The other replied, "Yes, but I landed on the returns."

———

In these days of high finance, it's interesting to note that Noah was the first financier: He was able to float a company when the whole world was in liquidation.

———

Executive ability: That's the art of getting the credit for all the hard work somebody else does.

He's the perfect businessman. When others look at a project and say, "How?" he looks at it and says, "How much?"

———

You must have positive thinking in business. My uncle kept thinking he'd never make it. Now he's positive he's not going to make it.

———

The sharpest business deal in this country was the Dutch purchase of Manhattan from the Indians. Peter Minuit had just conned Manhattan Island out of the Canarsie tribe and was standing with the sellers on the banks of the East River surveying his purchase. "Hold it," he hollered. "Isn't that Brooklyn over there?" The Canarsie chief snapped, "Listen, wiseguy, for twenty-four bucks you expect the place to be perfect?"

———

Flipping through her morning newspaper, the woman was attracted by a headline in the financial section. She read it with mounting perplexity, then turned to her husband and asked, "What makes the market go up and down?" "Oh, all kinds of things," he replied. "Commodity fluctuations. Inflationary pressures. International imbalances. Political tensions. Financial instability." She put down the paper and said, "Look, if you don't know, why don't you just say so?"

And how about the yuppie who married the corporate president's daughter and hung her nude picture over his desk? He didn't want people to think he had married her just for her money. "What's it like to be married to the boss's daughter?" he was asked. "Well," he said, "the morning after our wedding she made some greasy eggs, burnt toast, half-raw bacon, and crummy coffee. It was then I realized she couldn't cook either."

---

Tarzan came home in the afternoon and asked Jane for a triple Jack Daniel's. He sat down and in a few moments finished off the drink. "Let me have another," ordered the ape-man. After a moment of hesitation, Jane blurted out, "Tarzan, I'm worried about your drinking. Every afternoon you come home and proceed to get totally sloshed." "Jane, I can't help myself," Tarzan protested. "It's a jungle out there."

---

"My son is a good businessman," my neighbor said proudly. "He's so dedicated, he keeps his secretary near his bed in case he should get an idea during the night."

---

Sign on a store: "Don't be fooled by imitators going out of business. We have been going out of business longer than anyone on this block."

Humorist Mickey Freeman tells this story: Two partners own a clothing store. They take turns minding it. One day Harry, who's at the store, calls his partner at home. He says, "You got to come on down here and congratulate me. I just made a terrific sale—sold that awful electric purple suit with the big lapels." The partner comes to the store, sees Harry bandaged and bleeding, and says, "What happened?" "The customer's seeing-eye dog didn't like the suit," replies Harry.

---

The government is still trying to help small businesses. A little fellow used to make the rounds with a hand organ and a monkey. The government gave him a loan. Now he goes around with a steam calliope and a gorilla.

---

Two Seventh Avenue merchants were having their weekly crying session about business. One said, "Now take June. What a month. Only returns—horrible—and that was good compared to July. Even the customers who don't pay weren't buying." "Big deal," said his friend. "You think you got troubles? Let me tell you something. Yesterday I found out my son is a homosexual and my daughter is a lesbian! Now what could be worse than that?" "August!" came the answer.

The dress manufacturer sent this letter to one of his delinquent customers: "Dear Sir: After checking our records, we note that we have done more for you than your mother did—we've carried you for fifteen months."

———

"I have a hundred suits," the cloak-and-suitor was bragging, "and they're all pending."

———

"I buy a piece of merchandise for one dollar and I sell it for four dollars. You think 3 percent is bad?"

———

The big boss stood up before his board of directors and stockholders and said, "This year's financial report is being brought to you in living color—red."

———

Charlie Cohen and his son were traveling through Italy. They particularly loved Rome. The guide pointed out the Colosseum. "You see," Charlie lectured his son, "this illustrates what I've always told you. When you haven't got sufficient capital, you don't start to build."

———

Two businessmen were discussing a compatriot. "He used to work for me," said the first one. "I wouldn't trust him with my money. He would lie, steal, cheat—anything for a buck." "How do you know him so well?" "How? I taught him everything he knows!"

———

To get 10 percent out of him, you've got to be at least a fifty-fifty partner.

———

Forget the Depression—this bum went broke during the boom. He went bankrupt during his busy season.

———

"How much do you pay?" "Three dollars a week—but what can you do to make yourself useful around a butcher shop?" "Anything." "Well, be specific. Can you dress a chicken?" "Not on three dollars a week."

———

The efficiency expert scrutinized the salesman's expense account. "How the hell could you spend twelve dollars a day for food in Augusta, Georgia?" "Simple," the salesman answered, "you just miss breakfast."

———

Efficiency expert: a guy smart enough to tell you how to run your business—and too smart to start his own.

## Cads

His parents never struck him, except in self-defense.

———

They're speaking well of him lately—he must be dead.

———

Someday he'll go too far—and I hope he stays there.

———

What good is asking him to act like a human being? He doesn't do imitations.

———

He and I have a lot in common. We both think he's wonderful.

———

I owe everything I have to him: my ulcers, headaches, nausea . . .

## Cambridge, Godfrey
(see also Comedians)

Block busting is when one of our colored brothers moves into an all-white neighborhood and the white people are supposed to panic and start throwing bricks and bombs and burning crosses. Now the Negro who's living there is not afraid of bricks and bombs and burning crosses—he's afraid of another Negro moving into the neighborhood.

———

I remember we were the first black family on our block, and my mother came running in one day and shouted, "Look, they're moving in." I said, "Ma, do you know they are us?"

———

I got off the bus in Scarsdale by accident and in the fifteen minutes it took me to get another bus, property values dropped 50 percent. . . . I remember when I just got out of college and was looking for a job. I walked into this office building and there I saw my soul brother in the lobby sweeping and mopping the floor, and I asked him where the personnel office was. He said, "We don't hire colored help," and I said, "I'm hip . . ."

———

I remember a black guy who thought he was white. I ran into this cat on the train. There he was in his overalls, carrying an attaché case, and he sat down next to a white bejeweled Scarsdale dowager. She said, "Hmph.

Colored people," and he said, "Where? Where?" When this man goes to the store to buy a watermelon, he's so ashamed he says, "Wrap it up and put handles on it." You meet him on the street and ask him what he's got there. He says, "My bowling ball!" Did you ever see an oblong bowling ball? And he takes it home and he won't eat it in the dining room, 'cause he's afraid someone will see him through that big picture window. So he takes it into the closet and eats it, seeds, rind, and all, and when he drives from Scarsdale and reaches a Negro neighborhood, he acts just like the white people do. He says, "Lock your doors, colored people live here!" He ought to remember he used to be colored.

———

I keep telling all my white actor friends, "Go on, fool, keep tanning yourself, you'll be tanning yourself out of a job." And I have a whole lot of experience to prove it.

## Canada

Up in Canada they have an organization called the Royal Canadian Mounted Police. They have the reputation of always getting their man.

———

Did you hear about the Gay Mountie? He not only gets his man, he keeps him.

———

It gets so cold in the northern Canadian woods, the women wear mink girdles.

## Cannibals

It was opening night of the 232nd Planet Hollywood restaurant in Madagascar. Two Cannibals attended and were going over the guest list. "How about Roseanne for two?" "No, I don't want anything too heavy." "What about Madonna?" "I hate fast food." "Sylvester Stallone?" "We had Italian last night." "Arnold Schwarzenegger would be good." "I hate German food." "Judge Chan?" "An hour later we'd be hungry." "We could start with something small as an appetizer, like Dr. Ruth and Pia Zadora." "Hmmm— maybe. What about Bruce Willis?" "He's too tough." "What about David Letterman?" "Aren't you tired of ham?" "Yeah, you're right. Oooh, Anna Nicole Smith!" "No, I've got to watch my cholesterol." "Let's just have coffee, and Demi Moore for dessert." "Perfect choice."

———

Some people are vegetarians. Cannibals are humanitarians.

———

The cannibal loves his fellow man— with gravy.

———

The chief ate his mother-in-law and found she still disagreed with him.

The cannibal takes you seriously—or with a grain of salt.

———

The cannibal shows his hospitality by constantly having people for dinner.

———

In cultural exchange, the cannibal chief asked the U.S. State Department to send him a comic who tells dirty stories. He wanted to have some spiced ham for dinner.

———

CANNIBAL: I'm very hungry. FLIGHT ATTENDANT: Would you like to see the menu? CANNIBAL: No, the passenger list.

———

A young cannibal chief noticed a particularly beautiful young lady about to be placed into the burning kettle. "Wait," he shouted to the cooks, "I'll have my breakfast in bed."

———

The chief's wife sent a message to another tribal chief in the neighborhood: "Please come and visit Saturday night. We're having the Browns for dinner."

———

As one teenage cannibal said to his date: "Let's take a stroll down to the old campfire and see who's cooking."

———

Then there's the chief's son who studies at the University of Miami. The professor asked him, "Don't tell me you still eat people after all this education?" The son said, "Sure. But now I use a knife and fork."

———

One member of the cannibal tribe complained he was getting fed up with people.

———

The king asked, "What's for lunch?" The cook said, "Two old maids." The king screamed, "Leftovers again?"

———

The tribe had eaten the missionary and had thoroughly enjoyed him. The next day, one of the cannibals, poking through the dead man's belongings, found a magazine. He began tearing out pictures of men, women, and children, and cramming them into his mouth and chewing them. The chief watched him for a while and then asked, "Say, is that dehydrated stuff any good?"

———

Did I tell you about the cannibal who bought his wife a Valentine's Day gift? A five-pound box of farmer's fannies.

———

Then there's the chief who had hay fever from eating too many grass widows.

The husband came home after a hard day and asked, "Am I late for dinner?" The missus answered, "Yes. Everyone's already eaten."

---

The cannibal said to his wife, "I've brought a friend home for dinner." She said, "Fine. Put him in the deep freeze and we'll have him next week."

---

The two cannibals sat back and patted their stomachs. "That," one said to his host, "was an absolutely delightful meal." "I'm glad you liked it," said the other. "My wife certainly makes wonderful soup. But I'm sure going to miss her."

---

The missionary was captured by cannibals and thrown into the pot. Just when he was ready to give up, he noticed the cannibal chief fall to his knees and start to pray. "Are you a practicing Christian?" the missionary asked hopefully. "Of course," said the chief, "and be so good as not to interrupt me while I'm saying grace."

---

Did you hear about the cannibal who was expelled from school? They caught him buttering up the teacher.

---

A cannibal is somebody who lives off other people.

Why did the cannibal girl have to rush home? She was having her beau for dinner.

---

Cannibals are great. How can you resist people who love their fellow man?

---

If a politician found he had cannibals among his constituents, he would promise them a missionary in every pot.

---

A cannibal chief captured a newspaperman. The newspaperman cried, "I can do you good. I'm an editor." The cannibal said, "Good. Tonight you'll be editor-in-chief!"

---

The cannibal chief's daughter came home in good spirits from a holiday at the seashore. "Did you meet a handsome man on the beach?" "Did I ever. I've got him right here in my suitcase."

---

A cannibal is a guy who goes into a restaurant and orders a waiter.

---

My relatives must be cannibals. They've been living off me for years.

---

Two society leaders in one cannibal tribe were discussing their marital problems: "I don't know what to make of my husband these days," said one woman. The other offered, "Don't let that bother you—I'll send over my new book of recipes."

---

A cannibal extends an invitation to another cannibal. "Why don't you come over for dinner tonight? We're having my mother-in-law." The other says, "I don't like your mother-in-law." The first one says, "Okay, then, just come over for coffee and dessert."

---

Did you hear about the cannibal who had his mother-in-law and passed her in the woods?

---

Most people don't like drunks—but it takes a cannibal to like somebody stewed.

---

A cannibal mother pointed out a downed airliner to her small child and said, "It's like seafood. You just eat what's inside."

---

A cannibal came home late one night and his wife gave him a cold shoulder.

---

A man was shipwrecked and captured by cannibals. Each day one would take a dagger and puncture one of his veins, and some of the natives would drink his blood. Finally he said to the chief, "Look, I don't care if you eat me, I just hate getting stuck for the drinks all the time."

---

The cannibal cook asked the chief: "Shall I stew both these cooks we captured from the steamer?" The chief replied, "No, one is enough. Too many cooks spoil the broth."

---

Then there was the crooked crematorium owner who sold the ashes to cannibals as instant people.

---

Did you hear about the cannibal who ordered a pizza with everybody on it?

---

Did you hear about this cannibal's wedding party? They toasted the bride and groom.

---

The cannibal chief wrote to the head of the missionary society: "Please send more messengers from the Lord. The last two were delicious."

---

Comedian Roy Baxter explains it all: "This cannibal was so frustrated, he ate his heart out."

Roy asks and answers his own questions: "What do cannibals eat on Thanksgiving?" "Pilgrims." "What does a cannibal take for indigestion?" "Tummies."

One cannibal asked another, "Have you seen the dentist?" "Yep, he filled my teeth at dinner."

———

This cannibal ate a missionary because he wanted a taste of religion.

———

A newspaperman was captured and brought before the cannibal chief. "A writer, eh?" the chief said. "Fine, you'll make good alphabet soup."

———

The cannibal went into a bookstore and asked if they had a new cookbook he had read about entitled *How to Serve Your Fellow Man*.

———

A group of cannibals returned from a successful hunt. They placed the two captured men into a pot and started placing ice cubes around the pot. Two young children see this and look at each another: "Oh, no," one groaned, "not cold cuts again."

———

The chief's son was running around the tree chasing the visitor from the States. The boy's mother hollered, "How many times have I told you, don't play with your food!"

## Cars
*(see also Automobiles, Traffic)*

I just paid $8,500 for a used car that cost $7,250 when it was new. It cost me a lot of money for a second-hand car, but at least it gets me where I'm going—to the bank for a loan.

———

Those aren't dents in the fenders, they're old-age wrinkles. Why can't they make a car with fenders on the *inside*?

———

Now they make cars for every price range—except cheap.

———

If automakers want to increase sales, they ought to stop guaranteeing parts for the life of the car and start guaranteeing them for the life of the car payments.

———

Used-car principle: It's hard to drive a real bargain.

———

Every part of my car makes a noise, except the horn.

———

One thing about my old car: Vandals don't bother with it when I leave it on the street at night. They figure somebody's already beaten them to it.

———

My car is so dangerous to drive, it comes with a combination warranty and will!

———

The garage mechanic took a look at my bargain car and said, "Let me put it this way. If your car were a horse it would have to be shot."

———

A used car is all right as far as it goes.

———

I don't want a cheaper car. I want an expensive car that costs less.

———

My neighbor told me, "I think I'm finally gonna have to trade in that old car of mine. This morning I got passed while going uphill—by some punk kid on a skateboard."

———

My uncle complains: "I've had nothing but problems on that used car. The motor won't start and the payments won't stop. I was almost late for work today. My car's in the shop getting a wallet job."

———

Last year I deducted my used car as a religious expense, because whenever I drive it, I pray it'll reach my destination.

———

My automobile repair bills may be an example of a lemon putting the squeeze on you.

My car has a lot of options. I have the option of pushing it, towing it, fixing it, or junking it.

———

The best time to buy a used car is when it's new.

———

There are two things I hate about my used car: parts and labor.

———

If you want to improve the desirability of your present car, check out the prices of the new ones.

———

So far I've paid off three cars: my doctor's, my dentist's, and my plumber's.

———

Nowadays, if you want to buy a $10,000 car, it's easy. Just buy a $4,000 car on time.

———

New-car prices are so high, one dealer has a showroom and a recovery room.

———

I don't know anything about cars, but luckily I've got a good mechanic, and he believes in preventive maintenance. I bring it in every 500 miles so he can rotate the ashtrays and change the air in the tires.

———

An auto mechanic: That's a guy who stands behind his work—with a tow truck.

———

Nowadays every family needs two cars: one to drive while the other one's being recalled.

———

A good year for the automakers is when they sell more cars than they recall.

———

The key words in the auto industry are *lighter* and *heavier*. The cars are lighter and the payments are heavier.

———

A new-car buyer called an auto manufacturer: "Was it your company that announced that you recently put a car together in seven minutes?" The executive answered proudly, "Yes, sir, it was." The buyer said, "Well, then, I'd just like to let you know that I've got the car."

———

A new-car dealer whose business was in a lot of trouble went down to the beach to drown himself. He found a bottle, picked it up, rubbed it, and lo and behold, a genie appeared and asked what he wished most. The poor man thought a moment and said, "I'd like an imported-car dealership in a major city." The genie snapped his fingers and the guy found himself in Tokyo with a Chrysler agency.

———

Foreign cars have invaded the United States. The slogan is "Buy American," but the practice is drive foreign.

———

It's a funny thing about those foreign sports cars: Most of the people who can afford them can't fit into them.

———

There are so many Japanese cars being sold in America, my mechanic is learning to change spark plugs with chopsticks.

———

My brother the lover likes the Ferrari: "It gets more gals to the mile." Some of these foreign cars run on gas-o-hol. The luxury models run on champagne, and an economy model runs on cheap wine. They are now designing a garbage truck that runs on beer.

———

My neighbor bought an English-made automobile and after a month of careful computation concluded that he was not getting the phenomenally high mileage so often credited to such cars. So he took it to a local mechanic, who, after checking it thoroughly, pronounced it in perfect condition. "I love the car," my neighbor confessed, "but isn't there something I can do to increase its mileage?" "Well, yes," the mechanic said. "You can do the same as most foreign-car owners do." "What's that?" my neighbor asked. "Lie about it."

My dealer said, "Here's the good news: Your car is not one of those being recalled by Detroit. The bad news is, since it's Japanese, it's being recalled by Tokyo."

———

I don't know if it means anything, but I saw Santa Claus—and the reindeer were pulling him in a Toyota.

———

I like that new French car built along feminine lines. Everything's different: You don't put gas in a tank anymore—you just dab a little behind each headlight. And it's just loaded with features that appeal to women! Lavender-wall tires, a low-cut grille, and padded bumpers. You'll love it. They brought one into Detroit and three Ramblers chased it into an alley!

———

With all due respect to these automotive aliens, America leads the world in the number of automobiles produced. That tells us something about American workmanship. Of course, we also lead the world in the production of tow trucks.

———

My neighbor surprised his wife with a gorgeous new car. "It's beautiful," she gushed. "Let's go for a ride right now." He said, "We can't go anywhere in it for a while. I didn't have any money left for gas or insurance."

———

I bought a car with defective brakes. I told the dealer, "I don't want you to stand behind this car. I want you to stand in front of it."

———

In my neighborhood there are so many foreign cars that it has been two years since anybody has been bit above the knees.

———

Writer and TV personality Dick Cavett said, "I don't like to drive those small cars. Every time I stop at a light, I expect a little kid to come up and say, 'It's my turn.'"

———

The truck driver pulled up alongside one of those tiny foreign cars that was stalled on the highway and yelled, "Whatsa trouble, pal, need a new flint?"

———

Comedian Jack E. Leonard got a bill for sixty dollars for an auto tuneup and snapped at the mechanic, "Who does your tuning up . . . Leonard Bernstein?"

———

I love those ads that say the only thing you can hear in a Rolls-Royce is the clock. In my Rolls I hear everything but the clock—it stopped.

I remember when $150 was the down payment on a new car. Now it's the sales tax.

———

I think every new-car owner gets two shafts: one in the car and the other in the warranty.

———

I got a friend who really has a problem: How to get his car started in the morning and his wife at night.

## Carter, Jack
*(see also Comedians)*

The hi-fi is very old. God built the first speaker system from one of Adam's ribs.

———

God made Man before Woman, because he didn't want any advice on how to make Man.

———

Adam and Eve used to talk. ADAM: Ugh. EVE: Ugh. ADAM: Ugh. EVE: Ugh. ADAM: Ugh. EVE: Ugh, Ugh. Even then, Woman had the last word.

———

And the cavemen came, and they hit girls over the heads with clubs and carried them off. You could always tell the prettiest girl in the tribe: the one with the split lip, broken nose, black eyes. . . .

And the cavemen had no money. They used to use fish as money. And when they made a phone call, they'd drop the fish in the slot. That's why, even today, you hear operators say (hold nose), "Your number, please."

———

Conrad Hilton is redoing the Leaning Tower of Pisa as a hotel. He's calling it the Tilton Hilton.

## Celebrities

A celebrity is someone who works all his life to become famous enough to be recognized, then goes around in dark glasses so no one will know who he is.

———

A celebrity is somebody who is known by many people he's glad he doesn't know.

———

A celebrity is a person who's bored by the attentions of people who formerly snubbed him.

## Cemeteries
*(see also Death, Epitaphs)*

The man was crying as he knelt in front of the three tombstones lined up next to each other.

"Relatives of yours?" a passerby asked, just to be friendly. "This one is my first wife," the man offered. "She died from eating poisoned mushrooms. The second is my second wife.

She also died from eating poisoned mushrooms!" "What about the third?" the passerby asked. "Fractured skull." "How come?" "She wouldn't eat the poisoned mushrooms."

---

The town is so healthy that they had to shoot a traveling salesman to start the cemetery.

---

He was accused of stealing a car. He pleaded guilty with an explanation: "The car was parked outside the cemetery, so I thought the owner was dead."

---

"I can't find my husband's grave," the lady said to the caretaker at the cemetery. "His name is Charles Stein." The caretaker looked at his records. "I'm sorry, we have no Charles Stein buried here. The only Stein we have is Sylvia Stein." "That's Charles. He always put everything in my name."

---

On the tombstone for the old maid: "Who said you can't take it with you?"

---

Mr. Cohen belonged to an organization with many social benefits. Each person in the club was asked to buy a cemetery plot at a reduced rate—sort of a group plan so they could have a place to live when they died. When the organization found that it wasn't paying off too well, they asked the presi-dent to talk to the delinquent members. Cohen was first to be called. "You bought a plot twenty-five years ago," the president began, "and you haven't paid for it yet." The member looked askance. "I didn't use it," he answered. "Who stopped you?" was the topper.

## Charity

The jeweler was approached by a fund-raiser "for a very worthy cause." "Can I ask you something?" inquired the jeweler. "I have a brother who has six children to support, and he's not working. Would you call that a worthy cause? I have an elderly, unmarried sister who hasn't worked in thirty years. Would you call that a worthy cause? I got an uncle who's on relief. Would you call that a worthy cause? My father hasn't got food to eat. Would you call that a worthy cause?" "Of course," nodded the fund-raiser. "Well," said the jeweler, "I don't do a damn thing for these people. Why should I do something for you?"

---

The big game hunter was lost in the jungle. He had been missing for weeks. He built a little shelter and tried to stay alive. They sent a search party who got to the shelter just as he was ready to collapse from hunger and fever. The rescuers knocked on the door. "Who is it?" he asked weakly. "The Red Cross," came the brisk answer. "I gave at the office," the dying man said.

He announced his donation every year at the charity dinner: "Ten thousand." And he made out the check, but it always bounced. This year they insisted, "No checks. We don't tell you what to give, but it must be cash or keep your mouth shut." When donation time came, he stood up and hollered, "Two hundred dollars in cash and here it is—but don't deposit it until a week from Thursday."

---

I know one charity that collected $5 million and doesn't even have a disease yet.

---

At every one of the charity dinners, everybody gets a chance to take bows, tell jokes, and make speeches before he or she makes his donation. As one toastmaster said, "I'm not going to stand up here and tell you a lot of old jokes, but I'll introduce speakers who will."

---

At a certain affair recently, one member announced that he was making a donation of $1,000. Another proclaimed, "I'll give five thousand!" A third brought the house down when he cried, "I'm giving ten thousand." The pledges were always followed by an officer of the organization, who made a plea for a little extra dough: "Now who'll give more money, in the name of something they hold near and dear to them?" With that, the biggest donor got up and cried, "I now give five hun-

dred more for something I hold near and dear to me—the ten thousand I just gave you!"

---

The investigator for the Internal Revenue Service phoned the head man of a charitable organization and asked, "Did Mr. Frank Fump give you a $10,000 donation last year like he says?" "Not yet," the man answered gleefully, *"but he will."*

---

"I'm sorry," the secretary told the man collecting for the hospital fund, "but Mr. Adams can't see you today. He has a sprained back." "Well, tell Mr. Adams I didn't come here to wrestle him, I just want to talk to him."

---

I went to a very odd charity auction. Everybody was told to bring something they didn't have any use for. Sixty-eight women brought their husbands!

---

The shady lady visited the local community chest and offered, "Honey, I'd like to donate five grand to the chest." "Madam," said the chairman, "and I don't use the word loosely, we don't need that kind of money." The co-chairman poked him and said, "Take it, jerk—it's our money anyway."

---

Bob Hope, accepting still another plaque at a dinner, said that he had stopped letting such honors go to his head. "I just got a call from a fellow who said I'd been named Man of the Year by his organization because I was America's outstanding citizen, greatest humanitarian, and so forth. It was going to be the biggest dinner, the biggest civic reception ever. He set the date: April 2. I told him I was sorry, but I was going to be tied up that night. There was a short pause. Then he said, 'By any chance, would you have Red Skelton's phone number?'"

# Cheapskates
*(see also Money)*

He's so cheap, the only time he'll pick up a check is when it's made out to him.

When the check comes, he gets a slight impediment of the reach.

I'm sure you know about the cheap Texan who still has the first million he ever made.

They were trying to decide who was the stingiest man in town when someone talked about Jones.

"One day Jones was walking down the street and found a package of cough drops. That night he made his wife sleep out in the rain so she would catch a cold."

He's so stingy, he heats the knives so his wife won't use too much butter.

SUE: Are you saving any money since you started your budget system?
HELEN: Sure. By the time we have balanced it up every night, it's too late to go anywhere.

Sign on a Scotch golf course: "Members will kindly refrain from picking up lost golf balls until they have stopped rolling."

He's so cheap, he gets angry when gum machines won't take credit cards.

They stopped the crime wave in Scotland by putting up a sign over the jailhouse saying: "Anyone caught and put in jail will have to pay his board and lodging."

In Scotland they had to take the pay-as-you-leave cars off the streets when they found two Scotsmen starving in one of them.

"Stand behind your lover," said the Scotsman to his unfaithful wife. "I'm going to shoot you both."

"Good-bye," said McIntosh, "and don't forget to take little Donald's glasses off when he isn't looking at anything."

---

"My Scotch boyfriend sent me his picture." "How does it look?" "I don't know, I haven't had it developed yet."

---

A Scot was engaged in an argument with a conductor as to whether the fare was five cents or ten cents. Finally the disgusted conductor picked up the Scotsman's suitcase and tossed it off the train, just as they passed over a bridge. It landed with a splash. "What are you doing?" screamed the Scot. "Isn't it enough to try to overcharge me, but now you try to drown my little boy?"

---

HUSBAND: I suppose you won't go to the opening without a new gown. WIFE: I should say not. HUSBAND: I thought so, so I only got one ticket.

---

She's so cheap, she tells the waiter to wrap up the Chinese food that's left—says she has a Chinese dog at home.

---

Cheap is cheap, but she uses a substitute for margarine.

---

Somebody suggested he give his daughter cash as a wedding gift. "Oh, no," he said, "you can't get cash wholesale."

---

He even found a way to save money on his honeymoon. He went alone.

---

He's saving all his toys for his second childhood.

---

He tries to make every dollar go as far as possible—and every girl, too.

---

You get in five minutes late and he docks your pay. You get in five minutes early and he charges you rent.

---

When he pays his own check, he's treating.

---

He's always the first to put his hand in his pocket and the last to bring it out again.

---

If he were at the Last Supper he would ask for separate checks.

---

You've paid for dinner the last eight times. Let's flip for this one.

---

I'm looking for the cheapest guy in town: First prize is ten dollars—which the winner pays me! And don't call me collect. And I will not accept postage-due mail.

You think I'm cheap? Just because I refuse to pass the buck? Well, how about my brother-in-law? He thinks he's treating when he pays his own check. The last time I had dinner with him, he did pick up the check—and handed it to me. My brother won't even laugh unless it's at somebody else's expense.

I have a friend who's a two-fisted spender—both tightly closed.

My neighbor is so cheap, he even has a burglar alarm on his garbage can.

I know a guy so cheap, if he was a ghost, he wouldn't give you a fright.

My nephew recently bought some secondhand shirts cheap and changed his name to fit the monogram.

My cousin, before he was married, promised his fiancée the world, the moon, and the stars. On their honeymoon he took her to the planetarium. How's that for cheap?

My butcher is very unhappy. He's had Blue Cross insurance four years and hasn't been sick once.

My cousin doesn't always insist that his wife pay the dinner check. He sometimes offers to flip her for it.

I have a friend who is so cheap he tried to get a postage stamp wholesale. This guy took his girl for a taxi ride and she was so beautiful, he could hardly keep his eyes on the meter.

I know a guy who has a coin slot on his bathroom door for visitors.

How's this for a cheap bum: When his wife's kidnappers demanded ransom last December, he requested a 25 percent year-end discount.

I know a big spender who hands out IOUs to the drunken beggars on Delancey Street.

My country cousin is tighter than a train window: He got married in his own backyard so his chicken could have the rice.

My brother married a skinny girl so he could buy a small wedding ring.

While on an out-of-town sales trip, the stingy salesman sent his wife a check for a million kisses as an anniversary present. The wife, annoyed at her cheap husband, sent back a postcard: "Dear Charlie: Thanks for the anniversary check. The milkman cashed it for me just this morning."

———

The cheapest? The guy with a pay phone in his car.

———

It is said that I have financial arthritis: Every time I reach for a check, I wince. My mother-in-law says that when I break a dollar bill I sing "Auld Lang Syne."

———

I resent the fact that some people say I am still waiting for the Bible to come out in paperback.

———

The stingiest man I ever heard of was the guy who brought his bride a ten-cent sack of candy and took her on a bus ride for their honeymoon. When she was halfway through the candy he nudged her and remarked, "Honey, suppose we save the rest of the candy for the children."

———

I don't know what my brother-in-law does with his money, but I can tell you this: He doesn't carry it with him when we go out for a drink.

———

I don't want to say my neighbor throws cheap parties, but I don't know anybody else, other than the grocery, who charges a deposit on a beer bottle.

———

A miser might be pretty tough to live with, but he's a nice ancestor.

———

I have a friend who is really cheap: He found a box of corn plasters, so he went out and bought a pair of tight shoes. He also told his kids Santa Claus stopped making house calls.

———

The old farmer had survived the Great Depression and never gave up his frugal habits even when he came into some money. A TV salesman visited and told him, "You must be lonely. A TV set would be a great source of companionship." The guy wasn't interested. "But you might as well spend your money," the salesman argued. "You can't take it with you!" The farmer snapped, "Can't take a TV set, neither."

———

I'm looking for the cheapest man in town. A man of rare gifts. A man who lives poor so he can die rich. One who gives nothing away but himself.

———

There's an old legend that if you break a mirror you get seven years hard luck. My brother feels the same way about breaking a dollar. He told me he got his wife pregnant so they could fly on the family plan.

My brother was dining with me. He picked up the check, handed it to me, and said, "I wouldn't pay it if I were you."

---

My friend has worn an outfit so long it's been in style five times.

---

My broker is the only guy I know who tries to take the subway standby. He even went alone on his honeymoon.

---

My tough-spender cousin fell heir to a million dollars, and all his pals at the saloon he frequented heard about it. Worried that his sudden wealth would change him, one of his buddies was discussing it when my cousin strolled in. The buddy waved all the guys to the bar: "When he drinks, everybody drinks," he shouted. "When he smokes, everybody pays."

---

He's so tight, the only thing he's ever withdrawn from his bank is free ink from the inkwell.

---

This bum came up against the cheapest lady of them all. She counts her money in front of the mirror so she won't cheat herself. The only thing she ever gave away was a secret. A bum was cold and he had no place to sleep. In desperation he climbed up four floors of the tenement, knocked on the door, and asked Madam Cheapskate if she could spare a dollar or two for a bed. "Well," she answered, "bring it up and we'll see what it's like."

---

Cheap? After making a three-minute phone call to California, a New York tightwad's stutter was completely cured.

---

My neighbor asked me for a cigarette. I said, "I thought you'd stopped smoking." He said, "Well, I've managed the first stage—I've stopped buying 'em."

---

The cheapest of them all? This guy named himself chief beneficiary of his own will. He lived poor so he could die rich.

---

A modern-day miser is a man who can live within his income.

---

I know a man who likes his wife in clinging dresses—the ones that have been clinging to her for years. This guy is so stingy, he won't even pay attention.

---

A cheapskate I know went into a shopping center with his wife, leaving their child and carriage with the other carriages out front. Afterward, as the family started for home and had gone a few blocks, the wife screamed, "That's not our child!" The skinflint answered, "Shut your big mouth. This is a much better carriage."

Talk is cheap, so I'm sure it's nothing personal when they say I'm a big talker.

———

A big spender gave me a check for my favorite charity. I was about to put it away when I said, "You forgot to sign this." He said, "I know. I was hoping to keep my contribution anonymous."

———

A woman was complaining to her friend about her stingy husband: "Every time I need money I have to put on a big song and dance to pry it out of him. How come you don't have any trouble with that tightwad husband of yours?" Her friend smiled. "It's easy," she said. "I just tell him I'm going home to mother, and he gives me the fare."

———

Cheap? He remarried his wife so he wouldn't have to pay any more alimony.

———

This Wall Street big shot was showing his secretary a diamond ring he was giving his wife for her birthday. "Isn't it beautiful?" he asked. "Yes," said the secretary, "but I think your wife wanted a Rolls-Royce." "That's true," the big shot agreed, "but you can't get a fake of those!"

———

The first clerk said, "I don't know what that guy does with his money. He's broke again." "Was he trying to borrow from you?" asked the second clerk. "No, I wanted to borrow from him," said the first.

———

I asked a friend, "Will you tell me, please, how you manage that you are never pressed for money, but always have plenty of it?" He said, "That's very simple. I never pay old debts." I asked, "How about new ones?" "I let them grow old!" he said. Would you believe this bum goes to a drugstore and buys one Kleenex?

———

The big star wasn't sure he wanted to accept a Vegas hotel's offer of half a million dollars a week, but they clinched the deal when they threw in the continental breakfast.

———

If you lend my brother-in-law some money, he'll be indebted to you forever. He even bought his daughter a doll house with a mortgage on it.

———

A man called up his girl and asked which night she would be free.

———

This bum got on a bus and read the sign PAY AS YOU LEAVE. He's still riding!

———

And the winner in the cheapskate sweepstakes: the guy who married a girl born on February 29, so he had to buy her a birthday present only every four years.

---

When the man took his date home, she did not invite him inside. "Since we've been going Dutch all night," she groaned, "you kiss yourself and I'll kiss myself."

---

Had dinner with my brother. I don't want to say he's cheap, but before he picked up the check, the restaurant changed hands three times.

---

I know a fellow who made a generous contribution to a home for the aged, but he's still a cheapskate: He donated his mother and father.

---

Another guy I know is determined not to go without taking it with him: He's bought himself a fireproof money belt.

---

My brother was complaining to his pal, "I don't know what to do with my wife. She's always asking for tens and twenties." His friend asked, "What the hell does she do with all the money?" My brother said, "I couldn't tell you. I never give her any."

---

A comedian noted for his thriftiness was described this way: "He wouldn't offer to buy a round of drinks at an Alcoholics Anonymous meeting."

---

A girl at Roseland described her penny-pinching date: "He's tighter than a cummerbund around Jackie Gleason."

---

He talks through his nose to save wear and tear on his teeth. He tosses quarter tips around like manhole covers."

---

This character is so cheap. His nurse told me he was mad because he got well before all the medicine was used up.

---

Cheap? His money talks with a stutter.

---

He has a physical handicap: He's hard-of-spending.

---

This cheap bum and his wife visited one of the circus airfields where they charge fifty bucks a plane ride just around the town. The couple seemed hesitant until the pilot approached them and propositioned them. "I'll take you and your wife up for nothing. It will be a rough ride, but if you or your wife lets out one single word—one sound while we are up there—you pay double." They accepted the proposition and up they went. It was really a rough ride—dives, loops, turnovers. Finally they landed. "You win," the pilot admitted, "not a word or sound out of you." "No," the cheapskate said, "but I almost did say something when my wife fell out."

———

He is so cheap, he refused to go on the first trip to the moon. He won't go anywhere out of town unless he can stay with relatives.

———

My aunt is a very economical woman. She replaced the lightbulb in the refrigerator with a candle.

## Cheating

*(see also Bosses, Marriage, Sex)*

Guns don't kill people; husbands who come home early do.

———

All the world loves a lover, except the husband.

———

"You look great!" "Sure, I'm having a wonderful affair!" "Really? Who's the caterer?"

———

"Marta," Mrs. Davis said to her maid, "my husband is having an affair with his secretary." "I don't believe it," Marta answered. "You're just saying that to make me jealous."

———

Mr. and Mrs. Max Katz had been married thirty-two years. As they were sitting in a restaurant celebrating, Mr. Katz said, "You might as well hear it from me. See that blonde? She's my mistress." "You dirty dog!" Mrs. Katz exclaimed. "After all these years, you got a mistress?" "Wait a minute. See that redhead with the bangs? She's Pincus's mistress." "That little shrimp has got a mistress, too?" "And see that brunette? That's Levine's mistress." "Levine? That fat slob even has a mistress? You know something, Max? I like ours the best."

———

The wife found her husband in bed with her girlfriend. The argument that ensued was hot and heavy. "Let's play gin for him," the girlfriend suggested when they couldn't find a solution. "If I lose, I give him up. If you lose you give him up." "Well," the wife said, "to make it more interesting, let's play for a penny a point."

———

He never goes back on his word without consulting his lawyer.

———

"Did you sleep with my wife?" threatened the husband. "Not a wink," the man replied.

———

Comic Morty Gunty now laughs at his old trick of making a person-to-person call to himself at home so he could let his family know where he was without paying the toll charges. After arriving in New York, he put in a call to himself in Chicago so his mother would know he arrived safely. When the phone rang, his mother answered the phone. The operator asked if Morty Gunty was there. "No, he's not," his mother said, "and tell him to be sure to wear his sweater."

---

I wouldn't say he doesn't trust his wife, but she is the only lady in town who has a combination lock on her zippers.

---

The husband saw his wife going into the movies with a strange man, but he didn't follow them—he had already seen the picture.

---

Imagine that cheating sweetheart of mine! I've been going with her two years and I never knew she was married—until my wife told me.

---

For years I wondered where my husband spent his evenings. One night I came home early—and there he was.

---

Mr. and Mrs. Davis met his girlfriend accidentally. The wife acknowledged the introduction and said, "My husband has told me so little about you."

"I know a guy who's been wearing a girdle for three months—ever since his wife found it in the glove compartment of his car."—Henny Youngman

---

The doctor told my brother: "You won't live a week if you don't stop running around with women." My brother said, "Why? There's nothing wrong with me. I'm in great physical shape." The doc said, "Yes, I know, but one of the women is my wife."

---

There's one hotel in town that's strictly for cheaters. In fact, when a couple registers, they sign in as Mr. and Mrs. To-Whom-It-May-Concern. One guy followed his wife there. He broke into the room and found her making love to his best friend. "You'll pay for this!" he shouted. The friend said calmly, "I've got my American Express card. I never leave home without it."

---

Two doctors were talking. "I know you've been having a romance with my wife," one said. "What do you think of her?" The second doctor said, "Don't you know?" The first said, "Yes, but I wanted a second opinion."

---

Show me a man who kisses with his eyes open, and I'll show you one who wants to make sure his wife isn't around to catch him.

The poor soul went to see the psychiatrist and cried, "When I came home from the factory last night, I found my wife kissing another man! How can I prevent that from happening again?" The shrink advised: "Work more overtime."

———

Charlie told his friend, "I feel horrible. I'm going to be a father." His pal said, "Congratulations, but what's so horrible about that?" "Nothing, except my wife doesn't know about it yet."

———

The boss arrived at his office with a terrible headache. An employee told him, "A few days ago I had a terrible headache, too, but it didn't last long. My wife pulled me over to the sofa, gave me a big hug and kiss, one thing led to another, and presto! My headache went away." The boss put on his hat. "I've tried everything else," he muttered. "Is your wife home now?"

———

Two pals were drinking at the bar. "Why the sad look?" one asked. "It must be a girl." The other said, "Yeah, but I can't tell you about it." After a few more drinks, he loosened up. "Okay," he said. "I hate to tell you this, but it's your wife." His pal said, "My wife?" "Yeah." "What about her?" The depressed guy put his arm around him and said, "Well, buddy-boy, I'm afraid she's cheating on us."

A man told me, "I know my wife's incompatible, although I've never actually caught her at it."

———

The pretty model told me, "I knew that man couldn't be trusted. He's gone back to his wife."

———

My niece cried to me, "I see so little of my husband, I feel like I took his name in vain!"

———

One thing about the first man, Adam: He may have had his troubles, but he never had to listen to Eve talk about the other men she could have married.

———

"Just look at her," the headwaiter said about the girl at the bar. "She's had five husbands, including two of her own."

———

The captain was telling us, "My sex life has improved tremendously since my wife and I got twin beds." I asked, "How could that be?" He explained, "Hers is in Connecticut and mine is in Manhattan."

———

The obstetrician had just arrived at the hospital to help a woman who was about to give birth. "Will my husband be allowed to stay with me during the delivery?" she asked. The doc said, "Of course. The father of the child should always be present at the birth." The woman said, "Oh, God—he and my husband have never liked each other."

———

My brother told me, "Now that I'm a free man, sex isn't as much fun as when I used to cheat."

———

My neighbor lectures, "They say one picture is worth ten thousand words. I found that out in divorce court. My lawyer had ten thousand words and my wife had one picture of me and another woman."

———

I know I sound old-fashioned, but I just don't believe in trial marriages. I think they're very dangerous: If you're not careful, they could lead to the real thing.

———

My cousin told me, "When I met my wife, she didn't have a social life. In fact, she didn't start dating until after we were married."

———

You know there really is such thing as a happily married couple. It's any husband who's going out with another man's wife.

———

My neighbor and his wife make love all the time. That's why it's so difficult to catch both of them at home.

My sister overheard her neighbor talking about a married man with whom she was having an affair: "He's lazy, sloppy, not too bright, and very cheap, but I love him." That evening, at home, my sister confronted her husband and demanded, "Are you having an affair with our neighbor?"

———

The Indian was telling me that the squaws have been practicing a variation of the wife-swapping bit. It's called "passing the buck."

———

The husband is leaving for work in the morning and he says to his wife, "You know, you're the worst wife, the worst cook, the worst lover a man could have." He comes back that night and finds her making love to another man. "What are you doing?" he shrieks. She says, "I'm getting a second opinion!"

———

My friend came home unexpectedly and discovered his wife in her lover's arms. Drawing a gun, he walked toward the guilty couple. "Don't shoot!" his wife screamed. "Do you want to kill the father of your children?"

———

This short, fat, millionaire approached the beauty at the party. "Excuse me," he said, "I wonder if I could interest you in breaking up my marriage?"

The two salesmen approached the boss: "We weren't betting on whether your wife would have a boy or a girl; we were betting on which one of us it would look like!"

———

My neighbor told her friend, "I'm not a suspicious woman, but I don't think my husband has been entirely faithful to me." "What makes you think that?" "Well, my last child doesn't resemble him in the least."

———

"Of course I haven't been seeing another woman," said Adam. "You know perfectly well you're the only woman here." Eve was still suspicious. That night she sneaked over to where Adam was sleeping and quietly started counting his ribs.

———

Accused of having been seen with another man, the woman protested, "Darling, it was only my husband. You know you're the only one for me!"

———

The woman is happily married—her latest boyfriend likes her husband. And even after ten years of marriage, her husband finds her entertaining—when he comes home unexpectedly.

———

A man said, "You're the best little wife a guy ever had, even if your husband doesn't think so!"

———

The Wall Street executive told the lawyer, "Hell, give me the bad news first." Said the lawyer, "The bad news is that your wife found a picture worth a hundred thousand dollars." "That's the bad news? In that case, I can't wait to hear the terrible news." "The terrible news is that it's of you and your secretary."

———

The lawyer and his wife were taking a stroll on Fifth Avenue when the lawyer was greeted by a sexy blonde. "And how did you meet her?" the wife asked. "Professionally." "Yours," asked the wife, "or hers?"

———

I have a married girlfriend who loved to entertain but had to give it up—her husband started coming home.

———

The politician was late as usual. His opening line to his wife was, "I've just been talking to the senator, who agreed to do everything I want." The wife sneered, "Well, first wipe the senator's lipstick off your lips."

———

The movie producer came home unexpectedly and found his wife in bed with the onetime B-movie star. "Hey!" he screamed. "What are you doing?" The actor said, "To tell you the truth, not much of anything these days."

———

The loving couple was startled by a noise in the corridor. The woman got out of bed and cautiously opened the door just far enough to peek out. She returned to bed looking greatly relieved. "Relax, darling," she said. "Nothing to worry about. It was just my husband sneaking into your apartment."

___

You know your wife is being unfaithful when you notice your dog taking your pipe and slippers to a house down the street.

___

Florence and Emily, two pretty young housewives, arranged to have cocktails and lunch together. When they met, Emily could see that something serious was bothering her friend and said, "What's depressing you?" Florence sighed, "I'm ashamed to admit it, but I caught my husband making love." Emily said, "Why let that bother you? I got mine the same way."

___

The young, attractive housewife was a bit surprised when her husband's best friend dropped by one afternoon and offered $500 to make love to her. Thinking that the extra money would come in handy, she led him into the bedroom and fulfilled her part of the bargain. Later that afternoon, her husband returned from work. "Did my friend stop by today?" he asked casually. "Yes, he d-did," she stammered. "Why do you ask?" "Well," her spouse replied, "he was supposed to return the $500 I lent him last week."

___

The reporters asked the beauty, who was making it with the senator, "How come you never married?" She said, "I got nothing against marriage. Some of my best friends are husbands."

___

The wife screamed at the learned judge: "You bum! You miserable cheat! I know everything now!" The judge said calmly, "If you know so much, when was the Battle of Gettysburg?"

___

My neighbor told me, "Three nights a week out with the boys. Man, did the wife and I have an argument about that last night!" I asked, "How did it come out?" He said, "She agreed to cut it down to two."

___

A man came home and found his wife in bed with his partner. "What are you doing?" he shouted. She said to her bedmate, "See? Didn't I tell you he was stupid?"

___

I overheard a gal say to her girlfriend, "Helen, listen to this: That stinking husband of mine has been cheating on me. On Tuesday nights, when he's supposed to be playing poker with the boys, he's out with a young blonde. What do you think of that skunk?" Helen asked, "How do you know this?" The gal replied, "My boyfriend Harry told me."

———⊷———

My brother just had a nose job. He really didn't need it, but his neighbor's husband came home unexpectedly one night.

———⊷———

The man's friend told him that his gorgeous wife had four lovers. The man said, "Look, I know. But I'd rather have 20 percent of a good deal than 100 percent of a bad one."

———⊷———

A man was complaining to a friend about his marital woes: "My wife has started rationing sex. It's now down to once a week." "Oh, I wouldn't worry about that," his friend consoled. "I know some fellas she's cut off completely."

———⊷———

The judge said to the lady, "Your husband charges that you deceived him." The wife answered, "On the contrary, Your Honor, he deceived me. He said he was leaving town and he didn't."

———⊷———

When a man heard that his dearest friend was to marry a certain girl in West Centerville, he tried to halt the union. He went to his friend and said: "This marriage must not take place! Why, she's had an affair with every man in West Centerville." "Listen, West

Centerville isn't such a big town," replied the dope.

———⊷———

I've heard all the alibis, but this one takes the prize. She explained to her husband that more people drown in bathtubs than in the ocean or swimming pools—that's why he found her with a lifeguard in her bathtub.

———⊷———

The middle-aged lady had been reading all the stories about our permissive society and all the free love, switching, and cheating going on in the suburbs. She was interested. "Tell me," she asked the head of her women's club, "how do you start an affair?" "Always the same way," said the lady president. "First with Hatikvab, then the 'Star Spangled Banner,' and then the invocation!"

———⊷———

The husband came home and found his wife in bed with a midget. "I forgave you before," he screamed. "You promised only last week when I caught you that you would never cheat again."

"Now don't be angry, darling," she exclaimed. "Can't you see I'm tapering off?"

———⊷———

His wife had always talked about having a catered affair. He never paid any attention to her until he came home unexpectedly and found her in bed with the delicatessen man.

Sixty percent of the men cheat in America. The rest cheat in Europe.

---

The couple checked into a motel in Philadelphia opposite a railroad station. In the morning the husband went to see some clients and left his wife in bed alone. About 9:30 A.M. a train passed and the vibration knocked her out of bed. Ten minutes later another train passed, and again the vibration knocked her out of bed. Fifteen minutes later the same thing happened. She finally called the clerk downstairs and told him what she thought of his motel. "I don't believe it," he said. "Come up and see for yourself," she screamed. The manager came up full of apologies but still not admitting the lady's claim. "I'm lying in bed," she explained again, "and every time a train passed, the damn vibration knocked me out of bed." "I don't believe it," he repeated. "Okay," she said, "lie down and see for yourself." He was in bed five minutes when the husband came in. "What the hell are you doing in my bed?" he shouted. "Believe it or not," the manager said, "I'm waiting for a train."

---

The story is told that Noah Webster was embracing his chambermaid when his wife suddenly entered the room and caught him in the act. "Why, Noah," she said, "I'm surprised."

The great man of words quickly composed himself and said, "No, my pet, you are amazed. It is we who are surprised."

---

Two neighbors were drinking at the bar when one suddenly spoke up: "Do you like fat, sloppy women who roll their stockings down below their knees?" "I should say not." "Well, do you like women who always smell from garlic and have false teeth?" "No, of course not—sounds horrible!" "Then tell me, my friend, why are you always trying to date my wife?"

---

Comic Jack Carter tells this story: A man walks into a hotel and sees a woman in black sitting in a corner, crying. "What's the matter?" he asks solicitously. "I'm going to miss him," she says, and keeps on crying. The man asks who died. The woman says, "My husband. I knew he ran around, but I'm really going to miss him." The man asks, "When did he die?" "Tomorrow morning," the woman replies.

## Children

*(See also Adolescents, Babies, Family, Jokes for Children, Juvenile Delinquents, Kids)*

Uncle asked the eight-year-old if his two-year-old brother had started talking yet. "Why should he talk?" the kid groaned. "He gets everything he wants by yelling."

---

Their little baby was very quiet. He never spoke. They were pleased about this while he was a baby, but as he grew up he was also quiet and never once spoke. Finally, when the kid was eight years old and had never uttered a sound, all of a sudden he said, "Pass the salt." Shocked, the father said, "How come in eight years you never spoke?" The kid replied, "Well, up to now everything was all right."

---

The mother reprimanded her son for using a four-letter word. "But, Mother," the boy explained, "Tennessee Williams uses that word all the time." "So don't play with him no more."

---

The little girl walked into her mother's bedroom at three o'clock in the morning. "Tell me a story, Mommy," she whimpered. "For heaven's sake, it's three o'clock in the morning," muttered the sleepy mother. "Tell me a story," demanded the tot. "Look," suggested the mother, "why don't you wait until four o'clock when your father comes home and he'll tell us both a story!"

---

Cartoonist Al Capp once said, "Those parents who concern themselves with their children's problems are crazy. The problem of a nine-year-old kid cannot be solved in any way—except by becoming ten."

---

Humorist and writer S. J. Perelman: Nowadays you don't know how much you know until your children grow up and tell you how much you don't know.

---

I walked into my daughter's room the other night and said, "What about the prayers?" She said, "I'm saying them." I said, "I don't hear you." She said, "I'm not talking to you."

---

Tiny Tim's favorite children's stories:

•A Boy Scout, as of course you know, is supposed to do one good deed each day. "What good deed did you perform today?" asked a neighbor of a small Scout. "Oh," said the young hero, "Mother had only enough castor oil for one dose, so I let my sister take it!"

---

•Little Marie was sitting on her grandfather's knee one day, and after looking at him intently for a time, she said, "Grandpa, were you on Noah's Ark?" "Certainly not, my dear," answered the astonished old man. "Then why weren't you drowned?"

---

•Little Lydia had been given a ring as a birthday present, but much to her disappointment, not one of the guests at dinner noticed it. Finally, unable to stand their indifference, she exclaimed, "Oh, dear, I'm so warm in my new ring."

•Mother was instructing little Gertrude in regard to her manners as she was being dressed to return her little friend's call. "If they ask you to dine, say, 'No, I thank you, I have dined,' Mother said. But the conversation turned out differently from what Gertrude had anticipated. "Come along, Gertrude," invited her little friend's father, "have a bite with us." "No, I thank you," came Gertrude's dignified reply. "I have already bitten."

A lady who had just received an interesting bit of news said to her little daughter, "Marjorie, dear, auntie has a new baby, and now Mama is the baby's aunt, Papa is the baby's uncle, and you are her little cousin." "Well," said Marjorie incredulously, "wasn't that arranged quick?"

The teacher asked what a sweater was and one kid answered, "It's something I have to put on when my mother gets chilly."

Little Harry was asked by his Sunday school teacher, "And Harry, what are you going to give your darling little brother for Christmas this year?" "I dunno," said Harry. "I gave him the measles last year."

A little four-year-old girl and a three-year-old boy walked hand in hand up to the front of their neighbor's house. "We are playing house," the little girl said when the neighbor opened the door. "This is my husband and I am his wife. May we come in?" The lady was enchanted by the youngsters. "Do come in," she said. Once inside she offered the children some lemonade and cookies, which they graciously accepted. When a second glass of lemonade was offered, the little girl refused by saying, "No, thanks. We have to go now. My husband just wet his pants."

Every time I found a girl that I liked, I brought her home, but Mama always said, "I don't like her. She's not for you." Then I found a girl that looked like Mama, talked like Mama, and walked like Mama. I brought her home but lost out again—Papa didn't like her.

Here's a question for a PTA discussion: Should parents strike back?

"I'm trying something new," the young mother was saying. "This summer I'm sending my dogs to camp and my kids to obedience school."

There was a fascinating story in the paper recently. A nine-year-old girl played a chess tournament in Prague against fifteen of the world's greatest chess champions, all at the same time!

Would you believe it? She lost every game.

———

When a youngster hears a bad word, it goes in one ear—and out of his mouth.

———

"None of my kids are dropouts," my neighbor was bragging, "but they caused quite a few dropouts among the teachers."

———

"Why does it rain, Daddy?" "To make the flowers grow, and the grass and the trees." "So why does it rain on the sidewalk?"

———

The three-year-old bragged to her mom that she learned to write in school today.

"What did you learn to write?" Mom asked. "I don't know—I can't read."

———

"My, Grandpa, what a lot of whiskers! Can you spit through them all?" "Yes, sonny, I can." "Well, you'd better do it now, 'cause they're on fire from your pipe."

———

ALICE (age seven): Auntie, were you ever in a predicament? MAIDEN AUNT: No, dearie, but heaven knows I've tried.

———

"Did God make you, Daddy?" "Certainly, sonny." "Did He make me, too?" "Of course. Why?" "Well, He's doing better right along, isn't He?"

———

FOND MOTHER: Quiet, dear, the sandman is coming. MODERN CHILD: Okay, Mom, a dollar and I won't tell Pop.

———

My child is very sensitive. If he does something wrong, beat the child next to him and that will be punishment enough for him.

———

Last week I told my son about the birds and the bees. Now he wants to know about Brigitte Bardot.

———

The kids almost wrecked the house. When their parents arrived home, Mother wanted to know who started it. "It all started," one kid said, "when Charlie hit me back."

———

Kids rarely misquote you, especially when they repeat what you shouldn't have said.

———

Grandpa was doing some carpentry at home and asked his grandson to bring him a screwdriver.

The kid came back a few minutes later and announced, "I have the vodka, but I can't find an orange."

———

# Children's Jokes

JANE: Peanuts are fattening. JUNE: How do you know? JANE: Did you ever see a skinny elephant?

———

PASSENGER: What good is your timetable? The trains never keep time. CONDUCTOR: Well, how would you know they were late if it weren't for the timetable?

———

PASSENGER: Does this train stop at San Francisco? CONDUCTOR: Well, if it doesn't, there will be a big splash.

———

"How long can a man live without brains?" "I don't know—how old are you?"

———

"How did you enjoy the movie?" "Awful. I could hardly sit through it a second time."

———

"Do you understand why Robin Hood robbed only the rich?" "Sure—because the poor had no money."

———

There is a pupil in our class who is so thin that when he stands sideways the teacher marks him absent.

———

An autobiography is a history of motor cars.

"Did you buy any Christmas Seals?" "No, I wouldn't know how to feed them."

———

"Do you like codfish balls?" "I don't know. I've never been to one."

———

"This goulash is terrible." "That's funny—I put a brand-new pair of goulashes in it."

———

"How do foreign dishes compare to American dishes?" "They break just as easily."

———

"Which hand do you use to stir your tea?" "My right hand." "Funny, I use a spoon!"

———

"Do you believe in free speech?" "Sure!" "Good. Mind if I use your telephone?"

# China

An American standing at a bar in Hong Kong got into a conversation with the Chinese standing next to him. When the American asked what he did, the Chinese said, "Oh, I was a Chinese airman. I fight in Korea." The American asked him his name and he said, "My name is Chow Mein. I was a kamikaze flyer." The American said, "Who are you kidding, Chow Mein? I was a flyer, too, and I happen to know if you were a kamikaze flyer you wouldn't be here right now. That was a suicide squad!" The Chinese grinned and said, "Oh, me Chicken Chow Mein."

———

A tourist in China watched as three prominent Chinese were being buried. As the first casket was lowered, several Chinese women came forward, placing chickens, rice, bread, and wine on the coffin. "What's that for?" asked the tourist. "That is our custom," answered one of the mourners, "so that the body of the dead man will not go hungry." The same procedure was followed when the second casket was lowered. When the third was lowered, only a single cup of rice was placed on it. "Say," muttered the stranger, "how come they put so little food on that coffin?" The Chinese shrugged and said, "That was Sing Lee. He was on a diet."

———

When a Jewish kid gets bar mitzvahed in China, he says, "Today, I am a mandarin."

———

In China it's customary for a man never to take a girl out until he marries her. In the United States he never takes her out after he marries her.

———

# Chivalry
*(see also Marriage)*

"I noticed you got up and gave that lady your seat on the tram the other day," said one neighbor to another when they met on the corner. "Since childhood I have respected a woman with a strap in her hand," was the reply.

———

BOB: I saw a fellow strike a girl today. DICK: You didn't let him get away with it, did you? BOB: I went up to him and said, "Only a coward would hit a woman. Why don't you hit a man?" DICK: Then what happened? BOB: That's all I remember.

———

"See that girl over there?" "Yeah." "She's fresh from the country and it's up to us to show her the difference between right and wrong." "Okay, pal. You teach her what's right."

———

It's gonna be a typical American Christmas at our house this year. The tree comes from Canada, the ornaments from Japan, the lights from Taipei—and the idea from Bethlehem.

# Christmas

I gave my wife a gold watch for Christmas and she was surprised. She was expecting a chinchilla coat.

I gave my wife a $25 gift certificate for Christmas and it made her very happy. She used it as a down payment on a mink coat!

———

This guy received an envelope from his boss: "I am enclosing a little gift. Try it on for size. If it's too small, don't return it because I can't get it in a larger size." Enclosed was a check for $25.

———

Pianist and humorist Victor Borge says Santa Claus has the right idea: Visit people only once a year and you'll always be welcome.

———

I know a guy so cheap that on Christmas Eve he fires three shots in the air and tells his kids that Santa Claus just committed suicide.

———

Comedian Flip Wilson says, "When I was a kid I lost respect for Santa Claus. You see, everywhere I went I kept seeing the old boy in a different store. How can you respect a guy who can't hold a steady job?"

———

With inflation the way it is today, I went out and paid fifty dollars for a Christmas tree and brought it home. My wife wore it as a corsage.

———

May you have a Christmas you'll never forget—and a New Year's you won't remember.

———

I wanted to get my wife a bra for Christmas. It is a little embarrassing the way the salesgirls look at you. When they ask you for the size, you're torn between pride and reality.

———

One guy said he wants a size 7-1/4 bra. The salesgirl asked him how he got the measurement, and he said with his hat.

———

The great comic Red Skelton tells the story of the wealthy farmer who was not only rich but had a lot of money. He went to church on Christmas and after the services he said to the Reverend, "That was a damn good sermon, damn good." The minister was pleased but suggested, "It would be nicer if you didn't use such words to express yourself." "Can't help it, Reverend, but I still think it was a damn good sermon. That's why I put $500 in the collection basket." "The hell you did," said the minister.

———

Now you know how Santa feels, living in a whole world of takers and no givers.

———

Santa Claus is not so unique anymore. He wears that wild red outfit, boots, beard, a bag on his shoulder, and he works only one day a year. Do you know how many teenagers and hippies do the same?

———

With inflation today, I can't believe the prices they're asking for Christmas trees. It's true that only God can make a tree—but I wish he would investigate his salesmen.

———

The soldier boy was so unhappy. But it was Christmas, so I tried to cheer him up, Santa Claus and all that. "What Santa Claus?" he cried. "Twenty years ago I asked Santa for a soldier suit—now I got one."

———

Listen, I'm for Santa Claus. . . . Any guy who drops into your house only once a year and doesn't want to drink, eat, or stay over could be my friend for life.

———

Do your shopping now—before the prices go down.

———

My cousin told me, "I have no idea what gifts I'll receive for Christmas—but I sure know what I'm going to exchange this for."

———

My aunt lost her charge cards, so her husband put an ad in the paper offering a $100 reward for each card, no questions asked. The only catch is, the offer is not good until after the Christmas shopping season.

———

Our kids are so sophisticated today. My neighbor asked his six-year-old, "What are you gonna ask Santa Claus to give you this year?" The kid said, "Nothing. I'll use my charge plate."

———

Christmas worries me. That's when my wife always gives me presents I can't afford. I told my wife that the start of the Christmas shopping season makes my heart pound, my knees shake, and my pulse race. She said, "Thinking of all the money you're going to spend?" I said, "No, thinking of all the money you're going to spend."

———

It's too bad Election Day isn't held on Christmas: When we see some of the guys we elected, we could exchange them for something else.

———

Have you noticed that many people who laugh at kids for believing in Santa Claus are the same people who believe in campaign promises?

———

Can you imagine if the Christmas story happened today? The Three Wise Men would be fellas who got out of the stock market in time.

Ever wonder why Santa Claus goes "Ho Ho Ho"? Listen, if you had to work only one day a year, you'd laugh too.

———◦◦◦———

Just remember that the Christmas presents of today are the garage sales of tomorrow.

———◦◦◦———

Last year my beautiful wife gave me a smoking jacket for Christmas. It took me an hour and a half to put it out.

———◦◦◦———

I asked my dentist what he wanted for the holidays. He said, "All I want for Christmas are your two front teeth."

———◦◦◦———

What do you give a man who has everything? Shots!

———◦◦◦———

It was a slow Christmas: Santa Claus lost a bundle in the stock market.

———◦◦◦———

We all hope for the same thing at Christmas: that Santa will visit us and our relatives won't.

———◦◦◦———

Christmas shopping gives everyone who didn't go broke in the stock market crash a second chance.

———◦◦◦———

My favorite Christmas story is about my friend who took his little grandson shopping. They went to one department store and the lad dutifully climbed on Santa's lap. "Ho Ho Ho," Santa said. "What do you want for Christmas?" The kid said, "You better get a pencil and paper and write it down." "No, it's okay," Santa said. "I'll remember." The little boy recited his list and left. Grandpa and the boy went to another department store and another Santa asked, "Ho Ho Ho, what do you want for Christmas?" The kid screamed, "You dumb-dumb! I told you to write it down!"

———◦◦◦———

What my wife is giving me for Christmas is priceless: She's not giving me anything.

———◦◦◦———

Christmas is a time I'll long remember. I charged everything.

———◦◦◦———

I'm giving money for Christmas presents; it's the cheapest thing I could find.

———◦◦◦———

If you think it's the thought that counts, just try sending somebody a Christmas gift COD.

———◦◦◦———

It's always better to give than to receive. Then you don't have to bother exchanging it.

———◦◦◦———

This is the season when you buy this year's presents with next year's money.

———

I have a friend who didn't know what to give his wife, who has everything, so he decided to give her a husband who could afford it.

———

I just figured out why we're having so much trouble in the world: All the wise men are under Christmas trees instead of in Washington.

———

Happiness at this time of the year is a craps table in Atlantic City that will take gift certificates.

———

One kid looked up at Santa Claus and said: "Are you a politician?" Santa said, "Of course not. Why would you think I'm a politician?" "'Cause you always promise more than you deliver."

———

Santa Claus has the right idea: visit people only once a year and you'll always be welcome.

———

In Russia they have Santa Claus in department stores, too, but it's a little different: You sit on Santa's lap and *he* tells *you* what you're getting.

# Church
*(see also Religion)*

A minister asked a little girl what she thought of her first church service. "Well," she said after giving the matter some thought, "the music was nice, but the commercial was too long."

———

When the topless girl tried to enter the church, the vicar stopped her at the door. "But, Vicar, you can't stop me from going to church," she protested. "I have a divine right." "They're both divine," he said, "but that is not the question. You'll have to go home and put on something more respectable."

———

"There are so few people going to church these days," the chorus girl was saying. "In fact, in my church there are so few in the congregation, when our minister says 'Dearly Beloved,' I feel like I just got a proposal."

———

Sign over collection box in the vestibule: "GIVER: remember, you can't take it with you, so why not send it on ahead?"

———

"I will not give you the blessing this Sunday," the minister said to the congregation. "I don't feel you need it. The Lord said, 'Blessed are the poor,' and judging by the size of the collection, that covers all of you."

———

"How come I never see you in church anymore, Timothy?" "There are too many hypocrites there, Father." "Don't worry, son, there's always room for one more."

---

The minister reprimanded one of his congregation who always sat in the first row and fell asleep as soon as the sermon started. "You should feel complimented," the congregant explained. "If I didn't trust you, I couldn't sleep."

---

There are more old sinners than there are old preachers.

---

A clergyman was telling a very interesting story when his little girl interrupted, "Now, Daddy, is that really true, or is it just preaching?"

---

The preacher was telling his clan that there are more than seven hundred different kinds of sin. He was besieged with mail and phone calls the next day from people who wanted the list to make sure they weren't missing anything.

---

Coming out of church, Mrs. Peterson asked her husband, "Do you think that Johnson girl is tinting her hair?" "I didn't even see her," admitted Mr. Peterson. "And that dress Mrs. Hansen was wearing!" continued Mrs. Peterson. "Really, don't tell me you think that's the proper costume for a mother of two." "I'm afraid I didn't notice that either," said Mr. Peterson.

"Oh, for heaven's sake," snapped Mrs. Peterson. "A lot of good it does you to go to church."

---

Sign on a church in Portland, Oregon: "Come this Sunday, avoid the Easter rush."

---

A wealthy jazz musician decided to go to church one Sunday. After the service, he approached the preacher with much enthusiasm. "Reverend," he said, "that was a swinging sermon, man. I flipped my lid. That was the grooviest." "I'm happy you liked it," said the Reverend, "but I wish you wouldn't use those terms in expressing yourself." "I'm like, sorry, man, Reverend, but I dug that sermon so much," said the cat. "In fact, it sent me so much I flipped a C-note in the collection pot." The Reverend replied, "Crazy, man, crazy."

---

"I hear you went to the ball game last Sunday instead of to church." "That's a lie, and I've got the fish to prove it."

---

A small town is where people go to church on Sunday to see who didn't.

---

The drunken commuter collapsed in the subway. A clergyman rushed to his aid. Seeing the man's condition, he started to lecture him: "You're either going to heaven or the other place according to the life you intend to live." "I don't care where I go," gurgled the drunken commuter, "just so long as I don't have to change in Jamaica."

———

The minister was leaving the church to go to a different parish. "I'm so sorry you're going," the little old lady cried as she said good-bye. "I never knew what sin was until you came here."

———

She sang in church—and fifty people changed their religion.

———

"I advertised that the poor would be welcome in this church," said the minister, "and after inspecting the collection, I see that they have come."

———

He has some kind of religion—at least he knows what church he is staying away from.

———

GIRL PRAYING: Oh, Lord, I ask nothing for myself, but will you please send dear Mother a son-in-law?

———

The minister asked the congregation to raise their hands if they wanted to go to heaven. All did so except one. Then he asked who wanted to go to

hell. Nobody raised their hands. "Where do you want to go?" the minister asked the man who didn't raise his hand for either side. "No place," he answered, "I like it here."

———

The impatient teenager was bothered because she had to wait in line so long for confession. "They should be more efficient," she beefed. "They ought to have a fast line for those with three sins or less."

———

The pastor at a church was asked how many persons could sleep in the church building in case of an attack. "I don't know," replied the pastor, "but we sleep four hundred every Sunday morning."

# Churchill, Winston

A lady member of the House of Commons snarled at Mr. Churchill one night when they were in session: "Winston, you're disgustingly drunk." Churchill answered her like any good comic would reply to a heckler: "Madam, you are correct. I am very, very drunk, and you are very, very ugly! However, tomorrow, I shall be sober!"

———

The prime minister said it: "A fanatic is one who can't change his mind and won't change the subject."

Churchill on Clement Attlee of the Labor Party: "Attlee is a very modest man—and with reason."

Churchill on Sir Stafford Cripps of the Labor Party: "He has all the virtues I dislike and none of the vices I admire."

Lady Astor once said to Churchill: "If you were my husband, I'd poison your coffee." Churchill answered: "If you were my wife, I'd drink it."

Churchill was asked how he liked New York City during his visit there. This was his instant critique: "Newspapers too thick, lavatory papers too thin."

Too often the strong silent man is silent because he does not know what to say.

Churchill on a Socialist in the House of Commons: "He spoke without a note and without a point."

Playwright George Bernard Shaw had a running feud going with Churchill. He sent the prime minister a note saying: "I am reserving two tickets for you for my premiere. Come and bring a friend if you have one." Churchill replied immediately: "Impossible to be present for the first performance. Will attend the second if there is one."

Churchill on Prime Minister Ramsay MacDonald's speech: "He has the gift of compressing the largest number of words into the smallest amount of thought."

He was against peace at any price: "Look at the Swiss! They have enjoyed peace for centuries. And what have they produced? The cuckoo clock!"

Churchill was always fighting to get more and more protection for England—just to make sure. He used to accentuate his demands with the story of "the man whose mother-in-law had died in Brazil and, when asked how the remains should be disposed of, replied, 'Embalm, cremate, and bury. Take no risks.'"

## Cigarettes
*(see also Smoking)*

Winston cigarettes and transsexual Christine Jorgensen have the same claim to fame: It's what's up front that counts.

A well-bred man steps on the cigarette so it won't burn the rug.

The cigar-store Indian is now smoking cigarettes.

———

Filter-tip cigarettes have stopped people coughing, among other things, but they have caused more hernias by people dragging on them.

———

If those Winston cigarettes get any longer, only trombone players will be able to light them.

———

He's such a hypochondriac, he smokes only filter-tipped marijuana.

———

A nurse asked a bum coughing and smoking on the street corner, "How many cigarettes do you smoke a day?" "Oh, any given amount."

## Circumcision

Vaudeville, radio, and TV entertainer Eddie Cantor sent this telegram to producer Irving Thalberg after the birth of Thalberg's first son: "Congratulations on your latest production—I'm sure it will look better after it's been cut."

———

Circumcision: a surgical operation that has become a catered affair.

———

## Circus
*(see also Animals)*

I love circus people. Like the acrobat who married the tattooed woman because, "If I can't sleep in the middle of the night, I can sit up and look at the pictures."

———

Did you hear the story about the man on the flying trapeze who caught his wife in the act?

———

ELEPHANT: I'm getting sick and tired of working for peanuts.

———

I get shot out of a cannon. I get ten cents a mile and traveling expenses.

———

When I was ten I ran away with a circus, but the police made me bring it back.

———

The lions were so fierce that when the tamer went into the cage with the chair, he didn't get a chance to sit down.

———

The Barnum & Bailey Circus was playing Bridgeport, Connecticut, and the local paper sent its best reporter to interview the world-famous Tom Thumb, Barnum & Bailey's brilliant dwarf. The reporter found the room at the hotel and knocked on the door. It was opened by a towering giant who filled the doorway. "I'm a reporter," said the young man. "I want to interview Tom Thumb." "Glad to meet you," said the giant. "I'm Tom Thumb. Come on in." "You're nuts," said the reporter, looking up at the giant. "Tom Thumb's a dwarf." "Well," said the giant, "this is my day off."

---

The fat lady at the circus married the India rubber man, and in three weeks he erased her altogether.

---

Ad in *Show Business* magazine: "Lion tamer looking for tamer lion."

---

It was a bad year for the circus, and the owner called his troupe together to make his sad announcement. "I'm sorry to say there is only enough money to pay off three of you this week: Samson the strong man, Benny the bone crusher, and Ivan the knife thrower."

---

Ad in *Show Business* magazine: "Wanted: human cannonball. Must be able to travel."

# Clerks
*(see also Business)*

GIRL IN BOOKSTORE: Do you keep *The Divine Woman*? CLERK: Not on my salary!

---

YOUNG MAN: I want to buy a diamond ring. SALESMAN: Yes, sir. How would you like to buy one of our combination sets? Three pieces: engagement, wedding, and teething.

---

CLERK: Why, madam, these are the finest eggs we've had for months. CUSTOMER: Never mind, I don't want any eggs you've had for months.

---

SALESMAN: Of course, madam, we stand behind each bed we sell. NEWLYWED: Hmm. Thank you. Could you show me something else?

---

"I'd like to see something in silk stockings." "You men are all alike." "Is the color fast?" "Why don't you chase it and see?"

---

I have a brother who works in a department store. Yesterday he came home and said he was fired. He made a mistake and took a sign off a blouse counter and put it on the bathtub display. The sign read: "How would you like to see your best girl in one of these for a dollar ninety-nine?"

---

"Are you a clock watcher?" asked the businessman of the haggard graduate who had just applied for a job. "No," replied the average (but honest) student, "I'm a bell listener."

CUSTOMER: I'd like some rat poison.
CLERK: Will you take it with you?
CUSTOMER: No, I'll send the rats over to get it.

# Clothing

*(see also Dress, Fashion)*

Jack Spitzer, the Albany Ford dealer, told this tale: "A few weeks ago I went out on a hunting trip with a friend of mine who is in the clothing business. We were walking through the woods when all of a sudden a huge bear came out from behind a tree and leaped at me. I screamed, 'Help me, is that a bear?' My friend said, 'How should I know? Do I deal in furs?'"

———

I got a friend who has so many suits, he keeps one aside just for the moths.

———

His suit was so shiny, if it ever tore, he'd have seven years bad luck.

———

Comedian Robert King says, "The cleaners lost one of my best suits last month, and to my surprise I received a bill from them. When I phoned to ask about it, they informed me that they were sure they'd cleaned the suit before losing it."

———

I happen to have a suit for every day of the year, and this is it.

He had a suit on that was made in London, and he looked like he swam back in it.

———

When he bought the suit, it looked like a page out of *Esquire*. Now it looks like it was condensed for *Readers Digest*.

———

They gave away a penknife with every suit they sold. In case you got caught in the rain, you could slash your way out.

———

He had on a dinner jacket with dinner still on it.

———

He got a very expensive suit for a ridiculous figure: his!

———

At today's prices, clothes break the man.

———

"I would like a new mink coat," the wife demanded. Said the husband: "But you've only worn the one I gave you for two years." "You forget," reminded the wife, "for eight years the mink wore it."

———

If the shoe fits, it's out of style.

———

Clothes don't make the man, but a good suit has made many a lawyer.

———

His pants are tighter than his skin. He can sit down in his skin, but he can't sit down in his pants.

---

His pants are so tight, they wear out on the inside.

---

He is making suits out of awning material. Only trouble is, when the sun goes down, his pants roll up.

---

She wanted new clothes in spite of the fact that her closets were bulging with the best gowns in town. "Darling," she tried to explain to her husband, "I must have some new clothes. All the neighborhood has seen everything I own." "Well," the husband growled, "it'd be cheaper to move to a new neighborhood."

---

A dress shop received this note from a woman: "Dear sir, you have not delivered the maternity dress I ordered. Please cancel the order. My delivery was faster than yours."

---

The man put his high silk hat down on the seat next to him in the theater. When the fat lady came in, she sat down on the hat without looking. She jumped up immediately and they both eyed the black silk pancake. "Madam," he said to her icily, "I could have told you my hat wouldn't fit before you tried it on."

---

She is middle-aged when she chooses her shoes for comfort and her sweater for warmth.

---

Sign in lingerie shop: "Destiny may shape your end—but if it doesn't, we have the best girdles in town."

---

A girdle is the difference between facts and figures.

---

There's nothing so cold as a woman who's been refused a fur coat.

---

She doesn't have the legs for miniskirts—only the nerve.

---

If the skirts go any higher, my wife has a couple of blouses that will be just about the right length.

---

Clothes make the man poor—if he's married.

---

"What would go best with that tie?" "A long beard."

---

He's really in trouble. He told his wife her stockings were wrinkled—and she wasn't wearing any.

---

It was so hot in Miami, the women weren't wearing their mink stoles, just the appraisals.

---

HUSBAND: Another new dress? When am I going to get the money to pay for it all? WIFE: I may be a lot of things, but inquisitive I'm not.

---

She dresses to be seen in the best places.

---

The girls on the beach were wearing their baiting suits.

---

She looks like an unmade bed.

---

The way women's dresses are getting shorter and shorter, you never know what they'll be up to next.

---

The little boy got lost in the crowd. "Why didn't you hold on to your mother's skirt?" said the policeman who found him. "I couldn't reach it," the kid bawled.

The honeymoon's over when the groom stops praising his wife's clothes and starts pricing them.

---

Those short skirts are keeping us ignorant about what's going on in the world—I haven't read a newspaper or magazine on a subway in months.

---

Her Easter hat had so many flowers on it, two funerals followed her home.

---

Girls, here's a tip for a big buy on dresses: Milton Berle is having a sale on his old clothes.

## Cohen, Myron
*(see also Comedians)*

A bunch of nudists were walking down Fifth Avenue, and in the middle of them was a lone nudist with a long beard that stretched to the ground. A passerby asked one of the nudists why the man had such a long beard, and the nudist replied, "Well, someone has to go for coffee."

---

A big-business tycoon died and went to his eternal resting place. When he arrived in the other world, he was greeted by a salesman who used to visit him on Earth. "Max, old boy, I'm here for the appointment," said the salesman. "What appointment?" asked the businessman. "Don't you remember?" asked the salesman. "Every time I used to try to see you at your office, you'd tell me you'd see me here."

———

A frightened little man boarded a plane and took his seat right next to a big, burly Texan. The little man was so scared of flying that he threw up all over the Texan. Luckily, the Texan was asleep when it happened, but now the little man was more frightened than ever as to what the Texan might do to him when he awoke. Finally, the Texan did wake up, and quickly the little man said to him, "Feeling better now?"

———

A mother was telling a friend about her three sons. "Sammy is a doctor, Benny is a lawyer." Her friend said, "I'll bet you're proud of them." "And Joe is a silk manufacturer," the mother continued. Her friend looked at her and said, "A silk manufacturer?" "Yeah," the mother said, "and you know what? He supports Sammy and Benny."

## Cold Weather
*(see also Alaska)*

Winter is officially here in New York. The Italian pizzerias have changed to winter-weight olive oil.

———

I just arrived from Canada—I came in by dogsled. We had a woman driver.

She hollered, "Mush!" I hollered, "Mush," and while we were mushing, somebody stole my sled.

———

It was so cold in Winnipeg that the hens were laying eggs from a standing position.

———

It was so windy that one chicken had her back to the wind and laid the same egg twenty-seven times.

———

When I got home, my wife said, "Why don't you take off that purple sweater you're wearing?" I said, "What purple sweater? It's me. Boy, was I cold!"

———

It was so cold in Florida, they were selling frozen orange juice right off the trees.

———

It was so cold that the farmers had to milk their cows with ice picks.

———

When I received the contract to play Anchorage, I grabbed my tux and snowshoes, and off I skidded. North Pole nights are six months long. I arrived half-past January. The daytime is also six months and everybody stays up—that's why they have those Arctic circles under their eyes. But I wasn't disappointed about not playing Florida that winter, because I came back from Alaska with a color—blue.

Oh, I was a big hit. The only trouble is the audience was a little cold. I talked to one guy for an hour before I found out he was a snowman. I had a high-class opening at the club I worked. Everybody came to the premiere formal, sporting tuxedos with built-in parkas and patent leather snowshoes. The center ringside was reserved for eight: the mayor, his missus, and six huskies.

It's so cold in my house, even the janitor is banging on the pipes.

It was so cold when I was born, a penguin brought me instead of a stork.

It was so cold, I was looking for a girl with a high fever for a roommate.

She likes the cold weather. If it weren't for the goose-pimples, she'd have no figure at all.

It was so cold, I had to drink a six-pack of Prestone.

It was so cold, before she could say "I'm not that kind of girl," she was.

It was so cold, they had to chip me out of my waterbed. You think you've got problems? I've got a frozen zipper!

This weather is a wonderful experience for anyone who has ever wanted to live inside a Good Humor truck.

I was so cold, only my heartburn kept me warm.

I awoke to find two feet of ice in my bed—both of them belonging to my wife.

I can't believe my electric bill. I'm going to have to keep my thermostat at no more than sixty-two dollars a day.

A realtor has decided to put up condo igloos: He promises central refrigeration.

It's so cold, they're putting thermal underwear on the Statue of Liberty.

This is the time of the year for skiing, or as orthopedic surgeons call it, the busy season.

When you're zooming down a ski slope, there are two things you must never lose: your composure and your Blue Cross card.

I went to one ski resort that had three slopes: beginner, intermediate, and call-an-ambulance.

It's so cold, even my neighbor's wife is acting frigid.

# College

*(see also Education)*

"He's a perfect student. He is studying reading, writing, and rioting."

"My cousin is in medical school." "What's he studying?" "Nothing. They're studying him."

You can lead a girl to Vassar but you can't make her think.

My nephew sent me a note from college: "Dear Uncle, I'm doing well in everything except school."

"So you managed to escape from college?" "Yeah, I'm a fugitive from a brain gang."

"Would you like to buy a magazine?" "What's the idea?" "I'm working my brother's way through college."

"He wants to be a college man, so he put hair tonic on his slicker, trying to make a raccoon coat out of it."

"When you were in college, what did you go in for?" "Because it was raining."

"I want you to you know I got a letter at college. It said settle down and study or they'd kick me out."

"I'm taking three courses in college: French, Spanish, and algebra." "Let me hear you say 'good evening' in algebra."

"What is your son taking in college?" "Oh, he's taking all I've got."

"I'm going to enter the diplomatic service." "Domestic or foreign?" "Neither. I'm going to be president of a university."

INTERVIEWER: Tell me, Professor, you've taught for ten years at Yale, fifteen years at Oxford, nine years at the Sorbonne . . . What has been your biggest problem? PROFESSOR: Spitballs.

FIRST STUDENT: Congratulations! I hear you won a scholarship to Harvard Medical School. SECOND STUDENT:

Yes, but they don't want me while I'm alive.

How would I know the name of the school? I'm only a football player here.

If I'm studying when you come in, please wake me up.

I don't like to brag, but I'm putting a kid through college. He belongs to the guy who fixes my TV set.

Co-ed to girlfriend: I have a horrible feeling we are not being followed.

I saw six college kids stagger out of a bar and stuff themselves into the little car. One of them said, "Charlie, you drive, you're too drunk to sing."

Co-ed to her roommate: Frank is a perfect gentleman—but it's better than having no boyfriend at all.

He went through school by writing short stories—he wrote them to his father.

Sending a kid through college is very educational. It teaches his parents to do without a lot of things.

When the father questioned his son's marks at school, the answer was, "I don't care what anybody says, I'm just as smart as the next guy—who also flunked."

Two young college kids were having a slight argument talking about their relationship. "I don't mind your mother living with us," the fellow was saying, "but I do wish she'd wait until we get married."

Comic Larry Gore tells of a friend's son who is a conscientious objector. He refuses to go to a college and fight.

When my nephew goes back to college he can't decide what to take. It's a toss-up between the library and the dean's office.

The president of the college left like be came—fired with enthusiasm.

The trouble with college kids today is their sex habits. Too many youngsters start experimenting with their fingers crossed, which happens to be the wrong part.

They take only top students in this college. They must have an "A" in Pot.

The mother went to see her analyst and said, "I got a daughter in college. She doesn't use drugs, she's not pregnant, she doesn't drink, she got the highest marks in her class, and she writes to us every day. Tell me, where did we go right?"

---

My kid goes to an Ivy League college. Now he can write on toilet walls in Latin.

---

The personnel manager looked over the application of the college graduate: "I see you've never been in jail. Didn't you take any interest in college activities?"

---

The old man was bragging: "My son just made the Yale Picket Team."

---

One way to stop a student-protest movement is to make it a required course.

---

"I've dated the entire football team and I haven't made love to a single one of them," said the senior. "I'll bet it's that shy right end," answered her roommate.

---

Q: When your son finishes college, what will he be? A: About forty?

---

It took her four years to get a sheepskin—and one day to get a mink.

My sister worked her way through college as a chambermaid and graduated magna cum laundry.

---

I knew it was an Ivy League college. It had button-down windows.

---

COLLEGE APPLICANT: What courses do you have here? INTERVIEWER: Quantitative Chemistry, Philosophy, Contemporary Anthropology, Abnormal Psychology. COLLEGE APPLICANT: Now wait a minute. I don't know how to read yet. INTERVIEWER: Oh, another football player.

---

GIRL: Are you a freshman? BOY: That's up to you.

---

An American reporter interviewed an Eton schoolmaster. REPORTER: Do you allow your boys to smoke? SCHOOLMASTER: I'm afraid not. REPORTER: Can they drink? SCHOOLMASTER: Good gracious, no. REPORTER: What about dates? SCHOOLMASTER: Oh, that's quite all right as long as they don't eat too many.

## Comedians
*(see also individual names)*

How do you become a comedian? You take a mouthful of marbles and one by one you drop them. And when you've lost all your marbles, you're a comedian.

I became a comedian when my father gave me a rocking chair. I loved that rocking chair. I used it day and night. One day it broke, and when they discovered I was off my rocker, they knew I was a comedian.

———

People say I have a wonderful delivery: ten days for shirts and two weeks for sheets.

———

The last time he played a nightclub he was such a hit, the manager jacked up the price of sandwiches to twenty cents apiece.

———

When I was at the Palace, I drew a line two blocks long, but they made me erase it.

———

His jokes are original. But the people who originated them died years ago.

———

I wouldn't say his jokes are bad, but after every show he gives his writers a loyalty test.

———

He's got a lot of funny lines. Too bad they are all in his face.

———

The comedians are so young these days, the makeup men don't know which end to put the powder on.

———

The great humorist Ed Wynn died, and at his grave somebody said, "This is the first time you ever made us sad."

———

As a comedian, I feel I'm not getting the money I deserve, but I'm keeping quiet about it because at the present time I can't afford to take a cut.

———

Comic Henny Youngman says, "If you want to get the real dope about comedy, come to the real dope."

———

The big things lately have been the sick comics. Some of them are really sick—they're stretcher cases.

———

His act is so sick, his agent bills Blue Cross.

———

One sick comic went to a psychiatrist and was cured after six visits, but now the comic is out of work and the psychiatrist is making a fortune with his act.

———

They say great comedians are born. Well, I was born, wasn't I?

———

It was such a religious audience. After each joke they said, "Oh God."

When I finished my act they sat open-mouthed. I never saw so many people yawning at the same time.

---

He's a great comic; he just signed a contract with Warner Brothers. Now he's waiting for them to sign it.

---

A comedian is a guy who knows a good gag when he steals one.

---

His is the hottest act in town—every part of it is stolen.

---

"A comic is a guy who says funny things. A comedian is a guy who says things funny."—Ed Wynn

---

Take the case of Irving. Irving, to quote his own modest words, is a "highly famous comedian." He's on your radio station once a day, on your TV channel four times a month, and on his analyst's couch five times a week. He's like any other nice, normal, crazy mixed-up kid of fifty-three.

---

Irving was born of ordinary parents. His mama was a bearded lady and so was his papa. He was the only child of three brothers and sisters. He was a shy, retiring lad, the only kid who ever retired at sixteen without ever having worked. His mama coddled him because she saw something in him that nobody else saw. She saw that he was nuts. Whilst other kiddies were cutting out paper dolls, Irving was cutting up real live comedians.

When he was twelve years old and in the seventh grade, his favorite pastime was marbles. A bully began copping a couple from him every day, and when he'd lost all his marbles, he decided to go into show business. He figured anything's better than working. He scraped together all the money he could rob and bought a Joey Adams joke book. Then he bought another. And another. And another. And when he had eight, he traded them in for one Joe Miller book.

When he was fourteen years old and still in the seventh grade, the teacher caught this poor but dishonest boy stealing answers off another kid's test paper—a definite symptom of humorosis borrowiasis, otherwise known as joke-lifting. When the principal begged him to explain, he said, "Well, a funny thing happened to me on the way to the cloakroom. . . .

Years passed, but Irving didn't. Here he was, seventeen years old, and he'd moved to the sixth grade. When he married the principal, his mama suggested he quit school to earn enough money to keep him in joke books. Then he had a baby, which upset him because it was he who had it, not his wife. However, when the doctor commented that the baby had a better delivery than he did, he decided to forget his theatrical aspirations and invade the business world. He became a carpenter. One day he nailed together some nuts and bolts and screws and they all fell apart. "Goodly gracious," his mama shouted, "the boy's got a screw loose!" So back he went into show business.

Irving's family complained that he wasn't bringing any bread into the house. Corn, yes, but bread, no! But did that bother a staunch, fearless, talented, great show-must-go-on trouper like Irving? Yes! However, he laughed at them (which was the only laugh he ever got) and grabbed a little joke book and a lotta friends and began comedy-ing. Nothing happened. Then he collared an audience of his daddy's employees who'd laugh him up if he recited his income tax return. And he did. And they did.

Immediately he made up what little mind he had left and, upon hearing his mama say to his papa, "That Irving's a big joke," he announced, "Daddy dear and Mummy dear, I are going to be a comedian." "Better you should be a bum or something steady like a dope peddler," cried the family.

Irving wanted very badly to be successful. He tried and tried but he couldn't make it. Finally he divorced his old hag wife, grabbed himself a sexy chorine, and y'know what? He made it! But he found that it didn't help his career any. Somebody suggested he go to school so he could understand what the audience was talking about when they weren't listening to him. For years he went to school

at night, though he never learned anything because that particular school closed at 3 P.M. It was while he was going to school that he got his first break. The surgeon placed his arm in a plaster cast and in a few months he was as bad as new.

Poor Irving. He burrowed his pointed scalp deeper into his joke book until he began telling funny jokes until seven in the morning. Got so he couldn't crawl out of bed until he'd done three minutes of material. He actually began punning when he was alone. He was no longer a social joker. Eventually, in serious condition, he enrolled in GA: Gangsters Anonymous. They told him not to think about never making jests again, but just to promise himself that he wouldn't tell them for that day. They told him if he ever woke up at three in the morning with an uncontrollable urge to throw a punchline, he should call a certain number and they'd send Milton Berle over to sit with him until the spell was gone. One night after doing this, he fell into a stupor, talked in his sleep, and Berle wrote all his routines down and used them in his own act in Miami.

Irving became a has-been who never was. He became a neurotic. He did odd things like tell other comics they were good, and he said kind words about his confreres. When this occurred, well-meaning friends took him away.

'Tis said all comedians are neurotic because they have insecurity complexes. This is a lie. I know many clowns who are completely secure and are neurotic. However, I do resent people saying we are abnormal, poorly adjusted individuals who require psychiatry. And I am not alone in my resentment. My psychiatrist feels the same way.

Irving eventually recovered from his experience because he had faith that someday someone would recognize him. Several months later when he was walking down the street with his yo-yo, his kindergarten teacher stopped him and said, "Say, aren't you Irving?" Knowing he'd been recognized gave him confidence, and he grew and grew. When he'd started in show business he was only five feet, three inches, but soon his ego was six feet two.

Today, dear, sweet, stupid Irving has gone the way of all other successes. He has a Cadillac with a built-in Rolls. He is at home in country houses, winter houses, and a coupla houses that aren't exactly homes. He is a sports enthusiast and plays all games. Friends say he even likes the outdoor athletics. He makes ten grand a week. His hunting lodge in the Virgin Islands is so big he has to take a taxi to the bathroom. His faucets pour only champagne—domestic, of course, since he's always been chintzy with a buck. He has solid gold silverware and diamond inlays, and he takes weekly "humble lessons."

But, you ask, is he happy? Would he do it all over again? Was it all worth it? Do I think comedians can laugh happily ever after? Yes, he would, it was, and I do. . . .

# Commercials
*(see also Television, Advertising)*

They televised the entire ceremony at Sing Sing. Just as the convicted murderer was about to sit in the electric chair, the commercial came on: "You can be sure—if it's Westinghouse."

---

If not completely satisfied, return the unused portion of the can, and we will return the unused portion of your money.

---

If you have indigestion, do as thousands do—belch.

---

Use Jack Carter's big liver pills. One man I know used them all his life and finally died at the age of 103. Three days later they had to beat his liver to death with a club.

---

I don't know why they advertise bad breath—nobody wants it.

---

Our bras will support you in the manner to which you are not accustomed.

---

Girls, are you putting up a good front? Use our bras. The living bra for those who have been dead for years.

---

Don't kill your wife with washing. Let our product do it. Our product is never touched by human hands—just kick it into the washing machine.

———

Look, Ma, no cavities—but all my gums are gone.

———

Do you have teeth like the Ten Commandments? All broken? Use Adams' tooth powder and get a good paste in the mouth.

# Communism

*(see also Russia)*

A visitor to Hungary asked one of the natives, "How many people would you estimate are against the Communist regime here?" The native said, "Six." The visitor said, "Only six? Are you sure?" The native replied, "Yes, six: you, I, he, she, we, and they."

———

A Communist is a man who minds his own business at the top of his voice.

———

When Communists have each other as friends, they don't need any enemies.

———

Three prisoners in a Soviet prison were letting their secrets out: "I was put here for coming to work late," said the first. The second said, "I came to work too early. They said this proved I was an imperialistic spy." "I'm here," the third confessed, "because I arrived

exactly on time. This meant I owned an American watch."

———

When the Red arrived in hell, the devil asked him which section he preferred, Communist or capitalist. "Are you joshing?" he asked. "Communist, naturally; I know the heating won't work!"

———

A Communist is a person who wants to share his nothing with everybody.

———

Communist: One who borrows your pot to cook your goose.

———

The Moscow resident was sent to jail for five years for shouting "Down with Khrushchev." Anxious to make amends, when he got out he went around shouting, "Hooray for Khrushchev." He was sent back to jail for another five years.

# Composers

"Curse you, once more you are off your Beethoven."

———

"And again, my dear Gershitz, you have flown off your Handel."

———

"It seems to me the composer was under the influence of Gershwin when he wrote this number."

"No, it was cognac; I saw the empty bottle."

———

He may not be able to carry a tune, but he sure can lift them.

———

"He composes music in bed." "What kind of music could that be?" "Sheet music."

———

"What did you ever write?" "I wrote the score of the Army-Navy game." "What was it?" "Three to nothing."

———

"Everything he writes is no good." "I know; I tried to cash his check."

———

To write a hit song, you just take something composed by one of the old masters and decompose it.

———

"I have a wonderful ear. I can pick up anything that's musical." "Let's see you pick up the piano."

# Computers
*(see also Business, Office)*

To err is human; to really screw up you need a computer.

———

How can you tell when the dumb secretary has been using the computer? There is white-out all over the screen.

The guy was crying at the bar: "I don't understand my wife, I don't understand my boss. I don't understand my girl. I don't understand my kids. And now I don't understand my personal computer."

———

My biggest problem is reconciling my gross habits with my computer capacity.

———

Did you hear the story about the two computers that got married and had a baby? Its first word was "Data."

———

The young man fed into the computer dating service a request for a girl who didn't drink, smoke, swear, or have any bad habits. The computer blinked on and off and then flashed back a question: "Why Bother?" The next man at the same dating service entered his vital statistics and fed a picture of himself into the scanning port. The computer spit out the number of Dial-a-Prayer. Then there was this tall, dark, and rich gentleman who registered as a multimillionaire. The computer mugged him on the way out.

———

Women really love a computer. It's the one thing that will do exactly what they tell it to do.

———

My neighbor works at a company that is so stressful, even the computers have ulcers.

———

The computer has taken the place of labor, thinking, sex, productivity, and dating.

———

The machine can do more work faster than a human, because it doesn't have to answer the phone, and it never has to do its nails.

———

"This little computer," said the sales clerk, "will do half your job for you." The senior vice president decided, "I'll take two."

———

If you make a mistake, you're a bumbling idiot. If your computer makes a mistake, it's a malfunction.

———

My friend told me, "I had a tough time at the office today: My computer broke down and I had to think all day."

———

My uncle tells me about a fully automated bank in Miami. Seems somebody sent it a card saying, "This is a holdup," and the computer mailed the fellow $100 in unmarked bills.

———

One Wall Street executive tells me he has a solution to the twin problems of unemployment and low productivity: "I have invented a machine that will do the work of five men. It takes ten men to operate it."

———

I've got news for you: Computers do create jobs. Now it takes more people to correct each mistake.

———

It is good news when you are told the check is in the mail. It is bad news when you find out it was a recorded announcement.

———

Did you read in the *Wall Street Journal* about that big stockbroker who went to jail? They nailed him because his computer turned state's evidence.

———

Computers are getting all too human. Believe it or not, last week at an office party one of the computers got high on static electricity and tried to undo the printer's ribbon.

———

In Cuba they recently developed a brilliant new computer, but they ran into a problem. It was so smart, it defected to Miami.

———

"I knew it would happen," complained the office manager at the *Post*. "Now the computers want their own union!"

Computers are just like humans. When they make a mistake they blame another machine.

———

One thing a computer can't do as well as a secretary is spread gossip.

———

Another thing computers can't do even though they're mathematical geniuses is reconcile a woman's "present age" with her birth date.

———

They're into everything these days. Last week the computer won the football pool. It took the winnings, faxed out an order for multimedia software, and downloaded it. Now, every time you turn on a computer, you get cyber-sex screen savers, and it plays Beethoven's Fifth!

———

Some people just like to brag. A guy boasted about being fired and being replaced by a $250,000 computer.

———

Computers are getting wiser every day. A couple of college kids put cards into the machine to see if they were well matched—and the computer wound up with the girl.

———

A bachelor said he'd visited a computer dating office and listed specifications. He wanted someone on the small side, one who likes water sports, is gregarious, likes formal dress, and says little. "So," he sighed, "I drew a penguin."

## Confucius or Confused?

Chun King say, "Smart man his views always same like yours."

———

Cooing he stop with honeymoon but billing he go on forever.

———

Golf is game in which small ball is chased by man who too old to chase anything else.

———

City she full of teenage girls who have reached the dangerous age when their voices are change from no to yes.

———

Reckless driver he is person who pass you on road in spite of all you can do.

———

When women they kiss, she always remind me of prizefighter who shake hands.

———

Chasing pretty girl never hurt anybody—trouble is she come after catch them.

———

Platonic love he all same, like be invited to cellar for drink of ginger ale.

If you want proof that girls she are dynamite, just try to drop one.

———

If at first you not succeed, your father he own business.

———

An optimist he is man who marry his secretary and think he will continuing dictating to her.

———

Chun King say, "Smart lady she never let fool kiss her—or kiss fool her."

———

Every man he like to see broad smile, especially if broad she smile at him.

———

If any person he disagree with you, forget same. After all, he have right to stick to his ridiculous opinion.

———

Chun King say, "When hostess she not have enough chair for everyone, she give buffet dinner."

———

God he make universe and then he rested. He then make man and then he rested once more. Next he make woman—and nobody have rested ever since.

———

Chun King say, "Husband he living proof that woman can take joke."

———

Many husband he kiss with eyes open. He want make sure his wife's not around to catch him.

———

Mermaid she not so good. After all, she not enough fish to fry and not enough woman to love.

———

Tactless man is one who voice what everybody else is thinking.

———

Chun King say, "Wolf he is man with lot of pet theories."

———

Person who buy secondhand car, he know how hard it is to drive bargain.

———

Spinster she woman who know all answers, but nobody ask her questions.

———

When man he bring wife flowers for no reason, there usually reason.

———

Pedestrian he man who have two motorcar, one wife, and one son.

———

Chun King say, "Flirt she is girl who believe it is every man for herself."

# Cooking

*(see also Eating, Marriage)*

I got a wife who dresses to kill—and cooks the same way.

———

She runs the only kitchen in the world where flies come to commit suicide.

———

She got along fine in her cooking school until one day she finally burned something—her cooking school.

———

These days when you go into a restaurant and order a five-dollar dinner, the waiter wants to know: "On rye or white?"

———

The husband told his wife he wanted to be surprised for dinner, so she took all the labels off the cans.

———

His wife will put on anything for dinner, except an apron.

———

It takes her an hour to cook minute rice.

———

It took her the first three months of their married life to discover you can't open an egg with a can opener.

———

The only thing she knows about good cooking is which restaurants to go to.

My wife offered me some biscuits and said, "Take your pick." She should have said, "Take your saw."

———

She was a peculiar sort of a woman. She would let her son sit on her bread dough because she loved to watch her son rising in the yeast.

———

Then there was the woman who boiled her eggs for a half hour waiting for them to get soft. She was told to boil them for three minutes if she wanted them soft. So she boiled her potatoes for only three minutes, and she couldn't understand how they got hard so fast.

———

When Rosemary Wilson wrote *The Beautiful Wife's Cookbook*, Earl cracked, "They are making it into a TV series called 'The Survivors.'" I love Rosemary, but when she was on my radio show I said, "Rosemary Wilson's cookbook comes with 200 assorted get-well cards."

———

Comedienne Joan Rivers admits she's a terrible cook: "Yesterday I tried to make ladyfingers—and they turned out all thumbs."

———

Joan says her favorite recipe is a TV dinner, and her second favorite recipe is to warm it up. "The last time my husband had a hot meal was when a candle fell on his sandwich. I never realized how bad a cook I was until Betty Crocker threw a rock through my window. One time I served hors d'oeuvres on a Ouija board. The board spelled out, 'Don't eat the hors d'oeuvres.'"

Joan Rivers swears she made orange juice for her husband every single day on their honeymoon—and then she lost the recipe.

One guy complained about his wife's cooking: "I broke a tooth on it—and that was just the coffee."

You've heard about people who can't boil water. My wife can—she calls it soup.

Every time I meet a girl who can cook like my mother, she looks like my father.

Bob Hope says Phyllis Diller has the only dining-room table with a garbage disposal for a centerpiece.

Phyllis admits she's a lousy cook. "In my house we have Alka-Seltzer on tap."

Actor-comedian Don Adams says his mother was such a lousy cook, she brought him up on radio dinners.

Comic Pat Cooper says, "My wife broke our dog of begging from the table. She let him taste the food."

It still takes many housewives hours to prepare dinner. Do you think it's easy getting some packages out of the freezer?

Show me a beautiful, sexy wife who doesn't like to cook and I'll show you a couple who eat out a lot.

My wife discovered a great way to keep all her dishes, pots, and pans sparkling clean. She never uses them.

I won't say my wife is a bad cook, but the other night I sent her out to dinner and she burned the Diners Club card.

My wife has come up with a great formula to keep food costs down. It's her cooking.

My wife is really a lousy cook. The other night we had to call a repairman to fix our TV dinner.

I won't say my wife is a bad cook. On the other hand, I will say it. She has contributed recipes to a cookbook called *Condemned by Duncan Hines*.

———

My wife always has an excuse. I bought her a foreign cookbook and now she says she can't get parts for the meals.

———

I told my wife that for a new and exciting meal she should try the Galloping Gourmet's cookbook—so she boiled it.

———

She's a fast cook. She serves three-minute eggs in one minute and cooks minute rice in three seconds flat.

———

Comedienne Thelma Lee says: "There are some men who think we women run home from club meetings and put TV dinners on the table. First of all, I happen to be a very good cook, and my food melts in my husband's mouth—while it's defrosting. . . . You think the government has space problems? We women have space problems with the crummy freezers we're forced to use. You can't buy what you like to eat, you have to buy what fits. And I measure before I go shopping. I say, well, I have 2 inches here, 4 inches there. So I even found myself saying to the butcher, "I would like a chicken 2 by 4 by 7. And I would like you to take his left leg and wrap it around his neck, and if my calculations are right,

I can take four meatballs and put them under his armpit into the freezer!"

## Cooper, Pat
*(see also Comedians)*

I saw a hippie having his reflexes tested. A doctor hit the fellow's knee with a flower.

———

The moviehouse in my hometown showed second-run pictures. They were on TV first.

———

I complained to the landlord about my new terrace apartment. The sidewalk was blocking my view.

———

I walked away from a Las Vegas laundry machine for five minutes and somebody won my wash.

———

Liberace is afraid of the dark. When he goes to sleep he leaves his jacket lit.

———

I visited a Las Vegas hospital; the condition charts list the odds on the patients.

## Cops
*(See also Crime and Criminals)*

He was a great cop. Always assigned to headquarters, 'cause he had a head as big as a quarter.

"Calling car 66." "But we are car 99." "No, you're car 66." "How do you like that, we've been riding upside down!"

———

The cop requested duty on a motorcycle so that if there was any trouble, he could make a quick getaway.

———

On a policeman's examination one question was, "What would you do to disperse a crowd quickly and quietly?" The answer: "I'd pass the hat."

———

COP: Pardon me, Miss, but swimming is not allowed in this lake. GIRL: Why didn't you tell me that before I undressed? COP: Because there ain't no law against undressing.

———

Commenting on the recent police corruption in Chicago, humorist Mort Sahl said, "It's the only place where a kid can play cops and robbers by himself."

———

POLICE CHIEF: How did you learn so much about crime? CRIMINAL: I started in a small way. Picking midgets' pockets. CHIEF: How could you stoop so low?

## Cosby, Bill
*(see also Comedians)*

When I was a kid I never went to school; I always said I was sick. But I always managed to get better by 3:30, and I'd run into the kitchen and say, "Look, Ma, a miracle happened! I'm well! A little angel came and sat on my bed. She touched me with a wand and said, 'Go out and play.'"

———

We had a teacher in school who hated kids. He caught me reading a comic book in class and snatched it away from me. "You'll get this back at the end of the semester." I said, "Why, is it gonna take you that long to read it?"

———

I never liked doctors. They always keep their stethoscopes in the freezer.

## Courts
*(see also Crime and Criminals, Judges, Lawyers)*

"The court will give you three lawyers because of the importance of this case," the judge said.

"If it's all the same to you, Your Honor," the criminal said, "just get me one good witness."

———

This is the only country in the world where they lock up the jury and let the prisoner go home every night.

———

Woman to judge: "That's my side of the story. Now let me tell you his."

———

DEFENDANT: As God is my judge, I did not take the money. JUDGE: He isn't. I am. You did.

———

The scared defendant asked the irate judge what was the maximum penalty for bigamy.

"Two mothers-in-law," was the answer.

———

Woman juror to eleven exasperated men jurors: "If you men weren't so stubborn, we could all go home."

———

LAWYER: I'd like a new trial for my client. JUDGE: On what grounds? LAWYER: My client has dug up some money I didn't know he had.

———

A young man was brought before the judge for robbery. The case against him was strong. The judge turned to the alleged robber and scolded, "Well, what have you to say for yourself? Where are your witnesses? Don't you have any witnesses in this case?" "No, Your Honor," the prisoner said quietly, "not me. I never take along any witnesses when I commit a robbery."

———

JUDGE: Haven't I seen you before? TAILOR ON TRIAL: Maybe. So many men owe me money, I can't remember their faces.

JUDGE: Can't this dispute be settled out of court? DEFENDANT: Sure— that's what we were trying to do when the police interfered.

———

As a judge, when Goha hailed a husband before him for killing his wife, the husband in self-defense stated that he had caught his wife in the act of adultery. "Why did you not kill the man, the stranger who wronged you, instead of killing your wife?" asked Goha. "Because," the man answered, "if I had spared her, I would have had to kill a man a day; by killing her, I put an end to her adultery with only one murder."

———

A jury consists of twelve people who determine which side has the best lawyer.

———

She asked the judge for a divorce because her husband talked to her only three times in their five years of marriage, and she wanted custody of their three children.

———

The jury foreman stood up when the judge asked him if they had come to a decision. The foreman said, "We're all of one mind: temporarily insane."

———

In a little town in the West, a middle-aged woman was found guilty of killing her husband. But the judge suspended the sentence. He had compassion for her because she was a widow.

———◦◦◦◦———

The racket guy paid off the juror to hold out for a verdict of manslaughter. After two days and nights, the jury returned with the verdict he paid for. "I'll never forget you," said the hood. "You must have had a bottle of trouble—I mean, two days and nights." "I had plenty of trouble," the juror answered. "Everybody else on the jury wanted an acquittal."

———◦◦◦◦———

"I always had his best interest at heart," the wife told the judge. "So how come she married me?" the husband asked.

———◦◦◦◦———

"Is it true," the judge asked, "that you haven't spoken a word to your wife in five years of married life?" "Yes." "Explain yourself." "I didn't want to interrupt her."

———◦◦◦◦———

"Honest, Judge, I didn't desert my wife. I'm just a coward."

———◦◦◦◦———

"You've been acquitted on the charge of bigamy," the judge said. "You can go home now." "Oh, ah, Your Honor, sir—which home?"

The foreman of the jury announced, "Your Honor, we find that the man who stole the money is not guilty."

# Courtship
*(see also Dating, Kissing)*

She could have married anyone she pleased. She just didn't please anyone.

———◦◦◦◦———

ANN: We could never be happy, Dan. You know I always want my own way in everything. DAN: But after we're married you can still want your own way in everything.

———◦◦◦◦———

How can you tell if you're in love? You ask yourself, "Would I mind being destroyed financially by this person?"

———◦◦◦◦———

Courtship is a period when a man pursues a girl who is running toward him.

———◦◦◦◦———

HE: (sneaking up behind SHE and covering SHE's eyes) I'm going to kiss you if you don't know who it is! SHE: Abraham Lincoln? George Washington? Albert Schweitzer?

———◦◦◦◦———

MEL: If you refuse to marry me, I'll hurl myself off that 200-foot cliff. CAROL: Ah, that's just a bluff.

———◦◦◦◦———

FATHER: My boy, I never kissed a girl until I met your mother. Will you be able to say that to your son?

———

Never trust a girl who says she loves you more than anybody else in the world: It proves she's been experimenting.

———

All the world loves a lover—except the husband.

———

"Darling," she whispered, "will you still love me after we are married?" He considered this for a moment and then replied, "I think so. I've always been especially fond of married women."

———

My niece cried, "He is the man for me! He's handsome, he's sexy, he's smart, he's funny, he's strong, he's—" I interrupted, "He's married." She said, "So? Nobody's perfect."

———

This playboy talks about this playgirl: "The first night we met, we exchanged numbers. She gave me her phone number and I gave her my savings account number."

———

My nephew told me, "You know I used to go with this girl until I found out she spent $15,000 a year on dress-es." I asked, "So you broke up over that?" He said, "Yeah, now I go out with her dressmaker."

———

A rather homely young farmer, proposing to his sweetheart, confessed: "I know I'm not much to look at." "That's all right," she said. "You'll be out in the fields most of the time."

———

I was a judge at a pet show and was instructed to look for obedience, friendliness, loyalty, and good grooming. I told my instructors: Forget the pets—those are the makings of a great girlfriend.

———

Some people really know how to take the romance out of everything. I recently heard one doctor refer to Cupid as the world's first acupuncturist.

———

It's probably true that men don't make passes at girls who wear glasses. Often, though, they will make them at girls who drain them.

## Cowardice

MANLY: Put up your fists and fight like a man. WEAKLY: I'd rather put up my ears and run like a rabbit.

LUKE: Last week when that bear got out, you ran away and left me. You told me once that you would face death for me! DICK: Yes, I would—but that bear wasn't dead.

———

SHE: Don't be a coward, act like a man. HE: How do you like that? My life is in danger and you want me to do imitations.

———

SHE: You shouldn't be afraid of him. He's an ignorant savage and you're an educated, intelligent man. HE: What do you expect me to do? Beat him to death with my diploma?

———

Once there was a very brave lion tamer who was not afraid of the most vicious lions in the menagerie. But he had a wife who did not like him to stay out late, and one night he did stay out late. When he realized it was midnight, he was panic-stricken. He didn't dare go home, but if he went to a hotel, his wife might find him. So he went to the menagerie, crawled into the lion's cage, and went to sleep with his head resting on the largest lion. The next morning his wife began to hunt for him, and she looked all over town. Finally she came to the menagerie and saw her husband in the lion's cage. A look of contempt came over her face, and she snarled: "You coward!"

———

# Cowboys

He walked in with a gun on each hip, and she walked in with a hip on each gun.

———

There they stood, the Bicarbonate Brothers: Wild Bill Hiccup and Hopalong Acidity.

———

When I was out west I punched cattle for six months. Then the cattle started punching back.

———

The cowboys were digging and digging until they found their bonanza. Then they split it up and today they have the biggest bonanza split out west.

———

He rode a horse like he was part of the animal. I hate to tell you which part.

———

Definition of a cowboy: a boy whose mother was a cow.

———

Out west you ride a horse, and everything in front of you is purple and gold . . . and everything in back of you is black and blue.

———

CITY BOY: What is cowhide chiefly used for? COWBOY: To keep the cow together.

## Crazy

"It is an irrefutable fact," said the woman lecturer, "that throughout the world there are three men to one woman in every asylum." "True," a man in the rear shouted, "but who put them there?"

Dentist to patient: Your teeth are fine, but your gums will have to come out.

Man on phone to bank teller: "This is a stick-up. Send me fifty thousand dollars."

Youngster to mounted policeman: "Why can't you ride in a patrol car like the other policemen?"

"I could, only there isn't room for my horse!"

PROFESSOR: Does the question bother you? STUDENT: Not at all. The question is quite clear—it's the answer that troubles me.

MOTHER: If you don't stop playing that saxophone, I'll go crazy! SON: Too late, Ma, I stopped an hour ago.

"How did your backside get so cut up?" "The guy next door was hanging pictures in his flat. The wall is thin, the nails are long—and the guy is a midget."

The doctor had never seen such a fat patient. When she sat down on the chairs, the doc said, "Open your mouth and say moo."

The shy man jumped off the bus backward when he heard a man say: "Let's grab his seat when he gets off."

The doctor called the police. "Listen, a crazy man escaped. He weighs three hundred pounds and is three feet four inches tall." The cop said, "Are you kidding?" The doctor said, "I told you he was crazy!"

His latest invention was crossing a rabbit with a piece of lead. He hopes to get a repeating pencil.

"Who are you writing this letter to?" the attendant asked the patient. "To myself." "What does it say?" "How should I know? I haven't received it yet."

"Carrots are good for your eyes." "I don't believe that baloney!" "Did you ever see a rabbit with glasses?"

———

The stripper awoke after a high night and found herself with her clothes on. She yelled: "Ye gads—I've been draped!"

———

The girls around here are crazy about me. In fact, one girl has been trying to break my door down all day— I've got her locked in my room.

———

"All week long before the baby was born he brought his wife roses. A rose in the morning, a rose at night. Guess what they named the baby." "Rose?" "No, Max. It was a boy."

———

Never slap a guy in the face when he's chewing tobacco.

———

I can't understand it. No matter where a service station puts up a pump, they find gas.

## Credit

*(see also Money)*

Money isn't everything—except when you've mislaid your credit cards.

———

These days, if somebody pays you in cash, you get suspicious. You think maybe his credit is no good.

———

You have to give most American families a lot of credit—they can't get along without it.

———

He's steamed because the gum machine won't take credit cards.

———

A credit card is a printed IOU.

———

"Do you live within your income?" "Are you kidding? I can't even live within my credit cards."

———

A customer phoned a restaurant in New York to ask if they honored credit cards. "Not only honor, but also love and obey them," the manager answered.

———

The wife asked, "Why can't we pay our Diners Club bill with our American Express card?"

———

A little old lady walked into the credit department at Diners Club and demanded, "I don't care to bandy words with underlings about my overdrawn account. Take me to your computer."

Most department stores are willing to give a woman credit for what her husband earns.

———

Today's moneyless society won't seem really complete to us until we find a panhandler who accepts credit cards.

———

Credit cards have made buying easier, but paying harder.

———

Using a credit card is a convenient way to spend money you wish you had.

———

The main problem with paying by credit card is that Visa and Master Card don't accept American Express.

———

My wife is doing her best to stimulate the economy: She's the only one who has racing stripes on her credit cards.

———

A disgruntled would-be joiner wrote a long and sordid letter to the Diners Club claiming he couldn't understand why he was not acceptable. At the end he explained that he would like to get an answer and asked that it be addressed to the hotel on the letterhead. "This hotel," he said, "is one of my better creditors."

The funniest story going around Madrid, Spain, happened at one of the best nightclubs there. It seems that a certain newspaperman was attracted to a certain dancer at this club and asked if he might take her to another cabaret. The headwaiter said that such a thing could be arranged if the newspaperman was willing to pay for her time. At the moment the scribe didn't have sufficient pesetas and asked if he could cash a traveler's check. The headwaiter said no, but if the chap had a Diners Club card he would charge the date as dessert. And the deal was actually made!

———

The beggar stood on a street corner and asked a passing gentleman for money. "Not now," said the gentleman, "but I'll give you something on my way back." "Nope, that won't do," said the beggar. "Why you'd be surprised how much money I've lost giving credit that way."

———

CUSTOMER: I warn you, I won't be able to pay for this suit for six months. TAILOR: Oh, that's all right, sir. CUSTOMER: Thank you. When will it be ready? TAILOR: In six months, sir.

———

CREDIT MANAGER: Are you going to pay us something on that account? CUSTOMER: I can't just now. CREDIT MANAGER: If you don't, I'll tell all your other creditors that you paid us in full.

Creditor: a man who has a better memory than a debtor.

———

I met a fellow in Hawaii who told me he went there for respiratory trouble. He said back home his creditors wouldn't let him breathe easy.

———

My credit cards are in real bad shape. The only thing that will help right now is a cash transplant.

———

This year I'm determined to stay out of debt, even if I have to borrow money to do it.

———

I'm so used to buying with credit cards that when I bought something for cash, I signed all the dollar bills.

———

My neighbor is in big trouble: His credit is lousy. He even has to have a co-signer when he pays cash.

———

People who are too scared to steal, too proud to beg, and too poor to pay cash think credit cards are the answer.

———

I love the credit card commercials: "Tonight, steak in San Francisco. Tomorrow, teriyaki in Tokyo." Thursday, bankruptcy in New York.

———

The young wife said to her husband after looking over her budget: "If we miss two payments on the mortgage and one on the car, we'll have enough for a down payment on a color TV set."

———

I tried to use my credit card in a health food store, and the clerk told me they only accept natural cash.

———

With my credit cards, my wife has the world at her feet, while I have the creditors at my throat.

———

I admire the way my wife spends— she's a credit to her card.

———

Credit is a system of buying time with money you don't have.

———

Most people don't care how much they pay for something, as long as it isn't all at once.

———

The salesman tried to sell a refrigerator to the housewife: "Lady, you can save enough on your food bill to pay for it." She answered, "We are paying for a car on the carfare we save. We are paying for a washing machine on the laundry bills we save. We are paying for a TV set on the cost of the movies we don't see anymore. It looks like we just can't afford to save any more at this time."

No man's credit is as good as his money.

I know someone who pays cash every now and then just to throw the store management into a panic.

Two men were leaving a pub and one said, "You can't live with 'em and you can't live without 'em." The other agreed, "That's the way women are, pal." "Who said anything about women?" the first groaned. "I'm talking about credit cards."

I met my friend at a party and said, "You're looking a bit off color, pal. Anything wrong?" He said, "I'm afraid there is. I've had to give up drinking, smoking, and gambling." I said, "Hey, that's all to your credit." He cried, "It sure ain't. It's due to my lack of credit!"

My cousin told me, "My wife has the same attitude as the federal government: She never lets being in debt keep her from spending more."

With all the credit cards and mortgages available these days, anyone who isn't hopelessly in debt just isn't trying.

My neighbor says, "My wife must be a direct descendant of Teddy Roosevelt, the way she runs into stores yelling 'Charge!'"

Muggers are complaining that credit cards are hurting their business: They claim too few people carry cash these days.

I asked a bankrupt debtor why he went bankrupt. He answered, "I hate to owe money."

A large number of people are trying to keep up with the Joneses and a number of creditors are trying to keep up with them.

Credit: a device that enables you to start at the bottom—and go into a hole.

My car has something that will last a lifetime: monthly payments.

Education is a wonderful thing. If you couldn't sign your name, you'd have to pay cash.

Did you hear about the new credit cards for wives? It self-destructs after $100.

---

She likes guys who lay their cards on the table: Diners, American Express, Visa, MasterCard.

---

What this country needs is a credit card for taxpayers.

---

My friend has so many credit cards, he was bankrupt for six months before he knew about it.

---

Credit card: a convenient way to spend money you wish you had.

---

Eat, drink, and be merry, for tomorrow you may lose your credit card.

---

Credit card: instant debt.

---

Many a man is poor today because his credit card was good yesterday.

## Crime and Criminals
*(see also Cops, Courts, Judges, Lawyers)*

I always wondered what happens if a midget commits murder and is sentenced to die. Do they give him the electric high chair?

ROBBER: Okay, stick 'em down.
ROBBED: You mean stick 'em up.
ROBBER: Don't confuse me, it's my first job.

---

FINGERS: Whatever happened to Knuckles? He used to be in slot machines. ELBOWS: Oh, he went into bigger business. FINGERS: What's he in now? ELBOWS: Concrete.

---

He got caught stealing in the corset department and got sent up for a two-way stretch.

---

The crook with the greatest chutzpah I ever knew is the one who held up a bank with a nylon stocking over his head. He held up the first cashier and made him hand over $50,000. Then he proceeded to the next cashier and tried to open an account with the money.

---

Figures released today by the FBI show that for the first time there is now as much crime on the streets as there is on TV.

---

Organized crime in America takes in over $40 billion a year and spends very little on office supplies.

There's one neighborhood in the city so tough that the stop sign says, "STOP if you dare."

———————

There's one area in my brother's city where you can walk twelve blocks and not leave the scene of the crime. In this area even the candy stores have bouncers.

———————

The judge said to the bum, "You've committed six burglaries in a week." The bum said, "That's right. If everyone worked as hard as I do, we'd be on the road to prosperity."

———————

The victim said to the mugger, "But my watch isn't a good one—its value is only sentimental." The crook said, "That doesn't matter—I'm sentimental."

———————

The gangster handed his gal a beautiful mink coat. After admiring herself in it, she asked her fellow, "What is it worth?" He said, "Oh, five to ten, honey."

———————

"When you leave here," the host advised his pal, "start running and don't stop until you get home." Later that night the host got a call from the hospital, where his pal was lying beaten up and without his money. "I did what you said," the patient reported. "I ran and ran—and I caught up with a crook."

———————

The judge said to the character standing before him, "You can let me try your case or you can be tried by a jury of your peers." The bum asked, "What are peers?" The judge explained, "People of your own kind— your equals." The man said, "Well, I don't want to be tried by no car thieves."

———————

If crime doesn't pay, how come so many people want to be lawyers?

———————

One thief told me, "My lawyer just got me off for robbery. Now I have to rob somebody to pay his bill."

———————

The burglar said, "Don't be scared, lady. All I want is your money." She said, "Go away—you're just like all the other men."

———————

One resident of the city told me, "Security is pretty lax in my building. I lost the key to my apartment and a burglar loaned me his."

———————

One parking lot violator told the official he'd never forget him if he got him out of trouble with the police. And he didn't. The next time he was in trouble with the police, he called him again.

———————

This character told me he got a $100 parking ticket. I said, "That's pretty expensive even for this city. Why so high?" He said, "For parking on top of a police car!"

———

I don't want to say he was crooked, but he bribed the traffic cop with counterfeit money.

———

New York is a friendly town: If you want to shake hands, you must reach into your wallet pocket.

———

In the city these days, when you make your budget, you have to put a certain amount aside for holdup money.

———

The judge asked the police officer, "Why did you bring this man in? You say he's a camera fiend, but you shouldn't arrest him just because he has a mania for taking pictures." The cop said, "It isn't that—he takes cameras."

———

Number 32146, whom we'll call Blinky for short, was only recently taken from the mental ward of a prison and assigned a regular cell. It all dates back to the reason for his incarceration. Blinky was known as the Grandpa Moses of counterfeiters. He was so meticulous about copying a bill

that it took the eagle eye of a trained professional to detect his funny money from the real McCoy. For many months, Blinky worked on what he thought was a foolproof set of engravings for a $10 bill. His chore completed, he crumpled up his work of art, uncrumpled it, compared it with the original through a powerful magnifying glass, and decided to test it before going into volume production. Within two hours Blinky was arrested. "I defy you," he raged at the Treasury agent, placing both the original and the spurious bill side by side, "to tell me the difference between these two ten-spots." "There is no difference, Blinky," the T-man agreed, "and that's the trouble. Seems you made only one mistake. You copied your counterfeit from a counterfeit!"

———

This counterfeiter was going out of the business. So, in a last big fling, he made a $15 bill. He went into a candy store, bought a couple of fifty-cent stogies, and handed over the bill. The clerk looked at it for a moment, then went into the back of his establishment. He came out and gave him two $7 bills in change.

———

What we need is a slogan to encourage politicians to stay honest: "Make laws, not license plates."

———

I live in a very quiet neighborhood—very quiet. Where else can you hear people whispering for help?

———

I asked my nephew, who recently moved into a new neighborhood, "How much of a walk is it from your house to the nearest subway?" He said, "I don't know. I don't walk—I run."

———

The girl was screaming at her boyfriend. "You bum!" she cried. "You forgot what day it is!" He said, "Geez no, I didn't fuhget ya boitday. I even went to the jewelry shop to get you sometin'—but he was still open."

———

I'm tired of hearing people talking about my city's crime rate. We have four million people in New York and over a million of them have never even been mugged once.

———

One bank bandit was crying from his jail cell: "Twelve people out of 240 million find me guilty—and they call that justice?"

———

A street person was charged with stealing a pair of shoes. The judge said, "Stealing a pair of shoes, eh? Weren't you up here a year or so ago on the same charge?" The defendant confessed, "Yes, Your Honor. How long do you expect a pair of shoes to last?"

———

The magistrate said to the criminal before him, "The last time you were here, I told you I didn't want to see you again." The prisoner said, "I know, Your Honor. I told that to the policeman, but he wouldn't believe me!"

———

The accused strode forward at the end of the trial. "Your Honor," she said, "I wish to plead guilty." The judge demanded, "Why didn't you do so at the beginning of the trial?" "Because," the lady replied, "I thought I was innocent, but at the time I hadn't heard the evidence against me."

———

The next case had the judge furious: "I note that in addition to stealing money, you took watches, jewelry, rings, and pearls." The prisoner said, "Yes, Your Honor. I was taught that money alone does not bring happiness."

———

Crime is so bad in my neighborhood, the bank keeps its money in another bank. My neighborhood is so rough that when I called the police, there was a three-year waiting list.

———

The woman was charged with shoplifting. The magistrate asked if she had anything to say on her own behalf. She replied hopefully, "Yes, sir, I have. I take only American goods."

All this talk about crime finally got to me: I equipped my front door with a deadbolt, a multipoint lock, a double chain, and a device that electrifies the doorknob. Now I never have to worry about a burglar ripping me off when I'm away from home—because I can't get out of the house.

———

"I can't understand," said the defendant, "why I should be charged with forgery. I can't even sign my own name." The judge said, "You are not charged with signing your own name."

———

If the number of crooks in this country keeps increasing, I don't know where we'll put them all—our prisons and city halls are full.

———

I suppose it had to happen. . . . In the United States it is now as easy to buy a gun as it is to buy a politician.

———

A visitor told me, "This is a tough city. There's lots of stress. The other day I had a pain in my chest and I was fortunate—it was only a small-caliber pistol. Stress can kill you—a bullet you can get away from."

———

One prisoner said to his cellmate: "I am going to study and improve myself, and while you're still a common thief, I'll be an embezzler."

———

When Benny the burglar climbed out the window of the house, his waiting pal, Charlie, asked, "What did you get?" Benny said, "It's a lawyer's house." Charlie asked, "What did you lose?"

———

I'll tell you about my neighborhood. The most popular bumper stickers say, "Have you hugged your bail bondsman today?"

———

My cousin tells me he comes from a pretty rough neighborhood: The post office delivers arrest warrants in the mail marked "Occupant." That neighborhood is so tough, when you order in a restaurant they serve you broken leg of lamb. In school the kids were being taught, "An apple a day keeps the doctor away." One of the kids hollered, "That's all well and good, but what have you got for the cops?"

———

My mayor has announced that crime is down in the city: They've run out of victims.

———

One rich lady was arrested for shoplifting. She explained to the police: "I did it because I was depressed. I found out the body work on my Mercedes is going to cost $3,500."

———

With all the juvenile delinquency, muggings, killings, strikes, bombings, and uprisings going on, I think maybe the Indians should have had some stricter immigration laws.

———

As a kid, I lived in a neighborhood that was so tough, the school newspaper had an obituary column.

———

My apartment was robbed so many times I finally put up a sign that said, "We gave already!"

———

"You still say you're innocent," repeated the judge, "in spite of the proof that seven people saw you steal the necklace." "Your Honor," replied the prisoner, "I can produce seven hundred people who didn't see me steal it."

———

I'm always courteous. Just this morning I gave my place in a checkout line to a guy with only two items: a note and a gun.

———

The DA intoned, "Your Honor, look at the prisoner. In the past year he has committed many outrages—purse snatching, forgery, grand larceny, embezzlement, arson, kidnapping, and murder." "What do you have to say for yourself?" asked the judge. "Well," replied the young man, "nobody's perfect."

The thief put a gun in the ribs of the man walking on Fifth Avenue: "You're wasting your time," the victim said. "I'm a married man."

———

When it came time for the prisoner's release, the warden said, "I'm sorry, we seem to have kept you a week longer than we should have." The ex-con said, "That's okay. Just credit it to my account."

———

Because of the crime on Broadway, New York City pushed up theater time to 7:30 P.M. so people wouldn't be out too late. The restaurant owners complained that it hurt their business: "The only ones it helps are the muggers. They now get home earlier."

———

The crook pulled a gun on the cashier in the Chinese restaurant and said, "Give me all the money you got in the register—to go."

———

Everybody is conscious about crime in the streets. I asked one guy on Seventeenth Street and Broadway how I could get to Twenty-third and Lexington. "Easy," he explained. "You turn left on the next block, and if you make it . . ."

———

The FBI claims that organized crime in America has a yearly take of over

$50 billion, and it's going higher. What I want to know is, is it going public?

———

Comic Stanley Myron Handelman says, "My house was burglarized about ten times. Finally I figured I'm really going to get this guy. So I made believe I went out, turned off all the lights, and then hid in the closet. This guy thought I was out, came into the house, and stole two candles, my silverware, and a portable TV set. And the guy is really wise. He thinks he's gonna get away. But this time I got a complete description of him. He was average height and build and he was wearing a rubber mask of Charles de Gaulle."

———

Cop says, "Mrs. Snyder, your son just held up a bank and he shot the teller and killed two people in the bank. He ran outside and shot a police officer, then scaled a fence and broke into a building and attacked a woman on the third floor before we caught him." And she says, "I'm surprised. He's never that way at home."

———

Every politician is hollering about "our boys" in the penal institutions being treated badly. The whole idea is to make the prisoner feel at home, I guess so he'll want to come back again soon.

The big idea is to give him a home away from home. One warden really went a little too far. He had an inmate's wife make a slipcover for the electric chair.

———

Crime is getting so bad in some big cities, even the muggers travel in pairs.

———

I was going to read that report about the rising crime rate, but someone stole it.

———

A jeweler called the police station to report a robbery. "You'll never believe what happened, Sergeant. A truck backed up to my store, the doors opened, and an elephant came out, broke my plate-glass windows, stuck his trunk in, sucked up all the jewelry, and climbed back into the truck. The doors closed and the truck pulled away." The desk sergeant said, "Could you tell me, for identification purposes, was it an Indian elephant or an African elephant?" The jeweler asked, "What's the difference?" "Well," said the sergeant, "an African elephant has great big ears, an Indian elephant has little ears." And the jeweler said, "Come to think of it, I couldn't see his ears. He had a stocking over his head."

———

Central Park had a very slow night last Saturday, so these two muggers mugged each other.

Entertainer Dick Cavett picks on New York City: Like the time he told about being at the Shakespeare Festival in New York's Central Park, where crime is not unknown. He was watching a production of *Julius Caesar*. When Caesar got stabbed, eight people got up and left. Explained Cavett, "They didn't want to get involved."

———

I figured out why they're building the subway under Central Park. The subway is equated with pickpockets and perverts, while the park is associated with pushers and muggers. This is New York's way of getting it all together.

———

I know how New York's Forty-second Street got its name. It's called Forty-second Street because you can last only forty seconds without getting into trouble.

———

Crime is booming. A guy I know serving a term for burglary is eating his heart out because he's missing a very good year.

———

STICK-UP MAN: Your money or your life. MIKE: Take me life—I'm saving me money for me old age.

———

What a tough neighborhood I live in! In my neighborhood, no one ever asks you what time it is. They just take your watch.

He spent three months forging a check, only to have it come back from the bank stamped, INSUFFICIENT FUNDS.

———

"Hand over all your money or I'll blow your brains out," the thief said to the New Yorker. "Go ahead and shoot," the victim said. "You can live in this town without brains—but not without money!"

———

Even the cops in my neighborhood are afraid. The police station on my block is the only police station where the front door has a peephole in it.

———

I'm not worried about crime in the streets, but in my neighborhood they make house calls.

———

There's a new thing now, topless muggers. They do it that way so you won't remember their faces.

———

The delicatessen owner had been robbed so many times that he thought up a way to get even. He made one robber his partner. "If he's my partner I can steal from him," explained the storekeeper.

———

Walking home from work one night, my uncle was approached by a bum who pleaded, "Please, sir, if you don't mind, sir, can you spare the price of a meal? I have no work, no decent clothes. I have nothing in the world except this knife and this gun."

———

A stranger confronted a man on a dark street and asked, "Sir, have you ever been awarded a black belt in karate?" The other man said no. The first one then said, "In that case, this is a stick-up."

———

I know a burglar who is so helpful, if his clients don't have cash, he'll accept credit cards.

———

This snooty robber always insists that his loot be gift-wrapped.

———

He's a police reporter—once a week he reports to the police.

———

He was locked up for something he didn't do. He didn't wipe the fingerprints off the safe.

———

The crook's mother assured him, "I left everything in your room the way I found it: your gun, knife, blackjack."

———

The laws are strictly for the crooks. They lock up the witness and the jury, and they let the prisoner out on bail.

———

Under the laws of this country, a man is innocent until proven guilty. Then, if he isn't crazy, he is pardoned.

———

"We hang the petty thieves and appoint the great ones to public office."—Aesop

———

One guy walked over to me in front of my house and ordered, "Stick 'em down!" I asked, "Don't you mean, stick 'em up?" He answered, "No wonder I'm not making any money."

———

He's a modern Robin Hood: He steals from the rich *and* from the poor.

## Critics

"It was one of those plays in which all the actors unfortunately enunciated very clearly."—Robert Benchley

———

"He writes his plays for the ages— the ages between four and twelve."— George Jean Nathan

———

George Bernard Shaw sent Winston Churchill two tickets for the first night of his play *Pygmalion* with the note: "Here are a couple of tickets for the first night. Bring a friend—if you have one." Mr. Churchill replied, "Sorry, I cannot come to the first night but will come to the second—if there is one."

A critic is a man who knows the way—but cannot drive the car.

———

Drama critic Clive Barnes, reviewing a Broadway play: "I realized it was not a particularly distinguished play when, at the intermission, I found myself rushing up the aisle for a cigarette outside. It was not until I got out there that I remembered that I don't smoke."

———

The cast was well balanced—they were all rotten.

———

One of the shortest music criticisms on record appeared in a Detroit paper: "An amateur string quartet played Brahms here last evening. Brahms lost."

———

Another pithy review lasted much longer than the play called *Dreadful Night*. The account: "Dreadful night: PRECISELY!"

———

Irving Hoffman's critique killed a play. The producer went to his publisher and complained that Mr. Hoffman has very bad eyesight. "I may not see very well," Irving answered later, "but there is nothing wrong with my nose."

———

Go to any public square and see if you can find one statue erected to a critic.

———

This is the worst review I ever read. This actor did a one-man show and the critic wrote: "There were too many in the cast."

———

Heywood Broun on a play: "It opened at 8:30 sharp—and closed at 10:50 dull."

———

Alexander Woollcott: "The scenery was beautiful but the actors got in the way of it."

———

The show had one strike against it: The seats faced the stage.

———

Percy Hammond demolished one show. In closing he said, "I have knocked everything except the knees of the chorus girls—and God anticipated me there."

———

Dorothy Parker said about Katharine Hepburn, "She runs the gamut of emotion from A to B."

———

Heywood Broun was once sued by some actor named Stein for calling his performance "atrocious." The next time Mr. Broun reviewed Stein, he brushed him with, "Mr. Stein's performance was not up to his usual standard."

John Chapman said about a Mae West show, "Miss West has one more bust than she needs."

———

Don Rickles was discussing a new movie. "I came in late—but I wish I had missed it from the beginning."

———

Monty Woolley: "For the first time I envied my feet—they were asleep."

———

A critic is a legless man who teaches running.

———

A critic is a man who writes about things he doesn't like.

———

I never read a book before reviewing it—it prejudices me so.

———

The show got divided notices. We liked it, but the critics didn't.

———

The producer came to his wife and gleefully announced, "I think I got a hit." "How do you know?" "I met three of the critics and they each told me if I change one of the acts, I'll have a hit." "That's wonderful." "Yeah, but each picked a different act."

———

Two shipwrecked critics were drifting for weeks on a raft. The more frightened of the two started seeking forgiveness for his sins. "I've been a louse all my life," he said. "I've been cruel to actors. Too often I went out of my way to hurt them. If I'm spared, I promise—" "Just a moment," interrupted the other critic, "don't go too far. I think I see smoke from a ship!"

———

I saw the show at a disadvantage—the curtain was up.

———

If there is a hero in this book, he should kill the author.

———

The show had a cast of ten—buried in one plot.

———

Critic: one who finds a little bad in the best of things.

———

A critic on the *San Francisco Chronicle* brought back memories of the old Alexander Woollcott days with his neat scalping of a recent performance of the Royal Ballet in that city. The thrust went: "Nureyev danced as though he very much needed a vacation. I've seen better leaps from a popcorn machine."

# Daffy-nitions

ACQUAINTANCE: someone we know well enough to borrow from, but not well enough to lend to.

ALARM CLOCK: a small device used to wake up people who have no children.

ALIMONY: like pumping gas in another man's car.
—the high cost of loving.
—the pay-as-you-burn plan.
—fly now, pay later.

APOLOGY: the only way for a husband to get the last word.

BACHELOR DOCTOR: the answer to a mother's prayer for her daughter.

BANK: where you can borrow money, if you can prove that you don't need it.

BANKER: a gent who lends you an umbrella when the sun is shining and wants it back when it starts to rain like hell.

BARGAIN: what happens to all that money your wife has been saving you for years.

BEST MAN: the one who isn't getting married.

BIGAMIST: a man who leads two wives.

BOOKMAKER: a pickpocket who lets you use your own hands.

BRIS (circumcision): a surgical operation that has become a catered affair.

CHARACTER: a jerk with personality.

COMEDIAN: a person who knows a good gag when he steals one.

CONFERENCE: a group of men who, individually, can do nothing, but as a group can meet and decide that nothing can be done.

COURTSHIP: an entertaining introduction to a dull book.

COWARD: one who in a perilous emergency thinks with his legs.

———

DIAMOND: a chunk of coal that made good under pressure.

———

EDUCATION: something a boy spends years getting so he can work for a man who has no education at all.

———

EFFICIENCY EXPERT: If a wife did it, they'd call it nagging.

———

EGOTIST: a man who always talks about himself—when you want to talk about *yourself.*

———

EXTRAVAGANT: throwing out a tea bag after using it only once.

———

FLIRT: a girl who believes it's every man for herself.

———

FLIRTATION: wishful winking.

———

FRUSTRATION AND PANIC: Frustration is the first time you discover you can't do it the second time, and panic is the second time you discover you can't do it the first time.

———

GENIUS: the talent of a man who is dead.

———

HIGHWAY ROBBERY: the price of new cars.

———

HINDSIGHT: what a woman should have before wearing slacks.

———

HOLLYWOOD: where you put on a sport jacket and take off your brain.
HOLLYWOOD HOUSE: a swimming pool surrounded by mortgages.

———

HONESTY: fear of being caught.

———

IOU: a paper wait.

———

JANITOR: a floor flusher.

———

KLEPTOMANIAC: one who helps himself because he can't help himself.
—a real taker.
—one who steals the spotlight, and anything else he can carry.

———

LIBERAL: a man who has both feet firmly planted in the air; a man whose actions speak softer than words.

———

LONELY PERSON: a guy who can't admit that he finds himself poor company.

MARRIAGE: the hangover that lasts a lifetime.
—not a word—a sentence.
—a kind of friendship that is recognized by the police.

MINISKIRT: tempt-dress; the thigh's the limit.

MINK: a tranquilizer for women.

MONEY: the poor man's credit card.

MOTHER-IN-LAW: comes for a six-month visit—twice a year.

NOODNICK: a naked Santa Claus.

NUDIST: folks who grin and bare it.

ORATOR: the fellow who is always ready to lay down your life for his country.

ORGY: group therapy.

OVEREATING: the destiny that shapes our ends.

PEDESTRIAN: man with one car and a family of grown children.

PERFECT MAN: your wife's first husband.

PETTING: the study of the anatomy in Braille.

PHILANTHROPIST: one who returns publicly what he stole privately.

PHILOSOPHY: unintelligible answers to insoluble problems.

PRACTICAL NURSE: one who marries a rich patient.

PROTEIN: a call-girl too young to vote.

RACE HORSE: can take several thousand people for a ride at the same time.

RADICAL: anyone whose opinions differ from yours.

RELIGION: insurance in this world against a fire in the next.

ROTISSERIE: a Ferris wheel for chickens.

RUSSIA: where a guy can talk his head off.

SINNER: one who gets found out.

————

SOCIAL SECURITY: where the government guarantees you a steak in your old age—when all your teeth are gone.

————

SOCIALIZED MEDICINE: when women get together and talk about their operations.

————

SPINSTER: a woman who is unhappily unmarried.

————

STOCK MARKET: is like a sultan touching new bottoms too often.

————

TANGERINE: a loose-leaf orange.

————

TELEVISION: chewing gum for the eyes.

————

TOPLESS WAITRESS: wild waist show.

————

UNDERTAKER: the last guy to let you down.

————

UNTOLD WEALTH: that little bit the income tax people never hear of.

————

VICIOUS CIRCLE: a wedding ring.

————

VOCABULARY: something a man can use to describe a shapely girl without using his hands.

————

WRITERS: writers are born, not paid.

————

WOLF: a boudoir commando.

————

YAWN: a silence with an exclamation mark.

————

ZOO: a place where animals look at silly people.

## Dais

To many speakers, a speech seems to be something that makes you feel numb on one end and dumb on the other.

————

A proverb for all banquet speakers: "The mind cannot accept what the seat cannot endure."

————

Winston Churchill offers this advice to speakers on a dais: "Say what you have to say, and the first time you come to a sentence with a grammatical ending, sit down!"

————

Judge Jacob Braude said, "All work and no plagiarism usually makes a mighty dull speech."

George Jessel, toastmaster at so many banquets he's thinking of calling his autobiography *Dais Without End*, lives by the motto, "If you haven't struck oil in your first three minutes, stop boring!"

———

Lord Macaulay was being honored in London for fifty years of distinguished service to the crown. He began his speech of acknowledgment with these sad words: "Gentlemen, I understand that man inherited three basic vices: I must report to you that I quit one, and one quit me—but I still smoke."

———

At the Waldorf they had six daises, seating 140 prominent people at the General Omar Bradley tribute dinner. A very modest fellow sitting at NBC president Bob Kintner's table squinted at the six daises and said, "And on the seventh dais they rested."

## Dancing

Dancing is a rough thing for me. I got two left feet, and it's hard for me to find a girl with two right ones.

———

What bugs me about ballet is the fact that no matter how much I pay for seats and no matter how close I am to the stage, I can never hear a word they're saying.

If you're over forty, do yourself a favor and stay out of discotheques. At this age it's no longer dancing. It's committing suicide one bone at a time!

———

HE: Dancers run in my family. SHE: Too bad they don't dance.

———

After spending a romanceless weekend at a fancy resort, Sidney finally met a girl at the Sunday night dance. As he swung her around the dance floor in a swift rumba, he whispered in her ear, "Listen, baby, I have only one night left here." She whispered back, "I'm dancing as fast as I can."

———

I used to dance with Arthur Murray, but I found out I liked girls better.

———

A neighbor of mine and his wife took up the mambo very seriously, but I saw them the other night on the dance floor. While the wife was doing the mambo he was doing the samba. I asked him how come and he said he was trying to quit by tapering off.

———

The disco was jammed. On the dance floor, a pretty little redhead said to a young man, "Thank you for the dance." He said, "What dance? I was just pushing my way through to the bar."

These two old farmers wandered into the disco to watch the convulsions. "Look at 'em dance," one groaned. "If any of my dogs started actin' like that, I'd race 'em off to the vet to be pumped full o' worm powder!"

# Dating
*(see also Courtship, Kissing, Marriage)*

I had a friend who was dating a girl named Phyliss in a fake fur, until he found out it was really Phil—a fake her.

———

Comic Jamie DeRoy says, "I had a terrible time fighting off a blind date last night. He thought I'd given him the go-ahead because the second I saw him I turned green."

———

My blind date looked much better over the telephone.

———

What's the difference between a pig and a fox? About four drinks.

———

Comedian Morty Storm reports that he has no trouble making dates with girls. "My trouble is that they don't show up."

———

BOB: How did you do last night? FRANK: Great. I finally persuaded her to say yes. BOB: Congratulations! When is the wedding? FRANK: Wedding? What wedding?

"No more drinks," she said shyly. "I only drink to be sociable, and I'm feeling sociable enough right now. So let's go to bed."

———

The great comic Rodney Dangerfield explained the time he got no respect on a blind date. "I waited on the corner until this girl Louise walked by. I said, 'Are you Louise?' She said, 'Are you Rodney?' I said, 'Yeah,' and she said, 'I'm not Louise.'"

———

"My daughter is getting married," the woman announced, "and I hope she'll make her husband as happy as she's making my husband."

———

She likes going out with the chiropractor 'cause he always has a new twist.

———

Lots of men fought for her hand, but they quit when they saw the rest of her.

———

Love at first sight—is a labor-saving device.

———

She looked just like Monroe, and he was a great president.

———

What a date! I had more fun on a rainy day at the beach.

———

She is the kind of girl you take to the movies when you want to see the picture.

———

Once I dated a girl whose father was so rich, he had Swiss money in American banks.

———

CHARLES: Hello, darling, would you like to have dinner with me tonight? CURRENT GIRLFRIEND: Oh, I'd be delighted, dear! CHARLES: Okay. Tell your mother I'll be over at six o'clock and please not to have hash.

———

TED: The ex-debutante had a dance last night. NED: What's an ex-debutante? TED: A girl that came out last year and wishes she were back in this year.

———

SUITOR (to little brother): Here, take this quarter and go see a show. KID: No, I'll give you fifty cents to let me stay and watch.

———

"Resist the temptation," advised the moralist. "I would," sighed the girl, "but it may never come again."

———

The disgruntled lass was complaining bitterly to her roommate about last night's blind date: "Not only did the bum lie to me about the size of his yacht," she said, "but he made me do all the rowing."

## Daughters

She was only an upholsterer's daughter but she knew what to do on a couch.

———

She was only a railroad man's daughter but her caboose was the talk of the town.

———

She was only a cannibal's daughter but she liked her man stewed.

———

She's only a senator's daughter but she sure can advise and consent.

———

She's only a doctor's daughter but she's ready to make house calls.

———

She's only a lawyer's daughter but she knows how to break a guy's will.

———

She's only a hairdresser's daughter but she knows how to tease a guy.

———

She's only a travel agent's daughter but she cruises from bar to bar.

She's only a cab driver's daughter but she sure can take you for a ride.

———

She's only an actor's daughter but she'll make a play for anybody.

———

She's only a principal's daughter but, boy, does she have the faculties!

———

She's only a mechanic's daughter but she sure can fix your wagon.

———

She's only a tattoo artist's daughter but she's got designs on every guy.

———

She was only a suburbanite's daughter but she sure could go to town.

———

She was only a globetrotter's daughter but she certainly got around.

———

She was only a telephone operator's daughter but she was never too busy.

———

She was only a waiter's daughter but she sure could dish it out.

———

She was only a coin collector's daughter but she showed all the guys her quarters.

———

She was only a plumber's daughter but, oh, such fixtures!

———

She was only an artist's daughter but she didn't know where to draw the line.

———

She was only a stockbroker's daughter and all the boys got their share.

———

She was only a horseman's daughter but she never could say nay.

———

She was only a rancher's daughter but she horsed around with all the cowhands.

———

She was only a censor's daughter but she never knew when to cut it out.

———

She was only a postmaster's daughter but she liked to play with the males.

———

She was only an undertaker's daughter but there wasn't anything she wouldn't undertake.

———

She was only a credit man's daughter but she allowed anyone advances.

———

She was only a florist's daughter but she was potted all the time.

———

She was only a surgeon's daughter but she knew how to operate even better than Dad.

———

She was only a salesman's daughter but she gave out plenty of samples.

———

She's only an astronaut's daughter but she sure knows how to take it off.

———

She was only an electrician's daughter but you're in for quite a shock.

———

She was only an architect's daughter but, boy, was she built!

———

She was only a schoolteacher's daughter but she had no principals.

———

She was only a real-estate agent's daughter but she was easy to land.

———

She was only an optician's daughter but, boy, did she make a spectacle of herself!

———

She was only a real-estate salesman's daughter but she gave lots away.

She was only the dentist's daughter but she went around with the worst set in town.

———

She's only a violinist's daughter but she knows how to fiddle.

———

She was only a race car driver's daughter but she never put on the brakes.

———

She was only a sergeant's daughter but she never knew when to call a halt.

———

She was only an explorer's daughter but she always went too far.

———

She was only a Communist's daughter but everyone got his share.

———

She was only a baggage man's daughter but she knew all the grips.

———

She was only a stagehand's daughter but she had the loveliest props.

———

She was only a parson's daughter but she'll never go to heaven.

———

She was only a convict's daughter but she was never caught.

She was only a governor's daughter but what a state she was in.

———

She was only a lawyer's daughter but anyone could break her will.

———

She was only a politician's daughter but she said yes on every proposition.

———

She was only an air raid warden's daughter but was she good in a blackout.

She was only an artist's daughter but she never drew the line.

———

She was only a pitcher's daughter but you ought to see her curves.

———

She was only a farmer's daughter but all the traveling salesmen sold her.

———

She was only an innkeeper's daughter but they couldn't keep her in.

———

She was only a sculptor's daughter but her bust was the biggest in town.

———

She was only a grass-widow's daughter but she certainly wasn't green.

She was only a violinist's daughter but she liked to fiddle around.

———

She was only a builder's daughter, but what a terrific build.

———

She was only a bricklayer's daughter but she sure was well stacked.

———

She was only a wrestler's daughter but she sure knew all the holds.

———

She was only a boxer's daughter but she knew what to do in the clinches.

———

She was only a magician's daughter but she had a few tricks of her own.

———

She was only a car dealer's daughter but she had the best chassis in town.

———

She was only a pirate's daughter but she had a sunken chest.

———

She was only a pirate's daughter but she had a treasure chest.

———

She was only a schoolteacher's daughter but she certainly taught me a lesson.

# Death

*(see also Cemeteries, Epitaphs)*

The waiter dies and his wife is distraught. One day she meets someone who assures her that she can speak to her beloved husband through a medium. An appointment is made, the wife visits the medium, and the séance begins. She presses both hands on the table and calls out, "Sam—Sam, speak to me!" A haunting, whistling noise follows and then a faint voice cries, "I can't—it's not my table!"

"You know, in Egypt they have a peculiar superstition. They're afraid of burying people alive, so when a man dies they bury him for sixty days and then dig him up, place him on a cold slab, and have twenty beautiful girls dance around him for two hours." "What good does that do?" "Well, if he doesn't get up he's sure to be dead."

"Well," said the dying businessman, "you better put in a clause about my employees. To each man who has worked for me twenty years, I give and bequeath $50,000." "But," said the lawyer, "you haven't been in business twenty years." "I know it, man, but it's good advertising."

"There goes the funeral of a great polo player." "Yes, he rides just like he was part of the hearse."

The society snob died and was greeted by St. Peter. "Welcome. Glad to have you," he said.

"Thanks, but no," she said haughtily. "What's the big deal if you let anyone in here? This is not my idea of heaven."

I definitely believe in reincarnation. Did you ever notice how many dead people come to life every day at five in the afternoon?

The obituary editor of a Boston newspaper was not one who would admit his mistakes easily. One day, he got a phone call from an irate subscriber who complained his name had been printed in the obituary column. "Really," was the calm reply. "Where are you calling from?"

"My uncle loved crossword puzzles so much that on the day he died he asked to be buried six down and three across."

The actor died and it was standing room only at his funeral. "If he knew he would have had an audience like this," his agent remarked, "he would have died years ago."

St. Peter said to the newcomer, "I don't see your name on my register." When he looked farther down he said, "Oh yes, here it is. You're not due for twenty years. Who's your doctor?"

———

FAN: Why don't you write your life story? STAR: Not right now. My life story will be written posthumously. FAN: Good—make it soon.

———

"Dad, can my new boyfriend replace your partner who died this morning?" "It's okay with me, if you can arrange it with the undertaker."

———

There are two things we are sure of: death and taxes. Now if we could only get them in that order!

———

The son was sitting at the bedside of the elderly gentleman who was dying. "Where do you want to be buried," the kid asked, "in Forest Lawn or New York?" The old man got up on his elbow and answered, "Surprise me!"

———

Two corpses were laid out in the same room at the funeral home. One night after everybody left, one corpse sat up and asked the other, "What did you die from?" "Cigarettes," he answered, "I just smoked too many cigarettes." "What kind did you smoke?"

"Raleighs." "At least, did you save the coupons?" "Hell, yes! How do you think I got this coffin?"

———

Two friends were talking about the death of a man who owed them both money. They agreed it was too late to collect. "Isn't it funny," one said, "they say you can't take it with you, but you sure can take somebody else's."

———

Honoré de Balzac, the French novelist, was fond of the good life. When a stingy old uncle died and left him a great deal of money, Balzac's wit would not permit him to mourn; instead, he informed his friends of the news by announcing, "Yesterday, at five in the morning, my uncle and I passed on to a better life."

———

Who says you can't take it with you? My broker just opened an office at Forest Lawn.

———

Bob Hope said if he died and returned to Earth, he would like to ask for just three things: Al Smith's tolerance, Cardinal Cooke's heart, and Dean Martin's kidney.

———

Two pals were talking about the good old days. "Almost all our friends are gone," said Tom, "but the one I miss the most is Frank."

"Why Frank?" his friend asked. "Because I married his widow."

When one famous phony died, comic Red Skelton went to the funeral to find a huge crowd of people fighting to get into the funeral parlor. "Well," said Red, "it only proves what they always say: Give the public something they want to see, and they'll come out for it."

# Decorating
*(see also Antiques, Apartments and Landlords)*

My wife got rid of me because I clashed with the drapes.

Bessie was the one in the sisterhood who was the world traveler. "What do you think of Red China?" Sylvia asked her. "Please," Bessie said, "not with your yellow tablecloths."

"What do you think of the Colosseum?" "It's nice, but I like modern."

The interior decorator advised the rich Texan to paper his walls with thousand-dollar bills. "Nobody has anything like it." "Yeah," drawled the Texan, "but won't it clash with my solid gold floors?"

# Demonstrations

Remember the good old days when a demonstrator was someone who sold you potato peelers?

We now have a law that prohibits outside agitators from crossing state lines. I sent a copy of it to my mother-in-law.

The demonstration turned into a riot. One guy staggered out of the crowd carrying the limp form of a girl. "Here," said a cop, "hand her to me. I'll get her out of this." "The hell with you," said the guy. "Go and get one of your own."

Do you go back far enough to when a teenage protest was just a girl who said no?

Every place you go, all over the world, the college kids are demonstrating about something, picketing and complaining. They are learning to be the greatest mothers-in-law.

Remember the good old days when a demonstrator knocked on your door and tried to sell you a vacuum cleaner?

# Democrats
*(see also Politics and Politicians)*

I made so much money betting on the Democrats, I became a Republican.

Both candidates are ready and willing. Now if we could only find one that's able.

———

The Democratic state senator announced that he is perfectly familiar with all the questions of the day. The trouble is, he doesn't know the answers.

———

They elected him to Congress—anything to get him out of town.

———

The Democrats were pretty smart. Every place the Republicans went they left big tips and said, "Vote Republican." But the Democrats were smarter. They left no tip and said, "Vote Republican."

———

DEMOCRAT: Remember, the worm will turn. REPUBLICAN: So what, it's the same on both ends.

———

DEMOCRAT: The mayor stole the last election. REPUBLICAN: No, he didn't. DEMOCRAT: He did, too. REPUBLICAN: No, he paid spot cash for it.

———

Mike met his friend Joe, who was sporting three hats, one on top of another. "What's the idea?" demanded Mike. "I've decided to become a Democrat," replied Joe. "What are you wearing three hats for?" "A Democrat has one hat to cover his head, another he tosses in the ring, and one hat he talks through."

———

For twenty years two senators, one a Democrat and the other a Republican, quarreled every day. Finally a third party intervened. "Boys, this must stop," he said. "Let's have a drink together and make peace." The senators agreed, and when the drinks were served the impartial friend said, "Now make a toast to each other." Raising his glass, the Democrat said, "Here's wishing for you what you're wishing for me." "Oh, now you're starting in again," yelled the Republican.

———

The continual row between Democratic presidents and Republican congressmen over the budget reminded one senator of an Arkansas moonshiner who had been convicted a number of times. When he was again brought into court by the "revenoors," the judge told the culprit sternly: "Before passing sentence, I want to tell you that you and your sons have given this court more trouble than anyone else in the whole state of Arkansas. Have you anything to say?" The old fellow thought a moment and then said, "Well, Judge, I jest want to say that we haven't given you any more trouble than you've given us."

Senator Barry Goldwater, speaking about the Democrats, said that they didn't know how to give a proper dinner. He said that a proper dinner usually could be gotten from an Arizona Republican, and that it consisted of a steak, a bottle of whiskey, and a hound dog. When a somewhat insulted Democrat asked him what the hound dog had to do with the dinner, the senator replied, "Oh, he eats the steak."

# Dentists

*(see also Doctors)*

I recently heard of a dentist who had a television set installed in his operating room to distract his patients' attention. This led to some complications. For instance, one day a young boy called and said, "Mother says put her down for 'The Price Is Right' on Tuesday, and me for 'Captain Kangaroo' on Wednesday."

———

SON: Why is it that dentists call their offices dental parlors? FATHER: Because they are drawing rooms, son.

———

FIRST CANNIBAL: Have you seen the dentist lately? SECOND CANNIBAL: Yes, he filled my teeth at dinnertime.

———

The dentists' favorite marching song, so I understand, is "The Yanks are Coming."

———

TOM: I'd like to go to a woman dentist. DICK: Why do you want to go to a woman dentist? TOM: Because it would be a pleasure to have a woman say, "Open your mouth" instead of "Shut up."

———

A gangster went into a dentist's office and said to the dentist, "Pull my tooth." The dentist asked, "Which tooth is it?" And the gangster replied, "Find it yourself. I'm no stool pigeon."

———

MAN: Hey, that wasn't the tooth I wanted pulled! DENTIST: Calm yourself, I'm coming to it!

———

BUSINESSMAN: Yesterday I lit my cigar with a twenty-dollar bill. FRIEND: How extravagant! BUSINESSMAN: It was a bill from my dentist, and I wasn't going to pay it anyway.

———

A Tulsa, Oklahoma, oil man gushed into his dentist for an examination. The dentist dove into the millionaire's mouth and said, "Perfect, man, perfect! You don't need a thing." "Well, drill anyway, Doc," the patient drawled, "I feel lucky this morning."

The dentist examined the nervous lady and finally said, "It looks like I'll have to pull your tooth." The woman squealed, "I'd rather have a baby." The doctor countered, "Make up your mind, lady, before I adjust the chair."

———

I hate going to the dentist: the suffering, the excruciating agony—and that's just from filling out the insurance forms.

———

When a dentist is down in the mouth, the other fellow feels even worse.

———

The doctor complimented the lady: "You have very even teeth. It's the odd ones that are missing."

———

The dentist examined one of his patients and discovered his teeth were full of cavities. He asked, "Do you want me to fill them with gold or silver?" The patient screamed: "Gold or silver? I can't even afford to fill them with meat!"

———

The man went to see the country dentist at midnight in a panic. He had dropped his front bridge down the kitchen drain. The country doc walked into the man's house with a pipe wrench, removed the bridge from the gooseneck, and cemented the bridge back in place. Four days later the man was pleasantly surprised that his den-

tal bill was only $3, but was shocked that his "plumbing bill" was $485.

———

The first thing you learn from orthodontists is that buck teeth is the condition, not the price.

———

All my dentist does is make appointments for me to see another dentist. I really don't know if he's a dentist or a booking agent.

———

The modern dentist lives up to his claim, "It won't hurt a bit"—until the bill arrives.

———

I go to a dentist who charges only ten dollars a cavity: I gave him ten dollars and he gave me a cavity.

———

My niece told me, "Every time I go to the doctor's, he makes me take off my blouse. I think I'm going to find a new dentist."

———

My grandfather called his doctor and said, "Doc, I don't mean to be critical, but every time I eat I have to use tenderizer." He said, "Lots of people use tenderizer." My grandfather said, "In soup?"

———

My grandfather told me, "I'm at the age where biting into a candied apple brings me three things: memories, nostalgia, and a $100 bill from my dentist. My dentist really charges. Last week he put in a crown. I think it belonged to Queen Elizabeth."

———

Gold is now worth about $400 an ounce. I'll tell you how I found out. I was mugged by a dentist.

———

My dentist told me, "You've got nothing to worry about. I won't have to extract a single tooth. Of course, I'll have to take out the gums."

———

Do you ever get the feeling that your teeth are twenty years older than the rest of you?

———

I don't want to complain about my dentist, but last night I went to a dinner and swallowed 1,500 calories—and that was just in fillings.

———

My dentist is a wise guy. I said to him, "Tell me, Doc, how are the X-rays?" He said, "The X-rays are fine. It's your teeth that are no good."

———

I asked my dentist, "Doc, I need some advice. What should I do about all this gold and silver in my mouth?" He said, "Don't smile in bad neighborhoods."

———

You know you're a dental coward if you let your mustache grow long enough so no one can see that your teeth need work.

———

You know it's time to go to the dentist if no one tells you jokes because they're afraid you'll smile.

———

You know you're in trouble with your dentist when he keeps you seated till your check clears. How to get even? Bite down on his finger and tell him you thought it was a piece of cotton.

———

I just got my dentist's bill. I think he's pulling my leg, too.

———

"I've got good news and bad news," my dentist told me one day. "Which do you want to hear first?" I said, "The bad news." The doc said, "You have six teeth that have to come out." "And what's the good news?" "I broke eighty on the golf course yesterday."

———

My dentist relieved the swelling in my gums—and the swelling in my wallet.

———

I just paid my bill. Now there's a cavity in my bank account.

———

My aunt told me she owed her doctor $500. "I couldn't pay," she explained, "so I went to him and he took out all my gold fillings. Now he owes me $100."

---

My doctor's practice is so good he can't see another patient this year without getting into a higher tax bracket.

---

The pretty patient said to her dentist, "My, what graceful hands you have. They belong on a girl." The doc moved forward, smiling, and said, "All right, if you insist."

---

Today's dentists don't fool around. I won't say what happens if you don't pay a bill, but did you ever have a wisdom tooth put back in?

---

I went to see my dentist, Dr. H. H. Cooper, and found out my wisdom tooth was retarded. I asked how much this was going to cost me. He said, "To put it simply, just put your money where your mouth is."

---

I complained to my doctor that my teeth were turning yellow and asked him what to do. The doc said, "Wear a yellow tie."

---

I think my dentist is in big trouble: Last week he took out all my gold fillings and put in IOUs.

---

According to the latest survey, nothing gets an old dental bill paid like a new toothache.

---

And here's another bit of advice: Never go to a dentist who has his office soundproofed. I was sitting in the chair when my dentist stuffed cotton in his ears. I asked if the sound of drilling was that hard to take. He said, "No, but the sound of screaming is."

---

When the dentist says, "Open wide," you aren't always sure what he means: your mouth or your wallet.

---

No matter what you say about dentists, you've got to admit they keep up with all the new discoveries and progress going on in their profession. You go to a dentist's office and a receptionist gives you a form to fill out: Who are you insured with? Who insures them? Where do you bank? Do you have a safety deposit box? Do you pay your bills promptly? Are you an heir in anybody's will? They explain, "We've got the equipment here." They mean the billing computer.

The dentist said to his patient, "The bad news is you've got three cavities. The good news is your gold crowns have tripled in value."

---

Comic Ted Berkelmann reveals: "I know a dentist who has his new office almost completely equipped. All he's waiting for is a shipment of old magazines."

---

The next time you go to your dentist, try double-parking—that'll give you something to keep your mind off the pain.

---

I can never forget the Smith and Dale routine every time I go to a dentist's office:
DOCTOR: Don't worry, I'm painless.
PATIENT: Well, I'm not.

---

I asked my dentist to put in a tooth to match my other teeth, so he put in a tooth with four cavities.

---

The dentist said to his beautiful blond patient, "Honey, we can't go on meeting like this. You have no more teeth left."

---

FIRST MAN: She has teeth just like pearls. SECOND MAN: Yeah. She and Pearl got them at the same dentist.

---

PATIENT: Have you been a dentist very long? DENTIST: No, I was a riveter till I got too nervous to work high up.

---

"That's all right," the dentist said, "you don't have to pay me in advance." "What advance?" the patient answered. "I'm just counting my cash before you give me the gas!"

---

I finally broke my husband out of the habit of biting his nails. I hid his teeth.

---

He's a careful dentist. He pulled my teeth with great pain.

---

Her teeth are her own. I was with her when she bought them.

---

There is a rich Texan who has a different dentist for every tooth.

---

PATIENT: This may hurt a little. I don't have the money.

---

Her teeth are so far apart, when she smiles she looks like a picket fence.

---

Now I know why she smiles all the time. Her teeth are the only things that aren't wrinkled.

"I've got to reduce," she said to the dentist. "Will you yank out my sweet tooth?"

Sign in dentist's office: "Get your 1968 plates here."

# Diets

*(see also Exercise)*

A diet-conscious lady he knows once weighed 180 pounds but now weighs only 85 pounds—casket and all.

The prayer of a small girl: "Please, Lord, can't you put the vitamins in pie and cake instead of cod liver oil and spinach?"

This is a story that happened about seven hundred years ago in Asia. Nasreddin Hoca had a donkey with a voracious appetite. He wondered if by gradually reducing the animal's food every day it would be possible to condition the animal to get along without any food at all. This interesting experiment was continued for several weeks, but a few days after all food had been stopped, the donkey toppled over and died, to the great chagrin of Nasreddin Hoca, who sadly murmured: "What a pity that he should have died just when he was getting accustomed to hunger."

"No rich foods, no meat, no drinks," the doctor prescribed to his patient. "That should save you enough money to pay my bill."

Eat all you want of everything you don't like.

Sign in reducing salon: "Rear today, gone tomorrow."

If you are really set on losing weight, put the scale in front of the refrigerator.

"Take a look, Doc," she beamed. "I dropped twenty pounds." The doc looked and sighed, "You didn't drop them far enough."

The salesman and his wife arrived in California on a combined business-pleasure trip. He ordered the biggest and most expensive dinner he could afford. His wife made some fast calculations. "Frank," she warned, "that adds up to about 1,200 calories." "So what?" Frank answered. "I'll put them on my expense account."

No-Cal Hair Tonic—for fat heads.

The doctor told her she could eat anything she liked, and as much of it as she wanted for every meal. She chose strawberries and sour cream. When she came back to the doctor she was thirty pounds heavier. "I don't understand it," the doctor said. "Did you do what I told you? Did you eat strawberries and sour cream every meal and nothing else?" "Definitely," she said. "After every meal, I ate strawberries and sour cream."

———

Americans have more food to eat than people of any other nation on Earth, and more diets to keep us from eating it.

———

I just quit my onion diet. I lost ten pounds and twelve friends.

———

The best exercise to lose weight is to shake your head back and forth NO.

———

Diets are strictly for those who are thick and tired of it.

———

Dieting will not help him lose his fat head.

———

The best way to lose weight isn't nearly so much fun as the worst way.

———

Newest invention: a candy bar with lettuce inside, for women on a diet.

———

His doctor put him on a seven-day diet, but he ate the whole thing in one meal.

———

Dean Martin on the drinking man's diet: "I don't know about the rest of your body, but it sure makes your head lighter."

———

The second day of a diet is always easier than the first. By the second day you're off it.

———

He was put on a diet of chicken fat— it cuts the grapefruit.

———

The best way to stay on a diet is to keep your mouth and the refrigerator closed.

———

Well, it took a lot of willpower, but I finally gave up trying to diet.

———

Doctor to overweight patient: "Here, follow this diet. I want to see three-fourths of you back in my office for a checkup in two months."

———

We were standing on a local corner near one of those penny scales when a husband and wife approached. He jumped on the scale and dropped in a penny. "Listen to this fortune," he said enthusiastically to his wife as she peered over his shoulder. "It says I'm bright, resourceful, and energetic and that I will go on to great success." "Yeah," she retorted. "It's got your weight wrong, too."

———

Fat makes you more law abiding. For example, very few overweight men make successful bank robbers. They have too much trouble waddling away from the scene of the crime.

———

Comedienne Totie Fields says she's not overweight, she's just short for her weight. She should be seven feet eight inches tall.

———

There are minus twenty calories in a stalk of celery. It actually has five calories but you burn up twenty-five just chewing it.

———

Just when you get to the point when menu prices don't matter, calories do.

———

When I first met my wife, she was always on a diet. She had an hourglass figure, but now she's let the sand settle in the wrong end.

———

Today half the population is trying to lose weight. This applies to both men and women. One of the best ways to lose weight is to eat yogurt. It's a magic food made from unwanted milk.

I knew of a couple who went on a yogurt diet. They ate nothing but yogurt for six months. When they started, he weighed 264 pounds and she weighed about 130. But after eating yogurt for only four months, the husband lost 140 pounds and his wife disappeared completely.

———

In the interest of physical culture, I subscribed to one of those bodybuilding magazines. My mailman brought me 10-pound weights, then 20-pound weights, then 50-pound weights. And it was amazing; in less than three weeks, you should have seen the muscles on my mailman.

———

I have a friend who doesn't diet and never gains an ounce . . . he eats six meals a day. An average meal would consist of two steaks, four pounds of potatoes, three hamburgers, an apple pie, a malted, an ice cream soda, and a hot fudge sundae . . . and he still weighs the same 475 lbs.

———

When a woman goes on a drastic diet, she has either one or both of these objectives in mind: to retain her girlish figure—or her boyish husband.

———

Sandwich spread: what you get from eating between meals.

———

If you are thin, don't eat fast. If you are fat, don't eat—fast.

———

There are certain compensations for overweight women. Men do not suspect them and other women do not fear them as competition.

———

Travels of a french-fried potato: in your mouth a second, in your stomach four hours, on your hips the rest of your life.

———

I was on a cruise recently. And like almost every cruise I've been on, there were these adorable elderly little women. On this cruise there were two, in their mid-seventies. They were still wearing the muumuus they got when they were on their Hawaiian cruise. Well, they sit down to have coffee. And you know those little Sweet 'n Low packs you find in sugar bowls? As a rule one of these packets is too much for one cup of coffee. Now one of the women kept on opening packet after packet into her coffee. Finally her girlfriend said, "What are you, crazy? Just because it's free? Do you realize what you're doing? If you keep that up, you'll get artificial diabetes!"

———

Joan Rivers, who's dieting, boasts she lost two pounds last week. "But I cheated a little before I got on the scale. I shaved my head."

Even marriages change. Ten years ago I put my wife on a pedestal. Yesterday I put her on a diet.

———

Either she goes on a diet or we'll have to let out the couch.

———

The biggest thing to remember when you are dieting: what you see on the table must wind up on the chair.

———

You want to please a woman, tell her she lost weight. You want to displease a woman, tell her she needed to.

———

More diets begin in dress shops than in doctors' offices.

———

Funnyman Marty Ingels says he's been trying a new diet drink: two parts scotch and one part Metrecal. "So far I've lost five pounds and my driver's license," he says.

———

One woman got up in her weight-watching class and announced, "I just got rid of 175 pounds of excess flab. I divorced my husband."

———

A woman charged her husband with mental cruelty so severe that she lost thirty pounds. "Divorce granted," said the judge. "Not yet," the woman pleaded. "First I want to lose another ten pounds."

_____

He went horseback riding to lose weight and it must have worked. The horse lost 30 pounds.

_____

Comic Marty Allen says, "I've been losing weight and losing weight and I just found out why. My wife got a new rubber mattress, and at night I toss and turn and that's what's doing it. I'm erasing myself."

_____

Actress Sophia Loren says, "Everything you see I owe to spaghetti." She is the greatest ad against dieting. Sophia also says, "Show me a girl with a beautiful body, and I'll show you a very hungry girl." My secretary says, "Why should I go on a diet to lose weight? More people look like me than Sophia Loren. Right now I'm on a low-salary diet."

_____

You know you're ready for the diet bit when:

You wear two girdles—an upper and a lower.

It's hard to lose you in a crowd: You _are_ a crowd.

You're so fat they had to let out your garment bag.

Every time you sit on a bar stool, you have a hangover.

Blue Cross charges you group rates.

The phone booth fits you like a girdle.

Jumbo the circus elephant makes a pass at you.

A guy has to make two trips to put his arms around you.

They want you to model for duffel bags.

_____

Mrs. Plump was at a Weight Watchers meeting. She was sitting next to Mrs. Fatso, who was crying, "I think calories are very unfair! They keep hitting below the belt." Mrs. Plump said, "My husband insists I come here because he'd rather make love to a trim-figured woman." Mrs. Fatso said, "Well, what's wrong with that?" Mrs. Plump said, "It's just that he does it while I'm at these damn meetings."

_____

The first week of a diet is rough: I know, for I've undergone it. The second week is not nearly as rough, though, for by then I'm no longer on it.

_____

America is the land where half our salary goes to buy food and the other half to lose weight.

_____

Diet books can help you lose lots of weight. Just buy every one on the market and you won't have any money left to buy food.

_____

The "all you can eat" diet is for people who want to stay fat.

My aunt knew she was in trouble when she walked into Bloomingdale's and said to the clerk, "I'd like to see a bathing suit in my size," and the clerk said, "So would I."

———

Doctors will tell you that if you eat slowly you will eat less. It is particularly true if you're a member of a large family.

———

Somebody told me that it's always the people who are disappointed in love who are such compulsive eaters. So how come there are so many fat sultans?

———

Fat? I know a woman who used a hammock instead of a bra.

———

The Surgeon General and the entire medical profession tell us America is overweight. They're right. Now I know why we have so many fat heads in Washington.

———

A great diet is one in which you can eat anything you want with somebody else picking up the tab.

———

My niece goes to a great diet doctor who lets her eat anything she wants, as long as she pays his bills.

———

My sister lectures, "Even if you'll never pose for *Playboy*, it's not a bad idea to diet and try to get rid of your centerfold."

———

My sister-in-law wanted to buy a book on dieting. She goes to a bookstore, picks out a book, and asks the clerk, "How much can I expect to lose with this diet book?" The clerk looks at the book and says, "Fourteen ninety-five plus tax."

———

My fat uncle's doctor told him only an operation could get him thin. My uncle asked, "Is this operation really necessary?" The doc said, "You bet it is. I have three kids in college."

———

My neighbor's wife is so fat she has to wear stretch jewelry. She put on so much weight she had to take out her appendix scar.

———

A woman tearfully phoned a reducing salon to lament that her husband had given her a lovely present but she just couldn't get into it. The secretary gave her an appointment and then added, "Don't worry, madam, we'll have you wearing that dress in no time." She sobbed, "Who said anything about a dress? It's a Mercedes!"

———

Everybody has a diet they call their own. My brother-in-law's: You eat anything you want, but you must also drink two quarts of scotch a day. You don't lose weight, but you forget you're fat.

---

I went on a simple diet: There are only three things you can't put in your mouth: a knife, a spoon, and a fork. And if you use chopsticks, use only one.

---

I went to one of those fat farms, and they really work. The first day alone I was $500 lighter. I always feel a little silly going to a fat farm. There's something about spending $500 to take off what cost you $5,000 to put on.

---

My wife has a new diet that allows her to drink anything that comes from a blender. Last night, she drank two chickens and a pot roast.

---

The nice lady went to see the distinguished lawyer. "My husband is terrible," she cried. "It's been a nightmare these last two years. He neglects me something awful. Insults me all the time. Cheap? I don't even get pocket money. Why, he even skimps on money for food. I've already lost fifteen pounds!" The lawyer said, "Why don't you leave him?" She moaned, "First, I want to lose ten more pounds."

---

My wife said she plans to lose 180 pounds—ME!

---

I don't want to say my friend is fat, but he told me he is planning on opening a chain of fine restaurants across the country. He still hasn't decided if he'll serve the public.

---

My brother-in-law's got some body. His next job will be to model for beer kegs.

---

You know you're ready for Sweet 'n Low when you get a high electric bill just from the light that goes on when you open the refrigerator. Or when the mayor asks you to donate your pants as a shelter for the homeless.

---

You'd better start that diet when: You fall down and you rock yourself to sleep trying to get up. . . . You have no trouble watching your waistline—it's right there in front where you can see it.

---

Actor Marlon Brando claims he has a sylph-like figure. Who's to say there is no such thing as a big fat sylph?

---

Actress Shelley Winters is a big-hearted gal with hips to match. "Why should I go on a diet?" our gal Shelley says. "More people look like me than Joan Collins."

---

The hardest kind of diet pill to take is the one who keeps telling you how to do it. . . . The toughest part of dieting is not watching what you eat, it's watching what your friends eat.

---

My neighbor claims she keeps young by dieting, exercising, and lying about her age.

---

Comedian Buddy Hackett quit dieting—it made him irritable: "I was eatin' one egg every other day. I was hungry, irritable—a guy asks me what time it was, I throw him out the window."

---

Singer-actress Dolly Parton told me, "I'm glad I lost weight. It's the first time I've seen my feet in ten years."

---

On her vacation in Florida, Shelley Winters told me she had to leave; she was ejected from the beach for creating too much shade.

---

I won't say she's built like a truck, but I have noticed that nobody ever passes her on the right.

---

She's two inches taller than you are when she's lying down.

---

She's well-reared—and don't look too good in the front either.

---

They tell me you can't diet without exercise. When I was young I thought nothing of a ten-mile run—and still don't.

---

Now everybody has their own kind of aerobics: Lee Iacocca lifts his wallet. Princess Diana's daily exercise regimen consists of waving to commoners.

---

George Burns said, "First thing in the morning, I bend down and touch my slippers fifty times. Then, if I feel like it, I get out of bed and put them on."

---

Shelley Winters cries: "Forget the whales, save me!" Poor Shelley had to give up exercising: "I can't stand the noise."

---

In these troubled stock market days, the diet books should tell you the number of calories in fingernails.

---

Marlon Brando's weight problem may have to do with the fact that his doctor told him, "No more of those little intimate dinners for two—unless someone is eating with you." Marlon is very unhappy about losing 120 pounds. You can't blame him, she was a very beautiful blonde.

When she got married, they needed three relatives to give her away. Fat? She and the Statue of Liberty wear the same size dress. On the beach, she wears a six-piece bikini.

———

She has to put on a girdle to get into her kimono.

———

I won't say she's fat, but her charm bracelet has only old license plates.

———

My friend tells me there's a new course in losing weight through yoga. They teach you how to tie a knot in your neck so nothing can go down your throat.

———

My son-in-law started counting calories when he was told the only way he's allowed on the street is with a parade permit.

———

The new fashions keep our gals in shape: They have pants to make them look like boys and see-through blouses to prove they're not.

———

My doctor explained, "Jogging is better than romance for losing weight: You burn up the same amount of energy making love as you do jogging around the reservoir, except after two laps around the reservoir you don't want a cigarette." My doctor told me that every time you make love you lose about 200 calories. So far this year I've lost about 40 calories.

———

A recent report indicates that 34 million Americans are overweight. Those figures, of course, are round.

———

Exercise is good for you—not me.

———

The physical fitness people say there's nothing like getting up at 5 A.M., jogging five miles, and ending it off with an ice-cold shower. There's nothing like it, so I don't do it. The truth is, I don't need all that exercise— I can fall down by myself. In fact, the only exercise I get is bending to my wife's will.

———

One doctor told me I ought to do some swimming to stay in shape. He said it's good for the figure. I said, "Doc, you ever see a whale?"

———

Stay healthy and have a good brisk sit.

———

I have a modern diet that's taken twenty pounds off: I only eat when my wife cooks.

———

A man I know takes dozens of vitamin pills daily. "This blue one," he explained, "is for before dinner. The red one is for after dinner. And the yellow one—that is dinner."

Actress and businesswoman Jane Fonda preaches: "I'm all for yogurt, tofu, wheat germ, fish oil, and all those other good, healthy, and nutritious things. But, please, not while I'm eating!"

———

Carmine heard these two gals talking: "Gee, your husband is obese." "I don't know what that means, but to me, he's a big fat slob."

———

The two biggest sellers in any bookstore are the cookbooks and the diet books. The cookbooks tell you how to prepare the food, and the diet books tell you how not to eat any of it.

———

A fat man will never look old. There's no room for wrinkles.

———

I don't want to criticize my brother's weight, but his favorite food is seconds.

———

Eat, drink, and be merry, for tomorrow they may not be deductible.

———

Eat, drink, and be merry, for tomorrow ye diet.

———

My wife told me, "I bought all those exercise videos with Richard Simmons and Jane Fonda. I love to sit and eat cookies and watch them."

The wife was hollering at her husband: "You want to know where all the grocery money goes? Stand sideways and look in the mirror!"

———

The doctor gave the lady a bottle with 300 pills in it. "How many do I take a day?" she asked. The medic said, "You don't take any. You spread them on the floor and pick them up three times a day."

# Diller, Phyllis
*(see also Comedians)*

Phyllis Diller has a style all her own: masochistic humor.

———

My cooking is so bad, my kids refer to breakfast as morning sickness.

———

I once baked a rum cake that gave Fang a hangover.

———

Today my alphabet soup spelled "UGH."

———

I got my first laugh when my mother entered me in a baby contest.

———

When I was a kid we used to play Post Office. I was the Dead Letter Office.

———

I joined an astrology club and every week we meet and discuss the stars. This week we're discussing Paul Newman.

My mother-in-law buys her coats in a carpet shop. She wears a 9 by 12.

If Fang had a brain operation, it would be minor surgery.

Fang came home loaded one night, went into the closet, and said, "Third floor, please."

Fang is such a drag. He took his suit to the cleaners to be cleaned and depressed.

The only way I can get Fang out of bed in the morning is to wear a black dress and a veil, and sit on the edge of his bed and cry.

The doctor looked my body over. I said, "Is there any hope?" He said, "Yes. Reincarnation."

If I wore a peek-a-boo dress, it would be like turning in a false alarm.

Do I believe in witchcraft? I'm the result of it.

Everybody says I'm a beautiful person inside. Leave it to me to be born inside out.

"Phyllis has that rare beauty that drives men sane," says an admirer.

I call my neighbor Mrs. Clean. I finally found out why her laundry looks so much whiter than mine. She washes it.

I'll never forget my first fur. It was a modest little stole. Modest? People thought I was wearing anchovies.

Don't call a babysitter who knows your children. She won't come.

Don't taste the food while you're cooking it. You may lose the nerve to serve it.

It takes a heap of livin' to make a house a home.

Bob Hope says, "Phyllis Diller is the lady with a thousand gags. One thousand and two—I forgot her face and figure."

I can't work with my hair out of place. Do you have a screwdriver?

The other night a Peeping Tom begged me to pull down my window shade.

_____

My husband has always felt that marriage and a career don't mix. That is why he's never worked.

_____

When I go to the beach in a bikini, even the tide won't come in.

_____

My husband says he's learning karate to defend my honor. I told him to mind his own business.

_____

My husband once tried to run out on me, but the police arrested him for leaving the scene of an accident.

_____

I lost a beauty contest—and it was *fixed*!

_____

We're at a cheap hotel, but it has a continuous floor show—mice!

_____

Phyllis on her driving: "Who would give me a license? I got two tickets on my written test."

_____

My sister-in-law is so skinny, she has a striped dress with only one stripe.

_____

I found a great new weed killer, but it stains the carpet.

_____

Fang is so dumb. When he won his letter for high school, the coach had to read it to him.

_____

Fang had a terrible accident. He found a job.

_____

Fang said if they had used my figure for the hourglass, the day would be very short.

_____

Fang will not go on a picnic. He says we have the whole thing at home: bugs, dirt, tainted food. At our last picnic we wanted to play horseshoes, but his mother refused to go barefoot.

_____

When Phyllis was about three months pregnant, her neighbor asked her bluntly, "Are you going to have another baby?" "No," answered our heroine, "I'm just carrying it for a friend."

## Diplomats
*(see also United Nations)*

A diplomat is a guy who can convince his wife she looks fat in a mink coat or that she looks vulgar in diamonds.

_____

I asked one diplomat what his favorite color was and he said, "Plaid."

---

The definition of a diplomat: He talks interestingly for an hour and doesn't say anything. Or, it's the art of skating on thin ice without getting into deep water.

---

A diplomat is a person who can be disarming even though his country isn't.

---

A diplomat is a man who can tell you to go to hell so tactfully that you look forward to the trip.

---

Diplomacy is the ability to take something and act as though you were giving it away.

---

If you want to deceive a diplomat, speak the truth—he has had no experience with it.

## Divorce

*(see also Alimony, Marriage)*

There is only one quick relief from cold misery—a divorce.

---

Divorce often turns a short matrimony into a long alimony. And when it comes to alimony, my brother is dean of the club. "Paying alimony," says the dean, "is like paying for a subscription to a magazine that is no longer published."

---

Marriage always begins with a small payment to a minister and often ends with a large payment to a lawyer.

---

The girl who marries a man for his money sometimes has to divorce him to get it.

---

Another reason for so many divorces is that too many girls are getting married before they are able to support a husband.

---

To some women, marriage is always a gamble because they never know in advance how much their alimony will be.

---

Alimony payments often give a husband a splitting headache.

---

Marriage is the price men pay for sex. Sex is the price women pay for marriage.

---

Divorce is a legal recourse for a couple who are determined to prove that love can find a way—out.

---

"What's the name of your ex-wife?" "Plaintiff."

---

Man, was this guy hen-pecked: When he got a divorce, she paid the alimony.

———

The sexy wife of the busy tycoon just won a divorce, charging her husband with lack of attentiveness. "If anything happened to me," the stacked missus claimed, "my husband wouldn't be able to identify the body."

———

They all have different reasons for divorce. A woman cried to her lawyer, "I want to lose this guy. Last month he asked me for my finger size. Today he gave me a bowling ball!"

———

A woman wanted a divorce because she said her husband never took her anyplace. He explained to the judge: "I never go out with married women."

———

"I'd divorce him," said the bitter wife, "if I could find a way to do it without making him happy."

———

People get married before they know each other—and then get divorced when they do.

———

My marriage ended because we were incompatible. My wife hated me when I was drunk, and I couldn't stand her when I was sober.

They got divorced because of illness—they got sick of each other.

———

Some great philosopher said about divorce—I forget the philosopher's name—in fact, I forget what he said. But I say, divorce is useless. You get married for lack of judgment, you get divorced for lack of patience, then you remarry for lack of memory.

———

They separated because of religious differences. She worshipped money, and he didn't have a dime.

———

Two guys were talking. One said, "I got married because I was tired of going to the Laundromat, eating in restaurants, and wearing socks with holes." The other guy said, "That's funny; I got divorced for the same reason."

———

A woman said, "I want a divorce." The lawyer said, "Sure. For a nominal sum I will start proceedings." She asked, "How much is a nominal sum?" He said, "Five hundred dollars." She screamed, "Forget it. I can get him shot for less than half of that."

———

Divorce has reached new heights this year: Even couples who aren't married are going to divorce lawyers.

———

Actually my wife and I would have been divorced years ago if it weren't for the kids: She wouldn't take them and I wouldn't take them.

---

People living together without getting married is particularly disturbing to the guy who just got arrested for fishing without a license.

---

A man's wife complained she had nothing to do, so he signed her up for a bridge club. She jumps next Friday.

---

I said to my niece: "It's been rumored around town that you and your husband aren't getting along too well." She said, "Nonsense. We did have some words and I shot him—but that's as far as it went."

---

Last night a man heard his wife saying sexy things. When he looked around, he saw that she was on the phone.

"Honey," the new bride said, "I know that something is bothering you. I can tell. I want you to confide in me. Remember, we promised to share everything, for better or for worse." Her husband said, "But, dear, this time it's different." She said, "Nonsense. Together we can face anything. Now tell me what our problem is." He sighed, "Okay, if you insist. We have just become the father of an illegitimate child."

---

A man packed his suitcase and told his wife he was leaving her. "I'm sorry," he said, "but it just hasn't worked out. In the last six weeks since I've been back with you, we haven't been able to agree on anything." The wife replied, "You've been back seven weeks."

---

Two women were talking about a couple they knew. One said, "Ten months after they got a divorce, they're living together again." "What a shame," said the other. "Nowadays, even divorce fails!"

---

It may be true that marriage originates when a man meets the only woman who really understands him— but then, so does divorce.

---

A door-to-door salesman rang Mrs. Smith's bell and said, "If you have a rodent problem, I can solve it once and for all." She replied, "You're a little late. I divorced him last week."

---

My neighbor was telling her husband: "It seems to me that common sense would prevent many divorces." He answered, "It seems to me it would also prevent just as many marriages."

---

When you're divorced, everything you have is divided fifty-fifty: Your wife gets half and her lawyer gets the other half.

My uncle tells me, "After six years of marriage, my wife and I pondered whether to take a vacation or get a divorce. We decided that a trip to Bermuda is over in two weeks—but a divorce is something you always have."

The only grounds you need for divorce is marriage.

They were mispronounced man and wife.

For the man who has everything: a divorce.

I got custody of the kids—she got custody of the money.

Special cocktail: Divorce on the Rocks.

The only thing they had in common—was her.

They were married three years and the only time they were seen together was in court.

She didn't marry him for his money, but she sure is divorcing him for it.

Statistics prove that one out of every ten couples get divorced. The rest fight it out to the bitter end.

She divorced him because he had a will of his own—and it wasn't made out to her.

A divorce was inevitable. She was always complaining about the house-work—she didn't like the way he did it.

HUSBAND: I want a divorce. My wife called me a lousy lover. JUDGE: You want a divorce because your wife called you a lousy lover? HUSBAND: No, I want a divorce because she knows the difference.

The worst thing about a divorce is that somewhere, perhaps miles apart, two mothers are nodding their heads and saying, "See, I told you so!"

The Hollywood star was so senti-mental, she wanted to get divorced in the same dress in which her mother got divorced.

Reno, Nevada: The great divide.

The rapidly increasing divorce rate indicates that America is indeed becoming the land of the free. On the other hand, the continuing marriage rate suggests that it is still the home of the brave.

───────

My neighbor's wife cried, "I am completely opposed to divorce. I just don't like the idea of sharing my husband's money with a lawyer."

───────

He told me, "My wife and I had a fifty-fifty property settlement. She got the house and I got the mortgage."

───────

Divorce has done more to promote peace than the United Nations.

───────

Myron told me, "My wife and I were considering a divorce, but after pricing lawyers, we decided to buy a new car instead."

───────

The young matron appeared before the judge concerning a divorce. The judge said, "Your husband charges you deceived him." The wife declared, "On the contrary, your honor, he deceived me. He said he was leaving town, and he didn't."

───────

Zsa Zsa Gabor says, "A marriage license is still a very important document. Without one you can't get a divorce."

The divorce court was attentive as Zsa Zsa complained to the judge that her husband had left her bed and board. When she had finished, the husband rose to his feet and coolly replied, "A slight correction, your honor. I left her bed, bored." As they left the court she said to him, "Bye now, pay later."

───────

The judge declared the couple weren't fit to be tied.

───────

Pity the man who marries for love and then finds that his wife has no money.

───────

Ever since former talk-show great Johnny Carson made alimony so popular, marriage for a woman is turning out to be the greatest investment since AT&T.

───────

To find out if you're really in love, ask yourself: "Would I mind being financially destroyed by this person?"

───────

My friend Alan ran away from his wife. There's a big argument about what he should be charged with. She claims it's desertion. He says it should be leaving the scene of an accident.

───────

Zsa Zsa says, "Divorce is so easy nowadays that no one need hesitate about getting married." . . . "Getting divorced just because you don't love a man is almost as silly as getting married because you do." . . . Zsa Zsa just married her eighth husband. I wasn't invited to the wedding, but I have a standing invitation to the divorce.

The guy was explaining to the judge, "My wife can't even say her prayers without getting into an argument. In over thirty-five years of marriage, we haven't been able to agree on anything." The wife interrupted, "It's been thirty-six years."

The agitated caller yelled into the phone, "I want something to quiet my nerves." The man answered, "But I'm not a doctor, I'm a lawyer." She said, "Yes, I know. I want a divorce."

All I can say is, the man who said, "Talk is cheap" never said, "I do."

Things are speeding up in Hollywood. I just heard of a film star who started divorce proceedings three weeks before her wedding.

Two Hollywood gals were talking on the set. "My new husband is a doll," one said. "He doesn't drink or gamble, doesn't even look at girls, and is a great provider." The other said, "My God, how will you ever get a divorce?"

Divorce is the future tense of marriage. I know a woman who went to her bank and applied for a home improvement loan. The banker asked what she wanted the money for. She said, "To get a divorce."

The judge asked the lady, "Why did you shoot your husband?" She explained, "Well, your honor, you see, we couldn't afford a divorce."

"I want a divorce," the woman told the lawyer. "On what grounds?" he asked. "He's been unfaithful." "Can you prove it?" "I happen to know he's not the father of my child!"

Divorce is when the husband no longer has to bring the money home to his wife—he can mail it.

Divorce isn't as easy as it used to be. I know one couple who got a divorce—and the lawyer got the house.

Did I tell you about the nudist couple who got divorced because they were seeing too much of each other?

My friend Myron told me, "My wife would never divorce me. Why should she share her money with a divorce lawyer when she can stay married and have it all?"

I know one guy wants a divorce because he says the highlight of his marriage was the blood test.

I know one wife who tried so hard to please her chauffeur, her husband quit.

One man too cheap to get a divorce said to his milkman: "Don't you guys run off with wives anymore?"

My friend Myron said, "When I got married I said, 'I do.' When I got a divorce I said, 'Never again.'"

The two chief causes of divorce are matrimony and alimony.

Matrimony is a process whereby love ripens into vengeance or, in other words, alimony.

My neighbor reminds her husband when he starts getting stingy that her allowance isn't as big as her alimony would be.

One poor soul asked his lawyer, "If I don't pay alimony this month, can my wife repossess me?"

Divorce lawyer Marvin Mitchelson notes: "There are only two ways to avoid alimony. Either stay single or stay married."

The lady told her lawyer, "What makes my marriage more difficult than most is, it feels like it was made in hell."

My neighbor has the solution: "Before we were married, my wife and I signed a pre-nuptial agreement. If we ever get a divorce, she gets half of my nuptials!"

Who knows what puts marriages in trouble? Let's find out: My neighbor was telling me, "My wife and I frequently have words, but I never get to use mine."

Myron told me, "You think you have troubles? Two months ago my wife left me for good—and my mother-in-law didn't."

Marvin Mitchelson says, "An ideal marriage is one that never takes place."

———

Then there's the secretary who poisoned her boss. I asked, "Why?" She said, "When his wife called the office, he said he'd rather die than speak to her and asked me to take care of it."

———

She told him, "If you really loved me, you would have married somebody else."

# Doctors
*(see also Dentists, Psychology and Psychiatry)*

A doctor is where you go to get your health back and get back into debt.

———

Doctors bring out the money in us. They just took away the license of one of our best doctors—they claimed he was having an affair with his patients. That's too bad, because he's one of the best veterinarians in town.

———

The family doctor was speaking with the mother of four small children, one of whom he was treating for a cold. "Have you taken every precaution to prevent the spread of contagion in your family?" he asked. "Absolutely, Doctor," replied the mother in earnest. "We've even bought a sanitary cup and we all drink from it."

This banker went to a physician for a checkup. After a full examination, the doc said, "You're as sound as a dollar!" The banker said, "Am I really that bad off?"

———

"Who is your family doctor?" I asked my neighbor. He said, "I can't tell you!" I asked, "Why not? Don't you know his name?"

"Yes, Dr. Dick used to be our family doctor, but nowadays Mother goes to an eye specialist, Father to a stomach specialist, my sister goes to a throat specialist, my brother is in the care of a lung specialist, and I am taking treatments from a bank to pay for it all."

———

The lady said, "Doc, I'm afraid I'm turning into a sex maniac." The doc said, "Sit on my knee, dear, and tell me all about it."

———

You may not believe it, but I know one doctor's wife who is so jealous, she listens in on his stethoscope.

———

This lady player was in the doctor's office for a checkup. "Have you ever been X-rayed?" the doctor asked. She said, "Nope, but I been ultravioleted!"

———

The doctor was perplexed by his latest case. He had given his patient all kinds of tests, but his results were still inconclusive. "I'm not sure what it is," he finally admitted. "You either have a cold or you're pregnant." She said, "I must be pregnant. I don't know anybody who could have given me a cold!"

———

I asked Doctor Dick, "What's the difference between a specialist and a regular M.D.?" He explained, "The specialist has a bigger boat."

———

My doctor doesn't make house calls, but if you're sick more than five days he sends you a get-well card.

———

The pretty little girl said, "Doctor I think I'm becoming a nympho." "Well, lie down and tell me all about it."

———

I was at the hospital and a man in a mask took all my money. It was my surgeon.

———

All doctors are a little peculiar. One doctor was told by his girl that she wanted to break their engagement. First he insisted that she return all the gifts he gave her, then he sent her a bill for sixty-six house calls.

———

God heals. Doctors bill.

———

The sign in the doctor's office said: "The doctor is very busy. Have your

symptoms ready." . . . The patient said, "I don't feel good at all." The doc asked, "Do you smoke excessively?" He said, "No." "Do you drink?" "No." "Keep late hours?" "Nope." The doctor shook his head and said, "How can I cure you if you have nothing to give up?"

———

The maternity ward waiting room was full of nervous fathers-to-be up and down. One nervous man blurted out to another standing across from him, "I'm so annoyed! This had to happen on our vacation." "Vacation?" said the other. "What about me? We were on our honeymoon!"

———

The doctor said to the obviously pregnant lady, "Do you have a husband?" "No," she glared back at him. "I'm just carrying this for a friend."

———

Comic Gene Baylos told the doctor, "I've been losing my memory. What do you suggest I do?" "Pay me in advance."

———

The doctor asks, "First, let me start with your important medical history. Do you pay your bills promptly?"

———

I went for a complete checkup. The first thing the doctor did when I undressed was to examine my wallet. . . . I don't want to tell you what the final bill was, but this will give you a hint: One of my friends was in the hospital for two days and it cost him $2,800, and he'd only come there to visit me.

———

Doctors and lawyers are a lot alike. Win, lose, or draw, they get paid.

———

The doctor said, "I never met a disease I couldn't bill for."

———

Myron said, "Well, my doctor finally found out what I had—and he got every penny of it. . . . I just got out of the hospital. I'm okay, but my savings died.

———

My neighbor told me he went to the hospital to have his tonsils removed, but he swore he won't go back again. I asked, "Why?" He explained, "They also removed my wallet, my credit cards, my keys, and my car."

———

Medical costs are so high that it seems the first thing germs attack is your wallet. . . . Medicine has advanced to the point where an ounce of prevention is worth about $235.

———

Things have changed with doctors. They used to check our pulse, now they check our purse.

———

You may not be able to read your doctor's handwriting on a prescription, but you'll notice his bills are neatly typewritten.

———

The old-fashioned general practitioner's bedside manner went out with house calls. Today your doctor speaks in layman's terms: "Doc, you're charging me a hundred dollars and all you did was paint my throat." "What did you expect for a hundred dollars—wallpaper? NEXT."

———

"Doc, what should I do if my temperature goes up another point?" "Sell! NEXT."

———

"Doc, how can I avoid falling hair?" "Step to one side. NEXT."

———

"Doc, every bone in my body hurts." "Be glad you're not a herring. NEXT."

———

"Doc, what should I take when I get run down?" "The license plate number. NEXT."

———

"Doc, I think I've developed a split-personality." "Okay, which one is going to pay your bill?"

———

"Doc, should I file my nails?" "No, throw them away like everybody else. NEXT."

"Doc, I get this terrible pain in my back every time I bend over." "Don't bend over. NEXT."

———

"Doc, nobody ever pays attention to me." "NEXT."

———

"Doc, I think I've got a bad liver." "Well, take it back to the butcher. NEXT."

———

A doctor's office is a place where your symptoms are diagnosed after a thorough examination of your assets.

———

Some doctors believe in shock treatments—they dispense it through their fees.

———

George went to this doctor for an operation that added ten years to his life—and took twenty years off his savings account.

———

My doctor defends his high prices. "My stethoscope is from Cartier, my black bag is Gucci, my white gown is by Halston, and my operation room has an unlisted number. Somebody has to pay for it!" But rubber gloves from Malaysia?

———

Always check the parking lot at your doctor's office. If there's a Rolls-Royce in his parking space, you *know* who's going to pay for it.

My doctor is one in a million. He put me on my feet in no time. Made me sell my car to pay his bill.

———

Being a doctor is the world's greatest profession. In what other business can a man tell a woman to take all her clothes off and then send her husband a bill?

———

"My right foot hurts, Doctor." "Don't worry. It's just old age." "But I've had my left foot just as long. Why doesn't that hurt?"

———

DOCTOR: Look, Mr. Cohen, the best thing for you is to stop smoking, stop careening around the nightspots, stop drinking, and cut down on all those sweet and fattening foods. PATIENT: Doctor, honestly I don't deserve the best. What's second best?

———

The doctor was taking a stroll with his wife when they came face to face with a gorgeous blond package. She gave him a special greeting. "Who was your blond friend?" the wife asked a few minutes later. "Oh, just a young lady I met professionally," he answered nonchalantly. "Professional? Really? Yours or hers?"

———

I wouldn't say he was a bad doctor. In fact, he was a good diagnostician. He diagnosed your condition by feeling your purse.

A specialist is a doctor whose patients can only be ill during office hours.

———

DOCTOR: If I thought an operation was necessary, would you have enough money to pay for it? PATIENT: If I didn't have the money to pay for it, would you think the operation was necessary?

———

DOCTOR: You seem to be improving. I know your leg is still swollen, but I wouldn't worry about that. PATIENT: If your leg was swollen, I wouldn't worry about it either.

———

Any doctor can tell you the difference between an itch and an allergy. It's about $25 a visit.

———

The doc said to his patient, "I've got bad news and good news. The bad news is I amputated the wrong leg—I took off the good one. Good news is, your bad leg is getting better."

———

Nurse to doctor: "Do you remember Mr. Finekuchen, the patient who wouldn't respond to treatment? Well, he won't respond to his bill, either."

———

The doctor asked the airline pilot when he last had sex. "That was, let's see, 1955," the pilot said. "So long ago?" the doctor asked. "That's not so long," said the pilot. "Right now"—he looked at his watch—"it's only 2140."

———

Humorist Sam Levinson tells about the man who called his doctor for an appointment. The nurse suggested a date three weeks off. "But I may be dead by then!" "That's okay," she said. "You can always cancel the appointment."

———

My doctor only charged $10 for my X-rays but he talked me into 8 by 10 glossies for $35.

———

The noted doctor opened the patient's stomach and a bunch of butterflies flew out. "Say," the doctor said, "this guy was telling the truth."

———

A doctor opened his waiting-room door to a roomful of patients and asked, "Who's been waiting the longest?" "I have," said his tailor. "I delivered your suit three years ago and haven't been paid yet."

———

Patient tells doctor he has trouble with his ears. Says he coughs all night but can't even bear it. The doctor prescribes some medicine and the patient asks, "Will this make me hear better?" "No," said the doctor, "but it'll make you cough louder."

The elderly doctor sent his patient with a note to the young doctor in the office across the hall: "This will introduce Mrs. Gloria Osbin. She has been married for three years but has never achieved satisfaction. I was hoping you could help her."

Harassed surgeon to medical students watching a delicate operation: "Will the wiseguy who keeps saying 'Oops,' please leave!"

Here's Henny Youngman's favorite doctor joke. DOC: I am happy to tell you that you will probably live to be ninety. PATIENT: But Doctor, I am ninety! DOC: See, what did I tell you?

My doctor was writing a prescription with a thermometer. I said: "How can you write with a thermometer?" "Oops!" he said. "One of my patients must be walking around with my fountain pen stuck in him!"

The patient said to the doctor, "How can I ever repay you for your kindness to me?" He said, "By check, money order, or cash."

Money, in medicine, still talks. It's what doctors hear when they listen through their stethoscopes.

I asked my doctor if he could admit to any mistakes. He said, "Yes, I once cured a millionaire in only three visits."

The surgeon told the patient, "We'll need you unconscious for the operation. Would you prefer anesthesia or a peek at your bill?"

An old doctor in a small town finally took a vacation. He left his son, who was about to graduate from medical school, in charge of his practice. When the father returned, he asked his son if anything unusual had happened while he was gone. "I cured Mrs. Stephenson of that indigestion she has been suffering from for the past thirty years," the son remarked proudly. "Oh, no!" the father exclaimed. "That indigestion has put you through high school, college, and medical school!"

The doctor said, "My dear sir, it's a good thing you came to see me when you did!" The patient said, "Why, Doc? Are you broke?"

After undergoing extensive medical tests, a patient called the doctor to see if the results were available. "Not yet," said the medic. "Why not?" the patient demanded. "Because," the doctor snapped, "I haven't figured out what kind of an operation you can afford."

Dr. Rosee said to the beautiful young girl, "Okay, just take your clothes off." She said, "But it's my grandmother here who's ill." The doc said, "Oh, all right, madam, stick your tongue out."

The doc said to the pretty gal, "I suggest you curtail your running around, stop drinking, cut out smoking, begin eating properly, and get to bed early." She said, "Really?" He said, "Yes. Why not have dinner with me tonight? I'll see to it that you have the proper food and that you're in bed by 9:00!"

Listen, anyone can find a doctor these days—the caddies all have walkie-talkies. In fact, recent surveys show that on any given day, during office hours, four out of five doctors would rather be on a golf course.

I have confidence in my doctor. No matter what ailment I have, I'm confident he'll come up with a fee. A couple of weeks ago I complained to him that my nose was sore. He told me to stay off it for a few days. Finally he said, "I can't do anything for your problem. It's hereditary." I said, "Then send the bill to my father, will you, Doc?" After a while, the nurse called me: "You haven't paid your bill in two months and the doctor is upset." I said, "Tell him to take two aspirins and call me in a couple of weeks if he isn't feeling better."

The doctor said, "You have a severe, infectious, viral-type, influenza-ish sinus condition." The patient said, "Gee, Doc, sounds expensive. I've only got fifty bucks." The doc said, "You have a cold."

My doctor told me I shouldn't drink, smoke, overeat, or dissipate. What it all boils down to is this: Don't do anything that could interfere with paying his bill.

Medical costs are really rising nowadays. One doctor recently told me he's doing so well financially that now he can occasionally tell a patient there's nothing wrong with him.

The doctor felt the patient's purse and admitted there was nothing he could do.

We all think we are born free—until the doctor's bill arrives. I know one who has an exclusive practice: He only treats people with fat wallets. He just made a major breakthrough in medicine: He raised his fee to $150.

My doctor has come up with an easy payment plan for me. Now I automatically deposit my paycheck in his account.

I'm always a little nervous about going to see a doctor when I realize that doctors are usually described as practicing. I wouldn't mind, but they do most of it on the golf course.

---

Forget about house calls. No doctor will come to your house today unless it's to foreclose on the mortgage.

---

My family doctor is very meticulous—he always washes his hands before he touches my wallet.

---

A doctor is a person who acts like a humanitarian and charges like a plumber.

---

A new patient appeared in a doctor's office to explain, "Doctor, I'm disturbed. A week ago I came home to find my wife in the arms of another man, who talked me into going out for a cup of coffee. The next four nights, the exact same thing happened." "My good fellow," said the doctor. "It isn't a doctor you need; it's a lawyer." "No, no," insisted the patient, "it's a doctor's advice I want. I've got to know if I'm drinking too much coffee."

---

Two doctors were having a drink together. One noticed that the other was really getting loaded. The first doctor asked if anything was wrong.

His friend said, "Well, yes. Last night I got the ultimate rejection. I was in church praying for divine help, and a deep majestic voice answered, 'Take two aspirins and call me in the morning.'"

---

I had a peculiar thing happen to me: My doctor gave me a physical examination, then he put on rubber gloves to shake hands.

---

Surgeons appear to be getting younger all the time. I saw one this past weekend in a hospital with his rubber gloves pinned to his shirt.

---

Medicine is so specialized these days, one patient had to switch doctors when his athlete's foot moved from his right foot to his left.

---

If you have to go to the hospital, it may help you to remember that there is no such thing as a dangerous operation for less than $1,000.

---

The medic asked the lady, "What is the matter with your husband?" She admitted, "I think he is worrying about money." The doc said, "Ah, I think I can relieve him of that."

---

The doctor noted, "There goes the only woman I ever loved." The nurse said, "Why don't you marry her?" He said, "I can't afford to—she's my best patient!"

———

The young doctor asked, "Why do you always ask your patients what they have for dinner?" The old doc said, "It's a most important question. I make out the bills according to their menus."

———

My neighbor just came back from the doctor, and I asked, "Did he find out what you have?" He said, "No, he only charged me fifty dollars and I have a hundred dollars."

———

1 went to one young doctor fresh out of medical school. I don't think he's making too much money yet: His stethoscope is on a party line.

———

Listen, it's not always the doctor's fault. "Congratulations," said the nurse to the man who was pacing outside the maternity ward. "You're a bouncing father. We just tried to cash your check."

———

After being informed there was nothing wrong with his car, the doctor was handed a bill for $50. "If there's no damage, how come you're charging me fifty dollars?" he screamed. The mechanic said, "It's like this, Doc. You charged me fifty dollars for a visit last week and I didn't have anything wrong either."

My doctor told me there was nothing strange about my condition, except that it was so seldom encountered in a person who was still living.

———

I called my doctor to make an appointment and his beeper answered: "At the beep, leave your name, address, and credit reference."

———

The doctor told me, "Only an operation can save you." I asked how much it would cost. "Five thousand dollars." I said, "I don't possess that much money." The doc said, "Then we will see what pills will do."

———

The two young doctors were talking about their diagnoses: The first said, "You've cured your patient. What is there to worry about?" The second said, "I don't know which of the medicines cured him."

———

After the examination, the physician handed his patient a prescription and said, "Take this medicine after each meal." The poor soul said, "But, Doc, I haven't eaten in four days." The doc said, "Fine. The medicine will last longer. "

———

"I'm getting a little worried about myself, Doc," I explained. "I need something to stir me up, something to take me out of my state of lethargy and put me in fighting trim. Have you included anything like that in this prescription?" He said, "No, not in the prescription. You'll find that in the bill."

---

My uncle, who is eighty-five, sat before the doctor: "My wife just gave birth to a baby," he said. "Do you think I can do it again?" The doc said, "Tell me, do you think you did it the first time?"

---

Modern medical science has made a lot of progress with new miracle drugs. No matter what illness you have, doctors can keep you alive long enough to pay your bill.

---

Malpractice insurance is so expensive, doctors may go on strike to get public support for their cause. But it won't work: Nobody will be able to read their picket signs.

---

My brother-in-law tells me he is going to associate himself with some of the most famous and skilled medical practitioners in the country: He's going to be a caddie.

---

The Park Avenue doctor told the intern, "Doctor, I want you to look after my office while I'm on my vacation." The intern said, "But I've just graduated. I have no experience." Said the specialist, "That's all right, my boy, my practice is strictly fashionable. Tell the men patients to play golf and ship the lady patients off to Europe."

---

I think I first began to lose confidence in my doctor when I noticed the six-inch dollar sign tattooed on his chest.

---

My uncle was in the hospital recovering from surgery. After several days in a room on the fifth floor, he was being moved to the hospital's sixth floor. When I asked him why he was being moved, he told me, "Because I've just finished paying for the fifth."

---

Nowadays, the first thing a little boy learns to make with a toy doctor's kit is a bill.

---

A librarian was admitted to Doctor's Hospital for surgery. She got a get-well card from her associates that read: "If they take anything out, make sure they sign for it."

---

I know a surgeon who will take your appendix out for $500, even if you don't have one.

---

I heard one doctor tell a hospital patient, "You're fine now. Why, you'll be up and complaining about my bill in no time."

The best thing about Medicare is that it lets you have diseases that would ordinarily be beyond your means.

———

The young actor told his pretty nurse, "I think I'm in love with you. To tell the truth, I don't want to get well!" The nurse smiled and said, "Don't worry, I don't think you will. The doctor is in love with me and he saw you trying to grab me this morning."

———

"I'm going to operate on Mrs. Green," the doc told her nephew. "The fee will be ten thousand dollars." The nephew asked, "What does she have?" The doc said, "Ten thousand dollars."

———

When I was in high school I wanted to be a doctor, but that dream ended when I didn't make the golf team.

———

These days what four out of five doctors recommend is another doctor.

———

I went to my doctor for a physical. Now I know what M.D. stands for—Mucho Dollars.

———

The best way to tell real doctors from impostors is the way they hold medical instruments: A fake doctor doesn't know the proper way to grip a putter.

Yesterday, a man who charged that doctors are more interested in playing golf than in treating patients was attacked by a mob of angry doctors who beat him with their golf clubs.

———

I understand that greens fees will soon be paid by Medicare.

———

The wife was screaming at her husband: "I pinch and scrape and save pennies for a whole year, and then you go and blow it on your gallstones." He said, "You should be happy. The surgeon did a marvelous job. He operated just in time. One more day and I would have recovered."

———

A busy businessman suffering from insomnia was told by his doctor, "Instead of counting sheep, try telling each part of your body to go to sleep." That night, as he lay with his eyes open, he remembered and began trying it. "Toes go to sleep . . . feet go to sleep," he ordered. "Legs go to sleep . . . thighs go to sleep." He was up to his arms when his wife walked in wearing a sheer nightie. The husband sat up and hollered, "Wake up, everybody!"

———

I don't think we should pick on doctors anymore—they have their own problems. There are so many malpractice suits brought against them these days that now if you want a doctor's opinion on something, you have to talk to his lawyer.

---

These days there are three kinds of doctors: expensive, exorbitant, and "you gotta be kidding."

---

My doctor doesn't believe in acupuncture. The only thing he sticks me with is the bill.

---

The doctor said to my neighbor's wife in the hospital: "I don't care how good you feel. I'll release you when I think you're ready to be released and not a dollar sooner."

---

I heard a lady say, "My operation was so serious that when the surgeon finished operating, I was immediately put in the expensive care unit."

---

In America we spend billions of dollars a year just for health. No wonder we have so many healthy doctors.

---

The patient said to the pharmacist, "The doctor never mentioned that one of the side effects of this medicine would be poverty."

---

I have a friend who drowned while taking acupuncture treatments on a waterbed. Acupuncture is not new. As far back as thirty years ago it was big in my neighborhood in Brooklyn: Instead of a needle, they used an ice pick.

---

The last thing my eye doctor asked me to read on the chart was the figure 195 in very large type. He asked, "Is that clear?" I replied, "Very clear." He said, "That's good; that's the price of your new glasses."

---

A really smart doctor is one who can diagnose the ailment of a patient who doesn't smoke or drink and isn't overweight.

---

My doctor has a great stress test. It's called "The Bill."

---

Doc gave his patient a new "wonder drug" pill. The poor soul asked, "Will this relax me?" The doc said, "No. You'll just dig being tense."

---

A mother of five told a friend, "I've been going to a psychiatrist since I last saw you." "What's bothering you?" the friend asked. "Nothing's bothering me," the mother said. "But that's the only place I can lie down without being disturbed."

I was practically cured of back pains by acupuncture. When I phoned the doc that the pains had returned, the acupuncturist yawned, "Just take two thumb tacks and call me in the morning."

---

If a man still has his appendix and his tonsils, the chances are, he's a doctor.

---

"I wouldn't worry about your son playing with dolls," the doc told the middle-aged matron. She said, "I'm not worried, but his wife is very upset."

---

The thing that bothers me about doctors is they give you an appointment six weeks ahead, then they examine you, then they ask you: "Why did you wait so long to see me?"

---

The doctor said to Fatso, "You need more exercise, but you'll get that trying to earn the money to pay my bill."

---

I don't believe people who say doctors won't treat poor people. My father is poor and his doctor treats him—even though his fees are what made my father poor.

---

I told my doctor I lost my job. The doc said, "That's a coincidence. I was just going to tell you your condition is all cleared up."

There is one advantage to being poor: A doctor will cure you faster.

---

The patient said to the surgeon: "Look, I'm broke. Just cut out about fifty bucks' worth."

---

The doctor said, "Lady, in order to determine what's wrong with you, I'll have to give you a complete examination. Please get completely undressed." The woman looked at him coyly and said, "Doctor, you first."

---

Doctor to beautiful young patient: "I don't see anything wrong with you so far. Keep undressing."

---

Comic Pat Cooper says his doctor ordered him to stop smoking. The doctor added, "And since you're quitting, I'll give you five dollars for your gold lighter."

---

Talk about inflation. My doctor sent me a get-well card and in it was a bill for $20.

---

The doctor lost all his money in Las Vegas. He even gambled away the house and car. He knew he couldn't go home to his wife, so in desperation he decided to hold up a bank. But his bad luck continued because nobody could read his holdup note.

My doctor told me, "Nobody makes house calls anymore, except plumbers, TV repairmen, and burglars."

———

"I'm doing what I can," the doctor explained to the patient, "but you know I can't make you any younger." "The hell with that," said the impatient patient. "I'm not interested in getting younger. I just want to get older."

———

"I'm sorry," the doctor said to the stripper, "I don't have a brochure of scars to show you. You'll just have to take pot luck."

———

I feel awful tonight. I went to the doctor's office this afternoon to talk to him. As soon as I walked into the office, the nurse said, "Take off your clothes." I went into another room and there was another guy there with his clothes off. I said, "This is ridiculous. I only came in here to talk to the doctor and they made me take my clothes off." He said, "What are you kicking about? I'm the doctor!"

———

PATIENT: All the other doctors differ from your diagnosis in my case. DOCTOR: I know, but just wait—the postmortem will prove I'm right.

———

DOCTOR: Your husband will never be able to work again. WIFE: I'll go up and tell him right away. It'll cheer him up.

———

I was feeling a little run-down, so I went to visit a doctor someone had recommended to me. He looked me over and said, "Mr. Jones, I don't know how to tell you this, but you have only four hours to live. Is there anyone you'd like to see?" I said, "Yeah, another doctor!"

———

I know a doctor so egotistical that when he takes a woman's pulse, he subtracts ten beats for his personality.

———

"I don't get it," said one pretty girl as she took off her clothes. "I tell the doctor my sinus is bothering me and he asks me to strip." A naked redhead with a satchel on her lap replied, "My case is even more puzzling. I'm here to tune the piano."

———

"Calling Dr. Fink, calling Dr. Fink. Your patient refused to take the medicine you prescribed. He got well and went home."

———

A friend showed up at my party minus an appendix. "I didn't know you had appendicitis," I said.
"I didn't, but I had to run into my doctor's office to use his phone—and

how could I leave without buying something?"

———

"How are you feeling?" Dr. Gilbert asked his patient as the beautiful blond nurse stood by.

"I want to go home to my wife!" "Oh," the doc said, "still delirious, huh?"

———

The patient called the doctor at 2 A.M. He was distraught. "I can't sleep, doc. It's that bill I owe you. I can't pay it. It bothers me so much I can't sleep." The doctor said, "Why did you have to tell me that? Now I can't sleep!"

———

She met the doctor in the lobby. "Doctor," she groaned, "I feel terrible. My head hurts, my shoulder is killing me, it's hard for me to walk on my painful feet, and even my Adam's apple is rotten." "Well," the doctor suggested, "why don't you come around to see me." "Maybe," she said pensively. "Maybe next week if I'm feeling better."

———

A doctor is a success when he makes enough money to be able to tell a patient there's nothing wrong with him.

———

DOCTOR: You'll have to cut out women or liquor. PATIENT: Well, then, I'll give up liquor. I can always drink when I'm old.

The nearsighted doctor treated the patient for varicose veins for a year before he found out that the patient's fountain pen leaked!

———

"If my doctor could see me now with this champagne and caviar, he'd go crazy!" "Why, are you supposed to be on some kind of diet?" "No. I owe him $500!"

———

The girl told the doctor she was too embarrassed to get undressed, she was so shy.

"Okay," the doc said. "I'll put out the lights. You can undress in the dark."

When she was naked, she asked, "Where will I put my clothes?" as she groped in the dark.

"Right here next to mine," the doctor suggested.

———

The doctor rushed out of his study and instructed his wife, "Get me my bag at once!" "What's the matter?" she asked. "Some fellow just phoned and said he couldn't live without me." The wife thought a few seconds, then said, "Just a moment. I think that call was for me."

———

Back in East Texas, Old Man Jones confessed his troubles to the local doctor. "It's sort of ticklish to talk about, Doc," he apologized. "But I need some vitamins or something on account of when it comes to making love, I ain't got as much pep as I used to have." "Well, that's natural," the doctor said. "How old are you?" "Well, let's see. I'm a year older'n my wife and she's eighty-one. Guess I'm about eighty-two years of age." "And when did you first notice this lack of pep on your part?" "Well, the first time was last night. That wasn't so bad, but be dogged if we didn't notice it again this morning."

———

The woman ear and throat specialist was all in a tizzy. Seems she wanted to paint the throat of a very chic patient. The trouble was, she couldn't decide on a color!

———

DOCTOR: The check you gave me came back. PATIENT: So did my arthritis.

———

DOCTOR: All right, now what seems to be the matter with you? PATIENT: You studied for ten years. You tell *me*.

———

PATIENT: I sure hope I'm sick. DOCTOR: What kind of an attitude is that? PATIENT: Well, I'd hate to feel like this if I'm well.

———

The doctor said to the nervous new mother, "Now, don't worry about the baby. Just remember to keep one end full and the other end dry."

Never argue with a doctor. He has inside information.

———

The army doctor said to the young draftee, "I want a urine specimen." "Sure," the draftee said. "All right," the doctor said, "Fill that bottle over there." "From here??!!" exclaimed the draftee.

———

The doctor explained to the heart patient that he would be able to continue his romantic life as soon as he could climb two flights of stairs without becoming winded. The patient listened attentively and said, "What if I look for women who live on the ground floor?"

———

"The doc told me I'm in good shape for a man of sixty." "What's wrong with that?" "I'm only thirty-nine."

———

My neighbor tells me his wife switched doctors. "When she got pregnant, he told her it was all in her head."

———

Entertainer Virginia Graham tells about the meanest doctor in town: "He keeps his stethoscope in the freezer." . . . The doc asked Virginia why she gave up taking tranquilizers. She said, "I had to—I found myself being pleasant to people I don't even speak to."

———

Doctor Dick told me: "I cured a patient of being a hypochondriac. I told him his insurance didn't cover it."

———

Doctor Dick explains: "It's easy to spot a hypochondriac: He puts cough syrup on his pancakes. Instead of an olive in his martini, he has a Tums."

———

Two women were talking at tea: "You should see my doctor. He's marvelous." The other said, "Why should I see your doctor? There's nothing wrong with me." "My doctor's wonderful—he'll find something."

———

Last year, Americans spent more than $18 billion on medical care, and it's really doing the job. More and more doctors are getting well.

———

I visited my neighbor. "Did you recover from your operation?" I asked. "Not yet," he said. "The doctor says I still have two more payments."

———

I'm fascinated by our great modern doctors. The same operation can add ten years to your life and take ten years off your savings.

I don't think anyone should complain about the high cost of medical care—especially while they're still in the hospital.

———

A hospital bed is a parked taxi with the meter running.

———

Everything is so expensive. Hospitals really should use cheaper equipment—like an X-ray machine that takes four poses for a buck.

———

I really don't blame hospitals for trying to keep costs down, but I do think a coin-operated bedpan is going a little too far.

———

The doctor said to the young lady, "I'd like to give you a thorough examination. Take off your nightgown." The patient said, "But Dr. Schwartz found me perfect this afternoon." The doc said, "So he told me!"

———

After the physician checked the patient over, he asked, "Have you been living a normal life?" He said, "Yes, Doctor." "Well, you're going to have to cut it out for a while."

———

My aunt was telling her friends at the bridge club, "My doctor gives me a complete physical checkup for $250. Sure, it's a lot of money, but if he finds something wrong with me, it's worth it." One lady from the Bronx spoke up, "I don't know why people knock doctors. My doctor cleared up my rash in one treatment—and also relieved the swelling in my wallet."

———

The hypochondriac explained to his wife, "It was a delicate operation, in which the doctor separated me from my life savings."

———

Comedian Jan Murray says, "We are advised to get a second opinion before undergoing surgery, but they don't specify whether it should be from another doctor or your banker."

———

Comic Jack Carter tells me, "I asked for a second opinion and he billed me twice.

———

My doctor was leaving his crowded office to go out to move his car. He said to his patients, "Don't anybody get better. I'll be right back."

———

My neighbor cried to me, "Is my doctor expensive? He conducts open wallet surgery. Last week I ate nothing but hundred dollar-a-plate dinners—I was in the hospital. I had my first bath in bed in that hospital. A nurse washed me down, then gave me a wet cloth and said, 'You know what to do with this.' I didn't really, but for three days my room had the cleanest windows on the floor."

———

Myron's doctor is a specialist and charges $200 for a house call, $100 for an office consultation, and $50 if he gives you my advice by telephone. Myron asked politely, "I just wondered, sir, how much do you charge for passing a patient on the street?"

———

The great Milton Berle told me: "It's a good thing I'm covered by Red, White and Blue Cross." Uncle Miltie explained, "I was operated on at a great hospital—'Our Lady of Malpractice!' Five years ago they spent three million dollars on a recovery room. It hasn't been used yet." After the operation, the doc told Milton: "Soon your sex life will be terrific, especially the one in the winter."

———

This guy came to the emergency ward at the hospital and cried: "Help me. My backside hurts terribly." The doc asked, "What kind of work do you do?" He said, "At Coney Island. I put my head through a hole in the canvas and people throw baseballs at me, and

Doc, I haven't been able to sit down for a week." The doc asked, "What's throwing baseballs at your head got to do with your sitting down?" "The guy also rented out the back of me for a dart game."

———

Today's hospitals don't kid around. I won't say what happens if you don't pay a bill, but did you ever have tonsils put back in?

———

I gotta tell you, these hospitals swing. If you need mouth-to-mouth resuscitation, they get Cindy Crawford.

———

Advice to hospital patients: Before kissing the nurse, remove the thermometer from your mouth.

# Dogs
*(see also Animals)*

I've got a sheepdog. He doesn't have fleas—he's got moths.

———

I sold my dog for $100,000. I got two $50,000 cats for him.

———

They say barking dogs never bite. I know it and you know it, but does the dog know it?

———

"My dog may not be pedigreed and all that, but he's a hell of a watchdog. No stranger ever gets anywhere near our house without our Fido letting us know." "What does he do? You mean he growls and bites?" "No, he crawls under our bed."

———

They tell me that dog is worth $50,000. I still can't believe he could save up that much.

———

Great Dane: the kind of puppy that has the house broken before he is.

———

"I went to the dog races last night and I bet on a dog called Wise Guy." "How did you make out?" "He lost. He went all right up to the middle of the race, then he stopped and turned right back to where he started from." "What happened to him?" "He found out the rabbit he was chasing was a dummy."

———

"I've got a new dog, a dachshund. I entered him in the races last Saturday." "How did he make out?" "It was a circular track and he overtook himself."

———

My neighbor told me, "My dog was my only friend. I told my wife that a man needs at least two friends, so she bought me another dog."

# Dreams

WIFE: I dreamed you bought me a fur coat. HUSBAND: Well, go back to sleep and wear it in good health.

---

Never mind what my dreams mean, Doc, just get me their phone numbers.

---

He fell in love with the girl of his dreams—and she turned out to be a nightmare.

---

It doesn't hurt me if my wife dreams about being married to a millionaire, as long as she doesn't do it while she is out shopping.

---

I dream about beautiful girls, but you should see the kind I get.

---

"I dreamed last night that I was with Demi Moore. She was kissing me, hugging me—"

"Then what happened?" "Then it was time to get up. But I'm going to sleep early tonight."

---

I dreamed all night I was eating shredded wheat. When I awoke, half the mattress was gone.

---

The doctor gave the insomniac a handful of pills. "This red pill," he explained, "will make you dream of Heather Locklear. The pink one will make you dream of Cindy Crawford, and the yellow one will make you dream of Pamela Lee." "Good," said the patient, "I'll take two of each—and don't bother to wake me for two weeks."

# Dress

*(see also Clothing, Fashion)*

WIFE: Does she dress like a lady? HUSBAND: I don't know. I never saw her dress.

---

MARY: That dress is too tight for you. RUTH: It's tighter than my skin. MARY: How could anything be tighter than your skin? RUTH: I can sit down in my skin, but I'll be damned if I can sit down in this dress.

---

FIRST DRUNK: Look at that sign. SECOND DRUNK: Whazzit shay? FIRST DRUNK: Shays, "Ladies Ready-to-Wear Clothes." SECOND DRUNK: Well, ish damn near time, ain't it?

---

A woman may put on a golf suit and not play golf. She may put on a bathing suit and never go near the water. But when she puts on a wedding gown, she means business.

Two college roommates met on campus. "Say," asked the first, "what's the idea of wearing my raincoat?" "Well, you wouldn't want your new suit to get wet, would you?" he replied.

———

SHE: Do you believe that tight clothes stop circulation? HE: Certainly not. The tighter a woman's clothing, the more she's in circulation.

———

The sports fan was describing his date of the previous evening. "She wore one of those baseball dresses," he explained. "What's that?" his friend inquired. "A baseball dress? It had a diamond back, a grandstand view in front, and it showed a lot of beautiful curves."

———

GEORGE: Will you give me the address of your tailor? FRED: Yes, if you won't give him mine.

———

ANGELA: You certainly look cute in that gown. MILLIE: Oh, this? I wear it to teas. ANGELA: To tease whom?

# Drinking
*(see also Alcohol, Bars)*

My uncle adopted an eleven-day-old baby. Now his wife will have to get two bottles ready every night.

My brother-in-law is an occasional drinker—any occasion will do.

———

James Thurber said it: "One martini is all right, two is too many, and three is not enough."

———

He does not drink to his wife—he drinks because of her.

———

Talk about embarrassing moments. I saw a friend of mine really get loaded. He walked over to a gorgeous redhead at a party, introduced himself, and suggested she go home with him. And she did—she was his wife.

———

If you drink like a fish, swim, don't drive.

———

The drunk approached the girl at the bar. "I'll let you kiss me if you tell me what I've got in my hand." "A six-hundred-pound alligator," says the doll. "That's close enough," says the drunk.

———

Two drunks were riding a roller coaster when one turned to the other and said, "We may be making good time, but I've got a feeling we're on the wrong bus."

———

And speaking of drunks, two men were drinking in a bar, and suddenly one of them fell on his face. His buddy looked down and said, "That's what I like about you, Sam. You know when to quit."

———

Then there's the friend of mine who used the new martini-flavored toothpaste. He has 40 percent more cavities, but couldn't care less.

———

The drunk's hands were trembling when he went to see the doctor. "My God," said the medic, "how much have you been drinking lately?" "Not much. I spill most of it."

———

The fourth drink, and he said, "Y'know, one more drink and I'll feel it." And she said, "Y'know, one more drink and I'll let you!"

———

Several of the new cable TV stations show reruns of old TV series, like "Dick Van Dyke" and "Rowan & Martin's Laugh-In," except instead of running reruns of "The Dean Martin Show," they offer refills.

———

The lady was complaining about her husband's drinking. "We'd be rich today if whiskey came in deposit bottles."

———

I wouldn't say he drinks a lot, but he is the only guy in the world who doesn't see anything unusual about the Tower of Pisa.

———

The bus conductor asked the drunk if he got home okay last night. "Naturally," the poor soul said. "Why shouldn't I?" "Well, when you got up to give a lady your seat, there was only the two of you on the bus."

———

The temperance lecturer demonstrated the evils of drink by putting two glasses in front of him, one with water and the other with whiskey. He then produced a couple of worms, which he put in the water. They swam around happily. He took them out and put them in the whiskey, and after a few wriggles they both died. "That," explained the lecturer, "is what happens to your insides when you drink whiskey." He made his point. On his way out a little old lady stopped him and asked what brand of whiskey he had used. "Because," she said, "I've been bothered with worms for years."

———

There is a difference between a drunk and an alcoholic. The drunk doesn't have to go to meetings.

———

The drunk was stopped by a policeman as he staggered about the street at three o'clock in the morning. "Can you explain why you're out at this time?" asked the policeman. "If I could," said the drunk, "I'd be home by now."

———

Ice has great healing powers. It's a great pain reliever, especially when used in a glass of scotch.

———

He was called the town drunk. And that's not so bad, till you realize he lived in New York City.

———

With the price of liquor today, beggars can't be boozers.

———

Two drunks were weaving along the railroad tracks. One said, "I never saw so many steps in my life." The other said, "It's not the steps that bother me, it's the low railing."

———

The poor soul weaved into a local tavern, put his head on the bar, and asked for a double bourbon. "Don't be silly," said the barkeep, "you can't even lift your head." "Okay," said the drunk amiably, "then give me a haircut."

———

Drinker's advice: Never drink when you're driving. You might spill some."

———

The lush came home late and explained to his wife that he had just bought something for the house. "What did you buy for the house?" she asked. "A round of drinks," he answered.

———

Conditions were not good when Roosevelt ran for president, and this was his favorite story: A fellow was a big drinker. And he went to the doctor and said, "I can't hear and I can't see good." The doctor asked, "Are you a drinker?" "Yes, I'm a heavy drinker." "That's why you can't see and hear so good. You've got to stop drinking." A month later the doctor runs into the fellow and he's drunk again. "Didn't I tell you that drinking would interfere with your seeing and hearing?" he asked. "Doc, what I've been drinking is so much better than what I've been seeing and hearing lately, I decided to keep it up."

———

A drunk walked into an Automat, got change, then stopped in front of a slot marked "Cheese Sandwich." He dropped in coins, got a sandwich, and dropped in more coins, got another sandwich. After he had collected twenty sandwiches, the manager came over. "Don't you think that's enough?" he asked. "What?" cried the drunk, "you want me to quit in the middle of a winning streak?"

———

The shy character noticed a low-cut blonde sitting next to him alone at the bar. He gathered all his courage and sent a drink to her. She silently nodded her thanks. He repeated the same gesture six times. Finally, the drinks in him spoke up and he got up all the courage he could muster and mumbled, "Do you ever make love to strange men?" "Well," she smiled, "I never have before, but I think you've talked me into it, you clever, silver-tongued devil, you."

My cousin wrote, "I don't smoke, touch intoxicants, or gamble. I am faithful to my wife and never look at another woman. I am hard-working, quiet, and obedient. I never go to bars or places of ill repute and I go to bed early every night and rise with the dawn. I attend chapel every Sunday without fail. I've been like this for the past three years. But just wait until next spring, when they let me out of here!"

My neighbor really tried to go on the wagon last year and three bars sued him for nonsupport.

My brother joined a weightlifting class. Right now he's up to eight-ounce glasses.

One great thing about old Uncle Charlie: He never has a hangover—he stays drunk.

I asked the expert: "Tell me, what do you take for a headache?" He said, "Liquor the night before."

When you talk about heavy drinkers, my uncle has to win first prize: My poor old uncle drank a fifth of whiskey with each of his three meals, then took a nightcap at bedtime. When he finally died, the family tried to honor his last wish by having him cremated. It took them three days to put out the fire.

Nobody knew my boss drank—until one day he came in sober.

My father-in-law says he owes his success in life to a street corner orator he listened to one noon hour many years ago. He was a prohibitionist and he lectured on the evils of drink, pointing out how people ruined their health and spent all their time in saloons and their very last cent on liquor. My father-in-law was so impressed that the very next week he bought his first saloon.

My cousin the drunk thinks Beethoven's Fifth is a bottle of scotch.

Now they've got an organization called Teetotalers Anonymous. If you feel like going on the wagon, you call this number and two drunks come over to talk to you.

———————

At a party I heard the host ask, "Will you have a drink? We have scotch, rye, bourbon, and brandy." My uncle said, "Yes, please, that'll be fine."

———————

Our mayor is on a kick against smoking, sex, gridlock, and bribing. I hope he never gets to drinking.

———————

There are really no problem drinkers—except those who never buy.

———————

Drinking removes warts and pimples—not from me, but those who I have to talk to.

———————

My uncle's the nicest chap on two feet, if he could only stay there. His favorite drink is the next one.

———————

"I don't remember too much about last night," the drunk told me, "but we did get a ticket for riding three in the front seat." I asked, "What's wrong with three in the front seat?" He said, "It was on a motorcycle."

———————

The drunk went tearing around town honking his horn and running

red lights. It's a good thing he wasn't in his car at the time.

———————

My neighbor lamented: "A woman drove me to drink, and I never even had the courtesy to thank her."

———————

The drunk noted, "I always keep a supply of stimulant handy in case I see a snake—which I also keep handy."

———————

The lady said to the drunk, "Every time I see you, you have a bottle in your hand." He said, "You don't expect me to keep it in my mouth all the time, do you?"

———————

"Pour me a cold one," the teenager said, walking into the bar. The barmaid looked him over and said, "Get lost, kid. You want to get me in trouble?" The boy answered, "Maybe later. Right now all I want's a beer."

———————

A man ordered a martini "extra rare." The bartender said, "You mean extra dry." The man insisted, "I mean extra rare. I'm having it for my dinner."

———————

These two loaded gentlemen stood at the bar near closing time: "I got an idea," one lush said. "Let's have one more drink and go find sum broads." The other said, "Naah—I got more than

I can handle at home." The first guy said, "Great. Then let's have one more drink and go up to your place."

———

I don't want to say that guy drinks a lot, but he's two thousand swallows ahead of Capistrano.

———

A full-blooded Indian got a job as a bartender, but he was fired after five minutes. A customer asked for a Manhattan and the Indian charged him $24.

———

The drunk walked up to the parking meter, put in a quarter, and saw the dial go to sixty. "How do you like that?" he said. "I weigh an hour."

———

The brave fireman fought his way through the flames and rescued the man lying on the burning bed. When he carried him to safety he noticed the man was loaded. "Look what you did," he said to the drunk. "I hope that teaches you not to smoke in bed." "Who was smoking? It was on fire when I got in."

———

A guy was boasting of his grandfather: "He lived for ninety-four years and never once used glasses." "He had the right of it," nodded his brother. "I always said it was healthier to drink from the bottle."

"Stay out of that saloon, Mike," warned his friend. "If you go in, the devil goes in with you." "If he does," said Mike, "he pays for his own drinks."

———

The judge looked sternly at the defendant: "You've been brought here for drinking." The defendant answered, "Well, what are we waiting for? Let's get started."

———

Today there's a diet for everybody. The most popular is the drinking man's diet. It's hard to tell how many people follow it, because most of them don't know they're on it.

———

My alcoholic uncle is a baby at heart: He still gets his two o'clock bottle—and his three o'clock—and his four o'clock.

———

My uncle suggests a great recipe for a Christmas turkey: "Take a fifteen-pound turkey, add one quart of scotch, heat it, then pour a quart of gin over it, then a quart of Burgundy, then put it back in the oven for one hour. Then you take the turkey out of the oven and throw it out the window—but, oh, what a gravy!"

———

One way to cut down on drunk driving would be for the saloons to offer free home delivery.

A restaurateur I know has a new cocktail in his bar made with vodka and carrot juice. You get drunk just as fast, but it's great for your eyesight.

---

Two insomniacs were discussing their problem. "I've lost ten pounds in the last two weeks from lack of sleep," one victim said. "I don't know what to do." "I do," the other said. "I just take a martini every hour after dinner." "Terrific. And it works?" "No, but it keeps me happy while I'm awake."

---

My alcoholic uncle told me he's considering filling his swimming pool with martinis. He claims that'll make it impossible to drown, since the deeper you sink, the higher you get.

---

My alcoholic cousin tells me the staff at his favorite hotel are very considerate: "The morning after, they always serve my breakfast on the floor."

---

A recent survey shows that whiskey drinkers get more cavities than milk drinkers, but they go to the dentist in a better frame of mind.

---

My alcoholic uncle told me: "I haven't quit drinking, never. Everybody hates a quitter."

---

I will not think of my brother-in-law as an ordinary drunk, not after I heard he's donated his body to science, so he's preserving it in alcohol till they use it.

---

A heavy drinker was regaling his friends with his early life and the hard times he had. "Things were so bad," he recalled, "that sometimes I had to live for days on nothing but food and water."

---

To avoid a hangover—keep drinking.

---

Lovable clown Joe E. Lewis has been warned many times about his drinking. "Don't worry about a thing," is Joe's answer. "I'm responsible for a new surgical technique. After my last operation, instead of stitches they used corks."

---

The great W. C. Fields, well known for his light eating and heavy drinking habits, once said, "I never like to eat on an empty stomach." A friend once introduced him to brandied figs. Said Fields, "I never ate so much to drink in my life."

---

One of Jackie Gleason's fans was astonished to find the Great One imbibing pretty good at a bar. "I thought you were a man of regular habits," the man scolded. "I am," Jackie retorted. "Drinking is one of my regular habits."

"They say drinking shortens a man's life." "Yes, but he sees twice as much in the same length of time."

———

He only drinks to calm his nerves and improve steadiness; today he got so steady he couldn't even move.

———

Oil and alcohol do mix, but it tastes lousy.

———

"I went to a dozen different bars this afternoon, but I couldn't get what I wanted." "That's funny. What did you want?" "Credit."

———

He gets drunk on Scotch tape.

———

The Red Cross rejected his blood donation. His plasma had an olive in it.

———

He has no respect for old age—unless it's bottled.

———

The only way he opens a conversation is with a corkscrew.

———

I got a telegram from Joe E. Lewis, but I couldn't read it. The light was bad and I'm afraid to light a match around it.

———

It's a lie about how much Dean Martin drank. I knew him a long time and I never saw him take a drink until dinnertime. In fact, I had dinner at his house and you never saw such a banquet, but who can eat that much at eight o'clock in the morning?

———

Show me a man who can eat, drink, and be merry, and I'll show you a fat, grinning drunk.

———

DRUNK: Why didn't you wake me at seven-thirty? OPERATOR: Because you didn't get to bed until eight.

———

Joey Bishop says he gave Dean Martin a lighter—and he drank it in one gulp.

———

He drinks like a fish. Too bad he doesn't drink what a fish drinks.

———

Dean Martin cut his finger. It's the first time I ever saw blood with a head on it.

———

Problem drinkers—are those who never buy.

———

Dean Martin wants to buy Alcatraz. He always wanted a house on the rocks with water on the side.

Don't take another drink. Your face is already blurred.

---

Now that Alaska and Hawaii are states, the most popular American drink will probably be pineapple juice with ice in it.

## Drive-ins

I know a man so rich he goes to drive-in movies in a taxi.

---

Just think what a drive-in theater would be called if there was nothing on the screen.

---

The Catholics have a drive-in confessional. It's called the "toot and tell."

---

He was watching a movie at the drive-in theater with his girlfriend and somebody threw a brick in the window and hit her in the chest. It broke four of his fingers.

---

A drive-in is better known as a passion pit.

---

You go to a drive-in theater and what do you see? Sex, perversion, sodomy—and then you look at the screen.

---

My aunt went to a drive-in movie and became the first woman ever to be run over on the way to the bathroom.

No matter how bad the movie is at a drive-in theater, most patrons love every minute of it.

---

The husband and wife went to see the latest Julia Roberts movie at the drive-in. They were late arriving, and as they drove up to the attendant the husband said, "Will we get to see a complete performance?" "No, sir," he said, "you won't. But I reckon you'll come closer to it than in any other movie I can think of."

---

He showed her a lot of love and affection. He took her to a drive-in movie and let her peek into the other cars.

---

Pretty soon all the drive-in theaters will open up again—and people will quit watching movies again.

---

The owner of a drive-in theater said to his partner, "If business gets any worse, we'll have to start showing pictures."

---

At a drive-in theater, even after the murder mystery is over, nobody knows who did it.

---

I saw a championship fight at a drive-in theater but it was sort of confusing. Most of the time I was watching the wrong clinches.

A funny thing happened at this drive-in theater. A fellow drove in all alone.

This picture at the drive-in was so sad, there wasn't a dry windshield in the place.

There's a new drive-in theater screen: The manager puts one around each car.

When the teenager asked his old man for the car to take his girl to a drive-in theater, Pop said, "But it's so foggy!" The kid explained, "That's nothing. We've already seen the picture."

# Driving
*(see also Accidents, Automobiles, Cars, Traffic)*

My wife is such a bad driver, every time she loses control of the car, it goes back on the highway.

I gave my wife a car. She loves it so much, she's taking it to England. She wants to see what it's like to drive on the left side of the street—legally.

My wife is the world's worst driver. If she were an Arab, she'd come home with a dented camel.

My wife has a terrible sense of direction. She even goes against the traffic when she gets on an escalator.

The cop signaled the wife to the curb. "Okay," he sneered, "why didn't you signal what you wanted to do?" "Because," she answered, "there's no signal for what I want to do."

Best way to stop noise in a car is to let her drive.

It was one of those new low foreign cars. He stuck out his hand to make a left turn and ruptured the cop on the corner.

The latest model cars have modern devices to safeguard the lives of pedestrians. If a car runs over you, the exhaust sprays you with penicillin and a get-well card drops on your chest.

"My wife is the typical woman driver. I saw her driving down the street at only thirty miles an hour, but it was on the sidewalk. I ran into my building, shut the door, ran into the elevator, shut the door, ran into my closet, shut the door. It didn't help—she hit me!"

Lonesome George Gobel was asked to come up with a slogan over the Fourth of July weekend to encourage safe driving. George suggested: "Ladies and gentlemen, this is a holiday weekend. The National Safety Council estimates that 524 people will be killed. So far only 185 have been killed. Some of you folks aren't trying."

---

Sign in used-car lot: "If your headlights are out of order, don't stop to have them fixed at night. Just put your radio on real loud. This will help drown out the noise of the crash."

---

She's a great driver—gets twenty miles to a fender.

---

Is the white line in the center of the road really for bicycles?

---

My wife never stops for a red light when she's driving. She says, "You see one or two, you've seen them all."

---

Nothing confuses a man more than driving behind a woman who does everything right.

---

The woman driver made a right turn from the left lane and smashed into another car. "Why the hell didn't you signal?" the angry motorist screamed. "Sir," she answered haughtily, "why do I have to signal? I always turn here."

The husband complained that his wife ran over his golf sticks. "I told you," she said, "not to leave them on the porch."

---

When it comes to parking, she does a bang-up job.

---

Riding on the freeway is like Russian roulette: You never know which driver is loaded.

---

OFFICER: Miss, you were doing sixty miles an hour! SWEET YOUNG THING: Oh, isn't that splendid! I only learned to drive yesterday.

---

A man was driving an auto with his wife in the back seat and stalled his car on a railroad track with the train coming. His wife screamed, "Go on! Go on!" Her husband said, "You've been driving all day from the back seat. I've got my end across, see what you can do with your end."

---

The new owner of a used car was driving his purchase home. He was rapidly questioning the wisdom of his bargain when an officer roared at him, "Hey! You're blocking up traffic. Can't you go any faster?" "Yes, but I don't want to leave the car," was the disgusted reply.

---

Brought before a magistrate for speeding, the struggling young lawyer was asked to explain his haste. "What is your alibi for speeding at fifty miles an hour?" asked the judge. "Well, Your Honor, I had just heard, Your Honor, that the ladies of my wife's church were giving a rummage sale, and I was hurrying home to save my other pair of pants."

Three men were repairing telephone poles. A woman drove by in her car, and when she saw the men climbing the telephone poles, she said, "Look at those darn fools. You'd think I had never driven a car before."

"I got rid of that rear noise in my car," stated the motorist. "How did you do it?" "I made her sit up front with me."

## Drugs

Greenwich Village is a very unique place. Where else will you find signs that say KEEP ON THE GRASS?

For a business trip, try LSD in your IBM.

Comic Henny Youngman says his wife is hooked on LSD: Lox, Salami, and Danish.

CUSTOMER: You made a mistake in that prescription I gave my mother-in-law. Instead of quinine you used strychnine! DRUGGIST: You don't say? Then you owe me two dollars more.

CUSTOMER: I can't sleep at night. The least little sound disturbs me. I'm a victim of insomnia. Even a cat on our back fence distresses me beyond words. DRUGGIST: This powder will be effective. CUSTOMER: When do I take it? DRUGGIST: You don't. Give it to the cat in milk.

We got a new wonder drug. It's so powerful, you have to be in perfect health to take it.

DRUGGIST: Well, Charlie, did that mud pack improve your wife's appearance? CHARLIE: It did for a few days, but then it wore off.

"He's a great druggist, isn't he?" "Yes, but I think he makes the chicken salad a little too salty."

These new miracle drugs sound so good, I'm sorry I'm healthy.

## Dumb-dumbs and Slobbovia

America has now opened its borders to the independent kingdom of Slobbovia, as if we didn't have enough dumb-dumbs in Washington. The average Slobbovian politician never knows which foot he has in his mouth. If there's an idea in his head, it's in solitary confinement.

Did you hear about the Slobbovian grandmother who went on the pill? She didn't want to have any more grandchildren.

How does a Slobb make love? He hires a stand-in.

Do you know what they call anybody with an IQ of 80 in Slobbovia? Mr. President.

Slobey the Slobb went into the farm supply store and asked for six sticks of dynamite. The owner asked, "You want 'em to clear up your land?" Slobey said, "No, it's just that I'm going into town today and every time I go there, that wiseguy Dummy always comes up and yells, 'How are you?' and slaps me on the chest just to break the cigars he knows I carry there. Well, today when he does it, he's going to blow his damn hand off." This is the same guy who went to a doctor for an ulcer transplant.

Dumbrella, the mayor of Slobbville, proposed that a gondola be put in the Dopey Park Lake. One councilman

supported the idea with great enthusiasm: "Let's get two gondolas, male and female."

Slobbovians are loving people. Dan Dummy lived in a remote mountain village. One morning he was awakened by a postman delivering a letter. "You shouldn't have come all that way just to bring me one letter," he said lovingly. "You should have mailed it."

Did you hear about the Slobbovian skier with the frostbitten backside? He couldn't figure out how to get his pants on over his skis.

The newlywed asked his wife why she was cutting a block of ice into little cubes. The new wife said, "So they'll fit into the ice tray."

Dummy Stoopido passed a police station and noticed the sign that said, "Man Wanted for Bank Robbery." So he went inside and applied for the job. This is the same guy who spent hours looking for phone numbers in the dictionary.

Why don't Slobbovians throw dinner parties? They can't spell RSVP.

How does a Slobb increase his vocabulary? Easy—with a can of alphabet soup.

What can most Slobbovian kids do by the age of twelve? Wave bye-bye.

Most Slobbovians are as smart as they can be—unfortunately.

What do you call a Slobbovian with half a brain? Gifted.

A Slobbovian is going to the hospital for a minor operation: They're putting a brain in. His wife is going abroad. When she went to her doctor for shots, she slapped him when he asked to see her itinerary.

Why did the Slobb buy a hundred bottles of aspirin? He needed the cotton.

The kingdom of Slobbovia could have the biggest zoo in the world. All they have to do is build a fence around their country.

The mayor is such a lamebrain, he wears orthopedic hats.

Dummy gave his wife a washing machine for her birthday, but he had to return it: Every time she got into it, she came out black and blue.

A woman I know doesn't buy brooms because they don't come with instructions.

Dummy bought $3,000 worth of tires for his house because he wanted white walls.

This guy was going fishing and was buying bait. The store manager said, "I'll give you all you want for a dollar." Dummy said, "Good. I'll take three dollars' worth."

It's easy to spot a Slobb visiting this country: He asks what wine goes best with Alpo.

Slobbovian airlines are different: They show coming attractions of movies that will be shown on other airlines.

In Upper Slobbovia, thieves escaped with over half a million dollars from the Slobbovia National Bank. The papers said, "Police are baffled trying to figure out the motive for the crime."

The two Slobb hunters were driving into the woods when they saw a sign that said BEAR LEFT. So they went home.

The doctor told Slobbina, "You're pregnant. You're going to have a baby." She said, "Sorry, Doc, but the baby isn't mine."

Did you know they installed TV sets in all Slobbovian stadiums so the fans could see what was going on in their local bar?

———

Slobb drivers have never won the Indianapolis 500: They have to stop ten times to ask directions.

———

What happened to the Slobbovian water polo team? The horses drowned.

———

The mayor of Dumbville must be even smarter than Einstein was. Twelve people were said to have understood Einstein—the mayor nobody understands.

———

What do you call a pregnant Slobbovian lady? A dope carrier.

———

The mayor had this sign put up on the door of the dance hall: "All ladies and gentlemen are welcome—regardless of sex."

———

What do they call an intelligent man in Slobbovia? A tourist.

———

Two Slobbs froze to death in Upper Slobbovia: They went to a drive-in movie to see *Closed for the Season.*

Slobbina cried, "My boyfriend asked me to marry him and I'm so mad." "Why?" "Well, my mother married my father, my aunt married my uncle—so why should I marry a stranger?"

———

Did I tell you about Sam Slobb, who had a problem with spelling? He paid $50 and spent the night in a warehouse. . . . Or how about Bob Slobb, who wouldn't go out with his wife because she was a married woman?

———

Slobey told his wife, "I'll never work for that man again!" She asked, "Why? What did he say to make you so mad?" He said, "He told me I was fired!"

———

There were a Frenchman, an Englishman, and a Slobbovian all sitting with their girlfriends and enjoying themselves. The Frenchman said to his girl, "Pass the sugar, Sugar!" The Englishman said to his girl, "Pass the honey, Honey!" The Slobb, in the spirit of things, said to his lady, "Pass the tea, Bag!"

———

The Slobb told me, "I just bought a suit with two pairs of pants, but I don't like it." "Why?" "It gets awfully hot wearing two pairs of pants." He was so dumb he thought Einstein was one beer.

———

A Slobb applied for a job as a prison guard. The warden said, "Now these are real tough guys in here. Do you think you can handle it?" Dummy said, "No problem, sir. If they don't behave, out they go!"

———

I wouldn't say this guy was not a mental giant, but he thought a Band-Aid was a charitable organization for musicians.

———

Do you know they had to close down the library in Slobbovia? Somebody stole the book.

———

There was this guy in Lower Slobbovia giving evidence in a court case. He told the judge how he had seen a young girl beaten up by four muggers. The judge asked, "Why didn't you go to her aid?" Slobey said, "Your Honor, how was I to know who started the fight?"

———

The first dumb-dumb said: "I'm going to save my money and buy a Japanese radio." Answered the second dumb-dumb: "How are you going to understand what they're saying?"

———

The drunk was floundering down the alley carrying a box with holes in the side. He bumped into a friend who asked: "Whatcha got there, pal?" "A mongoose." "What the hell for?"

"Well, you know how drunk I can get, and when I get drunk I see snakes, and I'm scared to death of snakes. That's why I got this mongoose—for protection." "But," the friend said, "you idiot—those are imaginary snakes." "That's okay," said the drunk, "so's the mongoose."

———

My brother-in-law lost his job working a bank's hidden camera. He tried to get a holdup gang to stand closer together.

———

My nephew bought an inexpensive dictionary—it's not in alphabetical order.

———

Game-show host Bob Barker tells about a man who went home and complained to his wife. "I saw Tim Murphy downtown this morning and he didn't even speak to me. I guess he thinks I'm not his equal." His wife responded, "Why that stupid, brainless, conceited, good-for-nothing, moronic Tim Murphy! You certainly are his equal."

———

The train came to a sudden stop and the lady was thrown from her seat to the floor. "My goodness!" she said to the conductor. "What on earth happened?" "We hit a cow," he explained.

"Was it on the tracks?" "No, lady," said the conductor wryly, "we had to chase it across a field."

———

She thinks intercourse is the time spent between classes.

———

He's so dumb he thinks Shirley Temple Black is an African-American synagogue.

———

This dumb chronic says she's glad New York City has seven TV channels: "I can keep switching till I find a weather report I like."

———

Comedienne Phyllis Diller confides that nothing she does turns out right. "For instance, there are my twins. One is eighteen and the other is twenty."

———

He's the only person I ever knew who got up on the wrong side of the bed in a Pullman.

———

Most fishermen are superstitious, especially these two who hired a boat for a day's fishing and came back loaded with fish of all kinds. The guy at the pier congratulated them. "Thanks," one of them said. "We'd like the same boat again tomorrow." "Lucky for you, eh?" "Yes. Put a chalk mark on the side to show us where we were fishing today."

———

She thinks statutory rape means doing it standing up.

———

She is so dumb that when she rented a furnished room, the landlady left the VACANCY sign up.

———

She's so dumb, she takes off her sweater to count to two.

———

LADY: I want to mail this package parcel post. CLERK: Anything breakable, ma'am? LADY: No, but keep it right side up. It's a can of paint without the cover.

———

A farmer was driving his horse laboriously along a dusty road. He came to a man sitting beside the road, pulled his team to a halt, and called out, "How much longer does this hill last?"

"You ain't on no hill," the stranger called back. "Your hind wheels is off."

———

A man was staring at another man in the subway. "What are you staring at?" "I beg your pardon, but I . . . er . . . if it wasn't for the mustache, you know, you'd look just like my wife."

"But I have no mustache." "I know, but my wife has."

———

A: It's raining. Open the umbrella. B: Wouldn't do any good. It's full of holes. A: So why'd you bring it? B: I didn't think it would rain.

———

FIRST GUY: They fired my girl from her job at the bank. SECOND GUY: Yeah? How come? FIRST GUY: Well, when customers brought in money, she'd always say, "For me?"

———

"Fishing?" "No, drowning worms."

———

"What do you think of LSD?" "I think he'd make a great president."

———

I may have to find a new maid. When I lose the button off my shirt, she sews up the hole.

———

MISTRESS: It feels much colder in here. Has the temperature dropped? MAID: Yes mum, I'm sorry, I was cleaning the thermometer and I dropped it.

———

A friend told me one way to make housework easier was to use paper plates, but I found they clog up my dishwasher.

———

Woody Allen's hobby is to relax in a tub. "I stay there for hours," says Woody. "Sometimes I even fill it with water."

———

He wanted to write "Happy Birthday" on a cake. For three hours he tried to get the cake into his typewriter.

The only thing that can stay in his head more than an hour—is a cold.

———

It takes her an hour to cook minute rice.

———

The chorine was a little confused as she faced the lawyers on the witness stand. "Do you mind," she cooed to the judge, batting her baby blues, "if I tell my story in my lawyer's own words?"

———

"I was so surprised when I heard it," he screamed, "I couldn't believe my eyes."

———

He doesn't have an inferiority complex. He's just inferior.

———

If he said what he thought, he'd be speechless.

———

He has a brain—but it hasn't reached his head.

———

Offer that guy a penny for his thoughts—and you're overpaying him.

———

He's so dumb, he had the seven-year itch for eight years.

———

She had a 38 bust and an IQ to match.

HE: I suppose you think Barnum and Bailey are married to each other. SHE: What difference does it make, as long as they love each other?

———

He was so dumb, it finally sent him to the hospital. He threw a cigarette butt in a manhole and then stepped on it.

———

He was so dumb that it killed him. He bet his friend that he could lean farther out of a window. He won the bet!

———

He saw a moose head hanging on a wall and said to the host, "May I go in the next room and see the rest of it?"

———

The model was telling her friend about a strange man who got on at the same station with her and hugged her and kissed her until he had to get off. "Didn't you say anything to him?" asked her friend. "I should say not," said the model. "I never talk to strangers."

———

He was the flower of manhood—a blooming idiot.

———

He got an idea—beginner's luck.

———

The politician is so dumb, when you ask him his name, he calls a conference.

———

LOIS: Well, I'm falling in love, and I think I should go to a palmist or a mind reader. Which would you suggest? DORIS: You'd better go to a palmist. You know you've got a palm.

———

I lost my bank book, but don't worry. I took the precaution of signing all the checks as soon as I got them. Now they're no use to anybody.

———

She thinks a mushroom is a place to love.

———

She couldn't tell which way our elevator was going even if she had two guesses.

———

Why is it every time I wash ice cubes in hot water, I can't find them?

———

If anyone said hello to her, she'd be stuck for an answer.

———

He spent two weeks in a revolving door—looking for a doorknob.

———

They say it pays to be ignorant, so how come I'm broke?

I may look dumb, but that doesn't mean I'm not.

———

"This match won't light." "What's the matter with it?" "I don't know. It lit before."

———

He doesn't know the meaning of the word *defeat*—besides thousands of other words he doesn't know the meaning of.

———

He didn't know the meaning of the word *fear*—until he looked it up.

———

He changed his mind, but it didn't work any better than the old one.

———

She wouldn't accept tickets for a door prize. She says she doesn't need a door.

———

He thinks a naturalist is a crap-shooter who only throws sevens and elevens.

# E

## Ears

*(see also Eyes, Faces, Heads, etc.)*

The only time she washes her ears is when she eats watermelon.

---

All day long I heard a ringing in my ears. Then I picked up the phone and it stopped.

---

"That hat fits you nicely." "Yes, but what happens when my ears get tired?"

---

He's a big ear doctor. He only looks into big ears.

---

Her mouth was so big, every time she yawned, her ears disappeared.

---

Three little old ladies, loving but deaf, met at the supermarket. "Beautiful day," said one. "No, it's Friday," said the other. "Me, too," said the third. "Let's have a cup of tea."

---

My friend was bragging about his new hearing aid. "I can hear a leaf drop a block away. A drop of water is like an explosion. I can hear the tears in the apartment next door. It's the greatest hearing aid in the world." "What kind is it?" I asked. "It's a quarter to nine," he answered.

---

The doctors operated on a friend of mine for a constant ringing in his ears before they found out he was a bell-hop.

---

"You took the words right out of my ears," said the little boy to his mother.

"No, that's not right. It's you who took the words right out of my mouth."

"But I heard it before I said it."

## Earthquakes

I know it was a bad earthquake because my ZIP code changed three times.

---

After an earthquake, a Californian was walking around Nevada. A real-estate agent saw him and asked him if he was looking for a house, and he said, "Yes, I was wondering if it could have come this far."

---

An earthquake struck while a bride and groom were consummating their marriage. The bride quivered with delight. Afterward the groom turned to her and said, "I have to warn you, honey, it won't always be this good."

———

A crack in the earth said to another crack, "Don't look at me, it's not my fault."

———

It's a bad earthquake if you go visiting the next-door neighbors without leaving the house.
—If you can go surfing in your bathtub.
—If it causes $2 million in improvements in your local slums.

# Eating
*(see also Cooking)*

My wife never has to send out for junk food. She makes her own.

———

There's a simple rule to be followed when reading menus in fancy French restaurants: If you can't pronounce it, you can't afford it.

———

One restaurant customer said to another: "The service here is terrible, but you don't mind waiting, because the food is so poor."

———

I asked my wife, "Where am I when you serve those wonderful meals from which we always have the leftovers?"

A diner told his frantic waiter, "You know, I first came into this place in 1938." The waiter said, "I only got two hands. I'll get to your table in a minute."

———

Sam, my neighbor, said, "For the past two weeks I've been eating like a king: three wonderful meals a day." I said, "Your wife must be a good cook." Sam snapped, "What good cook? She's away visiting her mother. I've been eating at Joe's Diner."

———

My wife is such a lousy cook, every time she leaves the kitchen, she runs the risk of being arrested for leaving the scene of a crime.

———

The diner to the waiter: "What's my offense? I've been on bread and water for almost an hour."

———

My sister admits she's a lousy cook: "In my house we have Alka-Seltzer on tap."

———

The hostess asked the man, "Do you have a reservation?" He said, "No." She said, "Fine, then I'll give you immediate seating."

———

While dining at a restaurant, my neighbor yelled to the waiter, "What's this fly doing in my vichyssoise?" The waiter replied, "He's probably cooling off. It gets very hot in the kitchen."

My neighbor told his lady he would take her out to dine royally. Later she told her friends they went to Burger King and wound up at the Dairy Queen.

My wife is a lazy cook: She hires a hit man just to beat the eggs.

## Economy
*(see also Money)*

"Do you have any reliable rule for estimating the cost of living?" "I sure do. Take your income—whatever that may be—and add 25 percent."

Every child born in the USA is endowed with life, liberty, and a share of the government debt.

The trouble with today's economy is that when a man is rich, it's all on paper. When he's broke, it's cash.

"If all the world's economists were laid end to end, they wouldn't even reach a conclusion."—George Bernard Shaw

An economist always knows more about money than the people who have it.

We're living in a great economy. I never spent so much taxes in my life.

## Education
*(see also Children, College, Juvenile Delinquents, Kids)*

They have a new educational toy. It's a little too complicated for a kid, but it's designed to help the child adjust to the world of today. No matter how he puts it together, it's wrong.

I remember when aid to education used to be the father.

My son, who is nine years old, goes to a very progressive school. He dates his teachers.

Education is wonderful. It helps you worry about things all over the world.

Education is what a man gets when he sits in his living room with a group of teenagers.

Woody Allen says: "I had a terrible education. I attended a school for emotionally disturbed teachers."

Education is very important. A good education enables you to work for someone who has no education at all.

When better exams are made, they won't be passed.

"Whatcha been doing?" "Taking part in a guessing contest." "But I thought you had an exam in math." "I did."

———

PROFESSOR: Why the quotation marks all over this paper? STUDENT: Courtesy to the man on my right, professor.

———

"I would have passed my examination but for one thing." "What was that?" "The little boy who always sits in back of me was sick."

———

When school is out for the summer, the teachers are very happy to hand their Valium over to the parents.

———

"I spent $15,000 on my daughter's education," the businessman was complaining to his partner, "and she marries a bum who only makes $3,000 a year." "What are you complaining about?" the partner asked. "You're still getting 20 percent on your money."

———

I was a teacher in one of those progressive kindergarten schools. I didn't realize how progressive it really was until two of the kids got married last month.

———

One mother to another: "I never realized the value of education until the children went back to school."

A teacher is a person who used to think he liked children.

# Egotists

He's so conceited, he has his X-rays retouched.

———

He's carrying on a great love affair unassisted.

———

Zsa Zsa Gabor talking about her third husband, George Sanders: "When I was married to him, we were both in love with him. I fell out of love with him—but he didn't."

———

He likes you to come right out and say what you think—if you agree with him.

———

An egotist is a guy who tells you all the things about himself that you wanted to tell about yourself.

———

Muhammad Ali was explaining to me that he used to brag about being the greatest because it was good box office, and he was climbing and had to get attention. "Now," says the heavyweight champ, "I am not so show-offy. Don't misunderstand, I'm still the greatest, but I'm more modest about it."

———

I insist I am not conceited—although you realize, I have every right to be.

I'm afraid I'm unfaithful. I don't love myself as much as I should.

———

His head is getting too big for his toupee.

———

Every time he looks in the mirror he takes a bow.

———

Every time he opens the refrigerator and the light goes on, he takes a bow.

———

He's suffering from "I" strain.

———

He's a self-made man who adores his maker.

He's a guy who, when he reads a story and doesn't understand it, figures it must be a misprint.

———

When he hears a clap of thunder, he takes a bow.

———

I know I'm not the most handsome man in the world, but what's my opinion against millions of others?

———

"One of my chief regrets during my years in the theater is that I couldn't sit in the audience and watch me."—John Barrymore

———

Composer George Gershwin praised his mother by explaining, "She is so modest about me."

———

One columnist murdered a comic in his column without using his name. The comic threatened to sue. "But," his wife said, "he didn't mention your name." "That's it," he hollered, "nobody'll know it's me!"

———

He'll never change his religion. He thinks he's God.

———

Her body has gone to her head.

———

He has never said a kind word about anybody—that's because he only talks about himself.

———

Conceit is God's gift to little men.

———

The husband was primping in the mirror before leaving for his big speech. "I wonder how many great men there are in the world?" he mused. "One less than you think," said his wife.

———

He shaves in cold water because hot water steams up his mirror.

———

Every year on his birthday he sends his mother a telegram of congratulations.

---

The nicest thing about an egotist is, he never goes around talking about other people.

---

An egotist is a man who thinks he is everything you think you are.

---

I love people with big egos: To love oneself is the beginning of a lifelong romance.

---

He who falls in love with himself will have no rivals.

---

The only exercise egotists get is throwing bouquets at themselves.

---

The youngster gazed at his father's visitor, a man of large proportions, who looked like a whale in heat. "My boy, why are you looking at me like that?" the man asked. "Well, Daddy told Mother you were a self-made man." The guest said, "Right. I am a self-made man." "But," said the boy, "why did you make yourself like that?"

---

My brother-in-law claims, "At school, everybody hated me because I was so popular."

---

"I'm afraid I'm unfaithful," my aunt told me. "I don't love myself as much as I should."

---

My cousin says modestly, "They didn't give me looks, but they gave me an absolute monopoly on brains and talent." He doesn't want you to make a fuss about him—just to treat him as you would any other great man.

---

In an age when the fashion is to be in love with yourself, confessing to be in love with somebody else is an admission of unfaithfulness to one's beloved.

---

I haven't seen so much respect and admiration for one man since my brother stood alone in front of his three-way mirror.

---

People who think they know everything are very irritating to those of us who do.

---

A conceited person never gets anywhere because he thinks he is already there.

---

The reporter was passing along the river and heard sounds of someone struggling in the water. He recognized the man who was hollering, "Help! I'm drowning!" as a famous actor. The reporter said, "Geez, you're just too late to make the late-night edition. But don't worry. You'll have a nice headline all by yourself in the morning edition!"

---

"How's your new publicity agent?" I asked the actress. She said, "He's great. I've had him less than a month and already my house has caught fire once, I've been robbed twice, been in an auto accident, had three suicide notes from admirers, and now I've been threatened with kidnappers."

---

The opera star screamed on opening night: "What's with the ten bouquets of flowers?" The manager said, "They're wonderful." She yelled, "What's wonderful? I paid for fifteen!"

---

His girl adores him and so does he. I saw him at dinner and asked how he was coming along with his psychiatrist. He explained, "I used to be the most conceited, arrogant, egotistical, prideful person you ever saw, until I saw my shrink. Now you just couldn't meet a nicer, more humble guy than I am anywhere."

---

The newspapers carried a story about the nation's most beautiful actresses and the insignificant men they sometimes choose as husbands. My neighbor sighed. "I'll never be able to understand why the biggest shnooks always get the prettiest women," he said to his wife. "Why, dar-ling," she said, "what a very sweet compliment!"

---

My uncle never said an unkind word about anybody. That's because he never talks about anybody but himself.

## Egypt

This is a shaggy camel story: When the party got to Egypt midway on their world cruise, naturally the first wonder they decided to visit was the pyramids. Approaching a drive-it-yourself camel dealer, the tourists inquired how much it would cost to rent a camel. "That depends," the camel man said. "Do you want one lump or two?"

## Elections
*(see also Politics and Politicians, Presidents)*

The Britisher couldn't understand why we keep our bars closed on Election Day. "At home we keep the bars open," he said. "We figure nobody is going to vote for those candidates sober."

---

The sign in the voting booth in Moscow reads, "Vote Communist. The life you save may be your own."

---

To tell the truth, I do not believe in political jokes. Too many of them have been getting elected.

I never vote for the best candidate. I vote for the one who would do the least harm.

# Employment
*(see Bosses, Business, Labor, Office)*

"What's the big idea of hiring that cross-eyed man for a store detective?" "Well, look at him! Can you tell who he is watching?"

If at first you don't succeed, you're probably not related to the boss.

The four partners had a meeting about the stenographer who filled a sweater better than she did her job. "Which one of you took her out?" one of the partners asked. Three of them raised their hands, including himself. The man who didn't raise his hand was told, "Well, if you're telling the truth, *you* fire her."

The trusted employee had stolen half a million dollars over a period of years—and he was a relative to boot. When the big boss found out he fired him immediately. "I'm not going to put you in jail," he said. "I don't want a scandal—it would break your mother's heart, and it wouldn't help our firm either." The employee replied, "I admit I robbed you of a lot of loot, but I now have a big home, two cars, and every luxury I could want. I don't need a

thing. Why hire somebody else and have him start at the beginning?"

His idea was to get an employee who was not more than twenty years of age but with thirty years' experience.

He fired his secretary because of lack of experience. All she knew was typing, shorthand, and filing.

She failed the typing test but passed the physical.

She likes her job—lots of opportunities for advances.

She has a great future. She's really going places—with the boss.

The lady of the house reprimanded the maid: "Look at the dust on this desk," she said. "It must be at least two months old." "Then don't blame me, madam, I've only been here two weeks."

He gave the new maid the special list of dishes that his mother-in-law liked. "The first time you serve one of them," he said, "you're fired."

I just got a big television part—I'm gonna be scorekeeper on "Peyton Place."

———

"You never worked in a precision factory and you want two hundred a week?"

"Sure. The work is harder if you don't know how to do it."

———

My brother got a job as a lifeguard in a car wash.

———

My maid's idea of work is to sweep the room with a glance.

———

FIRST HOBO: I hate holidays. SECOND HOBO: Me, too. Makes you feel so common, when nobody ain't workin'!

———

The kid was playing hooky from school. The father told the kid to go out and get a job. The problem child decided to be a bookmaker in his neighborhood. Instead of money, he dealt in pebbles. One day another kid who was gambling with him came around with a big rock. "I better not take his bet," said the young bookmaker, "he must know something!"

———

The maid had been happily employed with the same family for ten years. One day the maid announced she was quitting because she was pregnant. The mistress said, "Rather than lose you, we'll adopt the child." A year later the maid again found herself "that way" and told her mistress, who again adopted the baby rather than lose her. This happened a third time. Help was hard to get, so the mistress again volunteered to adopt the child. And the maid said, "Oh, no, not me. I won't work for a family that has three children."

# Engagement
*(see also Courtship, Marriage)*

MARTHA: You know, you've been engaged to her a long time. Why don't you marry her? BOBBY: I've been thinking about it, but where would I spend my evenings if I did?

———

ED: So you broke your engagement to Evelyn. Why was that? BILL: Well, I was only doing to the engagement what it did to me.

———

RUSS: Are you engaged to marry Bob? NETTIE: Yes, I've promised to marry him as soon as he has made his fortune. RUSS: That isn't an engagement, that's an option.

———

If I had all the qualities you want in a man, I wouldn't be proposing to you.

———

When the two teenagers were turned down by the Marriage License Bureau, they asked, "Could you maybe give us a beginner's license?"

---

"The ring is nice," she said hesitatingly, "but it is small, darling." "So what?" he said. "After all, we are in love and you know the old saying 'Love is Blind.'" "Yes, but not *stone* blind."

---

"Be honest with me. Are you marrying my daughter for my money?" "To level with you, we're both taking a chance. How sure am I that you won't go broke in a couple of years?"

---

The period of engagement is like an exciting introduction to a dull book.

---

A man who had been going out with a young woman came to call on her one night carrying a little box in his pocket. At what he judged to be the right time, he pulled out the box, opened it, and showed his beloved an engagement ring with her name engraved inside. "I want you to be my wife," he said. "I don't know how to tell you this," she replied, "but I love another." "Tell me his name!" her suitor demanded. "No, no," cried the woman. "You're looking for a fight!" "I am not," shot back the man. "I just want to sell him this ring."

# England
*(see also British Humor)*

England is a country surrounded by hot water. But they always pull out of it.

---

Two lords were talking: "I hear they buried your wife." "Had to—dead, you know."

---

The English poet once was asked if he would teach his daughter several languages. "No," he replied. "One tongue is enough for any woman."

---

The English like to laugh at themselves: "It does get foggy here in London; in fact, I've been in only one city that was more foggy, but it was so foggy at the time, I couldn't see what city it was."

---

A young barrister was a candidate from a Lancashire town. "I'm very pleased to address a working-class constituency," he started. "It may interest you to know that I am a working man myself. In fact, I often work when you are asleep." A voice in the rear hollered, "You must be a blooming burglar."

---

"Ah, yes, my late wife was a most remarkable woman," the mild old Englishman told one of his cronies on a park bench in London. "A very religious woman," he continued. "Never missed a day in church, and at home it was prayers and psalm singing from morning to night." "How did she come to die?" the friend inquired. The Englishman replied, "I strangled her."

---

The elderly English couple had won a small fortune on the pools and were paying their first visit to the south of France. "Isn't this a beautiful place, dear?" asked the wife. "Glorious," agreed her husband. "Do you know, dear," he went on, "if anything happened to either of us, I'd like to spend the rest of my days here."

---

There's a university in England so conservative that it refuses to teach liberal arts courses.

---

A member of the faculty of a London medical college was chosen to be an honorary physician to the Queen. Proud of his appointment, he wrote a note on the blackboard in his classroom: "Beginning next month, I will be honorary physician to Queen Elizabeth." The next day when the professor returned to his classroom, he found the following line written below his notice: "God save the Queen."

---

A couple of GIs in Piccadilly were hoisting their third pint of bitters at a neighborhood pub when one nudged the other, saying, "Max, I think that highclassh, tony-lookin' gent hanging onto the bars stool there ish the Archbishop of Canterbury." "You're shtupid drunk," hicc'd the other, "What's the Archbishop of Canterbury gonna be doing here in a creepy bar guzzling beer?" "I'm drunk? I'm drunk?" yelled the first. "That'sh what I shaid. You're drunk." "Anyway, I say he's the Archbishop of Canterbury. You're crazy." Two pints of bitters later, Max reeled off his chair and teetered toward the high-class, tony-lookin' gent to see if he really was the Archbishop of Canterbury. When he asked the question, the man cursed him, his ancestors, his children, smacked him in the teeth, stepped on him, kicked him, told him to mind his own business and stalked out angrily. "Too bad," said Max, "now we'll never know."

---

After being injured in a cricket match (which wasn't cricket—it was crooked) the English sportsman went to a doctor, who put three stitches in his wound. "That'll be five pounds," the M.D. told him. "Five pounds?" howled the injured one, "for three stitches?" "That's right," smiled the doctor, "Boy," said the patient, "am I happy you're not my tailor."

---

After spending a year at Oxford, the son of an old English nobleman returned home for his summer vacation. "And now that you've spent a year at University, what did you find the hardest thing to deal with?" the old man asked. His son answered, "An old deck of cards."

————

A brilliant but homely English diplomat, sure he would land a position at the British Embassy in Washington, was heartbroken when he was nixed at zero hour. "I say, sir, but why was I turned down?" he asked his superior. "There's no doubt, Chauncey old man, that you're a whiz at foreign affairs," he was told, "but we cahn't possibly send anyone to Washington who doesn't look good before a TV camera."

————

A snobbish young Britisher who was so British he could barely talk visited Washington's home in Mount Vernon. He was promenading through the gardens when he spotted a hedge that looked like one he had back home in Stratfordshire on the Hertfordshire. "Ali, my good chap," he told the caretaker, "You see that hedge? George got that from jolly old England." "I don't doubt it," smiled the gardener. "As you probably know, he got this whole blooming country from England."

————

An American boasted to an Englishman about the speed of American trains. "In America," he bragged, "our trains are so fast that telegraph poles look like a continuous fence." "Ha," sniffed the Britisher, "that's nothing. I was on such a fast train in England last week that I passed a field of turnips, a field of carrots, one of cab-bage and then a pond. And we were going so fast that I thought it was broth.

————

BRITISH GUIDE (showing place of interest): It was in this room that Lord Wellington received his first commission. AMERICAN TOURIST: How much was it?

————

A man toddled into a London antique shop and offered for sale a piece of silk he claimed to be part of Sir Walter Raleigh's garment. The proprietor called his assistant: "Oh, Newton!" Newt shuffled forward, affixed his eyeglass, studied the silk, and wheezed, "It's Sir Walter's all right, but we have two yards of the same thing in our storeroom." Next day the man returned with a piece of the original ark, and again the owner called, "Oh, Newton!" and again Newt came forward, affixed his eyeglass, examined it, and said, "It's from the ark, but we have the rest of it in our storeroom." The following week the same man returned. He told the owner he had one of Nero's eyes and said, "And don't send for Newt. I have the other one in my pocket."

## Epitaphs
*(see also Cemeteries, Death)*

On a gravestone in the North of Scotland:

Dry up your tears and weep no more
I am not dead but gone before
Remember me and bear in mind
You have not long to stay behind.

———

From a Scottish graveyard:

Here lies I, Martin Elginbrodde
Have mercy o' my soul, Lord God,
As I wad do, were I Lord God,
And ye were Martin Elginbrodde.

———

Inscription on the tombstone of an old maid: And they say you can't take it with you. . . .

———

Here lies our Elvira Cohn: To virtue quite unknown, rejoice—be happy—have good cheer.
At last she sleeps alone.

———

If, after I depart this vale, you remember me and have some thought to please my ghost, forgive some sinner and wink your eye at some homely girl.—H. L. Mencken

———

Mrs. Billy Graham said if she had to select the words to be inscribed on her tombstone, she would borrow these from a road sign: END OF CONSTRUCTION—THANKS FOR YOUR PATIENCE.

———

Epitaph for a hippie: Don't dig me, man, I'm real gone.

———

Epitaph for a waiter: At last God caught his eye.

———

To a Husband from His Dear Wife: Rest in peace—till we meet again.

## Ethnic Humor

*I used to do a bit in vaudeville with five-time world boxing champ Tony Canzoneri. Tony explained that there are certain things you can't do in the ring anymore. "This you can't do." He demonstrated by putting his thumb in my eye. "And this is not allowed," he said as he hit me below the belt. "And, of course, you should never do this," he said as he kicked me in the shin. "And most important," he added, "no biting," which he demonstrated by taking a bite of my ear.*

*It's the same thing with ethnic humor. You use jokes like the following at your own risk. I record them here to show you the jokes, gags, and anecdotes that the ethnic groups are fighting.*

*Recently, New York State's Commissioner of Human Rights bemoaned the "alarming increase" in ethnic humor and warned that he was "prepared to proceed against offenders under the antidiscrimination law." Like my pal Canzoneri, I put these jokes here to warn you or alert you. If you insist on doing them at public gatherings, make sure you keep moving. Don't be a target.*

---

The unkempt Arab rug peddler was making his way down a Parisian boulevard trying to sell his wares. "Will you buy a carpet, monsieur?" he pleaded to a passing tourist. "No, no!" snapped the tourist, drawing back. "They stink!" The Arab drew himself up in proud indignation. "How dare you say that!" he cried. "I'll have you know, monsieur, that my carpets do not stink. It's me!"

---

How do you tell the bride at a Polish wedding? She's wearing something old, something new, something borrowed, something blue, something pink, something purple, something orange, something yellow . . .

---

"What is matched Puerto Rican luggage?" "Two shopping bags from the same store."

---

"How can you tell the difference between a Jew and an Italian?" "The Jew is the one in the Italian suit."

---

What is the difference between a Frenchwoman, an Englishwoman, and a Jewish woman's reaction when she is kissed in bed by her husband? The Frenchwoman says, "Oo la la, Pierre, your kisses are oo la la." The Englishwoman says, "Jolly well done. I say, Winston, your kisses are jolly well done!" The Jewish woman says, "You know, Sam, the ceiling needs painting."

---

They were hanging an Italian, a Jew, and a Pole. The Italian was first. The noose was loose and he slipped out, fell in the water, and swam away. The Jew was next. The noose was loose for him too, he slipped out, fell in the water, and swam away. The Pole cried out to the executioner, "Please tighten that noose—I can't swim!"

---

The little Jewish boy wanted to play with the Gentile kid next door. The Gentile kid said, "My father won't let me play with you because you're Jewish." The boy answered, "That's all right. We won't play for money."

---

The Catholic kid bragged to the Jewish kid, "My priest knows more than your rabbi!" The Jewish kid answered, "Sure, why not? You tell him everything."

---

The Scotsman, the Welshman, and the Englishman were left legacies by a friend on condition that each should put five pounds in his coffin. The Englishman put in a five-pound note. The Welshman put in a five-pound note, which he borrowed from the Englishman. The Scotsman took out the two five-pound notes and put in a check for fifteen pounds, payable to bearer. Three days later he was astonished to learn that the check had been presented and cashed. The undertaker was an Irishman.

---

The Irishman read so much about the evils of drinking that he gave up reading.

---

It all reminds me of my favorite story of the two pals having a gab session and one says, "Did you hear about the two Jews who got off a bus and one says to the other—"What is wrong with you?" interrupted his buddy. "Why must it always be two Jews? Two Jews, always we tell stories to abuse the Jews. They have enough trouble. Why don't you pick on some other nationality for a change?" "Okay," said his friend, "if that's how you feel about it. Two Chinamen got off the bus and one said to the other, 'Are you coming to my son's bar mitzvah?'"

---

"What would you call a six-foot-four Negro with a knife in his hand?" "Sir!"

---

"Why do Italians talk with their hands?" "Because they can't stand each other's breath."

---

Yom Kippur is the one day of the year when the Jewish people fast. Levy was surprised to see Cohen eating in a restaurant—and oysters yet! "Oysters? On Yom Kippur?" queried Levy with raised eyebrows. "What's wrong?" answered Cohen. "Yom Kippur has an 'r' in it."

---

Cross a Jew with a Pole—he's a janitor but he owns the building.

---

Sammy Davis, Jr., told the story of the Negro lad who goes to heaven and St. Peter stops him at the gate. "We only have heroes in here," says St. Peter. "But I'm a hero." "What heroic thing did you do?" "I was married to a white girl on the steps of Biloxi, Mississippi, City Hall at twelve noon!" "When did this happen?" "Two minutes ago!"

---

In Israel they have a slogan in the navy that goes: "Don't give up the ship—sell it."

---

How was the limbo invented? A Puerto Rican sneaking into a pay toilet.

---

Sammy Davis, Jr., says that years ago he got on a bus in the South and was told by the bigot driver to go sit in the back. "But I'm Jewish," Sammy protested. "Get off altogether!" shouted the driver.

---

The following lines were thrown by their own people, so don't holler:

Comedian Corbett Monica, Italian, says: "I'm trying to bring peace. I want the Italians and the Arabs to go to war. Nobody'll be hurt." He also says as soon as Italy heard that the Israelis were attacking Egypt, Italy surrendered.

———

One Polish man tells this one on the Poles. The couples insist on getting married in bathtubs because they want a double ring ceremony.

———

A Puerto Rican comedian whose name escapes me opens his show with: "I'm late because we had an accident at the house. Eight were hurt. The bed broke."

———

Show me a Jewish boy who doesn't go to medical school and I'll show you a lawyer.

———

Ahmed decides he needs a new brain, so he goes to the Cairo brain bank. The caretaker shows him the bottled brain of a German mathematician for $600. "Too expensive," Ahmed says. The caretaker leads him to the brain of an American nuclear physicist for $800. "Much too expensive," Ahmed replies. Finally the caretaker offers him the brain of an Egyptian general for $9,000. "Why should I pay that kind of money for the brain of an Egyptian general?" Ahmed protests. "But sir," the caretaker explains, "this brain has never been used."

———

Quoting humorist Irwin C. Watson: "I've been thinking that if I had to have a heart or a brain transplant and I was able to pick my donor, whose heart or brain would I want? And I decided I would want the heart or the brain of a bigot whether he be black or white— because I'd want a heart or brain that hasn't been used."

———

Fifty Puerto Ricans were arrested for sleeping in Central Park. They pleaded not guilty. Their defense was that they were having their room painted.

———

"Do you know what happened when the Ajax white knight came to Harlem?" "He was mugged."

———

A nymphomaniac is a Jewish girl who will go to bed with a guy after she's just had her hair done.

———

Did you hear about the new Italian university? It's called Whatsa Matta U.

———

How do you tell when an Irish patient is getting better? When he tries to blow the head off his medicine.

I knew a Southern bigot who happened to be a bed wetter. He used to go to his Klan meetings in rubber sheets.

———

How do you make a Hungarian cake? First you steal two eggs.

———

The missionary from good old England was trying to convert the Hindu to Christianity. "Tell me, wouldn't you like to go to heaven when you die?" The Hindu was not impressed. "Heaven can't be very good," he said, "or the British would have grabbed it years ago."

———

"Go with your sister?" the tourist said to the Mexican boy. "I won't even drink your water!"

———

What do 1776 and 1492 have in common? Give up? Adjoining rooms at the Poland Hilton.

———

Bob Considine tells the story about restaurateur Toots Shor, who learned to cope with problems early in life. As one of the few Jewish boys in a predominantly Catholic neighborhood in South Philadelphia, he found that his efforts to make friends with other kids were sometimes rebuffed—to the extent that they would chase him home like a pack of wolves closing in on a toothsome rabbit.

Toots learned to outwit them in a novel way. He discovered that by taking a shortcut through any Catholic church in his line of flight, he could gain a few yards and usually get home safely. "Those bums would have to genuflect when they passed the altar," Toots recalls, "and I didn't even break my stride."

———

Two black salesmen checked into a hotel in Georgia. One suggested they call room service and have them send up a couple of white broads. "Are you nuts?" the other screamed. "You gonna ask for white girls in Georgia?" "What's wrong? I want to love them—not go to school with them."

———

How do you keep a nice Jewish girl from having sex? Marry her.

———

Why does a Jewish wife close her eyes when having sex? She hates to see her husband having such a good time.

———

The British are the most diplomatic people in the world. Who else could smile at you when they serve you that coffee?

———

A Jew and a Christian were arguing about their heritage. The Jew said indignantly, "Why, when your ancestors were picking up acorns in the forest, mine already had diabetes."

A Catholic girl and a Jewish boy fell madly in love. But their religious beliefs interfered. The Irish Catholic mother advised her daughter to "sell him a bill of goods. Teach him the beauty and joys of Catholicism—make him be a Catholic." The girl did. She sold him and sold him, and the wedding date was set. One day before the marriage the girl came home and sobbed. "The marriage is off." "Why," said the mother, "didn't you sell him?" And the girl answered, "I sold him. . . . Now he wants to be a priest."

_____

An Israeli was bragging to his neighbor on the phone about Moishe Dayan. "The hell with Dayan," said the man. "Well," said the man from Tel Aviv, "how about Golda Meir, you got to admit that she's great." "The hell with Meir," he said. "Tell me—what nationality are you?" the Jewish gentleman asked quietly. "I'm Irish," he said proudly. "Then, the hell with Ella Fitzgerald," he said finally.

_____

It was a chip-in party—a reunion of old friends. The Englishman brought a cooked turkey; the Irishman brought a case of whiskey; the American brought a Virginia ham, and the Scotsman brought his brother.

_____

Ethnic humor is a vulgar caricature of a people that is put down here strictly as a comic history of a bygone era in comedy. Today it is rarely used, where once it was the rule of comedy. Even today, in the right hands and the right time and place, you could get killed.

_____

St. Patrick's is the day on which the Irish march up Fifth Avenue and stagger down Sixth Avenue.

_____

"What's an Irish seven-course dinner?" "A boiled potato and a six-pack of beer!"

_____

"How do you tell a bride at an Irish wedding?" "She's the one in the maternity dress."

_____

An Irishwoman who had reached the age of 102 was giving an interview about her longevity, when one of the reporters asked her if she had ever been bedridden. "Oh yis," she answered, "many times, me bye—and once on a sleigh."

_____

"Why is Santa Claus Polish?" "Who else would wear a red suit?"

_____

"Who has an IQ of 200?" "Poland."

_____

"What is a dope ring?" "Six Polacks sitting in a circle."

"What do you call removing a splinter from a Polack's behind?" "Brain surgery."

The Scotsman was awakened to find that his wife had died during the night. Frantically he called down to the maid, "Marta, boil only one egg for breakfast this morning."

"My Scottish boyfriend sent me this picture." "How does it look?" "I don't know. I haven't had it developed yet."

Tony opened his lunch box every day and found a peanut butter sandwich. Each day he threw it away hollering, "I no lika peanut butter sandwiches." After watching this for five days in a row, his co-worker asked, "If you no lika peanut butter sandwich, why you no tell your wife no make you peanut butter sandwich?" "What wife?" Tony screamed. "I make my own sandwiches."

"Was I brought here to die?" he asked when he opened his eyes in the hospital. "No," answered the Australian, "you were brought here yester-die."

The Irishman was really loaded. "Don't you know drinking shortens a man's life?" his doctor told him. "Yes," he hicc'd, "but he sees twice as much in the same length of time."

The Scotsman celebrated New Year's Eve with his wife. They got themselves drunk by going around in a revolving door all night.

"I wish you'd get something for that cough o' yours," the Englishman barked. "That's the second time you've blown out the bloomin' candle."

Tonto and the Lone Ranger were surrounded by Indians when the Lone Ranger turned to Tonto and said, "We're in trouble, Tonto." To which Tonto replied, "You mean *you're* in trouble, white man."

Comic great Dick Gregory says there is nothing to the rumor that Georgia is passing a law banning mixed drinks. "I'll say this about living in an all-white suburb," says Dick. "Crabgrass is not our biggest problem."

Two women met at Grossinger's: "What happened with your sons?" one asked. "Morris is in the dress business," she said. "He makes a fortune. Sends me the whole winter to Florida, gives me two hundred dollars a week just for spending money. A millionaire, that boy." "And Irving?" "He became a rabbi. By me that's not a business for a Jew."

When John married Theresa, they moved into a brand-new old flat in Harlem. The first pieces of furniture the husband brought home were a sewing machine and a full-length mirror. "What's all that junk?" the wife asked. Said the husband, "That's no junk. You take your choice. You take the sewing machine and go to work, or you take the mirror and sit down and watch yourself starve."

———

TEACHER: Now, children, I want you to write your name in your primers. ABE: Are you kidding? That will kill the resale value.

———

"How can you tell an Italian movie star from an American movie star?" "She's the one with the mustache."

———

"Who put the twenty-two bullet holes in Mussolini?" "Five thousand Italian sharpshooters."

———

You can always tell when you're passing a Scotsman's house—no garbage cans.

———

I don't believe the one about the young Scot who murdered his parents so he could go to the orphans' picnic.

———

"What happens to garbage in Italian restaurants?" "They serve it in Spanish restaurants!"

———

One thing you never heard of is a Puerto Rican suicide. You can't kill yourself jumping out of a basement window.

———

The Englishman laughs at a joke three times. Once when he hears it, once when it is explained to him, and once when he understands it.

## Etiquette

Etiquette is learning to yawn with your mouth shut.

———

Etiquette is knowing which finger to use when you whistle for the waiter.

———

Etiquette is the noise you don't make when you eat soup.

———

The well-bred man steps on the cigarette so it won't burn the rug.

———

Every time she throws a cup at her husband, she takes out the spoon.

———

He had the manners of a gentleman. I knew they didn't belong to him.

There is no man so bad that a woman cannot make him worse.

———

"Is my face clean enough to eat with?" "Yes, but you'd better use your hands."

———

Social tact is making your company feel at home, even though they wish they were.

———

"He's just bashful. Why don't you give him a little encouragement?" "Encouragement? He needs a cheering section!"

———

He eats with his fingers and talks with his fork.

———

He died an unhappy death. He was afraid his last breath would be a hiccough, and he wouldn't be able to say, "Excuse me."

———

"Do you know what to do with crumbs at the table?" "Sure, let them stay there."

———

"What is the first thing you do when you get up from the table?" "I put on my shoes."

———

"You know, I think there's something wrong with my boss's eyes." "How's that?" "When I went into his office this morning, he asked me three times where my hat was—and it was on my head all the time."

———

"Stop! Act like a gentleman." "Sorry, but I don't do imitations."

———

"This man is following me around, and he's been doing that for fifteen minutes. Tell him to stop."
"Don't be silly. That's the butler and he's trying to serve you cocktails."

———

"When I sneeze I put my hand in front of my mouth." "Really, Phil? Why do you do that?"
"To catch my teeth!"

———

My boyfriend is so polite, he always knocks on the oyster shells before he opens them.

———

Another thing: The next time you butter your bread, when you finish buttering it, don't fold it and then eat it.

———

He embarrassed us. He drank his soup and six couples got up and danced.

———

"When you yawn, you put your hand to your mouth." "What? And get bitten?"

She's very proper. She won't even look at things with a naked eye.

---

# Exaggerations

"Those Kansas cyclones must be terrible." "G'wan, down in Florida the wind was so strong it blew out the fuses."

---

Two men met at a race track and started a conversation.

"I've got a horse that's faster than any automobile."

"Faster than any automobile? Who was he sired by?"

"What do you mean?"

"What was his father's name?"

"I told you he was fast. Why, he is so fast, he ran away before he found out what his father's name was."

---

He's the fastest person imaginable. He can ring the front doorbell, go to the back door, and run through to the front of the house in time to let himself in.

# Executives

*(see also Bosses, Business, Employment, Office)*

He is so dedicated to his work that he keeps his secretary near his bed in case he gets an idea during the night.

---

A good executive is a man who believes in sharing the credit with the man who did the work.

---

An executive came home one night and slumped unhappily into his favorite chair. Noticing his state, his wife asked what was wrong. "Well," he moaned, "you know those aptitude tests I'm giving over at the office? I took one today and it sure is a good thing I own the company."

---

A good executive never puts off for tomorrow what he can get you to do today.

---

He's a perfect executive. When he's dictating to his secretary, he always ends a sentence with a proposition.

---

The big executive wolf had been chasing his secretary for weeks. "Tonight's the night," he warned her, "we go to my apartment." "I'm very didactic and pithy in my refusal of your derogatory, vituperative, and vitriolic proposition," she replied. "I don't get it," the big shot said. "That's what I've been trying to tell you!" she answered.

---

He doesn't believe in wasting time with secretaries. He uses the old saying, "If at first you don't succeed—fire her."

I hired a gorgeous secretary but I had to let her go. She came in the office one day and I told her to sit down and the silly girl looked for a chair.

Executive ability is convincing your wife you hired your pretty secretary for her ability.

"I have so many problems," said a corporate executive, "that if anything happens today, it'll be two weeks before I can worry about it."

# Exercise

Exercise kills germs, but we can't figure out how to make the damn things exercise.

A couple noticed that they weren't feeling as perky as they should, so they decided to consult a doctor. The doctor examined them and, finding nothing organically wrong, advised them to get more exercise. So the husband went out and bought himself a set of golf clubs, and a lawn mower for his wife.

Who knows from exercise? I get winded twisting the cap off the toothpaste.

The only exercise I get is putting my cuff links in my shirt.

When I feel like exercising, I lie down until the feeling goes away.

Running is when you use every muscle in your body. Incidentally, there are no muscles in the brain.

Running isn't as simple as it looks. Your feet have to control your stride; your feet have to control your balance. You might say, if you run ten miles a day, you've gotta have your brains in your feet.

The sheik hired a track star to run from the palace to his harem, about three miles away, to fetch one of his wives whenever he was in the mood. This happened three or four times a day. The sheik would nod and the track star would take off. This arrangement went on until the runner died at age thirty-six. The sheik lived to be ninety-six. The moral of the story is, sex doesn't kill you, it's the running after it that does.

The average executive will jog ten minutes for exercise and then take the elevator up to the second floor.

Joggers aren't very friendly. They pant rather than speak. My secretary says, "Jogging suits are really necessary for running. Otherwise you just look like you're late."

———◦◦◦◦———

When I was a kid, my only outdoor activity was chasing the Good Humor truck down the street. When I grew up I got my exercise hailing taxis. Now I take a cab to the Good Humor man.

———◦◦◦◦———

My neighbor's wife is a fitness fanatic who insists on teaching him some special exercises for every part of his body: To exercise his fingers, for example, she keeps making him take out his credit cards.

———◦◦◦◦———

"Why are you lying down? Are you tired?" "I'm lying down so I don't get tired."

———◦◦◦◦———

Actor-comedian George Wendt said it: "I get my exercise acting as a pallbearer for my friends who exercise."

———◦◦◦◦———

I get digital aerobics turning on the TV with the remote.

———◦◦◦◦———

"I get plenty of exercise," said the great Jackie Gleason. "Immediately after waking I always say sternly to myself, 'Ready, now. Up. Down. Up. Down.' And after three strenuous minutes I tell myself, 'Okay, boy. Now we'll try the other eyelid.'"

## Eyes
*(see also Ears, Faces)*

The height of embarrassment: Looking through a keyhole—and seeing another eye.

———◦◦◦◦———

My eyes were never any good—and I got a wife to prove it.

———◦◦◦◦———

He had bad eyesight until he was sixteen—and then he got a haircut.

———◦◦◦◦———

I lost my glasses and I can't look for them until I find them.

———◦◦◦◦———

I knew I needed glasses when I walked into the closet and said, "Down."

———◦◦◦◦———

I knew I needed glasses when I passed my wife and said, "Good evening, sir."

———◦◦◦◦———

It was so windy in Chicago, I spit in my own eye.

———

She had something that would knock your eye out—a husband.

———

"Do you close your eyes when you kiss?" "No, I have to be on the lookout for my husband."

———

I like to live in a small town. I don't have to keep an eye out for my wife—the neighbors do it for me.

———

Let's wash the windows, Mother. The neighbors are straining their eyes.

———

I'm not saying she's cockeyed, but she can look at a tennis match without moving her head.

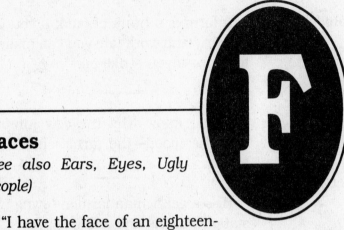

## Faces
*(see also Ears, Eyes, Ugly People)*

"I have the face of an eighteen-year-old." "Well, give it back—you're getting it all wrinkled!"

———

Is that your face or are you celebrating Halloween?

———

The last time I saw a face like that was on an iodine bottle.

———

She had a face like a flower—cauliflower.

———

She had a winning smile—too bad she had a losing face.

———

The only time her face gets washed is when she cries.

———

A man falls in love with a beautiful face and then makes the mistake of marrying the whole girl.

———

He has such a long face, the barber charges him twice for shaving.

———

She had an Early American face: She looked like George Washington.

———

Some girls have dishpan hands. She's got dishpan face.

———

She looks like a million—but nobody can be that old.

## Family
*(see also Babies, Children, Kids, Juvenile Delinquents, Marriage)*

Every family should have three children; if one turns out to be a genius, the other two can support him.

———

When I was six my family moved—but I found them again.

———

Her family was so exclusive, they didn't come over on the *Mayflower*, they had their own boat.

He didn't come from a good family—he was sent.

————

Our family had more trouble than a soap opera.

————

A family man is one who has replaced the money in his wallet with snapshots of the wife and kids.

————

She comes from such an old family, it's been condemned.

————

Actress Molly Picon tells about her childhood: "My grandmother raised eleven children in four rooms in Philadelphia." "How did she manage?" she was asked. "Easy. She took in boarders."

————

I came from a family of ten kids. I used to come home late so I could sleep on top.

————

Someone once asked my mother if everybody in our family suffered from insanity. She said, "No. We all enjoyed it."

## Farming

A farmer had such a pretty wife that he couldn't keep his hands off her, so he fired the hands and bought a tractor.

————

A farm is a hunk of land; if you get up early and work late you can make a fortune—if you strike oil.

————

Now I know why the cow jumped over the moon—the farmer had cold hands.

————

He's a gentleman farmer—owns two station wagons and a flower pot.

————

She was only a farmer's daughter, but she tried every salesman's samples.

————

"I heard you shot twelve ducks. Were they wild?"
"No, but the farmer was."

————

CUSTOMER: Is this milk fresh? FARMER: Fresh? Three hours ago it was grass.

————

SUE: My uncle can't decide whether to get a new cow or a bicycle for his farm. JOHN: He'd certainly look silly riding around on a cow. SUE: Yes, but he would look a lot sillier milking a bicycle.

————

"Why is this milk so blue?" "Because it comes from discontented cows."

————

"Name five things that contain milk." "That's easy. Ice cream, butter, cheese, and two cows."

# Fashion

*(see also Clothing, Dress)*

I like the suit you're wearing. Who shines it for you?

———

His suit looks like a million—all wrinkled and green.

———

I like your suit so much—like it was cut from an old sofa.

———

He rides the subway just to get his suit pressed.

———

My new blue serge suit picks up everything but women.

———

He looks like a torn page out of *Esquire.*

———

You like my suit? Very reasonable. Only two payments and a change of address.

———

My raincoat has a waterproof label; the label is waterproof—but not the coat.

———

"Who made her dress?" "The police."

———

"The suit fits you like a glove." "I wish it could fit like a suit."

———

It's terrible to see men looking like girls with their long hair and all. You can't tell the difference. I was sitting in a restaurant when a girl came in. I turned to the person at the next table and said, "Isn't it terrible how boys look like girls these days?" "That's my son," she said to the girl I was pointing at. "Oh, I'm sorry, I didn't know you were the mother," I said. "I'm not," my neighbor said indignantly. "I'm the father."

———

"How do you get into those tight pants?" "Very carefully."

———

Blue serge suits are very handy—for removing dandruff from your hair.

———

She's been married so many times, the wedding dress is her native costume.

———

A wise man never laughs at his wife's old clothes.

———

Gals who buy sweaters: "The right size is the tight size."

———

I gave her a three-piece sweater set for Christmas: two needles and a ball of wool.

———

Some women show a lot of style and some styles show a lot of women.

———

They say long dresses pick up germs. You should see what those short dresses pick up.

———

She always wears a play suit—but she means business.

———

If her dress were any shorter, it would be a collar.

———

Fashion note: Women will be wearing the same thing in brassieres this year.

———

Women's dresses keep going higher and higher; you wonder what they'll be up to next.

———

There are two types of sweater girls: the type that knits them—and the type that fits them.

———

"This dress is a little too long for me. Do you have anything shorter?" "Try the belt department!"

———

A new fur coat will do a lot for a girl and a girl will do a lot for a new fur coat.

———

There are millions of reasons why women dress the way they do—and all of them are men.

———

When the wife wears the pants, some other woman wears the fur coat.

———

The only thing getting longer in women's clothes—are the shoulder straps.

———

She talked him into buying her a new dress—then he tried to talk her out of it.

———

All a sweater does for her is make her itch.

———

Pajamas are great on a honeymoon—in case of fire.

———

Her dress kept everybody warm but her.

———

A woman's dress should be like a barbed-wire fence: serve its purpose without obstructing the view.

———

"This piece of lace on my dress is sixty years old!" "Beautiful. Did you make it yourself?"

Some of the bathing suits look like they haven't been delivered yet.

———◆———

She looks like she was poured into that dress—but forgot to say "when."

———◆———

Either her dress is too short—or she's in too far.

———◆———

If that dress she's wearing was cut any lower, she'd be barefoot.

———◆———

Actress Gina Lollobrigida doesn't like miniskirts. "It is better for men to discover," she says, "than for women to reveal."

———◆———

"I want a pair of shoes with low heels." "To go with what?" "A short, fat, bald millionaire."

———◆———

If women dressed to please their husbands, they'd wear last year's clothes.

———◆———

With those new miniskirts, and low-cut dresses, I don't know if she's trying to catch a man or a cold.

———◆———

Nobody asks her to remove her hat at the movies—it's funnier than any picture.

The latest in women's fashions are dresses made of newspaper. Can you imagine a man arrested as a masher just because he wanted to read the fine print?

———◆———

Comedian Fred Allen commented on a woman's hat: "There's a creation that will never go out of style—it will just look ridiculous year after year."

———◆———

Those stretch ski pants the girls are wearing this season come in three sizes: small, medium, and don't bend over.

———◆———

Your dress should be tight enough to show you're a woman and loose enough to show you're a lady.

———◆———

To women who wear slacks: "Does your end justify your jeans?"

———◆———

Those new paper dresses will be used to wrap some very nice packages.

———◆———

I think the fashion world is taking this designer label business a little too far: Would you believe Calvin Klein nasal spray? Gloria Vanderbilt designer aspirin tablets? Yves Saint Laurent arch supports? A truss with an alligator on it? Milk of Magnesia in a Halston designer Lalique bottle? Givenchy underarm spray? How about Ex-Lax by Gucci?

The fashion world is going way out this year. One clever Seventh Avenue dress designer is doing big business with a line of teenage maternity fashions in school colors. Just last week a big department store ran a full-page ad with the headline: MATERNITY DRESSES FOR THE MODERN MISS.

———

Everybody is dying their hair: One woman dyed it so many times, she has plaid dandruff.

———

A hooker had a little accident in Hollywood: She fell off her seven-inch platform shoes. She would have been injured, but her eyelashes broke the fall.

———

We've had slit skirts; now, how about something more practical—split jeans?

———

Slits in women's skirts now come in three different lengths: high, higher, and "not guilty, Your Honor."

———

With the dresses today, if a girl has to have her appendix taken out and she doesn't want it to show, they'll have to remove it through her nose.

———

My aunt explained why she finally decided to wear the mini: "If you're going to look ugly, you might as well look this year's ugly."

My niece told me, "I wore a see-through dress, but nobody wanted to."

———

My neighbor says, "I hope jodhpurs come back. They're the only pants that go out in the same place I do."

———

This year the newest thing in women's hairdos are men.

———

My neighbor went into a clothing store and the salesman showed him one suit for $1,200. He said it was made from virgin wool. My friend said, "That's nice, but I'd rather see something for about $200 from a sheep who fooled around a little!"

———

My wife says I've got to start dressing better: "It's embarrassing to have people drop coins in your coffee cup."

———

The annual best dressed list is upon us again. My friends are all excited: They want to know what to wear on the unemployment line.

———

Fashion is so important in this country, the president's wife just ordered a submarine to the coast of France to spy on the new spring line.

———

These days you can't judge a girl by the clothes she wears. There's not enough evidence.

———◦◦◦◦———

I sat at a dinner table with a girl last night whose dress was cut so low that I had to look under the table to see what she was wearing.

———◦◦◦◦———

This season, gowns that are in leave most of the wearer out!

———◦◦◦◦———

The most attractive thing about the latest fashions for women is that they won't last.

———◦◦◦◦———

Fashion is a personal thing. My sister is the only girl I know who wears prescription underwear.

———◦◦◦◦———

Designer jeans are great if you don't care about blood pressure below the waist.

———◦◦◦◦———

You can always tell a widow in Beverly Hills: She wears a black tennis outfit.

———◦◦◦◦———

I can't understand why women want to show their knees. Whoever said wrinkles were sexy?

———◦◦◦◦———

The credo of today's fashion is: If it's comfortable, forget it. A lady was hav-ing trouble with her new shoes at a fashionable salon. "They're not comfortable," she said. "I just can't walk in these shoes." "Madam," said the manager, "people who have to walk don't buy their shoes here."

———◦◦◦◦———

One fashion-conscious lady tried on a dress at a posh boutique and cooed, "It's very nice—but it's a lot less than I wanted to spend."

———◦◦◦◦———

No wonder they call it high fashion: Take a look at the price tags.

———◦◦◦◦———

Designer jeans prices are ridiculous. If I spend $150 for a pair of jeans, I expect a woman to be in them.

———◦◦◦◦———

The good news is, we're living in a time when millions of Americans are finally beginning to turn the other cheek. The bad news is, it's to show the designer label on their jeans.

———◦◦◦◦———

One model told the clerk, "I don't care about the style or color of shoes, but I want low heels." He asked, "To wear with what?" She said, "A short, plump, elderly millionaire. "

———◦◦◦◦———

The fashion maven was explaining why women's boxing never caught on:

"Did you ever hear of a woman putting on gloves without shoes and purse to match?"

———

A designer tells me women's clothes are getting more masculine and men's clothes are getting more feminine. Pretty soon you'll be able to save a fortune by marrying someone your own size.

———

My neighbor's wife always wants to buy a new outfit every time she's invited out. My neighbor thought he'd play a gag and accepted an invite to a nudist wedding. The gag was on him: She spent $3,000 on a body lift.

———

It's bikini time on the beaches. "I saw some of those new fashions," my sister notes. "I have earrings that cover more than that." Those bathing suits are really getting brief: I've seen more cotton in the top of an aspirin bottle. In fact, this year's bikini gives about as much coverage as a lapsed insurance policy.

———

My tailor made up six suits for the rock star for $18,000. That's not much, considering that the price includes batteries.

## Fathers

Father's Day is the day when father goes broke giving his family money so they can surprise him with gifts he doesn't need.

Father's Day and Mother's Day are alike, except that on Father's Day you buy a much cheaper gift.

———

I don't know why, but Father's Day never seems to grow up. It's like Mother's Day after taxes.

———

A father is a banker provided by nature.

———

My neighbor told me, "Every year my wife gives me the same present on Father's Day: a list of presents she wants for her birthday. This year my son gave me something I always wanted: the keys to my car."

———

I have good news and bad news. The good news is, the kids all got together and sent me a check for $100 made out to cash. The bad news is, they asked me to sign it and send it back.

———

My father told me about the birds and bees—he didn't know anything about girls.

———

My uncle is always unhappy on Father's Day because he never had any children to celebrate it with him. "Weren't you happy at home?" I asked him. He said, "Oh, sure. My wife laughs at everything I do—that's why we have no children."

DAD: The man who marries my daughter will need a lot of money. SUITOR: I'm just the man, then.

———

FATHER: You're getting too old to play with the boys. DAUGHTER (innocently): I don't have to anymore, father.

———

FATHER (to daughter's boyfriend): Remember, young man, the lights are put out in this house at eleven o'clock. BOYFRIEND: That's okay by me, sir.

———

FATHER: My son, I am a self-made man. SON: Pop, there's one thing I like about you. You always take the blame for everything.

———

"Who says that all men are born free?" wailed the young father as he received the doctor's bill.

———

"Mary, is that young man there yet?" "No, Father, but he's getting there."

———

My uncle is a little naive: He thinks a paternity suit is something you wear when your wife is pregnant.

———

The man who says he runs things around the house is probably referring to the lawnmower, the vacuum cleaner, and the washing machine.

———

That father of five children had won a toy at a raffle. When he got home, he called the kids together and asked, "Who should have this present? Who is most obedient? Who never talks back to your mother? Who does everything she says?" Five small voices answered in unison, "You can have it, Daddy."

———

Father admits he would never be what he is today without his family—BUSTED.

———

Father: The person who can't get into the bathroom, on the phone, or out of the house.

———

Every year my mom gave my dad the perfect Father's Day gift: She sent us kids to summer camp for two weeks.

———

My friend said, "I knew Father's Day was coming up when my daughter asked me what size cologne I wear."

———

Every father thinks he is the master of his home—but mostly he is the paymaster.

———

On Father's Day give Dad money—it's the one thing you can be sure he doesn't have.

———

Hollywood kids always have a problem on Father's Day. It's not so much a question of what to buy, it's who to give it to.

My brother-in-law the drunk told me the most embarrassing thing happened to him one Father's Day: "My wife had a scotch on the rocks as a nightcap, then went up to kiss Junior good-night. The kid opened his eyes and said, 'Mommy, you're wearing Daddy's perfume!'"

Last Father's Day was really something. I got up early and called my dad long distance. I wished him a happy Father's Day, and then we stayed on the phone for about an hour, reminiscing about my childhood and the great times we had together. Then, when we were ready to hang up, my father said six words that I'll never forget for as long as I live. He said, "By the way, who is this?"

# Gambling

They say that every election is a gamble, which is ridiculous. When you gamble, at least you have a chance to win.

—※—

I love to gamble, but I just can't throw my money around on gambling and drinking and women. I've got a government to support.

—※—

I just heard a touching story: There's a bookie down the street who changed his name to Red Cross just so his customers' losses would be tax deductible.

—※—

Atlantic City is now mad for gambling. My brother pulled into a parking space at one hotel and dropped a quarter in the meter. Three little wheels spun around, and he lost his Chrysler.

—※—

I was lucky in Atlantic City—I got a ride home. I just hope they have more luck with my money than I did.

—※—

Las Vegas: Now there's a town for my money. They've got some pretty classy hotels there. You have to wear a tie to lose your shirt.

In Vegas you can't beat the climate, the people, the food—or the slot machines.

—※—

I go to Atlantic City once a month to visit my money—and leave a little interest. Money isn't everything, but if you stay there long enough, it's nothing.

—※—

My neighbor put four kids through college. Unfortunately, they were his bookmaker's kids.

—※—

I'd probably do more gambling if I had a better bookie. The one I've got now had me bet on Harold Stassen in five elections.

—※—

When I do gamble I like to play the horses, but before I bet I always talk to people who know horse flesh—trainers, jockeys, my butcher.

—※—

At the track, I met my very dejected uncle, who was tearing up his stubs. "Why so sad?" I asked. "I've got reason to be sad," he lamented. "I came here today with enough money to choke a horse, but I made a terrible mistake." I asked, "What was that?" He said, "I didn't choke him—I bet on him."

———————

When you enter Nevada, they have big signs that say: KEEP NEVADA GREEN—LOSE!

———————

Gambling is a sure way to get nothing for something! I learned how to make a small fortune in Atlantic City: Go there with a big one.

———————

They now have five-dollar slot machines. They're for the man who has everything—but not for long.

———————

Most hotels have signs in the rooms that say: HAVE YOU LEFT ANYTHING? In Atlantic City the signs say: HAVE YOU ANYTHING LEFT?

———————

Gambling has done wonders for Atlantic City: It's the first time I saw slot machines that take welfare checks.

———————

A lot of people are planning to spend their vacations in Atlantic City. Which is appropriate. A vacation is where you get away from it all—all your money, your savings, your stocks.

———————

Atlantic City is jumping. I walked away from an Atlantic City laundry machine for five minutes, and somebody won my wash.

———————

The trouble with hitting the jackpot on a slot machine is that it takes so long to put the money back in.

———————

I'm going back to Atlantic City this weekend. I hope I break even. I need the money.

———————

My neighbor told me, "Gambling brought my family closer together: I lost all my money and we had to move into one room."

———————

The only way to win at blackjack is to use a real blackjack.

———————

They even have slot machines in the men's room in Las Vegas. If you don't win, you don't go.

———————

I went into a drugstore and asked for some aspirin. The clerk said, "I'll toss you double or nothing." I ended up with two headaches.

———————

Everybody in Las Vegas has a system to beat the system. I asked one maven, "What do I do? One day I lose, one day I win." He said, "Jerk, play every other day."

———————

In Vegas, even the houses of worship are a game of chance. At one church on the strip, the priest calls the bingo numbers in Latin so the atheists can't win.

———

Gamblers are nice people. I have a friend who always observes Be Kind to Animals week: All the money he earns he gives to the horses.

———

Drinking and gambling are a powerful parlay in Nevada: "But we have it under control," one friend told me. "Monday night, at my Gamblers Anonymous meeting, we all get drunk. Then Tuesday night, at Alcoholics Anonymous, we have an all-night poker game."

———

One loser approached me and said, "I know, I know, I owe you $300." I said, "It's only $200." He said, "It's gonna be $300."

———

It is estimated that Americans spend over $7 billion a year on games of chance alone—and that doesn't include weddings.

———

Gambling in Las Vegas or Atlantic City is a little ridiculous. You take your money out of the bank and pay your own transportation to bring it to them.

———

In Reno, you can get rid of your wife and your money at the same time.

———

My uncle is a loser. He pumped $150 into the first machine he saw and never won a nickel. He *did* win 100 packs of cigarettes.

———

It was their first time in Vegas, and the elderly couple couldn't wait to try it all. They pulled slot machines and played bingo, craps, roulette, blackjack with all kinds of exuberance. After each thrilling excursion, they returned to their rooms to recuperate and count their losses. The fourth night, the husband said, "Honey, I'm too tired to go again. Let's just send them a check."

———

Las Vegas has had a steady increase in population since the 1960s. This is because half of the people who visit there can't afford to leave.

———

Vegas is the type of town where celebrating a blessed event is getting three sevens on the slot machines.

———

My brother had a rough weekend in Atlantic City: "I went for $600 at the tables—and that was just the dinner tables." Remember when people went to Atlantic City to get tanned—instead of faded?

———

My neighbor groans he hasn't been having much luck playing the horses: "Yesterday the nag I bet a bundle on ended up in a photo finish with the truck that waters the track."

———

Gambling is basically a foolish vice. It's kind of like diving into an empty swimming pool! The chances that you'll hit bottom are about the same.

———

A man once saw a priest blessing a horse at Aqueduct, which convinced him to bet a bundle on the nag. When the horse ran out of the money, he remarked to the priest, "Father, it looks like a blessing doesn't work at the track." The priest replied: "My son, I wasn't blessing that horse, I was giving him last rites."

———

Las Vegas has the only hotels in the world where if you call down for room service, they send up three slot machines and a change maker.

———

My sister suggests: "The best way to prevent your husband from gambling is for you to spend it first."

———

I know a guy who only made mental bets. He lost his mind.

———

Atlantic City has one major advantage for New Yorkers over Las Vegas. You don't have to go so far to lose your money, and you can hitchhike home.

———

You've heard about the war on poverty? Vegas is where you go to surrender.

———

My neighbor told me, "The last time I was in Las Vegas I lost my car, my watch, and my money. I lost everything but my good-luck charm."

———

This big gambler made his way to the blackjack tables every night and left his wife in the room. One night, while in the middle of a hot game, the bellboy hissed in his ear, "Mr. Davis, your wife is upstairs making love to your friend." The man yelled at the dealer, "Hurry up with this deal. This is positively my last hand."

———

The last time I was in Atlantic City, I was approached by a frantic-looking stranger who asked, "Can you let me have twenty-five dollars? I've got no place to sleep and I haven't eaten for two days." I said, "How do I know you're not going to take the money and gamble with it?" The guy said, "No way. Gambling money—I've got."

———

Bernie explained, "Don't misunderstand, I have enough money to gamble with. Now if I could only borrow some to live on."

———

Everybody advises, "Don't gamble unless you can afford to lose." But if you can afford to lose, why gamble?

———

I actually overheard one New Yorker standing next to a slot machine with his eyes upward mumbling, "Please, if you're listening, God, I know you don't approve of gambling, but just this once, let me break even."

———

Please let it be known that I am dead set against gambling. I'll bet two to one they'll never legalize it in New York.

———

Casinos have every known game of chance to remove you from your money: Keno, craps, poker, bingo, blackjack, slot machines, roulette. One seventy-year-old gambler said to his wife, "Enough already, let's go upstairs and make love." She said, "I don't like the odds."

———

You want to get away from it all? Go to Atlantic City. There they get it all away from *you*.

———

Gambling has done a lot for Vegas's economy. It's the only place in the world where a roulette table takes Social Security checks.

———

At the deli at Resorts International, I asked for a hot roll, they brought me fresh dice.

———

At the bar, one sad gambler sat next to Jack Davis, the president of Resorts: "I've been playing craps for a whole month without a winner," he complained. Jack asked, "Then why don't you stay away from the tables?" The guy growled, "Are you nuts? And give up twenty years of experience as a crapshooter?"

———

There's a sign at Trump's Taj Mahal that says, "We'll give you 8 to 5 you enjoy your stay."

———

I really had a swinging time in Atlantic City. Roulette, blackjack, craps—shows you what you can do with an old bank account if you're handy.

———

The Trump Hotel is really elegant. The waiters, waitresses, busboys all look so important. Why not? Last week they were customers. . . . Last week's pit boss is this week's pastry chef. He changed jobs when they caught his hands rolling the dough.

"I'm positively through with gambling forever." "Forever? I don't believe it." "Is that so? I'll bet you five dollars I'll quit."

---

"Let's go and play some poker." "No, thank you. I don't play the game." "I was under the impression you played poker." "I was under that impression myself once!"

---

Two guys were arguing. Said the first guy, "You don't even know where you are! I'll wager you twenty dollars you're not even here, and I'll prove it." Said the second guy, "All right, go ahead." "You're not in St. Louis?" "No, I'm not in St. Louis." "And you're not in Chicago?" "No, I'm not in Chicago." "Well, if you're not in St. Louis or Chicago, you must be someplace else, and if you're someplace else you can't be here." Suddenly the second guy snatches the money. The first guy said, "I didn't lose! Give me back my money." "Whaddaya mean?" "You took the money right out of my hand." "I did not." "You did." "Listen, you said I wasn't here, I was someplace else. And if I was someplace else I couldn't have been here."

## Gardening

She was only a gardener's daughter—but she was potted all the time.

---

He was a good tree doctor, even if his bedside manner was a bit wooden.

---

A green thumb? She bought a hanging fern and the rope died!

---

He planted a rock garden and by the next morning two of them were dead.

---

I tried my hand at gardening once, but it all looked like something out of Peter Pan: It never grew up. Gardening doesn't run in my family either. The first time I saw pictures of the surface of the moon, I thought it was my brother's backyard.

---

His idea of science fiction is *Better Homes & Gardens*.

---

If you give a weed and inch, it will take a yard.

---

What do you get when you cross a rambling rose with a pansy? A flower that smells sweet, wears too much color, and skips.

---

A weed is a plant with nine lives.

---

Gardening is truly getting down to earth.

Money may not grow on trees, but let me tell you, trees grow on money!

———

I don't think my gardener has a very green thumb either. He seems to bury seeds instead of plant them.

———

In suburbia real status is having a thick green lawn. We lived next door to a psychiatrist who had a terrific lawn. He used reverse psychology. He planted weeds and let the grass take over.

———

There was a Slobbovian gardener who was jumping up and down in his vegetable patch when a passing tourist asked him what he was doing. The Slobb replied, "Planting mashed potatoes."

———

Sylvia was eager to order seeds from the gardening catalog for her new country house. As she was ordering the seeds her husband pointed out, "Darling, those flowers take two years to bloom." "I know that, dear," she replied. "I'm using last year's catalog." Next she proceeded to go outside and instruct the gardener to turn the cucumber seeds inside out before he planted them. "Whatever for, madam?" he asked. "So instead of all those nasty little bumpy warts," she replied, "they'll have cute little dimples instead."

## Gays and Lesbians

The Canadians have their first gay Mountie. He not only gets his man, he gets to keep him.

———

When Pearl found out her nephew was gay, she rushed over to console her sister. "It's not all bad," her sister Sylvia said. "At least he's dating a doctor."

———

A homosexual is someone who doesn't believe in mixed marriages.

———

His father wanted a boy and his mother wanted a girl, so he split the difference.

———

What do you call two gay men named Bob? Oral Roberts.

———

When Bruce got his degree as a dentist, he became a true Tooth Fairy.

———

They have a new gay doll named Bruce. You wind him up and he totally ignores Barbie and takes Ken to the movies.

———

Have you heard about the new gay motorcycle club in the village? They're calling it "Hell's Hairdressers."

———

I went to dinner in the Village with my wife the other night. She got three propositions, I got four.

———

New York has now hosted the Gay Olympics with competitive categories in Male, Female, Butch and Bi. Sounds more like "bewitched bothered and bewildered" to me.

———

They had a Drag race in the village with three different categories: High Heels, Pumps, and Slingbacks.

———

This male couple had a fight and decided to break up. As he was packing, Kenneth said, "I'm taking all the Babs and Bette CDs with me." "Yah," said Doug. "Well, you know what you can do with them." "Don't you dare try to make up to me," cried Kenneth.

———

Why do so many gay men have mustaches? To hide the stretch marks.

———

Did you hear about the gay stock boy who got fired for drinking on the job—at a sperm bank?

———

One of the country's top Mafia dons is gay. When he gives you the kiss of death, it includes dinner, dancing, and champagne.

Being homosexual kept Terry out of the Marines, so he became a majorette in the WAVEs.

———

Last month a "lavender boy" won the Golden Gloves. Of course, they were four buttoned and came to the elbow.

———

Did you hear about the Dutch boy who stuck his finger in the dyke—and she beat him up!

———

What's the difference between a lesbian and the whales? No one is trying to save the lesbians.

———

What does a lesbian bring on the second date? A U-haul. What does a gay man bring on a second date? What second date?

———

What is hell on earth? Five blind dykes in a fish store.

———

Did you hear about the Australian sailor who left Victoria for Sydney?

———

After twenty years of marriage a man confessed to his wife, "I have a young gay lover." "I can't believe this," she cried. "What's he got that I haven't got?"

———

In West Hollywood, the gay and lesbian community is very politically active. They have petitioned the governor for the right to elect their own mayor, their own chief of police, and their own homecoming queen.

———

A Martian landed in San Francisco and the first building he walked into was a gay leather bar. He walked up to the bar and as he was trying to say, "Take me t—" they did!

———

Two college girls went away to Europe on a summer vacation. One of them was secretly gay. As they checked into their hotel room on the first night, she turns to her friend and says, "I have a secret about myself I think I should tell you. Let me be frank with you—" "Oh, no," cries the other girl as she jumps up on the bed. "Let me be Frank, you can be Alice!"

———

What do you call a lesbian Eskimo? A Klondyke.

———

There is a new gay Chinese restaurant in Greenwich Village. The specialty of the house is Sum Yung Gae.

———

What can a roll of Life Savers do that a man can't? Come in five different flavors.

———

Did you hear about the gay Jewish weightlifter? He's always off in some corner pumping Myron.

———

"Hey, Mervin," a gay kid called out to his roommate. "Did the rabbi come yet?" "No, but he's starting to moan."

———

A young Jewish lesbian decided to emigrate to Israel from New York, because she missed the Hebrew tongue.

———

Did you hear about the businessman who got drunk and spent the night in a biker bar in the Village? He woke up with a queer taste in his mouth.

———

They arrested several transvestites in Greenwich Village yesterday. They were all booked on charges of male fraud.

———

"Did you hear about Pearl's son, Sammy?" Sylvia said to Bea. "No, what happened?" "He moved to San Francisco and turned prematurely gay."

———

The thing that impresses me most about New York is the number of women who don't wear brassieres and the number of men who do.

———

Would you call Christine Jorgensen the original odd couple?

The very beautiful debutante married one of those "lavender boys," but she didn't know it. She awakened the first day to find breakfast on the table and the house spic and span. He served lunch and dinner, made the beds, and did the marketing. After a sumptuous dinner that he prepared with his own delicate little hands, she looked at him adoringly and said, "Darling, if you could only make love!"

When one of the actors in a Broadway show was suddenly taken drunk, the director had to make a fast replacement and called one of the chorus boys to do the lines. The dancer swished on and said his lines in a voice so high only dogs could hear him. "No, no!" screamed the director. "Try it again, but come on like a man!" "Gracious," the dancer lisped, "for $200 a week he wants me to do character parts."

## Gold Diggers

The gold digger advises: "A woman should never chase after a man—unless, of course, he's getting away."

A gold digger loves a man for all he's worth.

She knows a good thing when she sues it.

A great way for a girl to get a mink is to find a wolf and skin him.

After all, if he's got what it takes, she's taking what he's got.

One gold digger said to the other, "He's old enough to be your grandfather." "But he's rich enough to be my husband," replied the other.

They met in a very interesting way. He opened his wallet and there she was.

"Your heart is harder than steel," said the amorous millionaire to the beautiful chorus girl. "Nothing can soften it." "Try diamonds," she replied.

"One day I told her about my rich uncle. The next day, she was my rich aunt!"

Half the women in this country are working women. The others are working men.

The easier she is on the eye, the harder she is on the pocket.

It's like they always say: "A gold digger is only as strong as her weakest wink."

From the Gold Diggers' Handbook: A woman is known by the company who keeps her—or the corporation, franchise, and subsidiary. Every gold digger must have her standard: the gold standard. A man and his money are some party. There are only two kinds of men a gold digger should date: foreign and domestic. Look for a man who's tall, dark, and has some. Always marry a man with a strong will—made out to you.

She has an interesting way of getting a new wardrobe. She starts by taking the old one off.

My niece doesn't mind if a man loves her and leaves her—if he leaves her enough.

A Hollywood sex symbol married a rich, short old man. A reporter asked her, "What could you possibly see in him?" The star replied, "He has the rarest quality of masculine virility." "What is that?" asked the reporter. "A hundred fifty million in the bank," she said.

"It's not true that I married Jonathan because his father died and left him a fortune," the gold digger snapped at her sister. "Of course not, Donna," said her sister. "You would have married him no matter who left him the money."

My best friend went broke last year on junk blondes. He should have seen the last one coming when she introduced herself by saying, "How much did you say your name was?"

# Golf

The teacher said: "Johnny! Remember what happens to little boys who use bad language playing marbles!" The kid said, "Yeah, Teach, they grow up and play golf."

The club grouch was unhappy about everything—the food, the assessments, the parking, the other members. The first time he hit a hole-in-one, he complained, "Dammit, just when I needed the putting practice!"

The wife came into the bedroom and found her husband hugging his golf bag. "What's going on?" she asked. "You told me I had to choose," he answered, "and this is my choice." She followed her husband to the country club and watched as he had a terrible day with the clubs. "How can you prefer this to making love to me?" she cried. "Ah, come on honey," he said. "This is for money."

Sam married a beautiful twenty-two-year-old redhead, and before they left on their honeymoon he thought he would be completely honest. "Look, I have a confession to make. Golf is the most important thing in my life. I sleep golf, I dream golf; golf is all I think about twenty-four hours a day. Just golf. I just wanted to set things straight." She said, "Good. I also have a confession. I'm a hooker." "Oh," he said, grabbing her wrists. "I can fix that. Just hold your left hand over your right hand, like this."

---

My neighbor was crying because her husband left her for the sixth time. I said, "Don't be unhappy. He'll be back again." She said, "Not this time. He's taken his golf clubs."

---

I was playing golf with my dear friend, the priest. I watched as he bowed before each shot and mumbled a few words. After a very poor performance on the front nine, I stared over the course, turned to the priest, and asked, "Father, would it help me to pray a little, too?" He said, "I'm afraid not, my boy." I said, "Why not?" He said, "Because you're such a lousy putter."

---

Charley was lining up his putt on the sixth green when suddenly a woman dressed in a bridal gown came running toward him. "This is our wedding day," she shouted. "How could you do this to me?" "Listen, Sarah," the golf nut said. "I told you only if it's raining—only if it's raining."

They're saying golf is so popular that it has replaced sex. Of course, it's the guys over sixty who are saying it. Take my neighbor, who is over seventy. He told me, "My sex drive has turned into a putt." This is the same husband who will walk through thirty-six holes of golf but won't get up to get his own glass of water.

---

Sunday is the day we all bow our heads: Some are praying and some are putting.

---

My neighbor's wife wanted a new caddy, so he sent her a sixteen-year-old boy.

---

My doctor told me, "Golf is healthy. It matters not whether you win or lose. What matters is whether I win or lose."

---

The doctor told Al: "You look pretty run down. . . . I suggest you lay off golf for a while and get in a good day's work at the office."

---

Some golfers are just natural cheaters. My brother-in-law cheats so much that the other day he had a hole-in-one and he marked a zero on his scorecard.

---

There was one golfer who told the truth: He called another golfer a liar.

Nothing counts in golf like your opponent.

———

"I'm sick and tired of being left alone every weekend!" the wife cried. "If you think you're going to play golf today, I'll—" "Nonsense, darling," the husband said as he reached for the toast. "Golf is the furthest thing from my mind. Please pass the putter."

# Gossip

A gossip is a person who will never tell a lie—if the truth will cause more damage.

———

Most people can keep a secret—it's the person they tell it to who can't.

———

Raquel told Gloria at the manicurist's: "Ellen told me that you told her the secret I told you not to tell her." Gloria said, "Gee, and I told her not to tell you that I told her." Raquel said, "Well, I told her I wouldn't tell you she told me, so don't tell her I told you."

———

Make someone happy today. Mind your own business.

———

At any party, don't talk about yourself. It will be done when you leave.

———

Four women met every week in each other's houses to play bridge. One day, one of the women said, "Instead of playing, let's talk. You don't know this: I'm a kleptomaniac, but I swear I never took anything from any of your homes." The second lady said, "I'm a nymphomaniac, but I never made a play for any of your husbands." The third said, "I'm a dipsomaniac, but I never stole any of your booze." The fourth said, "I'm a gossip, and I can't wait to get to the beauty parlor."

———

A good gossip can't believe everything she hears—but she can repeat it.

———

Two ladies entered a restaurant. One noticed a familiar face at the other end of the room. "Do you see who I see sitting over there?" she said to her friend. "Tell me, do you believe that terrible story about her?" Her friend replied eagerly, "Yes, what is it?"

———

I never repeat gossip, so please listen carefully the first time.

———

Plastic surgery is a science that can do anything with a nose except keep it out of other people's business.

———

Hear no evil, see no evil, speak no evil—and you'll never be a success at a cocktail party.

## Habits

Mrs. Traum was so happy. "I've cured my husband of biting his nails." "After all these years?" I said. "Tell me how." "I hide his teeth," she revealed.

———

Want Ad: Pretty girl, college graduate, good typist, wants job as secretary. No bad habits—willing to learn.

———

"I just can't break my wife of the habit of staying up till four or five in the morning." "What the hell is she doing?" "Waiting for me to come home."

## Happiness

True happiness is when you marry a girl for love and then find out later she also has money.

———

Happiness is a man with a wife to tell him what to do—and a secretary to do it.

———

You want to make someone happy today? Mind your own business.

A guy is never happy until a girl comes along and makes him miserable.

———

Dr. Albert Schweitzer: "Happiness is nothing more than good health and a bad memory."

———

Happiness is midway between too much and too little.

———

They say that money doesn't bring happiness, but I'd like to be able to find out for myself.

———

Happiness is fitting into your jeans and then realizing they're your daughter's.

———

Maybe money won't buy you happiness, but at least it will keep you company while you're looking for it.

———

The guy stormed out of the house after an argument with his wife. "You'll be back," she yelled after him. "How long do you think you'll be able to stand happiness?"

Two lady shoppers were having high tea. Packages were piled all around them—they had obviously been taking full advantage of the postholiday sales. One of the ladies lifted her wineglass in salute to her companion and said, "Whoever said that money can't buy happiness just didn't know where to shop."

One star I know has three swimming pools: one with salt water, one with fresh water, and one with Perrier.

Perhaps it's just as well that money can't buy happiness. Considering today's prices, most of us couldn't afford it anyway.

Happiness is seeing your favorite girl in a two-piece outfit: slippers.

The only really happy people are married women and single men.

Happiness is when your girl sees you out with your wife—and forgives you.

Happiness is your secretary becoming pregnant and her boyfriend marrying her.

Happiness is signing your marriage license with disappearing ink.

Happiness is an income tax collector allowing you to list your wife's hairdresser as a dependent.

Happiness is the income tax man accepting your mistress as a deduction.

Happiness is when your wife gets in the wrong line at the bank and makes a deposit.

Happiness is a martini before and a nap after.

Money can't buy happiness, but it will get you a better class of memories.

It's true that money can't buy happiness, but it sure goes a long way toward the down payment.

My neighbor told me, "There's only one thing that keeps me from being happily married: my wife."

A woman gets married to make two people happy: herself and her mother.

I asked my girl to marry me and she said no—and we lived happily ever after.

My first wife and I were happily married for five years. Then she lost her job.

———

For twenty years my wife and I were very happy—then we met.

———

"What happened?" I asked my down-in-the-mouth neighbor. He said, "I had a rough battle with my old lady: She promised she wouldn't talk to me for thirty days!" I said, "Well, then, you should be happy!" He cried, "What happy? This is the last day!"

———

A solicitous wife is one who is so interested in her husband's happiness that she hires a detective to find out who is responsible for it.

———

A guy is never happy until a girl comes along and makes him miserable.

———

Happiness is a No Tipping sign.

# Health

*(see also Diets, Exercise)*

Humorist Emil Cohen tells about the man who meets a friend he hasn't seen for a long time and asks, "How do you feel?" "Terrible. I have hardening of the arteries, high blood pressure, dizziness, arthritis, bronchitis." "I'm sorry to hear that. What have you been doing?" "Same thing I've been doing for the last twenty years. Still selling health foods."

———

"And last but least," the lawyer read the will aloud, "to my nephew, Charlie, who has always told me that health is more important than wealth, I leave the entire contents of the closet in my study: my sunlamp."

———

Mark Twain said it: "The only way to keep your health is to eat what you don't want, drink what you don't like, and do what you'd rather not."

———

Studies show that having a pet is good for your health. A dog keeps the doctor away, especially if it's big enough.

———

Quit worrying about your health—eventually it will go away.

# Hecklers

*(see also Insults)*

One good way to save face is to keep the lower half shut.

———

Next time you give your old clothes away, stay in them.

———

There's a bus leaving in five minutes. Get under it.

———

Find yourself a home in a wastebasket.

———

I don't know what I'd do without you, but I'm willing to try.

———

If you had your life to live over again, don't do it.

———

Do you have a chip on your shoulder, or is that your head?

———

Sammy Davis, Jr., to a pest: "If you're ever in California, sir, I do hope you'll come by my house and use my pool. I'd like to give you some drowning lessons."

———

Jack E. Leonard, annoyed by a noisy ringsider, finally exploded. "Sir, I have a terrible toothache that's killing me—but compared to you it's a pleasure."

———

Milton Berle had a practice of picking on somebody at the ringside smoking a cigar. Pretending to wave the smoke away, he would groan, "What are you smoking? An old army blanket? Don't you ever inhale?" Hugh Herbert was ready for him and shouted back, "Not while you're in the room!"

———

Why don't you phone me sometime, so I can hang up on you?

Don Adams says he has a sure way of squelching a nightclub heckler. If someone is giving him trouble, he signals for an offstage phone to ring, then he feigns answering it, turns to the heckler, and says, "Pardon me, sir, it's your doctor. Your spare mouth is ready."

———

Milton Berle quieted a ringside woman heckler by saying, "You did the same thing to me in 1946. I never forget a dress."

———

It's all right to drink like a fish—if you drink what a fish drinks. In your case, brain surgery would be only a minor operation.

———

Thelma Lee was heckled by some bore who yelled, "Hey, baby, take off your clothes." She squelched him with a line from *Kismet*, "Don't work up an appetite if you have no teeth."

———

Some overexcited broad screamed at the great Dizzy Dean, "If I were your wife I'd give you poison," and he answered, "If you were my wife I'd take it." This line has been credited to everybody from Winston Churchill to Rin Tin Tin, but it sounds like our Dizzy.

———

I hear they just redecorated your home—they put new padding on the walls.

Someday you'll go too far—and I hope you stay there.

———

I won't ask you to act like a human being. I know how good you are at imitations.

# Hijacking

Everybody is so nervous on airplanes nowadays. On one champagne flight, every time the cork popped, the pilot changed course.

———

Did you notice they rarely hijack a 747? They know they can't feed that many in Havana.

———

About that plane, the 747: It's so large it takes four hundred passengers, twenty crew members, and a dozen guys to hijack it.

———

The airplane hijackings are making a lot of people very nervous. On the flight here from Miami I got up to go to the washroom and the whole crew surrendered.

———

The skyjacker boarded a Miami-bound plane and ordered the pilot to "take me to Miami or I blow up this plane." The pilot answered, "But that's where we're going—it's on our schedule." The armed man replied, "I know.

But I've tried three times, and each time I wound up in Havana."

———

After one recent skyjacking a woman walked into an airline office in New York and asked for two chances on a ticket to Miami.

# Hippies

*Every generation has its rebellious youth, drug subculture, and philosophical searching. But few generations had the marvelous innocence and wonder of the hippies during the late 1960s and 1970s.*

———

I went to one weird hippie wedding. The bride didn't throw her bouquet, she smoked it.

———

The hippie bride was bragging to her hippie groom that their new apartment will have one bath. "Do we really need that many?" he asked.

———

The hippie couple had their apartment redone in early slob.

———

I noticed a hippie on Sunset Strip who was wearing one shoe. "Lose a shoe?" I asked. "Nope," he grumbled, "but I found one."

———

Hippie girl to hippie boy: "Of course I love you. What a dumb question. I love everybody."

---

There are now over fifty thousand hippies who dress alike, look alike, smell alike. And what's their big beef? Conformity.

---

Most of them haven't had a bath in so long they are on the critical list of Lux.

---

If you look at them, they got that far-off look—and if you ever smell them you know why they are far off.

---

Hippies say they want to love everybody—and they miss very few.

---

A hippie was walking down the street with a cigar box under his arm when he met another hippie who asked, "Hey, man, what's cookin'? Where you goin' with that cigar box?"
"I'm movin'."

---

This is comedian Jack Carter's favorite hippie story: A married couple of hippies was blessed with a child through natural birth. A friendly policeman helped them deliver the child in the park, and as the officer brought the little babe to life by slapping it gently on the rear, he heard the screams of this hippie couple yelling, "Police brutality, police brutality!"

## Holidays
*(see also Christmas)*

APRIL FOOL'S DAY

Today is April Fool's Day. Did you ever get the idea that political elections should be held today? The biggest April Fools are the politicians. According to FBI estimates, only a small number of career criminals will be caught this year. The rest will be re-elected.

---

It's April Fool's Day, so don't take any wooden nickels, even though they're worth more than the real ones.

---

My neighbor warned me, "Be careful about the practical jokes you play today. My mother played a practical joke on my dad and he reminds me of it every time my birthday rolls around."

---

The landlord told my neighbor, "It's April Fool's Day and I've decided to raise your rent." My neighbor beamed, "Now that's swell of you. I was wondering how I could raise it myself."

---

The groom was enjoying his honeymoon. He was at the bar in his hotel, having drinks, when a friend asked, "Where's your bride?" The groom said,

"She's upstairs with my best friend making love." The friend said, "What are you going to do about it?" "Nothing. April Fool! He's so drunk he thinks he's me!"

---

The man complained to the slumlord in his building, "There's no ceiling in my bedroom." The slumlord answered, "That's okay, the man upstairs doesn't walk around much!"

---

How did I know it was April 1? My neighbor took his car for a walk and left his girl to be washed and polished.

---

April Fool's Day is when your brother sleeps on his waterbed wearing a life jacket.

---

It's April Fool's Day, the day the dumb-dumbs sound smart. Like the dope who picked a guy's pocket in an airplane and made a run for it. . . . Or the garage mechanic who told the women's libber, "You have a short circuit." She answered, "Well, don't just stand there like a dummy. Lengthen it."

---

COLUMBUS DAY

Columbus and his men came over on the *Nina*, the *Pinta*, and the *Santa Maria*. Today, all Americans are in the same boat.

---

I'm very proud and thrilled to celebrate Columbus Day with every Italian in the world, but between you and me, what's so great about Columbus discovering America? It's so big, how could he miss it? In fact, discovering America is like discovering Orson Welles in a telephone booth.

---

Columbus discovered America for one reason: He wanted to give the rest of the world a place to borrow money from.

---

When Columbus came to America in 1492, everybody thought the world was flat—and the way prices are going, it soon may be.

---

Don't get me wrong. America is still the land of opportunity. The only foreigner who didn't make any money here was Columbus.

---

Times sure change. Before Columbus found us, America was controlled by the Indians, who hunted and fished so much that they didn't have time to work and worry. Columbus changed all that. Now that the white man controls the nation, he works and worries so much that he doesn't have time to hunt or fish.

---

You can't blame the Indians for not getting too excited about Columbus

Day. Five hundred years ago, when the Indians were running this country, there were no taxes, no national debt, no foreign entanglements, and the women did all the work. What they can't understand is how white men thought they could improve on a system like that.

--- * ---

FOURTH OF JULY

Thanks to our founding fathers, every child born in the USA today is endowed with life, liberty, and a share of the government debt.

--- * ---

Every American still has a chance to become president of the United States—that's one of the risks he or she has to take.

--- * ---

When John Hancock signed the Declaration of Independence, it was the first insurance policy he wrote that guaranteed that all men are created equal. I wonder if he intends to pay off on Mickey Rooney.

--- * ---

Nathan Hale said, "I only regret that I have but one life to give for my country." His wife said, "Before you give your life, let's talk to John Hancock about insurance."

--- * ---

Patrick Henry said, "Give me liberty or give me death." His wife said, "You'll drop dead before you get a divorce from me."

--- * ---

Abe Lincoln is known for his Gettysburg Address, which is very surprising. It didn't have a ZIP code.

--- * ---

How about Honest Abe's living in a log cabin? No lights, no heat, no running water. I think I have the same landlord!

--- * ---

NEW YEAR'S DAY

Millions of people will start the New Year by drinking to somebody's health—while they ruin their own.

--- * ---

My brother-in-law welcomes in the New Year. "Everyone has to believe in something: I believe I will have another drink."

--- * ---

Me, I don't go out on New Year's Eve. Why should I spend all that money on things I won't even remember?

--- * ---

A toast to the New Year! May all your troubles last as long as your New Year's resolutions.

--- * ---

I'm not making New Year's resolutions this year. I've got a few left over from last year I never used.

--- * ---

A New Year's resolution: Starting next month, I resolve not to procrastinate.

My friend made a resolution: "From now on I'm just going to have a little scotch in the afternoon—and in the evening a sexy Italian will do."

My uncle reminds you to watch the drinks if you're driving, "because they have a tendency to spill if you make a turn."

At the stroke of midnight, I want you to give a long, smoldering, passionate kiss to the one you love the most—and if your husband is handy, give him a kiss, too.

I think I know why we celebrate on New Year's Eve. It gives us time to recall the past year and then drink enough to forget it.

The drunk told me: "I never drink on New Year's Eve. That's amateur night."

THANKSGIVING
Have a happy Thanksgiving. You sure have a lot to be thankful for. If nothing else, be glad you're not a turkey.

In my house we're not having a new turkey this year. We've still got some left over from last year.

I try to be grateful for little things, like my lifetime pension lasting out the week.

My neighbor was complaining, "Grateful? What have I to be grateful for? I can't pay my bills." I told him, "Well, be grateful that you aren't one of the creditors."

And most of all, let us be grateful that we live in the United States of America, where a man can still do as his wife pleases.

Thanksgiving is a day for happiness: Money can't buy happiness, but it helps you look for it in many more places. And even if happiness could be bought, there would still be those who would try to chisel on the price.

Thanksgiving is when turkeys that have fattened up all year go to the chopping block. With humans, it's April 15.

Oh, I'm grateful and all, but as long as the pilgrims were making the effort to come over here and make a big meal, why did it have to be turkey? Why not lamb chops? Or a corned beef sandwich?

---

### VALENTINE'S DAY

My neighbor got this Valentine: "Roses are red, violets are blue my alimony check is six weeks overdue."

---

Valentine's Day is named after St. Valentine, the patron saint of lovers, florists, candy companies, and divorce lawyers.

---

My uncle told me, "My wife is on a diet, so I got her what I consider a very thoughtful Valentine gift: I sent her a lettucegram."

---

"Dear Joe," she wrote. "Be my Valentine. Words cannot express how much I regret having broken off our engagement. Will you please come back to me? Your absence leaves a space no one can fill. Please forgive me and let us start all over again. I need you so much. Yours forever, Sylvia. P.S.: By the way, congratulations on winning the lottery."

---

### WASHINGTON'S BIRTHDAY

George Washington was first in war, first in peace, and the first to have his birthday juggled to make a long weekend.

Father's Day is dedicated to George Washington. There are hundreds of hotels, motels, and boardinghouses all over the country that have signs that say GEORGE WASHINGTON SLEPT HERE. No wonder he was called the father of our country.

# Hollywood and Beverly Hills

Two Hollywood ladies were bragging. "Charles and I made our money the old-fashioned way," said one. "We were born rich." "You gotta be kidding," said the other. "My Irving is so rich, he bought his son a kiddie car with a built-in telephone." "Yeah? Well, Charlie built me a house with seven dining rooms—one for each course!" "Is that so? Well, Irving bought his son a set of trains—the Pennsylvania and the Central." "Really? At parties, my husband serves only money. . . ."

---

Beverly Hills is Hollywood's show-off place. Even their motorcycle gang is different: It's not every gang whose members ride chauffeur-driven motorcycles.

---

Beverly Hills matrons never look you straight in the eye. They're too busy searching your face for signs of a facelift.

---

A panhandler on Rodeo Drive: "If you don't have cash, sir, how about lending me your American Express gold card for the day?"

This film star is really upset. Her secretary didn't keep the records straight, and now she finds she has had two more divorces than she has had weddings. One handsome actor told her, "I'd love to be married to you someday." She said, "Okay. I'll put you on my wedding list." One impatient wolf insisted on a date. She put him off with, "You know I'm going to be married tomorrow. Call me in about three weeks."

Then there was the Beverly Hills society girl who only partially returned affection: She returned all the love letters but kept all the rings.

Even grandmas are different in Beverly Hills: "My daughter married a big producer," one was bragging. "They even have four cars." The second grandma said, "That's wonderful. Do they have any children?" She said, "Yes, they have a little boy—a beauty. He's fifteen months old." Her friend asked, "Does he walk yet?" She said, "You joking? With four cars, why should he walk?" The other said, "My grandson, only three years old, God bless him, has already had five fathers."

You know you're down and out in Beverly Hills when: Your wife starts asking for the household expense money in traveler's checks. . . . You start carrying cash again. . . . You're invited to a screening and it turns out to be a police lineup.

Hollywood. Land of the stars, the has-beens, the would-like-to-be's, playground of the rich, the famous, and the phoniest. I finally figured out what the Hollywood Hills are made of: bull.

Things aren't always what they appear: A $1 million house in Beverly Hills could be a $600,000 house with a $400,000 burglar alarm system.

I saw this sign in a Beverly Hills shop on Rodeo Drive: "Japanese and Arabic spoken here. Cash understood." Beverly Hills is where the poverty level is a two-car garage.

Two old stars met at their club in Beverly Hills: "I say, Tony, old boy," said one, looking morosely into his drink, "as your best friend I hate to tell you this, but your wife is fickle." His pal said, "Oh? So she's thrown you over, too?"

The producer came home and found his wife in the arms of his leading man. "I beat the hell out of her," he told me. "Didn't you hit the guy?" I asked. He said, "Hell, no, he's the star of my picture."

They're talking about the woman shopper on Rodeo Drive who was arrested for vagrancy because she was carrying only three credit cards.

Some folks have said that Hollywood people are not real. That's not true. Some of them may be phonies, but they're real phonies.

A Hollywood producer received a story entitled *The Optimist*. He called his staff together and said, "Gentlemen, this story is great, but the title must go. It's got to be switched to something simple. We're intelligent and know what an optimist is, but how many of the morons who will see the picture will know he's an eye doctor?"

Did you hear about the elephant who appeared in so many jungle pictures he went to Hollywood? He just had his tusks capped.

A Hollywood star never cheats. Who is he going to find who he loves as much as himself?

"Who made her dress?" "The police."

The Hollywood gals never cheat—they just have unlisted husbands.

A Hollywood couple I know has finally ironed out the divorce settlement. Now they can go ahead with the wedding.

Why did the famous drinking actress leave her dress on the floor all night? She was in it at the time.

How does an actor in Hollywood know when he's getting old? There are more lines in his face than there are in his script.

Beverly Hills is a pretty expensive town. There was an old lady who lived in a shoe—it's all she could afford for $90,000.

In Hollywood, they get married in the morning. That way, if it doesn't work out, you haven't wasted a whole day!

Hollywood had a power failure. The street lights, radio, and Liberace's jacket went out.

I know a Hollywood youngster who is very proud. He has the most parents at PTA meetings.

———

Hollywood is a place where you spend more than you make, on things you don't need, to impress people you don't like.

———

What do you give a newly married Hollywood couple? About three months.

———

God created Hollywood because he felt sorry for actors. He gave them a place in the sun and a swimming pool. The price they had to pay was to surrender their talent.

———

The best acting in Hollywood is done by the stars congratulating the Academy Award winners.

———

The actor was divorced for the fourth time. He never could hold an audience.

———

One actress reported that the wire wheels were stolen from her Rolls-Royce and the police didn't seem properly sympathetic. When she asked why, the cop shook his head and said, "Crime is relative. Who's the bigger thief, the kid who steals them? Or Rolls-Royce, which gets $500 a wheel for them?"

The Hollywood teacher told the actress's son, "Tell your mother to come to school next month." The kid said, "I can't tell my mother." The teacher asked, "Don't you know where she's going to be next month?" The boy said, "I don't even know *who* she's going to be next month."

———

I love Hollywood. It's the only place in the world where they take you at facelifted value.

———

One actress wouldn't acknowledge her plastic surgeon at a Beverly Hills party. He sniffed, "How do you like that? She's lifting my new nose at me."

———

You have no idea what class is until you've visited Beverly Hills. Where else can you find monogrammed garbage? Talk about class: One producer's wife told me, "We've got cats here that won't scratch because they might chip their nail polish, and dogs that are paper trained on fifty-dollar bills!" And if you think all of this is too much, they've got the only fire hydrants that you have to open with a corkscrew.

———

There's a new deodorant for sale in Hollywood that gives off the odor of chlorine. It's for people who want others to think they have a swimming pool.

Beverly Hills is a fabulous place. This town is so rich, every Christmas they distribute food baskets to people with only one swimming pool. And where else do traffic lights come in decorator colors? In fact, Beverly Hills is so chic the breadline has a complimentary caviar bar, and the unemployment line has a complimentary car wash.

———

In Hollywood psychiatrists advertise: "Two couches—no waiting."

———

One Beverly Hills mother was telling her friend, "My son has never gone to a psychiatrist." The friend said, "Really? What's wrong with him?"

———

An underprivileged child in Hollywood these days is a child with only one set of parents.

———

In Hollywood schools are different. It's the only place where truancy officers work from a surfboard.

———

There's a shortage of water in Beverly Hills at the moment: Two Perrier trucks collided.

———

Recipe for making chicken soup in Beverly Hills: "Bring the Perrier to a slow boil . . ."

———

The nightlife in Philadelphia starts at about 10 P.M. and runs to about three in the morning. The nightlife in New York starts at midnight and runs until about seven in the morning. In Hollywood, the nightlife starts at ten in the morning and ends at three in the afternoon.

———

You know you're down and out in Beverly Hills when:

You see your 8 by 10 glossies in the post office.

Thieves break into your house and leave something.

The organist at your daughter's wedding has a monkey with a tin cup.

The local thrift shop refuses your clothes.

Your friends' answering machines won't take your calls.

They want to use your house to shoot a remake of *Tobacco Road*.

The authorities pick you up for wearing polyester.

You see your accountant on "Lifestyles of the Rich and Famous."

———

You know you're still on top in Beverly Hills when:

You've got two chauffeurs. One only makes left turns.

Your kid's kiddie bank has a vice president.

Your kid's nurse has a maid.

You have a chauffeur-driven sled.

Your kiddie car has whitewall tires.

You have an air-conditioned baby carriage.

You have an unlisted Social Security number, an unlisted wife, and an unlisted ZIP code.

"Who made her dress?" "The police."

———

Would you believe even AT&T in Beverly Hills has an unlisted number?

———

The Beverly Hills police cars are Mercedes. The fire trucks are convertibles.

———

This Beverly Hills star can afford a dentist who makes house calls. The star's husband was on a diet, so he hired someone to swallow for him. This star has more money than she can spend—but a sleep-in TV repairman?

———

The Hollywood Hills are alive with the sound of con artists.

———

Hollywood is where the people accept you for what you're not.

Hollywood is over a hundred years old, and that ain't easy in a town where even the senior citizens claim to be under thirty. In fact, the only time you're over thirty-six here is when you're listing your bust measurements. It's the only place in the world where they have live-in plastic surgeons.

———

I like the people in Hollywood. It's the Hollywood in people that I don't like.

———

Hollywood is a small town bordered on the north by producers, on the south by starlets, on the west by agents, and on the east by ulcers.

———

This producer hesitated at offering a once-famous movie actress a part in his newest picture: "Darling," he cooed to the star, "you may not want to play this role. It calls for a lovely but immoral prostitute who runs from the arms of one bum to another, a woman who lies and cheats, a real witch. Tell me, how do you feel about it?" She said, "Feel about it? It's the first decent part I've been offered in years."

———

Hollywood is where the wedding cake outlasts the wedding.

———

This bride walked into her new home. She turned to her new husband and said, "John, darling, this house looks familiar. Are you sure we haven't been married before?"

———

These Hollywood kiddies were playing house. One said, "We're going to have a big family. I want three fathers and three mothers."

———

In Hollywood they don't ask, "How's your wife?" They ask, "Who's your wife?"

———

Beverly Hills officials have passed a law banning sex in restaurants, because they're afraid it might lead to smoking afterward.

———

Have you heard about the latest hit TV show in Hollywood? It's called "Bowling for Alimony."

———

There are four things that every genuine Beverly Hills star must have: a Japanese gardener, a Filipino houseboy, a French maid, and a Mexican divorce.

———

I love Hollywood: It's got everything under the stars, including the starlets.

———

Did I tell you about the expectant father who wanted to name the baby Oscar, because it was his best performance of the year?

Hollywood is where the movies are running longer and the marriages are running shorter. In Beverly Hills they figure the marriage has a chance of succeeding if the couple leaves the church together.

———

Two Beverly Hills princesses were discussing their boyfriends. "My new boyfriend is a dream," said one. "He doesn't drink, gamble, or even so much as look at another girl." The other said, "Gee, how will you ever get a divorce?"

———

Beverly Hills, it's a helluva town: The kids' bunk beds don't have a ladder to get up to the top bunk; they have a little self-service elevator. One kid is now working on his fifth father by his fourth mother, and I'll say one thing for him: He never talks back to his dad. Why should he? He hardly knows the man. The kids there don't play good guys and bad guys, they play clients and agents.

———

I know one actress who never got an Oscar, Emmy, or Tony—but she's had every Tom, Dick, and Harry.

———

In Hollywood film circles everybody lies, but it really doesn't matter because nobody listens.

———

It was a bitter Hollywood divorce and a rough custody battle: She got the children and he got the scrapbooks.

———

Hollywood is a place that seems to forget that wives are like cars: If you take care of them, you don't have to get new ones all the time.

———

One actress said: "I have so many movies where I've played the role of a hooker, the producers don't pay me in the regular way anymore: They just leave cash on my dresser."

———

I wouldn't say she's a fickle actress, but she does have a wash-and-wear wedding gown.

———

In Hollywood it's usually the little things that break up a marriage: the little blondes, the little redheads, the little brunettes . . .

———

The swinging actress was complaining to her director: "You're not photographing my best side." He answered: "I can't. You're sitting on it."

———

In Beverly Hills an amicable divorce is one in which the husband gets to keep anything that falls off the moving van as it leaves the driveway.

The movie extra was fast becoming a problem to the director. He refused again and again to jump from the cliff into the water. Screamed the extra: "No, I won't do it. There's only two feet of water at the bottom of that cliff!" "Of course," said the director. "Do you think I want you to drown?"

———

DIRECTOR: You have never been kissed before? ACTRESS: What am I, a character actress?

"Who made her dress?" "The police."

———

"Here is where you jump off the cliff." "Yeah, but suppose I get injured or killed?" "Oh, that's all right. It's the last scene of the picture."

———

"Every day at the studio I rub elbows with some of the biggest stars." "You mean when you're serving the soup?"

———

A Hollywood couple got married—and their lawyers lived happily ever after.

———

The accepted custom is to ask a girl's father for her hand in marriage, but in Hollywood you ask her husband.

———

The pretty girl said, "I won first prize and a movie contract." "What did you enter?" I asked. She replied, "A producer's apartment."

Everybody is going to Hollywood to find fame and fortune. Listen, Johnny Carson can't marry everybody.

---

Joan Rivers is unique. She's the first woman to divorce him without marrying him first.

---

As one motion picture star told me, "They say you can't take it with you, and as a divorcee I know it's true. I can't take it with me because my wife took it with her."

---

Joan Rivers has never forgotten her mother's advice: "Trust your husband, adore your husband, and get as much as you can in your own name."

---

Somebody asked singer Kenny Rogers how many bathrooms were in his Holmby Hills mansion. He said proudly, "I can seat sixteen."

---

The Hollywood producer said proudly, "Everything I owe, I owe because of my wife. I married a girl who majored in selfish."

---

Singer Dolly Parton told me, "When I was just starting, I vowed to become a star or bust." Boy, did she keep her vow. . . . Can you imagine Dolly with a chest cold? She must buy industrial-strength Vicks by the case. "Of course my feet are tiny," Dolly says. "Things just don't grow in the shade." "My only problem," says our gal, "is that I have to paint my toenails from memory."

---

Hollywood is where the girls marry for love—and divorce for money.

---

Milton Berle was explaining that the reason some Hollywood stars postpone their weddings is because they have trouble finding babysitters.

---

Two actresses who hadn't seen each other for years were catching up on things at the Beverly Wilshire Hotel. "I haven't seen much of Marvin lately," one said. "Oh!" said the other. "Then you didn't marry him?" She said, "Yes, I did."

---

She walked into the lobby of the Westwood Marquis with her cleavage down to her ankles and her hips moving on fast forward. "We should all pray for that woman," one actor said. The other looked up and said, "Believe me, I have, but she prefers her husband."

---

Did you read where Dolly Parton had her chest insured for $1,000,000? And that was just against theft. . . . Now that she's a Hollywood star, what will they ask her to impress in the cement in front of Mann's Chinese Theater?

Hollywood isn't exactly a swinging town. No matter how hot it gets in the daytime, there is nothing to do at night.

———————

Woody Allen said of the film capital: "The only cultural advantage is that you can make a right turn on a red light."

"Who made her dress?" "The police."

———————

Hollywood brings out the Hollywood in people. It gives them a chance to show off their best assets—and anything else they want to show off. Liz Taylor showed up at one party wearing all her wedding rings, one for each finger. The other two fingers were ready and willing. Singer Tom Jones showed up in a new pair of pants, which come in three sizes: tight, tighter, and intravenous. You've heard of "wash and dry"? His pants were "wash and choke." Joan Rivers showed up in open mouth and tight pants. Calvin Klein kept following her around, trying to scratch his name off her jeans.

———————

I always thought everybody in Beverly Hills was worth millions—or at the very least owed millions—until I saw the picture *Down and Out in Beverly Hills* and read the Bantam book of the same name: "You know you're down and out in Beverly Hills when Gloria Vanderbilt follows you around, trying to scratch her name off your jeans."

You know you're still doing great in Beverly Hills when: Your kid's piano teacher is Vladimir Horowitz . . . when you serve chocolate-covered caviar at cocktail parties . . . when the bracelets the cops use are 14-karat . . . when the kid says to the teacher, "A note from my parents? Do you realize that requires six signatures?" . . . This producer has music in all his elevators: live bands. Would you believe he has solid gold silverware?

———————

You know you're down and out in Beverly Hills when "package deal" means you're trying to get the store to gift wrap the stuff you just shoplifted.

———————

My favorite all-time Hollywood character is the king of the malaprops, Samuel Goldwyn: "I can tell you in two words: im possible." . . . "A verbal contract isn't worth the paper it's written on." . . . "Let's bring it up to date with some snappy nineteenth-century dialogue," and his greatest, "Gentlemen, include me out."

———————

I know a very unusual show business couple there. They had a baby *after* they got married.

———————

The real star of the town is the Beverly Hills Princess: She is uncompromising when it comes to romance. She wants a man to love her as much as she does. What do you call a BHP on a waterbed? The Dead Sea. Did I tell you about the BHP bride who vowed to make her husband happy even if it took every dollar he had? What are the three happiest days in the life of a BHP? When she gets her diamond ring, when she chooses her China, and when she gets her divorce.

"Who made her dress?" "The police."

---

Why is a Beverly Hills Princess like her husband's car? It's tough to turn either of them on in the morning. How does a BHP make chicken soup? First she boils two cups of Perrier. The daughter of a BHP was going off to college and a friend asked, "What is she taking?" "Twenty-two pairs of jeans and forty-three blouses." The first words a BHP says? "Gucci—Gucci—Gucci."

---

If Hollywood is the factory, Beverly Hills is the showcase. Alan King describes Beverly Hills as one of the richest and swankiest areas in the country: "It's a great place to live, provided you never need a policeman or a fireman in a hurry. They come by appointment only." It's a place where, if an actor's wife looks like a new woman, she probably is.

In Beverly Hills, the banks must keep only new bills on hand. Their clients absolutely refuse to accept any bill that's been used. Interest rates are now so high, it's a heartening sight to go to Beverly Hills and see people standing in line for mortgage stamps. One of the banks failed. You should have seen the mess, with a run on a bank with valet parking. There is one bank that is so exclusive, they don't take a picture of bank robbers, they take an oil painting.

## Honeymoon

*(see also Brides and Grooms, Marriage)*

You can always tell when the honeymoon is over. He phones to say that he'll be late for dinner. She has already left a note to tell him that it's waiting for him in the refrigerator.

---

The two grooms met in the coffee shop of Honeymoon Hotel. "Where's your wife?" one asked. "She's in her room smoking. Where's yours?" "She's hot, too, but she's not smoking."

---

The bride and groom were having a wonderful time, so they decided to stay another week. The new husband wired his father, "It's wonderful here. Please send fifty dollars." The old man wired back, "Come on home. It's good anyplace."

---

They just got married—the farmer's daughter and the traveling man. She was sweet and naive but ready. He was kind and gentle and wanted his timid new bride to get a chance to get ready for bed, so he retired to the bathroom and gave her thirty minutes. When he came out he was amazed to see her completely dressed—coat, boots, and all—sitting there waiting for him. "What's wrong? Why are you dressed?" he asked. "Ma said we'd be going to town about eleven o'clock," she answered.

———

My brother told me, "I'll never forget my honeymoon. My wife put on her sexiest negligee, snuggled up close, and in a very shy voice said, 'Dear, now that we're married, can I do anything I want?' I said, 'Anything you want.' 'Anything?' 'Sure, anything.' So she went to sleep!"

# Hospitals
*(see also Doctors)*

Recently I was sick for two weeks and got a card that said, "Get well quick." It was from Blue Cross.

———

There's this busy hospital clinic where patients can come for free medical treatment. Lots of elderly people who have nothing to do just come to tell the doctor their troubles. One such woman went every day. There was nothing wrong with her. But the doctors humored her, listened patiently, and actually looked forward to her visits. One day she didn't show up. Next day, her doctor asked, "Where were you yesterday? We missed you." "I'll tell you the truth," she replied. "I was sick."

———

DOCTOR: Nurse, where's the man who belongs in this bed? NURSE: He couldn't get warm, so I put him in with that lady who's in 104.

———

What ever happened to good old-fashioned medicine? I can remember when the first thing that happened when you were rushed to a hospital was they took your pulse. Now all they take is your Blue Cross number.

———

I know a doctor who is so independent he won't even make hospital calls.

———

It now costs more to go to the hospital than it once cost to go to medical school.

———

The patient was leaving the hospital and wanted to see his bill. The doctor told him, "Sorry, old man, you're not strong enough yet."

———

Private hospitals have other strange ways of making money, like selling tickets for the visitor's hour.

I don't think anyone should complain about the high cost of medical care, especially while they're still in the hospital.

---

My friend Myron told me, "When I was in the hospital, I had a day nurse and a night nurse. In the afternoon I rested."

---

My brother told me he just returned from minor surgery at Doctor's Hospital. "What kind of treatment did you get?" I asked. He replied, "The nurses said, 'How's our leg today?' or 'How's our back today?' But when I touched our thigh, she slapped our face."

---

Hospital costs are so high these days it's become impossible for a patient to be ill at ease.

---

A hospital's a place that keeps you three days if you have big troubles—and three months if you have big insurance.

---

I know hospital costs are out of hand, but I never thought I'd see a self-service operating table.

---

The patient was complaining about the hospital food: "I hope the doctors didn't go to the same school as the cooks."

After she visited her uncle in the hospital, a woman took the nurse aside and asked, "Confidentially, is he making any progress?" The nurse said, "Not at all. He's not my type."

---

After two weeks in a hospital, I realized how bad my wife's cooking is. When I was discharged, I hated to leave, the meals were so good.

---

## Hot Weather

It's been so hot in New York, the Statue of Liberty traded her torch for an ice cream cone.

---

It was so hot and dry in Central Park, I saw two trees chasing a dog.

---

It's been so hot lately, the chickens have been laying hard-boiled eggs.

---

Hot? Even Heather Locklear has been taking cold showers.

---

Rodney Dangerfield says, "On hot days like these I just want to go out in the backyard and take off all my clothes, but the birds would leave, my dog would run away, and the property value would drop."

Please make this a safe summer. Riding on the Belt Parkway is like Russian roulette: You never know which driver is loaded.

———

Air conditioning is that marvelous invention that helps you keep cool until you get the electric bill.

———

I'll tell you what kind of luck I've had during this heatwave: My electric bill this month was $117,000! It was a mistake, of course, but the electric company said to go ahead and pay it and they'd take it off next month's bill.

———

Summer's the time for reruns on TV. A rerun is also what you get from drinking the water in Mexico.

———

Summertime is great for beaches. I had a chance to go to a nude beach, but I turned it down. I like to wear a hat to keep the sun out of my eyes.

———

It was so hot that Myron says he bought a steak in the supermarket, and by the time he got home, it was well done.

———

It's so hot and sticky, even muggers won't work in this humidity.

———

It's so hot that for the first time Madonna's sex drive is in park.

———

It's so hot, even Sharon Stone is willing to sleep alone.

———

I can tell it's going to be another hot summer in New York. Yesterday I passed by Grant's tomb and the window was open.

———

It's been so hot that Cher's been lifting her skirt for other reasons.

———

Hot? At the Lincoln Memorial in D.C., Abe was wearing Bermuda shorts.

———

It's so hot, my neighbor's glad his wife is frigid.

———

My brother likes this hot weather. He's hoping it will thaw out his wife.

———

Joan Rivers screams about hot weather: "Humidity is just another plot against women. It makes things droop years before they're supposed to!"

———

The water shortage has helped this summer: Bars are now serving scotch and milk, and prisoners are being given bread and wine.

You know it's really hot when you wake up in the morning to a tingling sensation and then you realize your waterbed is percolating.

―――

The drought is going to kill off a lot of good sex for the creative young marrieds: Instead of a waterbed, they'll have to use the old-fashioned mattress.

―――

Now there's a new slogan: "Be patriotic—bathe with a friend."

―――

The drought is so bad, armored cars are now delivering bottled water.

―――

It was so hot in New York, the tough guys were tossing men into the harbor stuffed in seersucker sacks.

―――

It was so hot, instead of carrying a torch, the Statue of Liberty was holding a glass of iced tea.

―――

One reason I'm glad I'm not an Arab: How'd you like to be tooling down the highway and have your camel boil over?

―――

Hey, don't slave over a hot stove in weather like this. Do it the easy way: Rush home and toss a couple of TV dinners on the sidewalk.

―――

They got air conditioning everywhere now, even in the steamrooms. And with the new buildings without windows, they now have the air conditioning going all year round. Now you don't have to wait for the winter to catch a cold.

―――

It was a hundred degrees outside. The car was unbearably hot inside, but the windows were rolled up. "Will you please open the windows?" the husband pleaded. "Are you nuts?" the wife screamed. "And let our neighbors know our car isn't air-conditioned?"

## Hotels

I stayed at one hotel in Puerto Rico that was so large, by the time you got to your room you owed two days' rent.

―――

One night a rather tipsy gentleman from the city checked into the hotel. A half hour later he was back at the reception desk demanding to see the manager. "Sorry," said the clerk, "but the manager is not in the hotel. Is there anything I can do?" "I must talk to someone about my room. It's awful." "Is it the bed?" questioned the concerned clerk. "No," replied the drunk.

"The bed is the best little ol' bed I've ever seen." "The towels?" "Best darn towels I've ever seen." "No hot water?" "Greatest little ol' hot water anywhere." "Then," cried the clerk, "what is wrong with the room?" "It's on fire."

———

Some of the hotels are feeling the economic pinch this year. I hear that one hotel owner is stealing the towels back from the guests.

———

Imagine if Howard Hughes and Garbo ever had a romance. It would be the biggest mystery since Twiggy bought a bra.

## Hunting

"Once I shot a buck." "You did?" "Yeah, then I shot two bucks, then I shot three bucks, and then I shot five bucks." "Then what happened?" "Somebody hollered, 'Cheese it, the cops,' and I dropped the dice and ran."

———

"Son, do you like steeplechasing?" "I don't know. I never chased any."

———

"How do you know you hit that duck?" "I shot him in the foot and in the head at the same time." "How could you possibly hit him in the foot and head at the same time?" "He was scratching his head."

"While we were hunting, a big animal passed by me." "Reindeer?" "No, it just poured, darling."

———

"I shot this tiger in India. It was a choice of me or the tiger." "Well, the tiger certainly makes the better rug."

———

"If an elephant charges you, let him have both barrels at once." "And the gun, too, as far as I'm concerned."

———

"While we were hunting, I could have shot a bear." "Why didn't you?" "I didn't like the look on his face. He wouldn't have made a good rug."

———

"I shaved every morning." "You mean to tell me you shaved while you were hunting?" "Yeah, I had a lot of close shaves."

———

"I went hunting and shot a raccoon." "Was it a big one?" "Was it a big one? I found two college boys in it."

———

"Say, boy, did you see a fox run by here?" "Yes, sir." "How long ago?" "It'll be a year next Christmas."

———

"Why was he arrested?" "For shooting quail." "Doesn't he know quail aren't in season?" "Well, when they are in season, the quail aren't around, and there are lots of them when it isn't the season. If the quail don't obey the rule, he won't either."

# Hypochondriacs

The hypochondriac was crying to the doctor that he had a fatal liver disease. "That's silly," the doctor explained. "How would you know? With that disease there is no discomfort of any kind."

"My symptoms exactly."

He won't kiss a girl unless her lipstick has penicillin in it.

———

It's easy to spot a hypochondriac. He's the guy who can read his doctor's handwriting.

# I

## Indians

Did you ever realize that the American Indians are the only ones ever to be conquered by the United States and not come out ahead?

———

Comic Jack Carter's story: A man walking along the highway sees an Indian lying down with his ear to the ground. He goes over and hears the Indian say, "Small wheels, Cadillac, color green, woman driving, two children in the back, a California license plate." The man says incredulously, "You mean to say you can tell all that just by putting your ear to the road?" The Indian says, "Ear, nothing; that car ran me over a half hour ago."

———

I can't understand why the Indians want to reclaim five thousand miles of California. They'd never be able to send smoke signals in the smog.

———

Comedian Dick Capri says his wife is an Italian Indian: sort of Siouxcilian.

———

John Wayne says he defeated so many Indians in his movies he gets hate mail from Jane Fonda.

## Inflation

"The cost of living," says comic Lee Tully, "is ridiculous. I asked for fifty cents' worth of Swiss cheese and they wrapped up eight holes."

———

The price of a penny postcard went up from a nickel to six cents.

———

Inflation means you never had it so good—or parted with it so fast.

———

You can console yourself with one thought: The money you don't have isn't worth much anyway.

———

What used to cost five dollars to buy now costs twenty-five dollars to fix.

———

I shop at a friendly grocer. They not only deliver, they arrange financing.

The young housewife picked out three apples, an orange, two pears, and a banana and handed them to the grocery clerk. "That'll be $4.75," he barked. She handed him a five-dollar bill and started to walk out. "Wait, you forgot your change," he called to her. "That's okay," she said sweetly. "I stepped on a grape on the way in."

---

We're told that money isn't everything. The way things are going, it soon won't be anything.

---

Even inflation has its bright side. Now there's hardly enough candy in a five-cent candy bar to be fattening.

---

I wanted to join an organization that fights inflation, but they raised their dues.

---

We have the highest standard of living in the world. Too bad we can't afford it.

---

The bride was near tears as she explained to her mother that, although she had followed the recipe explicitly, there hadn't been enough meat to go around. Her mother spotted the trouble quickly. The recipe, in Grandmother's faded handwriting, began: "Get about fifty cents' worth of rump roast."

Sign in supermarket: NOBODY UNDER $2 ADMITTED.

---

Sure, two can live as cheaply as one, but now it costs twice as much. What goes up—must keep going up.

---

Rodney Dangerfield said, "The cost of living is going up—and the chance of living is going down."

---

Joan Rivers said, "Women who complain about inflation should go to Italy. That's where a girl really feels the pinch."

---

I handed a bill to the cab driver and asked, "Do you have change for a dollar?" "Are you kiddin', mister?" he barked. "These days a dollar *is* change."

---

Inflation is really here. I gave my nephew a nickel and the kid asked, "What is this, a medal?"

---

"Darling," the husband announced happily, "I got good news. We don't have to move to a more expensive apartment. The landlord just raised our rent."

---

Inflation: mini-money.

---

Inflation: That's when you pay a quarter for a nickel penny candy.

A dollar doesn't go as far as it used to, but what it lacks in distance, it makes up in speed.

———

Who says kids don't know the value of a dollar? They must—that's why they ask for ten.

———

Look at it this way. If the buck really loses its value, think how good you will feel when you send your ex-wife her monthly alimony check.

———

There is one consolation in inflation: The money you haven't got isn't worth as much as it used to be.

———

In the good old days, what you paid for a car, you now pay for the insurance.

———

My insomnia is so bad, I can't even sleep when it's time to get up.

———

The doctor told his patient after a thorough examination, "You're sound as a dollar." The patient got panicky. "Please, doctor, don't scare me like that."

———

It now takes twice as much money to live beyond your means as it used to.

———

Inflation that used to be creeping is now jogging.

———

I saw a TV commercial the other night that said, "Please don't buy our product. It costs so much to make it, we can't afford to sell it."

———

Inflation is getting worse. The grand prize in this year's lottery is an all-expense-paid trip to your supermarket.

———

The guy who blew a fortune in the market may have just returned from a trip to the supermarket.

———

Statistics prove that the best time to buy anything is a year ago.

———

A sign in the gift shop read: "For the man who has everything: a calendar to remind him when the payments are due.

———

My neighbor told me, "I made two big mistakes last year. The first big mistake was starting a new business. The second was starting it in a fire-proof building."

———

"I wouldn't mind the rat race," a friend told me, "if I could just have a little more cheese."

Many of us would be delighted to pay as we go—if we could only catch up with paying where we have been.

---

I lead a life of wine, women, and song. It's cheaper than gas, food, and rent.

---

Just remember: A two-dollar bill is not only unlucky, it won't buy anything either.

---

My neighbor's wife can never figure the prices in the supermarkets. It upsets her. She says one store tried to buy back at twice the price all the groceries she bought there the week before.

---

A bargain is anything these days that's only a little overpriced.

---

The dollar is worth nothing these days. The value of the buck is so low, police caught a man passing counterfeit bills and gave him a ticket for littering.

---

I'm independently wealthy. Thank God I have enough money to last me the rest of my life—unless I have to buy something.

---

The high cost of gasoline may wind up saving us money. By the time you fill the tank, you don't have any money to go anyplace else.

---

Sign in a midtown restaurant: "Our prices have not gone up since yesterday."

---

Remember the good old days when you spent ninety dollars on a meal and a plane ride came with it?

---

A husband poring over the checkbook said, "Honey, we can make it through the rest of the year, providing we don't buy anything, eat anything, or turn anything on."

---

The most common cause of car sickness is still the sticker price on the window.

---

The cost of living is always the same: all you have.

# Insults
*(see also Hecklers)*

He's got a photographic mind—too bad it never developed.

---

I don't mind him being born again, but did he have to come back as himself?

---

He's the kind of friend you can depend on: always around when he needs you.

⸺◦⸺

He never says an unkind word about anybody—because he never talks about anyone but himself.

⸺◦⸺

If I gave you a going-away present, would you?

⸺◦⸺

Clean-cut? He once asked a hooker if she'd like to have some fun. When she said yes, he took her bowling.

⸺◦⸺

If you were a building, you'd be condemned.

⸺◦⸺

I can read you like a book, how I wish I could shut you up like one.

⸺◦⸺

He was the kind of kid who made his parents wish that birth control was retroactive.

⸺◦⸺

If I don't get in touch with you in a year or two, please show me the same consideration.

⸺◦⸺

I'm responsible for bringing together all the people who love and respect you. They're waiting outside in the phone booth.

⸺◦⸺

Some of you may not recognize him tonight. He came disguised as a human being.

⸺◦⸺

I feel like making small talk. Let's discuss your IQ!

⸺◦⸺

You know, you'd make a perfect stranger.

⸺◦⸺

You're really not such a bad person—until people get to know you.

⸺◦⸺

He doesn't have an enemy in the world. He just has a lot of friends who don't like him.

⸺◦⸺

You're okay in my book, but I only read dirty books.

⸺◦⸺

You're a man who has no equals—only superiors.

⸺◦⸺

It's been so long since you paid for anything, you still don't know prices have gone up.

⸺◦⸺

At least you give your wife something to live for—a divorce. Look at your face—was anyone else hurt in the accident? You have a lot of talent—but it's in your wife's name.

I think the world of you, pal, and you know the shape the world is in right now!

———

I'm proud to be a friend of yours, pal, and it isn't easy being a man's only friend.

———

It's good to see you—it means you're not behind my back.

———

You're a good egg—and you know where eggs come from.

———

You're not yourself today, and I notice the improvement.

———

He knows a lot; he just can't think of it.

———

He looks the same as he did forty years ago—old.

———

He knows how to break up a party—he joins it.

———

I don't know what makes you tick, but I hope it's a time bomb.

———

I'll never forget the first time we met, but I'm trying.

———

I looked high and low for you, but I didn't look low enough.

———

If you have your life to live over again, do it overseas.

———

You are a humble and modest man—and with good reason.

———

You are a man of rare gifts. You haven't had one in years.

———

Your folks never told you the facts of life, because they never thought you would have to use them.

———

In her own eyes, she's the most popular girl in town—in the country. "You know," she told me with characteristic modesty, "a lot of people are going to be miserable when I marry." I said, "Really? How many men are you going to marry?"

———

The lady diner said to one waiter, "Why aren't you in the Army?" He snarled, "For the same reason that you're not a Rockette."

———

Comic Wilson Mizner about Hollywood producer Jack Warner: "He has oilcloth pockets so he can steal soup."

———

Have you ever wondered where people in hell tell each other to go?

———

You're a real magician. You just made an ass out of yourself.

———

He's suffering from bottle fatigue.

———

You know I'm forming an attachment for you. It fits right over your mouth.

———

Comedian Don Rickles blasted a ringsider: "The schmuck wears a wash-and-wear suit—and gets a gravy stain on his silk tie."

———

If there's ever a price on your head, take it.

———

You have a ready wit. Let me know when it's ready.

———

Groucho Marx said, "I never forget a face—but in your case I'll make an exception."

———

Don Rickles saw actor Ernest Borgnine in his audience and yelled, "Look at that face! Quick, call up Allstate. I think I've found an accident."

———

Don't get such a big head. Remember, even a pair of shoe trees can fill your shoes.

———

WIFE: When I was sixteen I was chosen Miss America. HUSBAND: In those days there were very few Americans.

———

Find yourself a home in a wastebasket.

———

There's a girl I would like to take home to mother—her mother.

———

The lush blonde turned blond lush was the pest of the night. I looked down at her plunging neckline and sneered, "Be careful, honey, or you'll spill that dress all over your drink."

———

Director Billy Wilder listened to an actor sing, and told him, "You have Van Gogh's ear for music."

———

A prominent entertainer paid $1,000 for a toupee. Funnyman Pat Cooper marveled, "Even Jesse James didn't have a price like that on his head."

———

You can write the story of his life on a piece of confetti.

———

The comic's wife told the agent she was going to have a baby. "Wonderful," he said. "I hope you have a better delivery than your husband."

## Insurance

The lady sent a letter to the insurance company: "I'm happy to announce that my husband, who was reported missing, is now definitely deceased."

─────

"But lady, you can't collect the life insurance on your husband. He isn't dead yet." "I know that—but there's no life left in him."

─────

Jack Benny likes to play on the fact that he keeps his back toward the check. "It's true I have a slight impediment of the reach when a check comes," he said. "In fact, I don't want to tell you how much insurance I carry with Prudential, but all I can say is, when I go, they go."

─────

My father-in-law is in the insurance business. He sold me a twenty-year retirement policy. At the end of twenty years, he retires.

─────

He sold me group insurance, but the whole group has to get sick before I collect.

─────

I'm a believer in insurance, but honesty is the best policy if you don't have general coverage.

─────

What really hurt Humpty-Dumpty wasn't that he had a bad fall, it's that he had recently let his accident policy lapse.

─────

My insurance company is pretty good, but they're reluctant to pay off claims: My policy has a $500 debatable.

─────

I'm paying so much insurance to take care of the future that I'm starving to death in the present.

─────

A few weeks ago I tried to get some health and accident insurance. I had to go to three doctors and get three estimates on what it would cost to fix me up before I could get any insurance.

─────

My neighbor told me, "After years of nagging, I finally bought one of those annuities but, of course, I didn't read the small print. Now I've discovered that to be eligible for compensation I have to be run down by a herd of wild animals on Fifth Avenue. Then I collect three dollars a week. If I lose my hair, the insurance company helps me look for it. And they take marvelous care of my wife: All maternity costs—after the age of eighty-seven."

─────

My job provides me with a real good health insurance policy. For instance, should I ever come down with yellow fever, the insurance company will repaint my bedroom so that I don't clash with the walls.

———◦◦◦———

They have a new kind of fire and theft insurance: They only pay you if your house is robbed while it's burning.

———◦◦◦———

A woman asked her insurance agent, "Should my husband die overnight, what would I get?" He said, "That depends on how the evidence is presented to the jury."

———◦◦◦———

My neighbor told me, "I had a policy on my first husband." I asked, "What did you get out of it?" She said, "My second husband."

———◦◦◦———

Those were memorable days in the early history of our country. . . . Nathan Hale saying, "I only regret that I have but one life to give for my country." Patrick Henry saying, "Give me liberty or give me death." John Hancock saying, "Have I got a policy for you!"

———◦◦◦———

Taxes and life insurance are just about the same thing: You pay out the money, and someone else has the fun spending it.

———◦◦◦———

In every insurance policy the big print giveth and the small print taketh away.

My house is thoroughly insured. For instance, if a burglar gets hurt robbing me, he can sue.

———◦◦◦———

My friend Myron has so much life insurance that he can make his wife's day just by sneezing.

———◦◦◦———

This man went to his insurance agent to report that his car had been stolen and he would like to get his money immediately. The president was polite but firm: "Sorry, we do not give you money. We replace your car with a new one." The indignant man screamed, "If that's the way you do business, you can cancel the policy on my wife!"

———◦◦◦———

A broker lectures: "Honesty is the best policy—except when trying to collect on your insurance policy."

———◦◦◦———

The broker received a phone call from an excited woman. "I want to insure my house," she said. "Can I do it by phone?" The broker said, "I'm sorry, but I'd have to see it first." The woman cried, "Then you'd better get over here right away—because the place is on fire."

———◦◦◦———

This insurance adjuster was annoyed. "How come," he asked the man who sent for him, "you didn't call the police the minute you discovered your car had been stolen?" The man answered, "Well, for one thing, my wife was in it!"

———

A manufacturer was considering joining a lodge, but first he asked the president, "Does your lodge have any death benefits?" The prez said, "It sure does. When you die, you don't have to pay any more dues."

———

I asked my neighbor's wife, "When will your husband's leg be well, so he can return to work?" She said, "Not for a long time." I said, "Why? I thought it was almost well." She explained, "It was—but then compensation set in."

———

A woman awoke to find a burglar going through her jewelry box. "Jules," she whispered to her husband, "stop that thief." He said, "Suppose he's armed?" She said, "Please. That jewelry isn't insured—you are."

———

Today the only guy who likes to see a girl fully covered is her insurance agent.

———

Sex is like life insurance: The older you get, the more it costs.

———

The newest policy is no-fault auto insurance: If you have an accident, you call the insurance company, and they tell you it isn't their fault.

Life insurance is a system that keeps you poor so you can die rich.

———

I have a very reliable insurance company. In all the fifteen years they have been insuring me, they never missed sending me the bill.

———

When I was sick my wife sat up all night reading to me—my insurance policy.

## Inventions

Humorist Irwin C. Watson tells this story: Talking about women's liberation brings to mind the people who always say that behind every successful man there's a woman. Well, once I went to check up on this and I found some interesting stories. You know that when Thomas Edison was getting together what was then called the incandescent lamp, he spent thirteen years trying to find the right filament, the right gas, and the right container to make this thing glow. And one day, at about three in the morning, he finally made it glow. And he ran out of the barn, across to the house, up three flights of stairs to his wife's bedroom, and said, "Darling, look!" And she woke up and turned over and said, "Would you turn off that light and come to bed?"

———

He crossed a carrier pigeon with a parrot so it could deliver messages verbally. The first day he tried it out, it turned up three hours late. "What kept you?" asked the inventor. "It was such a lovely day, I decided to walk," the bird explained.

———

Did you hear about the guy who crossed a carrier pigeon with a woodpecker so that when messages are delivered, it can knock on the door?

Did you hear about the guy who crossed a dog and a hen and got pooched eggs? How about the guy who crossed an electric blanket and a toaster and got a machine that pops people out of bed?

———

Benjamin Franklin may have discovered electricity, but the man who invented the meter made all the money.

# Jail

I entertained the inmates at Greenhaven State Prison. The guys loved me. They even voted me an honorary sentence.

---

It's easy to do a show in jail; that's one audience that won't walk out on you. Never worry when they walk out on you. It's when they walk toward you that you should worry.

---

A college football team arranged a match with the guys at Sing Sing Prison to help them in their rehabilitation program. As the two captains were about to toss for sides, the college captain said: "Hey, just a second—you've got fifteen men on your side."

---

As he was strapping the convict into the electric chair, the warden asked, "Have you a final wish?" "Yes," answered the book-of-etiquette victim with a sly glance at the prison matron, "allow me to give my seat to a lady."

---

A convict, telling how he got into jail, said, "I had the car so long that I completely forgot I had stolen it when I reported it stolen."

---

"I know," the Sing Sing captain smiled. "That's why we're in prison. We cheat."

# Judges
*(see also Courts, Crime and Criminals, Lawyers)*

The judge said, "I've known lawyers who sometimes tell the truth. They'll do anything to win a case."

---

I broke a mirror, which means seven years bad luck—but the judge let me off with five.

---

The judge said to the defendant, "Have you anything to offer the court before I pass judgment?" The defendant responded, "Nope. My lawyer took every last penny."

---

The judge said to the defendant, "Have you got a lawyer? The defendant said, "No but I have a few good friends on the jury."

The judge said to the lady defendant, "Why did you shoot your husband with a bow and arrow?" Said she, "I didn't want to wake the kids."

---

The judge looked down at the accused man, a hardened criminal charged with a terrible crime. "Given the gravity of the crime, the court sees fit to appoint you three attorneys." The defendant said, "To hell with that, Your Honor, just get me one good witness."

---

"This is the fifth time I've had you in this court. Aren't you a little bit ashamed?" "Your honor, haven't I seen you five times? Do I criticize you?"

---

It takes a thief to catch a thief, and a judge to let him go.

---

The judge said to an aged prisoner of seventy, "The sentence is thirty years penal servitude." In tears, the prisoner said to the judge, "Your Honor, I won't live long enough to serve the sentence." The judge responded kindly, "Don't worry. Just do the best you can."

---

The truth will set you free—unless you're a criminal. Then it takes a judge.

---

The judge said to the drunk, "Thirty days or fifty dollars." The drunk thought about it for a moment and then said to the judge, "Better give me the fifty, Your Honor. That will keep my wife from asking me where I was last night."

---

A judge asked a woman her age. "Thirty," she replied. "You've given that age in this court for the last three years." "Yes. I'm not one of those women who says one thing today and another tomorrow."

---

A judge is a man who ends a sentence with a sentence.

---

The judge told the bum, "You've been brought in here for drinking." The guy says, "Okay, let's get started."

---

"This is the third time you've appeared before me. I order you to pay a $100 fine." "Your honor, don't I get a discount for being a steady customer?"

---

The judge said to the defendant, "Aren't you embarrassed to be seen here so often?" "Not at all," said the man. "This place seems very respectable to me."

---

The plaintiff cried to the judge, "My house was robbed the other day—and what really ticked me off is that this guy stole my $5,000 alarm system."

———

The defendant's lawyer said, "To save the state the expense of a trial, Your Honor, my client has escaped!"

———

While putting on their robes, the judges were saying to each other: "What would you give a sixty-two-year-old prostitute?" "Oh," said the colleague, "about thirty bucks."

———

Judge Edelstein gave the killer 200 years. The convict said, "I'm lucky I didn't get life."

———

Mr. Schneider stood up in court. "As God is my judge, I do *not* owe my ex-wife any money." Glaring down at him, the judge replied, "He's not, I am, and you do!"

———

"You're charged with public drunkenness. What's your plea?" "Not guilty. Why, I'm as sober as you are, Your Honor." "Thirty days. Next case!"

# Juvenile Delinquents
*(see also Adolescents, Kids)*

America will never be invaded. Our juvenile delinquents are too well armed.

———

The delinquents of today are the same as the delinquents of fifty years ago, only they have better weapons.

———

Strike your child every day. If you don't know why, he does.

———

He could go to any reform school in the country on a scholarship.

———

When he goes to school, the teacher plays hooky.

———

Never give your kid his full allowance. Keep some to bail him out.

———

Our juvenile delinquents today are well educated. When they write dirty words on the toilet walls, they're in Latin.

# Kids

*(see also Adolescents, Children, Education, Juvenile Delinquents)*

Youngsters today are more advanced than ever. Recently I did a show for a bunch of Cub Scouts—and they all brought their wives.

One ambitious kid asked his father if he could do any work around the house to help make himself some extra money. The old man told him he couldn't think of anything. "In that case," the kid said, "how about putting me on welfare?"

The hardest part of telling young people about the facts of life is finding something they don't already know.

I'm not worried about what kids know today—I'm just worried about how they found out.

One Scout told me, "I don't know why parents get upset about sex education in schools. It's like chemistry, except they don't let you experiment."

I think kids should learn about sex the same way I did—with a pair of high-powered binoculars.

Two kids were discussing their future. "Now that your old man has given you the car, does he still give you a weekly allowance?" "No." "Then how do you pay for gas?" "Simple. When the tank is near empty, I let the old man drive it."

The most important thing to learn about rearing children is how to protect yourself.

Pop got this letter from his son, who was camping upstate: "Dear Dad, I have come to the conclusion that it is time for me to stand on my own two feet. I shall call collect Sunday night to explain. Love, Stanley."

Kids have it made today—their mothers drive them everywhere. They drive them to school, to their friends' houses, to the movies, to dancing lessons. . . . I know one kid who wanted to run away from home and his mother said, "Wait, I'll drive you!"

What's the use of teaching your kid to talk when in a few years you'll wish he'd shut up?

My accountant was telling me, "Not only is my son Donald the worst-behaved kid in the class, but the teachers complain he has a perfect attendance record."

Pop said, "It's all my fault. All my life I worked and slaved to provide a safe and beautiful home for our kids to grow up in; a friendly, happy place to bring their friends; a secure refuge against the storms of the world. And now that they've grown up, they won't leave."

Charlie and Frankie were playing on the beach in Atlantic City. "I'm really worried," Charlie said. "Dad slaves away at his job so I'll never want for anything, and so I can go to college. Mom spends every day washing and ironing and taking care of me when I don't feel well. I'm worried!" Frankie asked, "What have you got to worry about?" "I'm afraid they might try to escape," said Charlie.

A kid walked into the living room and spoke to his father. "Pop," he said enthusiastically, "I've got great news for you." The old man smiled and asked, "I'm glad. What is it?" The kid said, "Remember you promised me $100 if I passed in school?" Pop nod-ded. "Well," the son said, "I'm sparing you the expense this year!"

Parents were stricter in the old days. One day I said, "Mom, my shoes are too tight." She said, "Why don't you fold your toes?"

A mother used to cry over her baby's first haircut. She still does, only now it's over the price.

Okay, so the kids are back in school. Back to the three R's: reading, writing, and rioting. In my day the kids had shoulder bags—now they have holsters. Instead of crayons they carry mace. I saw a gun shop having a "Back to School" sale.

In one school, instead of a guidance counselor, they have a parole officer. Instead of overtime, the teacher's union is now asking for combat pay. Talk about tough high schools. At the front door, they search you for weap-ons. If you don't have any, they hand one to you.

In some schools kids don't enroll any-more—they're fingerprinted. No more is it called art appreciation class: Today the kids major in graffiti. In one school, the students even kept the teacher after school.

A lot of young high school kids are graduating pregnant cum laude. Even the nursery rhymes are coming into modernity: I heard a little fifteen-year-old say, "Mary had a little lamb." Her friend said, "Yes, but Gloria had a daughter."

Energy in youth is confusing. The same kids who are too tired to help with the dishes can wait up all night for the box office to open for a rock concert.

Warren, age eight, was asked by his grandfather, "What's the first thing you notice about a girl?" The boy replied, "Well, that all depends on which direction she's facing."

First day back in school, my neighbor's kid was asked to write a paper entitled, "How I Spent My Summer Vacation." The kid told the teacher, "I'm not making any statement without my lawyer here!"

The old man was hollering, "You young kids, with your wild ideas about sexual experience and free love! Let me tell you, it may be free, but it's not love. It's just plain free lust. What's this world coming to?" His wife said, "Calm down! You can't change things. Why are you so angry?" He said, "Because I'm not part of it!"

There's no such thing as "kids" anymore. With sex education being taught in grammar school, a minor becomes a major before he can spell. One little girl I know carries an umbrella with mistletoe in it.

The class assignment was to write a short paper called "Things I'm Thankful For." One fourth-grade boy said, "First my glasses. They keep the boys from punching me—and the girls from kissing me."

My neighbor and his wife told me, "We decided to have children because we felt there might be something missing in our lives. Now we're sure of it: We're missing our freedom, our privacy, and our sanity."

A father decided to teach the facts of life to Myron, his ten-year-old son. He sat down and nervously explained all about the bees and the flowers. When he finished, the old man suggested that the boy pass on this information to his eight-year-old brother. Myron went to his younger brother's room and said to him, "You know what married people do when they want to have kids? Dad says that bees and flowers do the same thing!"

A father knows his kids are growing up when his daughter starts applying lipstick and his son starts wiping it off.

Shortly after my neighbor had a new baby, her five-year-old daughter was sitting with her friend Myrtle. "Do you think you'll have a baby soon?" Myrtle asked. "Have a baby?" the little girl screamed. "I can't even tell time yet!"

———

When my kids became wild and unruly, I just used a nice, safe playpen. Then, when they finished, I climbed out.

———

A teacher knows he's in trouble when he tells his kids the facts of life—and the kids correct him.

———

Our schools don't need more money; they must learn to save money. They can start by teaching driver education and sex education in the same car.

———

Students are in favor of discipline in school: They want the teachers to do exactly what they tell them.

———

The principal said to her second-grade teacher: "You just can't send thank-you notes to your pupils when they stay home because of illness."

———

The parents of a ten-year-old boy were concerned about the introduction of sex education in the school and were worriedly discussing the possibility that their youngster might have to attend classes in the subject. The kid overheard their discussion and disposed of the problem neatly by saying, "I don't want it if there's any homework."

———

"I'm trying something new," the young mother was saying. "Next summer I'm sending my dogs to camp and my kids to obedience school."

———

My nephew came over to the house the other night. He asked me to help him with his arithmetic. After two hours, he said to me, "If it takes you so long to do fourth-grade work, what am I gonna do next year?"

———

Parents have to learn to see the best in things. For instance, if your daughter comes home from college with a little bundle in her arms, be glad when it's laundry.

———

My neighbor said, "My nephew who took violin lessons is now a conductor." I replied, "Great. Does he conduct the Philharmonic?" He snapped, "What Philharmonic? He's a conductor on the A train."

———

A teenager asked a clerk in a Beverly Hills department store, "If my parents like this blouse, can I return it?"

The father yelled, "Always you ask me questions! What would have happened if I asked so many questions when I was a kid?" His son said, "Maybe you'd be able to answer some of mine."

My eight-year-old nephew wonders, "If teachers are so smart, how come they're still in school?"

Two kids talking: "We had a spelling bee at our school last week." "So what? Yesterday our school had a cockroach that did calculus."

The way our young kids are behaving these days, now it's the parents who are running away from home.

Poverty is hereditary: You can catch it from your children.

Parents spoil their kids these days. I bought my kid a spacesuit—cost me $28—and you know something? He won't go!

The youngster hollered at his dad, "I didn't ask to be born." The old man answered, "If you had, the answer would have been no."

My neighbor told me: "I'm so proud of my son the college graduate. He got his first job." I said, "Great. When did he graduate?" He said, "Twelve years ago."

"Maria," Mom said to her eight-year-old. "Have you given the goldfish fresh water?" The youngster replied, "No, Mom. They didn't finish what I gave them yesterday."

Pop said to his daughter, "You usually talk on the phone for two hours, but this time it was only forty-five minutes. Why?" She said logically, "Well, this time it was a wrong number."

Sending a kid to college is educational for the parents. It teaches them how to do without a lot of things.

If you have any good advice to give to your kids, do it while they're young enough to still believe you know what you're talking about.

A man used to sing his children to sleep until he heard one of them whisper to another, "If you pretend to be asleep, he stops."

Every time my daughter smiles at me, it brings a tear to my eyes. I just can't forget how much those braces cost.

————

Teenagers today are people who express a burning drive to be different by dressing exactly alike.

————

A woman's neighbor consoled her: "I wouldn't worry about your son flunking second grade." The mother said, "Well, I do worry—and so does his wife."

————

College is an institution that really does prepare its students for the real world: Right off the bat it puts them in debt.

————

Mother said to her little boy, "Every time you are naughty, I get another gray hair." The kid said, "Gee, Mom, you must have really been a wild swinger when you were little—look at Grandma."

————

"Did you hear about Myron? He's supporting two wives." "Myron is a bigamist?" "No, his son got married last month!"

————

For most kids an unbreakable toy is something you use to smash those that aren't.

————

A wealthy stockbroker's son was overheard saying, "I haven't finished learning about the birds and the bees. Now my dad wants me to learn about the bulls and the bears."

The boy who had just been graduated from college went to work for his father. "Go out and sweep the sidewalk," the father commanded. "But, Dad," the lad protested, "I'm a college graduate!" "Oh, I forgot about that," the father said. "I'll come out and show you how."

————

The little boy told his mom when he came home from school one day that he was in love with a girl classmate. Mom asked, "Now how do you know you're in love?" The kid said, "She told me."

————

Teacher asked an eleven-year-old pupil why he didn't do his homework. "I did," he replied. "Only I made it into a paper airplane and it was hijacked to Cuba."

————

The neighborhood kids were in their front yards when a fire truck zoomed past, with the station mascot sitting on the front seat. The children began discussing the dog's duties. "They use him to keep the crowd back at a fire," said a five-year-old girl. "No," said another, "they carry him for good luck. A six-year-old boy brought the argument to an abrupt halt. "They use the dog," he announced firmly, "to find the fireplug."

————

"Tell me, son, do you like your new nurse?" "No," said the youngster, "I hate her. One of these days I'm gonna grab her and bite her on the neck like Daddy does."

A Sunday school teacher asked, "Who was the first man?" and one youngster volunteered that it was George Washington. "It was Adam," the teacher said. "Oh," the kid answered, "Sure—if you count the foreigners."

Humorist Archie Campbell says his little boy, ten years old, came home from school and said, "Daddy, what is a sweater girl?" Being quick on the draw, as a good father should be, he said, "Well, son, a sweater girl is a girl who works in a factory where they make sweaters." Then, looking at the boy, he said, "By the way, where did you get a question like that, anyway?" The son replied, "Never mind that question. Where did you get that answer?"

Comedian and actor Dick Van Dyke collects kid stories. Here are some of his favorites: A girl thought it would be nice if God helped her with her arithmetic, but her mother said, "God can't help you with your math . . . ask Him to give you more patience to do your studies." The girl looked puzzled and then said, "Oh, God doesn't know the New Math either?" Some kids seem to regard God as a celestial Santa Claus. Four-year-old Betty slipped into bed without saying her prayers one night, explaining to her mother, "There are some nights when I don't want anything." In a classroom, a teacher asked, "Why do you suppose we no longer offer burnt offerings to God?" A boy answered, "Air pollution."

Kids of kindergarten age love any kind of story, from Superman to the Good Samaritan. One teacher told me she was relating the Good Samaritan story to her class, making it as vivid as possible so the children would realize what was happening. Then she asked the class, "If you saw a person lying on the roadside all wounded and bleeding, what would you do?" A thoughtful little girl broke the hushed silence. "I think I'd throw up," she said.

One of my favorite stories comes from Fort Worth, Texas, where the First Baptist Church of Forest Hill was holding a special Mother's Day service. The pastor was giving corsages to the oldest mother, the mother with the most children, the youngest mother, and so on. A five-year-old girl became more and more concerned because her mother hadn't received anything. Finally she whispered loudly, "Don't worry, Mother. If they give one for the fattest mother, maybe you'll win it."

Rodney Dangerfield admits his father wasn't very fond of him: "He taught me to look both ways when crossing the street—up and down."

The three-day-old baby was screaming in his crib while his older brother of five watched with interest. "Has he come from heaven?" Johnny asked his mother. "Yes, dear." "No wonder they threw him out."

---

LADY (to little boy): My dear, does your mother know you smoke? SMALL BOY: Madam, does your husband know you speak to strange men?

---

"Dad, you were born in California, weren't you?" "Yes." "And mother was born in New York?" "Yes." "And I was born in Indiana." "Yes, son." "But, Dad, isn't it funny how we all got together here?"

---

"Where's your mother, sonny? I've come to wash her bay window." "You're too late, mister. She took a bath last night."

---

TEACHER: Now, Johnny, what stirring speech did Paul Revere make when he finished his immortal ride? JOHNNY: "Whoa."

---

In the presence of the camp owner and two counselors, the parents were signing the necessary documents to send their boy to camp. Watching was the younger brother, who finally looked up with tears in his eyes and asked, "Daddy, why are we selling Robert?"

---

Actress-comedienne Roseanne says today's kids can talk their way out of anything: "My daughter had C's and D's on her report card, and she insisted they were vitamin deficiencies."

---

"Can any of you children name the fifty states?" the teacher asked her third-grade students. One clever youngster called them out in alphabetical order. "Wonderful," exclaimed the teacher. "I certainly could not have done that at your age!" "Sure," hollered one kid, "back then there were only thirteen of them."

---

The little boy was complaining to his father about his mother. "She makes me go to bed when I'm wide awake—and wakes me up when I'm sleepy."

---

A seven-year-old boy was being taught the proper way to ask a girl for a dance by the teacher in the dance instruction class. A half hour later the kid asked the teacher, "Now, how do I get rid of her?"

---

Comic Freddie Roman reports: "My wife has really pushed our kid. I think it's great that mothers want the best for their kids. But there's such a thing as overdoing it. My son's ten years old and I still remember the birth announcement my wife sent out: 'Mr. and Mrs. Freddie Roman proudly announce the birth of their son, Dr. Alan Roman.'"

———

An eight-year-old girl walks into a bakery shop and says, "My mommy found a fly in the raisin bread." And the baker says, "Bring back the fly, I'll give you a raisin."

———

The five-year-old boy says to his friend, "My father can beat your father." The friend says, "Big deal. So can my mother."

# Kissing

*(see also Courtship)*

Two models were comparing boyfriends. "Sometimes I'm suspicious of him," said one. "He kisses my hand." "Oh, but that's the way a man with experience kisses," the other answered. "I don't know. A man with experience should have better aim than that."

———

Never let a fool kiss you—or a kiss fool you.

———

A kiss is like faith, hope, and charity. For a girl it's faith, for a married woman it's hope, and for an old maid it's charity.

———

"Where did you learn to kiss like that?" "I used to blow the bugle in the Boy Scouts."

———

I learned to kiss by blowing up footballs.

———

"And what did Flo say when you kissed her?" "What do you think she is, a ventriloquist?"

———

"I could never let a man kiss me unless I was engaged." "Damn it! Just my luck." "But I am engaged."

———

It's no fun to kiss a girl over the telephone—unless you're right in the booth with her.

———

Kissing is an expression of affection that gets two people so close together they can't see anything wrong with each other.

# Labor

*(see also Bosses, Business, Employment, Office)*

I'm strictly for labor unions; they protect their people. My furnace broke down and I can't get it fixed. The furnace repairman says that his union won't permit him to work in an unheated house.

Nobody wants to make house calls anymore. I called an exterminator and asked him if he could kill rats. He said, "Sure . . . when can you bring them in?"

I went into the deli for lunch and, after waiting twenty minutes for a waiter, called one over and told him that I had only one hour. He growled, "I don't have time to discuss your labor problems now."

The waiter told the boss, "We want a guaranteed annual wage, a guaranteed annual bonus, a guaranteed pension plan, and we would like a guarantee that you won't go broke."

A steam shovel was digging at an excavation when a union official stomped in. He said, "A hundred men could be doing that job with shovels." The contractor agreed but added, "Why not a thousand men with teaspoons?"

There are still people who will do an honest day's work, but they want a week's salary and fringe benefits to do it.

Nothing helps a sick employee get well like running out of sick benefits.

"We've got the greatest union in the world," the husband told his wife after dinner. "Why, what happened?" she asked. He explained, "Well, I've got good news and bad news. First the good news. I got $50,000 severance pay." "That's just great," said the wife. "Now, what's the bad news?" He said, "Wait till you find out what they severed!"

The unions protect their workers and their wives—in both cases, by putting more men on the job.

God needed only six days to create the world—but then, that was before labor unions.

———

My TV repairman took out his diamond-studded screwdriver and his platinum tweezers, twisted a few controls, and said, "That'll be $185." I said, "What could you possibly have done to warrant a $185 charge?" He explained, "Three things: I coagulated the circuit rectifier, I gold-watered the azalea bushing, and I let my wife go shopping at Saks."

———

In union there is strength—and in unions even more strength: The handsome young union house painter attracted the lady of the house. She asked him to drop his brush and come make love to her. The union man complied. An hour later the same thing happened. At noon he took out his lunch box and started to eat when the lady beckoned him again. He said, "Nope, not now, madam. I'm on my own time."

———

A New York sign painter who made a specialty of lettering signs for union strikers was picketed by men who wore signs saying: "These signs were not painted by the firm we're picketing."

———

My neighbor told his son, "Learn a trade, and then you'll be able to go out on strike."

One lady called up the owner of a restaurant: "Would you mind calling my husband, Andy, to the phone? He's the waiter." The boss said, "Andy the waiter? Does he work for me?" She said, "Yes, of course, but at present he's outside picketing the place."

———

The only work my neighbor's ever done full-time is picket.

———

Myron was called to the office by the supervisor for talking back to his foreman: "Is it true that you called him a liar?" "Yes, I did." "Did you call him stupid?" "Yes." "Slave driver?" "Yes." "And did you call him an opinionated, bull-headed egomaniac?" "No, but would you write that down so I can remember it?" Myron's boss hated him so much, just before he fired him, he gave him a raise so he would be losing a better job.

———

The chief called his assistant into his office. "Frank," he started, "I want you to slow down. Take it a little easier. Stop pushing yourself. What I'm saying is you're fired."

———

The electrician knocked on the back door and said to the lady who answered, "I came to install the TV cable." The woman said, "I didn't order any TV cable, mister." He said, "Are you Mrs. Davis?" She said, "No, I'm Mrs. Rosen. Mrs. Davis moved away last year." The electrician screamed, "How do you like the nerve of some people? They call us, say they want TV cable right away—and then they move!"

---

The latest statistics show that there are over a million people who are idle in New York. Fortunately, most of them work for the government.

---

One city employee mentioned, "Maybe it's true that hard work won't kill a person—but you never heard of anyone who rested to death either."

---

The waiter asked the owner, "If I take this job, will I get a raise every six months?" The owner said, "Well, yes, if you do a good job." The waiter said, "I knew there was a snag to it someplace."

---

The shop steward asked the porter what he was doing. "Sharpening pencils," the porter said. "Ain't allowed," said the steward. "That's a job for a carpenter."

---

The old politician said to his son, "When I was your age I was working twelve hours a day, with half an hour for lunch, six days a week—and believe me, I loved it and worked hard every minute." The kid said, "Please, Father, be more discreet in voicing your antilabor, union-baiting senti-

ments. You'll never get re-elected with radical statements like that."

---

Things are tough in the job market. I met a guy who said he just lost his job. "Where did you work?" I asked. He said, "The unemployment office."

---

You think you've got problems? We have a plumber who no longer makes house calls.

---

The new man on the road crew told the foreman he hadn't been given a shovel yet. "So what? You're getting paid, aren't you?" "Sure, but all the other guys have something to lean on!"

---

Two Hollywood actors were talking. One said, "We have to picket tomorrow. Shall I pick you up in the Jag or the Rolls?" The other said, "We're striking against deplorable living conditions. You'd better make it the Jag. It's a small car."

## Lawyers
*(see also Courts, Crime and Criminals, Judges)*

A license to be a lawyer makes stealing legal. Today, when you get done paying the lawyer, you don't have anything left to pay the judge.

---

I consulted a lawyer to find out if I needed a lawyer. He said no and sent me a bill for $300. Two days later, I was at a party and met another lawyer. I told him how all I did was ask the first guy if I needed a lawyer and he socked it to me for $300. "Can he do that?" I asked. "Yes," the second lawyer said. The next morning he sent me a bill for $300 for legal advice.

Every lawyer has a meter going, and he doesn't even drive a taxi. He says, "Hello," it costs $25. "How are you?" is at least $40. Even a call girl doesn't charge $175 an hour. I know one lawyer who charges you if he dreams about you. Thinking about you while going up in an elevator is double time. One attorney received a birthday gift from a client. He didn't like it. He sent her a bill: "For time spent while returning your gift: $150."

A friend told me, "Boy, do I have an expensive lawyer. He handled my medical malpractice suit and I wound up owing the doctor a liver and a kidney and my attorney an arm and a leg."

The client said to his attorney: "Say, man, your bill is ridiculous. You're taking four-fifths of my damages. This is extortion." The lawyer replied quietly, "I furnished the skill, the eloquence, and the necessary legal learning for your case." The client said,

"Yeah, sure, but I furnished the case itself." The lawyer sneered, "Anybody could fall down a hole."

The guy told the judge: "My doctor says I can walk, but my lawyer says I can't."

The butcher pushed open the door marked PRIVATE and stood before Forster, the attorney: "If a dog steals a piece of meat from my shop, is the owner liable?" The lawyer said, "Of course." The butcher said, "Okay, your dog took a piece of sirloin steak worth twenty dollars about five minutes ago." The lawyer said, "Is that so? Then just give me another twenty dollars and that will cover my fee."

A lawyer is a learned gentleman who rescues your estate from your enemies—and keeps it himself.

You can't live without lawyers—and you sure can't die without them.

A businessman was involved in a lawsuit that dragged on for years. One afternoon he told his attorney, "Frankly, I'm getting tired of all this litigation." The lawyer replied, "Nonsense. I propose to fight this case down to your last nickel."

The two attorneys were talking. "As soon as I realized it was a crooked deal, I got out of it." "How much?"

---

What's the best way to save a marriage? Go out and price a few divorce lawyers.

---

"I know the evidence is strongly against me," the crook said, "but I have $75,000 to fight the case. Can we win?" "As your attorney, I assure you that you'll never go to prison with that kind of money."

---

I'll tell you how smart my lawyer is. He never graduated from law school. He was so smart, he settled out of class.

---

The judge leaned over the bench and said to the prisoner, "How come you can't get a lawyer to defend you?" The defendant said, "As soon as they find out I didn't steal the money, they won't have anything to do with me."

---

"Before I take this case," the counselor said, "you'll have to give me a hundred-dollar retainer." Myron agreed: "All right. Here's your one hundred bucks." The lawyer said, "Thank you. This entitles you to two questions." Myron screamed, "What! Isn't that awfully high for just two questions?" The attorney said, "Yes, I sup-

pose it is. Now what's your second question?"

---

A lawyer is a man who helps you get what's coming to him.

---

"I borrowed $2,000 from my father so I could study law," the young attorney said. "My first case was when my father sued me for $2,000." The kid now works for a law firm—making loopholes. This same young counselor was advising his pretty new client, "When we go to court, I want you to wear a short skirt." She protested, "But they're not in good taste." He said, "Do you want to be acquitted, or do you want to be in good taste?"

---

The lawyer said to his client, "Now, madam, I will take your case, but do you think it's advisable for you, a mother of twelve children, to accuse your husband of neglect?"

---

If you want to make a short story long, tell it to a lawyer.

---

When you go into court, you are putting your fate into the hands of twelve people who weren't smart enough to get out of jury duty.

---

A lawyer and a doctor were arguing about the relative merits of their professions. "I don't say," said the doc, "that all lawyers are thieves, but you'll have to admit that your profession does not make angels of men." The lawyer answered, "You're right. We leave that to you doctors."

———

The two cellmates were talking. One said, "Me? I robbed from the rich and gave it to my lawyers."

———

Would you believe there is a lawyer's referral service with the slogan, "Our lawyers can relate to your particular problem: Most of them have been in jail, too."

———

The attorney said, "Are you sure you're telling me all the truth? If I'm going to defend you, I've got to know everything." "Yeah, I told you everything." "Good. I think I can get you acquitted. Your alibi is excellent. Now, are you sure you told me everything?" The defendant said, "Yeah, all except where I hid the money."

———

Talk is cheap—if lawyers don't do the talking.

———

The law is a system that protects everybody who can afford to hire a good lawyer.

———

Norman had just won his first case, and the client, a man acquitted of a burglary charge, came over to congratulate him. The client said, "Thanks a lot. I'll drop in on you sometime!" The lawyer said, "Fine—all I ask is that you make it in the daytime."

———

The lawyer was walking down Fifth Avenue when he saw two cars collide. He rushed over and yelled, "I'm a lawyer. I saw the whole thing—and I'll take either side."

———

Harvard University claims it produces most of the nation's lawyers and politicians: That's a good enough reason to close the place down.

———

The attorney said to the judge, "One hundred thousand dollars isn't nearly a big enough settlement, Your Honor. After all, my client deserves something, too."

———

"If we win this case," said the client, "I'll pay you $3,000." The lawyer agreed, "Okay. Get some witnesses." The man hunted up several witnesses and won the case. "Now that we've won," the lawyer said, "how about my $3,000?" The client agreed, "Okay. Get some witnesses."

———

The pickpocket was crying: "I should have been a lawyer. Crime sure as hell pays them."

———

Where there's a will, there's a lawsuit.

———

The divorce attorney was telling the couple, "Your husband gets custody of the car, you get custody of the house, and I get custody of the money."

———

This lawyer and his wife were walking in Central Park when a robber stuck a gun at them. "Tell him you're a lawyer," the wife snapped. "There's supposed to be honor among thieves."

———

My neighbor told me: "I asked my son the lawyer for some advice. Yesterday I received a bill. I said to him, 'You'd charge your own father?' He replied, 'But Dad, didn't you notice the 50 percent discount?'"

———

He's such a great lawyer, he got the jury so confused they sent the judge to jail.

———

Some men are heterosexual, some are bisexual, and some don't think about sex at all—they become lawyers.

———

My lawyer's great. I broke a mirror, which means seven years hard luck. He got me off with five.

## Laziness

For my brother, laziness is a career: He never puts off till tomorrow what he can put off forever.

———

My neighbor's wife was complaining about her man. "He's so lazy. He's been sitting there all day doing nothing." I asked, "How do you know?" She answered, "I've been watching him."

———

My uncle refuses to drink coffee in the morning—it keeps him awake all day. He has a watch that tells how many days till his retirement. Lazy? When he leaves the house, he finds out which way the wind is blowing and he goes in that direction. If his ship ever did come in, I doubt if he'd bother unloading it.

———

The lazy man cries, "Everything gets easier with practice, except getting up in the morning."

———

I know a bank robber who was so lazy he made carbon copies of the holdup note.

———

I have the laziest friend of all: He married a widow with five children. The first thing he does when he gets up in the morning is take a sleeping pill. He finally fell off the couch and had to be taken to the hospital in an ambulance. The doctor examined him and reported, "I'm afraid I've got some bad news for you, sir. You will never be able to work again." The poor soul said, "Thank you, Doctor. Now what's the bad news?"

The laziest guy in town? He listens to the weather on the morning show and won't go to work if it's raining anyplace in the country.

The directions on his medicine say, "A teaspoon before going to bed," and in one day he uses seven bottles.

He has the seven-year itch and is already nine months behind in his scratching.

His idea of cleaning house is to sit in a corner and collect dust.

I know a man who's so lazy, he always goes through a revolving door on somebody else's push. Automation could never replace him—they still haven't found a machine that does nothing.

Women have a tough life. They have to clean, cook, and sew, and that's very hard to do without getting out of bed.

My neighbor told me, "I couldn't work if I wanted to. All my life I've had trouble with my back: I can't get it off the bed. Besides, I've found that the hardest thing in the world is doing nothing: You never know when you're finished." I went to see him and found him in bed, as usual. "Why are you lying down?" I asked. "Are you tired?" He said, "No, I'm lying down so I don't *get* tired."

How about the hillbilly who was reclining under a tree? I said, "Hey there! Your house is on fire." He said, "Know it," without moving. "Well, why don't you do something about it?" He said, "Doin' it now. Bin a-prayin' for rain ever since she started."

My uncle Charlie's very superstitious: He won't work any week that has a Friday in it. Some people would call him a failure. He isn't—he just started at the bottom and liked it there.

The laziest man I know is also the richest. He's an oil man from Texas who bought his wife a yacht for Christmas so he wouldn't have to wrap anything.

"Doc," a man said, "if there's anything wrong with me, don't give me a long scientific name. Say it so I can understand it." The doctor said, "Very well. You're lazy." The patient said, "Thanks, Doc. Now give me a scientific name, so I can tell my boss."

———

Lazy? His wife has kept her promise to keep the kitchen spotless. They eat out.

———

Lazy? He counts calories not because he wants to lose weight but because he doesn't want to have any excess energy.

———

The boss told the young office clerk, "I think you're the laziest person I ever met. I don't believe you do an hour's work in a week. Tell me one single way in which this firm benefits from having you here." The young man said, "Well, when I go on vacation, you don't have to hire somebody to take my place, and no extra work is thrown on the others."

———

The news that Steve had lost his job got around quickly, and Myron asked, "Why did the foreman fire you?" Steve shrugged, "You know what a foreman is—the one who stands around and watches the other man work." Myron asked, "What's that got to do with it?" Steve explained, "Well, he just got jealous of me. People thought I was the foreman."

Lazy? Coffee doesn't keep him awake, even when it's hot and being spilled on him.

———

The guy told his boss, "I'm late because the escalator got stuck." The boss said, "Why didn't you walk up?" He said, "I couldn't. It was going down!"

———

"My father pays our rent," complained the woman to her husband. "My mother buys our clothes and my aunt pays for our groceries. My brother helps with the children's school fees, and my sister arranges our holidays. I'm ashamed that we can't do better." "I know how you feel," soothed her husband. "You have at least two uncles who give us nothing."

# Leno, Jay
*(see also Comedians)*

*For years comedian and talk-show host Jay Leno has been doing comic bits about stupid signs. He has a book out about it entitled* Real But Ridiculous Headlines From America's Newspapers, *and here are a few of my favorites:*

———

"Thieves Steal Burglar Alarm" . . . "Post Office Paychecks Get Lost in Mail" . . . "Blind Cabby Forced to Abandon Driving" . . . "Several Items Reported Stolen From Empty Store" . . . "Condom From Stretch Product

Line" . . . "Lebanese Chief Limits Access to Private Parts."

ADS: "Step into Joyce Shoes made from genuine fake eel skin" . . . "Don't be fooled—accept only imitations" . . . "Eight bagels for $1.49—limit 3" . . . "White Flower 2 day sale—Friday only" . . . "The best things in life are FREE and here's how to get them! Send check or money order for $5.99 to: Home Value Coupons" . . . "Toilet phones for sale—sit down and talk."

More Leno news: "Braille dictionary for sale—must see to appreciate" . . . "Must Sell: health food store due to failing health" . . . "Farmer looking for wife with good tractor—if interested, please send picture of tractor" . . . "CRIME: Sheriff asks for 13.7% increase" . . . "Mayor says D.C. is safe except for murders" . . . "First annual going out of business sale at Randy's Camera Shop."

"Bush orders Army troops to U.S. Virgins" . . . "If bases close, prostitutes would likely be out of work" . . . "Horny man indicted on sex charge" . . . "Boys Town will buy orphanage with girls" . . . "Smaller families require less food" . . . "Attorneys don't want ban on lawyer-client sex" . . . "Mimes banned for abusive language."

"State will poison rivers so it can count dead fish" . . . "Animal rights group to hold meeting at steakhouse" . . . "Woman scolded for killing husband" . . . "Nude scene done tastefully on radio play" . . . "Iraq invades Kuwait; students may lose parking" . . . "Police kill youth in effort to stop his suicide attempt."

"Theft suspect unable to take off with stolen pigeons in his pants" . . . "Con sends death notes to judges after learning to write in prison" . . . "Cemetery plots for sale: 2 Butler County Memorial Park, *never used*, $2,850.00" . . . "Rockland incumbents lose; deceased candidate re-elected" . . . "Dentists charged in death, sent back to VA to practice."

## Lies

Remember, the person who agrees with you . . . will lie about other things, too.

With most men, a lie is a last resort. With a politician, it's first aid.

I asked my neighbor, "Have you seen one of those instruments that detect falsehoods?" He said, "Seen one? I married one!"

The only people who make love all the time are liars.

An honest politician is one who's never been caught.

———

What do you tell a guy who is wearing a new suit that looks like a Salvador Dali copy, when he asks you how you like it? Try: "That suit is really you." Or: "I don't care what anybody says—I like it. But what the hell do I know?" He'll take the lie as a compliment.

———

My friend's wife is a great gal, except she just can't be trusted. Even if she *told* me she was lying, I still wouldn't believe she was telling the truth.

———

You've just concluded a passionate love scene with the temporary love of your life. She doesn't want you to go home to your wife, and cries, "You're only interested in me for one thing!" Be ready with the lie of your life: "That's the one thing my wife wishes I was interested in *her* for."

———

Sometimes the truth can be rougher than a lie. My neighbor confided to me: "I told my wife the truth. I told her I was seeing a psychiatrist, two plumbers, and a bartender."

———

Cynthia cured her husband from coming home early in the morning. I asked her how she did it. "Easy," she explained. "Last night when I heard him fumbling downstairs, I yelled, 'Is that you, Myron?'" "How did that help?" I asked. She said, "My husband's name is John."

———

Lies can be used for good instead of evil: My boss received offers from four publishers for the fiction rights to his expense accounts.

———

My neighbor says, "The only time my husband tells the truth is when he admits he's lying."

———

It's always the best policy to tell the truth, unless, of course, you are an exceptionally good liar.

———

The way my brother-in-law handles the truth, he should work for the weather bureau.

———

My friend said, "I don't trust my wife. Last night she didn't come home at all, and this morning, when I asked where she had been, she told me she spent the night with her sister Carol." I asked, "What makes you think she didn't?" He said, "I know, because I spent the night with her sister Carol."

———

"My husband is a liver, brain, and lung specialist," said the butcher's wife.

# Losers

Talk about losers, He took this gal to the Tunnel of Love at an amusement park and she told him to wait outside.

---

My neighbor told me, "I was in Atlantic City for only three days and lost my car, my watch, and my money. I lost everything but my good-luck charm."

---

My friend always bets on number 8. At the races he put a bundle on the number 8 horse and always lost. In Atlantic City his chips were always on number 8—always lost. I asked, "Why always 8?" He said, "It's my lucky number."

---

A loser? When his bookie's place burned down, the only thing the firemen saved were his IOUs. . . . He's the only person who can buy artificial flowers and have them die on him. . . . He crossed in front of a black cat the other day and it's had bad luck ever since.

---

A friend told me, "As a kid I was very dull and really a loser. I used to belong to this teenage club that liked to hold wild parties at my house. I wouldn't have minded, but they would never invite me."

---

I suspected my marriage was in trouble from the first day: Her parents sent me a thank-you note.

When I was a baby, my parents bought me a carriage with no brakes.

---

I know a girl who was so ugly, she never made *Who's Who* but was featured in *What's That?*

---

I went to a computer dating service, and they sent me the number of Dial-a-Prayer.

---

I went to a psychoanalyst for years and it helped. Now I get rejected by a much better class of girls.

---

My parents didn't want me. They put live teddy bears in my crib.

---

I was kidnapped when I was a kid. Soon as my father got the ransom note, he sprang into action—he rented out my room.

---

When I was born, my father gave out cigar butts.

---

Even my bank doesn't have confidence in me. I have the only checks in town with three things printed on them: my name, address, and "insufficient funds."

---

No wonder I have no confidence in my looks: On Halloween my parents sent me out as is.

———

I remember the time I had an operation. While it was going on, I heard the doctor tell the nurse, "I'll take all calls."

———

My parents spent ten years trying to find a loophole in my birth certificate.

———

My brother was such a loser that in school during fire drills, his teacher told him to stay in his seat.

———

Talk about losers: I went to a real wild party at a nudist camp. My luck, everybody got drunk and started putting their clothes on!

———

My neighbor is a real loser. He has a slight impediment in his speech—his wife.

———

My uncle claims he's so hen-pecked, his parakeet gets to talk more than he does.

———

I'll give you a loser: He's so hen-pecked, he still takes orders from his first wife.

———

I know another man so hen-pecked he never knows what he and his wife are arguing about—she won't tell him.

He's such a loser, on his wedding night she told him they were seeing too much of each other.

———

You're a sure loser when your junk mail arrives postage due.

———

It's not a matter of whether you win or lose, it's whether you can deduct your losses.

———

Sign at Las Vegas dice table: SHAKE WELL BEFORE LOSING.

———

A born loser is a guy whose ship comes in, but it's loaded with relatives.

———

I hung up my stocking last Christmas and all I found was a note from the health department.

———

I was an unwanted child from birth. I had to take a taxi home from the hospital.

———

Are you ready for the loser of the year? He got a letter from a magazine sweepstakes telling him he may owe them a million dollars.

———

My brother proposed to his girl, saying, "Marry me and I'll go to the ends of the earth for you." After the wedding she said, "Okay, now you keep your end of the bargain."

———◦◦◦◦◦———

Last week my brother the loser called up to get the right time. The recording hung up on him.

———◦◦◦◦◦———

A loser is a guy who's been unlucky in two out of two marriages: His first wife left and the second one won't.

———◦◦◦◦◦———

My brother's a born loser. When his ship finally came in, he was waiting at the train station.

———◦◦◦◦◦———

I know a guy who's so thick-headed, he'd make the perfect contestant for a game show called "Strike It Poor."

———◦◦◦◦◦———

My wife wants her sex in the backseat of a car—and she wants me to drive.

———◦◦◦◦◦———

This character I know has a twin sister and she forgot his birthday.

———◦◦◦◦◦———

My bank demands my identification—even when I deposit money.

———◦◦◦◦◦———

Even as a kid, my luck was bad. On my tenth birthday my father bought me a bat. The first day I played with it, it flew away.

My education was dismal. I went to a school for mentally disturbed teachers.

———◦◦◦◦◦———

My parents did not love me. They bronzed my baby shoes with my feet still in them.

———◦◦◦◦◦———

I have no luck with women. The other day I asked a girl to see her apartment, and she drew me a sketch.

## Luck

Comedian Henny Youngman tells of a poor fellow, a real hard-luck guy Henny and some friends wanted to help out. The sad man had a lot of pride, so they decided the best way to avoid embarrassment for him would be to hold a raffle and make all the tickets the same number as his, so he couldn't possibly lose. Shaking the stubs up in a hat, one of the group held it out for him to draw. The number he pulled out was 6-7/8.

———◦◦◦◦◦———

You think you're unlucky? Did you hear about the single girl who is pregnant? She goes to a small town far away from the big city and leaves a phony forwarding address. Then she checks in at a small hospital using a false name, of course. She doesn't tell a soul where she is—neither family nor friends—and then she gives birth to quintuplets.

This guy is so unlucky, he opened a fortune cookie and found a summons.

———

This guy is so unlucky, he opened a fortune cookie and found his draft notice.

———

This guy won $1 million on his lottery ticket. I asked, "Are you deliriously happy?" He said: "Yes! Yes! Yes!" I asked, "What is the first thing you are going to do?" He answered, "Tell my friends it wasn't me!"

———

The question is always being asked by some people: Is it really bad luck to have a cat walk behind you? And I think it all depends on whether you're a man or a mouse.

———

He had tough luck. He had a check for ten dollars and the only person who could cash it was a fellow to whom he owed nine dollars.

———

It's always bad luck when thirteen people are drinking at the bar and you are picking up the check.

———

On doctors: I went to a doctor for a kidney condition. Of course, you never know how a doctor will deal with kidneys. You don't have to get 100 percent in every subject to be a doctor. You can get 65 in one subject and zero in another and you're a doctor because it averages out okay. He might have gotten 35 in kidneys, zero in liver. That's why, when I go to a doctor, I don't want to see his degree, I want to see his report card.

# Marriage

*(see also Brides and Grooms, Cooking, Courtship, Divorce, Engagement, Honeymoon, Sex)*

The matchmaker said to the young man, "I have a girl for you with $50,000." The chap said, "Can I see her picture?" The matchmaker snapped, "With $50,000 we don't show pictures."

---

The marriage agent said, "I will be honest. She squints and has false teeth." The applicant said, "False teeth? Are they gold?"

---

A woman told the marriage broker she wanted a man with a nice business. The man he found insisted, "I'm a businessman. In my business I get samples. How do I know if she's any good? Find out if she'll give me a sample." "But she's a good girl," said the broker. "No samples, no deal," the businessman insisted. The broker told this to the girl, who screamed, "He's a businessman? Well, I'm a businesswoman. Samples he wants? References I'll give him!"

---

A young woman brought her fiancé, Rocky, home to meet her parents. The old man asked his prospective son-in-law about their future. Rocky said he would keep his bride in the manner to which she had become accustomed. "How?" asked her father. "I'll move in with you!" Rocky answered.

---

She said, "You look like my third husband." He asked, "How many husbands have you had?" She said, "Two."

---

She waited for him outside his office on February 29. "It's a leap year," she smiled. "Come on, my parents and my lawyer say we should get married." He tried to change the subject. "Tell me," he said with a rather painful smile, "how's that diet of yours going?" She said, "Just fine. Last week I lost eight pounds." He said, "That's wonderful. How did you do it?" She said, "I had your baby."

---

"Are you proposing to Charlie this leap year?" Sylvia asked her friend Ruth. She said, "No, my feelings toward him have changed." Sylvia asked, "Then will you return his diamond ring?" Ruth said, "No, my feelings toward the diamond ring have not changed."

She said, "All I want in a husband is a man who is good-looking, kind, and understanding. I don't think that's too much to expect from a millionaire."

The wealthy lawyer put all his stocks and bonds and money in his daughter's name, but of course she fell for a jerk. There was nothing he could do but look up his prospective son-in-law and tell him, "Sylvia is going to be a wealthy girl in her own name. If we let her bring you her extensive dowry, what can we expect from you in exchange?" The young lover said cheerfully, "I'll be glad to give you a receipt, sir."

A man in love is incomplete until he has married. Then he's finished.

"Darling, you have deceived me," the young bride said to her husband shortly after the marriage. "But I told you I was a millionaire, and I am," the groom answered. "Yes," the bride retorted. "But you also told me that you were seventy-four years of age and in poor health, and now I've discovered that you are only fifty-six and fit as a fiddle."

"Did you hear they've got a new product that cuts down on a man's sexual urges?" I asked my neighbor.

He said, "So what's new with that? I married one thirty years ago."

A fellow was testifying in court about the serious injuries he received in a loading platform accident. He said: "Ever since I fell off that loading platform, I have been unable to have marital relations more than five times a week." The judge leaned over and said: "Tell me, where is that loading platform?"

Some marriages are made in heaven—but so are thunder and lightning.

You know what it means to come home to a wife who will cook for you, love you, take care of you, adore you? It means you're in the wrong house.

Marriage is a lot like the Army: Everyone complains, but you'd be surprised at the large number that re-enlist.

The difference between sex for money and sex for free is that sex for money usually costs a lot less.

When it comes to broken marriages, most husbands split the blame—half his wife's fault and half her mother's.

The wife said to her husband, "Sylvia next door tells me that her husband makes love to her three times a day. Why don't you do that?" He said, "I would, but when I run into her I usually have garbage in my hand."

---

It's not letting a wife have the last word that worries most husbands, it's getting around to it.

---

Attorney: "For many, divorce is a great relief. The only problem is, you have to get married to enjoy it."

---

The only time my wife pays strict attention to what I say is when I'm asleep.

---

Hard work is the soundest investment: It provides neat security for your wife's next husband.

---

The secret of a happy marriage is to find someone you could be happy arguing with.

---

My wife practices the rhythm method. That means she won't make love unless there's a drummer in the room.

---

My wife is allergic to money. As soon as it gets in her hands, she gets rid of it.

---

There are still more marriages today than divorces, which proves that preachers can still outtalk lawyers.

---

Marriage is like a lottery. The trouble is, you can't tear up your ticket if you lose.

---

My wife sure knows how to spend money. She's extravagant. I mean, who tips at toll booths? My wife is easy to please: She'll go anyplace for dinner except her own kitchen.

---

Everybody is always trying to find a cure for marriage: My neighbor bought a book, *How to Be a Boss in Your Own Home*—but his wife hasn't permitted him to read it.

---

I know one husband who doesn't permit his wife to have her own way. She has it without his permission.

---

Outside of maybe making love once in a while, the average housewife doesn't want to work anymore.

---

A husband is what is left of the lover after the nerve has been extracted.

---

I wish I could have as much fun when I go out as my wife thinks I have.

There is probably a good reason why the husbands of the ten best-dressed women of the world are never listed among the ten best-dressed men.

———

Two dowagers met on the street, one wearing an enormous pendant. "This," announced the wearer proudly, "is the world-famous Plotkin diamond." "I've heard of the Hope diamond," said her amazed friend, "and the curse that goes with it. I've also heard of the Koh-i-noor diamond, but never the Plotkin diamond." "Not only is this a fabulous diamond," she replied, "but it has its own curse that goes with it—Mr. Plotkin."

———

I believe the young people today are getting married much too young. Imagine having your father drive the car on your honeymoon.

———

Helping with the dishes and housework makes for a happier marriage. It's too bad more wives don't do it.

———

They say opposites attract. That's why I married a girl with money.

———

The judge asked one witness, "What did you do before you were married?" "Anything I wanted to," was the answer.

———

The old-fashioned couple used to stay married. Nowadays, the old-fashioned couple is the one that bothers to *get* married.

———

A wife lasts only as long as a marriage, but an ex-wife is forever.

———

My neighbor's daughter asked him, "Daddy, what does a woman do when she loses interest in sex?" He said, "She gets married."

———

Definition of a guy who's been married five times: spouse broken.

———

The only difference between in-laws and outlaws is that outlaws don't want to live with you.

———

A gentleman is one who holds the door open while his wife lugs in the bags of groceries.

———

A woman told the shopkeeper, "I want a small revolver for my husband." He asked, "Did your husband give you any indication of the make he prefers?" She said, "No, he doesn't know yet that I'm going to shoot him."

———

Marriage is the only war in which you sleep with the enemy.

I was married by a judge. I should have asked for a jury.

———

My neighbor told his wife, "If you really loved me, you would have married somebody else."

———

Me and my wife go fifty-fifty on everything: I tell her what to do—and she tells me where to go.

———

The guys were playing golf at the Concord Hotel and saying only good things about their wives. "I just love being with my wife," Schwartz said. "She has such a way about her. And our credit cards are in her name, so I never leave home without her."

———

Marriage is a game you must know how to play: During the marriage vows, one groom said to the rabbi, "Hurry it up. We have an appointment with the marriage counselor in an hour."

———

You know you've made a bad marriage if you go in for wife swapping and you have to throw in the maid.

———

My cousins tried to save their marriage for the sake of the children—and they are the children they tried to save it for.

"I was a fool when I married you," he snarled. "I know," she answered, "but I was too infatuated to notice at the time."

———

"Darling," the young wife said hesitatingly, "I hardly know how to tell you, but soon there will be a third sharing our little home." The husband was ecstatic. "Sweetheart," he cried, "are you sure?" She said, "Positive. I had a letter from my mother this morning saying that she would be here next Saturday!"

———

In Afghanistan, Mullah was crying because his donkey died. His neighbors roasted him, "Mullah, it's not nice you should grieve more for your donkey than for your wife, who died last summer." He answered, "When my wife died, you consoled me that you would find me a younger and prettier wife—but so far no one has suggested finding another donkey."

———

In Saudi Arabia, after a violent sandstorm had disrupted service, this sign appeared in telephone booths: "Until further notice please limit calls to four wives."

———

The poor soul said to his wife, "Look, dear, we're low on money now. We're just going to have to cut down on luxuries. If you would learn to cook, we could fire the chef." She answered, "In that case, if you would learn to make love, we could fire the chauffeur."

———

My wife lets me run things in our house—errands.

———

My neighbor told me, "When I first met my wife, she was a schoolteacher. I used to write her passionate love letters—and she'd send them back corrected. I must be the only man in the whole world who returned from his honeymoon and received a report card. It said, 'Dick is neat and friendly and shows, a keen interest in fun and games.'"

———

A diplomatic husband to his wife, "How do you expect me to remember your birthday when you never look any older?"

———

A woman asked the clerk at the fur shop, "Will a small deposit hold it until my husband does something unforgivable?"

———

My wife is exactly like life insurance: The older she gets, the more she costs.

———

Marriage is a romantic story in which the hero dies in the first chapter.

———

Let's face it, men, you really need a wife. . . . Think of all the things that

happen that you can't blame on the government.

———

Wives are the opposite of fishermen: They brag about the ones that got away and complain about the one they caught.

———

My neighbor's wife told her husband, "You certainly made a fool of yourself at the party. I only hope no one realized you were sober."

———

My sister says, "My husband is a very versatile man. He can do anything wrong."

———

The angry wife confronted her husband and said: "That twenty-dollar bill that was in your pants pocket last night—did you steal it out of my purse this morning?"

———

The angry husband screamed, "Supper's not ready again? That's it—I'm going out to a restaurant!" The wife said, "Wait just five minutes." He asked, "Why? Will it be ready then?" She said, "No, but I'll go with you!"

———

They can never forget the time they first met—but they keep trying.

———

Remember the old-fashioned wedding ceremonies and the little flower girls? The flower girls are now the couples' own kids.

---

You can usually tell early on if a marriage is going to work. This last wedding I went to is a good example: About halfway down the aisle, the bride stopped and asked if anyone in the audience had an aspirin.

---

The nice lady said to the psychiatrist: "It first occurred to me that our marriage was in trouble when my husband won an all-expense-paid trip for two to Las Vegas—and he went twice."

---

You can always tell when a marriage is shaky: The partners don't talk to each other during the TV commercials.

---

"Irving," the new bride cried, "when you married me you promised to love, honor, and obey." He said, "Yeah, but I didn't want to start an argument in front of all those people."

---

The wife says, "Hoping our marriage will improve is like leaving the night light on for Jimmy Hoffa."

---

My neighbor told me, "We had a church wedding because my wife's parents didn't want to miss bingo."

---

Here's what you need to have a very happy marriage: The first thing is to establish who's boss. In my house what I say goes. The trouble is, when I raise my hand, my wife never calls on me.

---

"Do you and your wife ever have a difference of opinion?" my friend asked. I said, "Sure we do, but I don't tell her about it."

---

They have all kinds of books on marriage, like *How to Make Your Marriage Work*. Then there's the sequel: *How to Make Your Wife Work*.

---

During a lifetime, a man goes through three economic stages: What he spends on his date is charity, what he spends on his wife is tribute, and what he spends on his ex-wife is ransom.

---

My wife was an immature woman: I'd be in the bathroom taking a bath, and she would walk right in and sink my boats.

---

Ours was a small wedding: just her parents, my parents, and the obstetrician.

---

Home is where the husband runs the show, but the wife writes the script.

---

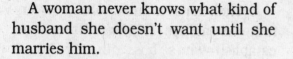

A woman never knows what kind of husband she doesn't want until she marries him.

My neighbor brags that his wife deserves all the credit for stopping him from gambling away his salary: She spends it before he gets it.

A playboy enjoying his feast at the deli insisted that no matter what anyone else says, the most dangerous food of all time is the wedding cake.

The average man has probably thought twice about running away from home—once as a child and once as a husband.

All most men want from their wives is affection, admiration, encouragement, and the ability to live grandly on an inadequate income.

A wife is a woman who always says, "I'll admit I'm right, if you'll admit you're wrong."

Wife to husband as they leave a marriage counselor's office: "Now that we're back on speaking terms, shut up!"

The most trusting husband we know is the one who thinks his wife spent the night in church because she came home with a Gideon Bible in her hand.

"Say, that's a beautiful sable," I told my neighbor's wife. "Must have cost you a fortune." "No," she said, "it only cost a kiss!" I asked, "One that you gave your husband?" She said, "No, one that he gave the maid."

My wife cooks religiously: Everything she serves is either a burnt offering or a sacrifice.

The couple was having an argument: She hollered, "If it weren't for my money, this furniture wouldn't be here!" He answered, "If it weren't for your money, I wouldn't be here!"

The wife was complaining to her friend: "No wonder I'm sick of marriage. Tommy hasn't made love to me once since the honeymoon." "Why not divorce him?" "Because Tommy isn't my husband."

My neighbor told me, "I'm all upset. My wife hasn't spoken to me in a week—and I can't remember what I said to make her shut up."

Old saying: He married her to get rid of her.

A fellow asked his girl's father for her hand in marriage. Pop asked, "Well, the point is, do you think you can make her happy?" The suitor said, "Heck, man, you ought to have seen her at the motel last night!"

———

Her husband demanded, "Is there another man, Shirley?" And she said, "No, of course not. Only you and Pat and Oscar and Henry, as always."

———

Young wives are more practical nowadays. I know one who was so economical that she went without her honeymoon so that her husband could save up for alimony.

———

"I don't want to say my wife's cooking is bad," says my neighbor, "but every time somebody drops food on the floor, the dog runs and hides."

———

It's no wonder my wife feels so much at home at the race track. After all, she is a nag.

———

A bachelor has nobody to share his troubles with. But then, why should a bachelor have troubles?

———

Adam would never have taken a wife if God didn't put him to sleep first.

———

A bachelor's a man who believes that one can live as cheaply as two.

———

A wife can usually live within her husband's income, provided he has another one for himself.

———

Two guys downing martinis: "Did you hear Joe's wife got another baby?" "Another baby? That's her eighth. "Yeah, he wants to get her a special gift, but he doesn't know what." "How about a stop sign?"

———

Slapping the groom on the shoulder, the bride's father said cheerfully: "My boy, you're the second happiest man in the world."

———

My sister-in-law says: "Husbands are like fires. They go out when unattended."

———

My wife has her own way of keeping our kitchen immaculate: She never goes in it.

———

My neighbor embraced his daughter lovingly and said, "Your young man told me today he wanted you as a bride and I gave him my consent." The daughter cried, "Oh, Dad, it's going to be so hard leaving Mother!" Dad said, "I understand perfectly. Just take her with you."

———

When kids today go dancing, it's a little crazy. The kids don't look at each other, don't talk to each other, don't touch each other—it's like being married.

The only form of gambling allowed by the church is marriage.

My sister suggests: "The best way to hold on to a husband is to treat him as you would any other pet: Give him three meals a day, plenty of affection, and a loose leash."

The lady cried, "My husband accuses me of overdrawing our checking account. I haven't overdrawn. He has underdeposited."

My neighbor told me, "I can honestly say that since I married my wife, I haven't looked at another girl. I'm completely discouraged."

Two men were discussing their wives. One said he loved his wife very much, but every time they got into an argument, she became historical. "You must mean hysterical," his friend corrected. "No, historical. She keeps bringing up the past."

My neighbor was told that his wife ran away with his best friend. He said,

"Anybody who would take her away *is* my best friend."

My neighbor told me he's marrying a girl with a $100,000 a year income. I said, "And you told me it's a love match." He said, "It is. I love money!"

For a man, marriage boils down to two adjustments regarding give and take: When it comes to money, you give, she takes. When it comes to orders, she gives, you take.

Polygamy would never work in this country. Think of four wives in a kitchenette.

The cop stopped the couple driving seventy-five miles an hour. The signs on the windshield and the back of the car announced JUST MARRIED. The officer said, "I should give you a ticket for speeding, but I figure, why add to your troubles?"

A couple were dining out on their wedding anniversary. The husband lifted his glass for a toast and said, "I can't think of anything good to say. We have rotten kids, we lost our house, we don't have a car." His wife interrupted, "But you have me." The husband replied, "You're not listening. I'm trying to think of something good to drink to."

A woman's hardest years are those before she finds a husband. A man's hardest years are those after he finds a wife.

———

My sister-in-law told me: "My idea of an unbalanced budget is one in which I find I'm spending less than my husband is earning."

———

If it weren't for marriage, people could go through life thinking they had no faults at all.

———

My wife says, "I admit my husband is more intelligent than I am. The proof is that he was smart enough to marry me—and I was dumb enough to marry him."

———

A man can say anything he pleases in his own home. Nobody listens anyway.

———

A practical nurse is one who's married to a rich old patient.

———

A young minister was called on to perform his first wedding ceremony. After the rites, the bashful couple just stood there. The nervous parson knew he had to get them started back up the aisle, so habit dictated his next words. "It's all over now," he told the couple. "Go—and sin no more."

———

I said to my neighbor: "The trouble with you is you don't relax. You take your troubles to bed with you." He said, "What can I do? My wife refuses to sleep alone."

———

JOHN: I wish my wife were a dentist. HARRY: Why? JOHN: I'd love to have her say to me, "Open your mouth," instead of her usual, "Shut up."

———

I'm not having any trouble meeting expenses. My wife keeps introducing me to new ones.

———

I went to a Mob wedding recently. It was the only time I ever saw the groom cut the wedding cake with a switchblade.

———

The fat lady at the circus married the Indian rubber man—and in three weeks he erased her altogether.

———

The paradox of marriage is that a man hitches up to one woman to escape many others, and then chases many others to forget the one he's married to.

———

My neighbor told me, "I'm really getting absent-minded. Just the other day I kissed a woman by mistake." I said, "You thought it was your wife?" He said, "No, that's just it. It *was* my wife!"

A husband is a person who is under the impression that he bosses the house, when in reality he only houses the boss.

———

My neighbor notes: "I subscribe to the theory that people should never get married on Sunday. It's just not right to gamble on a holy day."

———

My neighbor describes a family man as one who has several mouths to feed and one big mouth to listen to.

———

The man who holds the car door open for his wife has either a new wife or a new car.

———

The women's lib organization is advocating that wives be paid for housework. My neighbor says he's agreed to pay his wife—if she comes in only on Thursdays.

———

The newlyweds had just sneaked off to the honeymoon resort. After dinner, the groom went to bed, but the bride pulled up a chair and sat gazing out the window at the stars. "Aren't you coming to bed?" asked the husband. "No," she announced. "Mother told me this would be the most beautiful night of my life, and I don't want to miss a minute of it."

———

WIFE: When are you going to get window shades for the bathroom? The neighbors will see me if I take a bath. HUSBAND: Don't worry about it. Take your bath. If they see you, *they'll* buy shades.

———

My sister believes, "All men are alike, which is probably why the mother of the bride always cries at the wedding."

———

Second wives always work out better. Like the ads say, when you're number two, you try harder!

———

"Today is my birthday," Alice told her neighbor, "and Harry served me breakfast in bed." The neighbor said, "You're lucky. I had to go to the hospital and have a baby to get breakfast in bed."

———

I won't say she married for money—but the ceremony was performed by an accountant.

———

It was a perfect marriage—he was old and she was frigid.

## Matchmakers

The Lonely Hearts Club had a big sign over the reception desk: "We accept only young ladies of the highest moral standards."

The young suitor asked politely: "Do you happen to have the names and addresses of the rejects?"

———

A matchmaker takes a young man to meet a girl and her family. As they're leaving, the matchmaker says, "Wonderful people, aren't they? Cultured, dignified, educated, rich. Did you see their silverware? Pure sterling." The young man says, "Maybe they only borrowed it to make a good impression." Matchmaker says, "Ridiculous. Who would lend anything to those thieves?"

# Miami

I saw a real hero during a Miami fire. He rescued fourteen mink coats and sixty-five canes.

———

So many people move to Miami to enjoy their golden years, there are more old people in the parks than there are pigeons.

———

In Miami, every time you hear an ambulance go by, you know another prune has been pitted.

———

Everybody talks about how everyone else retires in Miami—you know, the ambulances meet the planes, etc. I heard a conversation between an elderly man and woman. She said, "So,

Irving, you want to take a walk to the corner?" He said, "Yes. That's a good idea. And while we're there we'll pick up a shower cap for Sylvia." She said, "Listen, why should we do everything in one day?"

———

This character from the North was in Miami enjoying the sunshine. "How do you tell the summer from the winter down here?" he asked a native. "Simple," answered the local. "In winter we get Cadillacs, Rolls-Royces, and Lincolns. In the summer we get Fords, Volkswagens, and stuffed shorts."

———

There are three ways to travel to Miami when you get on a plane: first class, tourist, and prisoner.

# Mistakes

The greatest mistake of my life is the number of temptations I've resisted successfully.

———

The carpenter ran up to the paymaster and said, "Hey, I'm short four dollars." "I know," said the man with the money. "We overpaid you four dollars last week, but you didn't complain then." "Well," said the carpenter, "I don't mind overlooking one mistake. But when it happens a second time, it would be dishonorable to keep silent."

———

Will Rogers told about the doctor who operated on people for gallstones who died of pneumonia. "Not my doctor," Will said. "If he operates on you for gallstones, you die of gallstones."

## Mistresses
*(see also Cheating)*

My friend Herb has a perfect explanation for keeping her but not marrying her: "When she's my mistress and I buy her a mink, she is so grateful. Once we're married, she feels it's coming to her."

———

A mistress is like a wife, only you don't have to do the dishes.

———

She is known by the company that keeps her.

———

A mistress doesn't care for a man's company—unless he owns it.

———

A mistress is a good time that was had by one—and all.

## Money
*(see also Alimony, Bankruptcy, Bills, Business, Divorce, Economy, Gambling, Gold Diggers, Rich People, Taxes, Vacations and Travel, Wall Street)*

Money isn't everything—but it sure keeps you in touch with your kids.

———

If you saved money in the old days, you were considered a miser; nowadays, you're a wonder.

———

I've got enough money to live the rest of my life—unless I want to buy something.

———

It's true that money can't buy love, but it makes shopping more fun.

———

Whoever said money can't buy happiness—doesn't know where to shop.

———

Money may not buy happiness—but it rents it as often as you want.

———

Money may not buy you happiness but it gets you a better class of enemies.

———

Money can't buy happiness but it can make being miserable a lot more fun.

———

Maybe money can't buy happiness—but poverty brings misery right to your door.

———

Be sure and save your money. You never know when it may be valuable again someday.

———

The salary we used to dream of is the one we can't live on today.

Last winter my wife was pestering me that I wasn't saving enough money, so I decided to let her handle the money. It was unbelievable. After two months she informed me that she had saved enough for us to go skiing for a week. She had made reservations at a nice resort, deluxe room. Everything was fine but it started to bother me. As we waited to go down the slope I couldn't control myself any longer. I asked, "Where did you get this money from?" She said, "I got rid of something we never used." And off we went down the slope . . . and just as everything seemed perfect I had an accident and broke my foot. When my wife visited me at the hospital she seemed upset. I said, "What's the matter? I'll be out of here in no time." She said, "I hope so. Do you remember when I told you I got rid of something that we never use? Well . . . it was our Blue Cross hospital coverage!"

Money may not be able to buy love—but it will sure put you in a good bargaining position.

It's just as well that money can't buy happiness. With today's prices we couldn't afford it anyway.

What do Poland and the U.S. have in common? In the U.S. they will not accept zlotys when you want to buy something. In Poland they will accept zlotys, but there's nothing to buy.

My neighbor and his wife are having money troubles. The only time they make ends meet is in bed!

Mark Twain once made an inspiring New Year's resolution: "I am going to live within my income this year even if I have to borrow money to do it."

My wife and I like the same things—only I like to save it and she likes to spend it.

Comedian George Kirby dug up an old Chinese proverb that says: "A man who squeezes a dollar seldom squeezes his wife." Well, judging by the way money is being thrown around these days, wives are getting all the squeezing they can handle.

There are more important things in life than money—but they won't go out with you when you're broke.

Making money isn't the real problem in life—the problem is passing it.

There are more things in life than money—but you need money to impress girls like that.

"You've got to admit," she said to her husband, "that spending money is my only extravagance."

———————

Money is only important if you haven't got it.

———————

A special curse: You should have a lot of money—but you should be the only one in your family with it.

———————

Comic Harry Hershfield told of a needy man asking a friend to lend him $100. The friend was silent. The needy one said: "You owe me an answer." The friend replied: "Better I owe you an answer than that you owe me $100."

———————

"I won't lend you the money because it's raining in Tokyo. Yes, that's a reason. If I don't want to lend it, one excuse is as good as another."

———————

A dollar goes very fast nowadays, but not very far.

———————

This handsome young actor married an elderly lady with millions: It was a marriage made in Chase Manhattan. . . . He loves her company: It does $6 million a year. He explained to his pals in the show: "The great thing about money, it never clashes with anything you're wearing." He told them, "I keep a diary of all our good times together. It's called a bank book."

———————

The very handsome young man amazed the very rich dowager with a proposal of marriage. "What?" she gasped. "You really want to marry me? Why you silly, sweet young man, you've only known me for three days." The young suitor said, "Oh, no, it's much longer than that. You see, I've worked for two years in the bank where you have your account."

———————

The young man said, "The Boy Scouts have the right idea. I help little old ladies across the street to my place. You should see all the merit badges—made of gold."

———————

I know a man whose wife was twice his age but two thousand times his bank account. But pretty soon she started to complain, "You're making it with other girls. This must stop." He said, "Calm down. Don't I let you pay the bills? Don't I let you buy all my clothes?" She said, "Yes, of course." He said, "Well, what are you grumbling about? I only use the others for love-making!"

———————

Carmine Santulli tells me: "My wife has the personality and mannerisms of a flea: When she gets on my back, I can't shake her off. The only way I can get her off is to use a special potion. It's called money."

———

A budget is a plan that enables you to pay as you go—if you don't go anywhere.

———

A budget is a complete record of how you manage to spend more than you earned.

———

The wife was crying to her mother, "We always have too much month left at the end of our money!"

———

What's the big fuss about Jackie and Ari Onassis spending $20 million a year? They're still the only couple I know who stay within their budget.

———

So Jackie and Ari spend $20 million a year. Big deal—so does Rhode Island.

———

Definition of budget? A family quarrel.

# Mothers and Mothers-In-Law

To Mom on Mother's Day:
You surely are a winner.
One question do I ask:
What time is Sunday dinner?

I appreciate the chance to visit my mom on Mother's Day. It's like taking a refresher course in guilt.

———

My mama was an extravagant saver. She saved more than my father earned. My father was always strictly business: Every year he had her Mother's Day card notarized.

———

My neighbor told me it took his wife three hours to get her new mink coat for Mother's Day: one hour of shopping and two hours of tantrums.

———

The woman said to her husband, "Is it true that money talks?" He said, "That's what they say, dear. Why do you ask?" She said, "Well, I get so lonely during the day, I wish you'd leave a little here to talk to me!"

———

I don't think my dad was too happy when I was born. On Mother's Day he sent my mom a sympathy card.

———

My mom will always remember the Great Depression: It was the day I was born.

———

Let's hear it for Mom—the only woman with a Ph.D. in laundry.

———

I asked my friend, "What did your mom get for Mother's Day?" He said, "A new washer/dryer." I said, "What happened to her old washer/dryer?" He said, "She divorced him last year!"

———

I never could have achieved the position in society that I now hold without my mother—but honestly, I don't hold that against her.

———

The most remarkable thing about my beautiful mom is that for years and years and years she served the family nothing but leftovers. The original meal has never been found.

———

I can remember my mom and dad taking me to exotic, faraway places—and trying to leave me there.

———

All mothers are champs at giving advice. This little old lady was held up by a rough character with a gun. She wasn't a bit scared. "You should be ashamed of yourself, robbing a poor little lady like me," she protested. "A man your size should be robbing a bank."

———

Mother's Day is a little confusing in Hollywood. Most kids play it safe out there. They send a card to their current mother, their previous mother, their original mother, and just to make sure, they also deliver one to the leading lady of their father's new picture.

———

My neighbor said, "I don't know what to get my wife for Mother's Day. First she wanted a mink, then she wanted a silver fox. It was ridiculous. The house is full of animals."

———

I remember when my dad came home on Mother's Day and glowed, "Guess what I brought home for the one I love best?" Mom said, "Cigars, razor blades, cuff links, and golf clubs."

———

My friend Myron tells me, "Last year on Mother's Day the whole family got together for a big dinner, and afterward, when Mom started to clean up, I said to her, 'Don't bother with those dishes. Today is Mother's Day. Leave them. You can always do them tomorrow!'"

———

The whole family met at Mom's house on Mother's Day. "What's for dinner?" Pop asked. "Take out!" Mom said. The old man asked, "What kind of take out?" Mom said, "ME!"

———

Mother noted, "The trouble with getting money as a Mother's Day gift is that you can't take it back and exchange it for something larger!"

———

This year the card company is out with a new line of greeting cards for Mother's Day. They come in two sizes: regular and unwed.

___

My wife suggested we dine someplace where we haven't eaten before for Mother's Day. "Good idea," I said. "How about home?"

___

Years ago my mom told me not to send her any Mother's Day gifts. She didn't want to be reminded.

___

The new bride gushed to her mother, "My husband is very good to me. He gives me everything I ask for." Mom said, "That merely shows you're not asking enough."

___

The woman shouted over the phone, "Hello, Mama, I got great news! I just won $10,000 in the state lottery! One of my tickets won!" Her mother said, "That's wonderful, but what did you mean 'one of my tickets'?" The daughter explained, "I bought four and one of them won." "Dummy," said her mother, "why did you need the other three?"

___

I'm tired of hearing jokes knocking mothers-in-law. I happen to have the greatest mother-in-law in the world and I'd say that even if she weren't looking over my shoulder as I write this.

___

He who fights and runs away—will return when his mother-in-law leaves.

___

In a Peruvian village a donkey kicked to death a peasant's mother-in-law. When she was buried, the whole male population of the village flocked to the church. After the funeral, the priest expressed his joy to the peasant: "Your mother-in-law was liked very much. I have never seen so many people in any church." The peasant said, "They didn't come for the funeral. They came to buy the donkey."

___

For Mother's-in-Law Day, do something nice for the lady: Take her out to dinner, send her flowers, divorce her daughter.

___

My mother-in-law is very well informed: She can complain on any subject.

___

I won't say my mother-in-law's bad. It's just that she's so nearsighted, she nagged a coathanger for an hour.

___

My pal left his wife because of another woman—her mother.

___

Statistics prove that Japanese women make the best wives. They care for you, pamper you, feed you—and your mother-in-law lives in Osaka.

———◦◦◦———

My mother-in-law needed a blood transfusion, but we had to give up on the idea. We couldn't find a tiger.

———◦◦◦———

Song title: "Fly Me to the Moon— And Don't Call Me Till Your Mother Leaves."

———◦◦◦———

My neighbor's mother-in-law had just come for a visit. His little son was ecstatic: "Now Daddy can do his trick!" he yelled with glee. "What trick is that?" his grandmother asked. "Well,"

the boy answered. "Daddy said that if you stayed a week, he'd climb the walls. I never saw anyone do that before!"

———◦◦◦———

Two young college kids were having a slight argument about their relationship: "I don't mind your mother living with us," the guy was saying, "but I do wish she'd wait until we get married."

———◦◦◦———

My mother-in-law should get the meddle of honor.

———◦◦◦———

No man is really successful until his mother-in-law admits it.

# New York

New York is one of the busiest cities in the world, where something is always happening—most of the time it goes unsolved.

---

We bought Manhattan Island from the Indians for $24. Now it costs that much to park here.

---

New York is a city where you can get away with murder, as long as you don't park next to a fireplug.

---

One councilman came up with a solution to relieve New York's parking and traffic problems: encourage car theft.

---

I asked a subway guard, "What's the best way to get to Queens?" He called me a cab. . . . I don't know why people knock the subway. After all, it's a landmark. The first car started running in 1900. It just got to Grand Central yesterday.

---

Two sardines decide to take a trip into Manhattan. One says, "Let's take the subway." The other sardine says, "What, and be squeezed in like people?"

---

New York City streets are safe. It's the people you have to watch out for.

---

In New York zoos, animals are kept behind bars—for their own protection.

---

Comic Henny Youngman told me, "I ate at an outdoor cafe—and a busboy mugged me."

---

New Yorkers basically keep to themselves. If it weren't for the muggings, there'd be no personal contact at all.

---

In New York, they don't give you the key to the city. They show you how to pick the lock.

---

New York muggers are up to date—they've even started taking credit cards.

---

A man was stopped by a mugger in a downtown alley. The man, who didn't have any money on him, was afraid the mugger would hurt him, so he said, "Could I write you a check?"

The mugger said, "All right, but I'll need to see two forms of ID."

---

In another jam-packed bus, the young lady was having difficulty fishing for a half dollar in her purse to pay her fare. The man next to her volunteered. "May I pay your fare?" She stammered, "Oh, no, I couldn't let you do that. After all, you're a total stranger." He said, "Not really. You unzipped me three times."

---

New York City is one big gridlock: The traffic sign on Fifth Avenue says: "No stopping—no standing—no parking—no kidding."

---

Our one-way streets help. On a one-way street, the motorist is bumped from the rear only.

---

A warning sign on upper Broadway says, "Beware of children going to and from school, especially if they are driving cars."

---

Anybody in New York who speaks good English must be a foreigner. Anybody who doesn't speak English at all must be a cab driver.

---

Some New Yorkers are complaining. They wish the city would collect garbage as often as it collects taxes.

---

This sign seen in New York: "Keep New York clean. Trash New Jersey."

---

In New York everybody runs. You're either a jogger running to keep your figure, or a pedestrian running to keep your wallet.

---

New York isn't the safest town for criminals. One guy held up a bank, and on the way to the getaway car he was mugged!

---

The new laws warn you to drive carefully: The life you save may belong to a pedestrian on his way to remove his car from the parking space you're looking for.

---

New York: The only place where you can park as long as you want to, but you don't want to.

---

A lot of people don't think New York is a friendly city. That's not true. Where else would a mugger knock you down, take your wallet, and then tell you to "have a nice day"?

---

Whenever you're feeling hostile toward a burglar, just remember this: He's the only man in America who still makes house calls.

You know what a mugger is? He's a guy who steals your money without getting elected.

———

Talk about tough neighborhoods. Where I grew up, nobody asked you for the time. They just took your watch.

———

Marvin said, "My house has been broken into so many times, we just put up a sign that says, "We already gave."

———

Crime is so bad in this neighborhood, when you call the cops, there's a three-week waiting list.

———

A very ugly woman was stopped by a mugger who frisked her quickly and said, "You don't have any money." The ugly girl said, "Just keep doing what you're doing and I'll write you a check."

———

I love New York. Where else can you find his and hers muggers?

———

The muggers decided in order to reduce violence and increase tourism they would go union. As of this fall, when a man mugs you he simply hands you a card, takes your money, and tells you to perform two self-inflicted wounds.

———

For years, New York Governor Mario Cuomo has vetoed the death penalty so many times, New York's electric chair has been declared safer than New York subways. Now Con-Ed will come out with several new models.

———

New York is the only town in the world where you can park your car, walk two blocks, and find your hubcaps for sale.

———

New York is unique. Where else can you buy mutual funds with your welfare check?

———

In New York people from all walks of life—run.

———

There are some classy places in New York: At the Plaza they wouldn't let you into the steamroom without a tie and jacket. At the Waldorf you have to shave before you can enter the barbershop! At the Pier, even room service has an unlisted number.

## Obscenity

My wife got the strangest call the other night. She turned to her neighbor and said, "It's an obscene call. What shall I do?" "Quick," answered the neighbor, "ask if he's got a friend."

———

Did you hear about the Indian chief who set fire to the telephone booth? He wanted to send an obscene phone call.

———

Broadway is really on a Sodom and Gomorrah kick. Where else can you buy a copy of *The Machine,* and if it says abridged, it means all the clean parts have been taken out?

———

Everybody complains to the post office about getting unsolicited mail, pornographic pictures, and dirty magazines. What I want to know is, who do you complain to if you didn't get any?

## Office

*(see also Bosses, Business, Clerks, Labor, Secretaries)*

The clerk brought this letter of recommendation to the office manager:

"To whom it may concern: This is to certify that Mr. Jan Franklin has worked with us for two days and we were fully satisfied with his work, except that on his last day of work he was dismissed on account of not being on time, dishonesty, vulgarity, bad temper, inefficiency, and a habit of stealing. We wish him all success in life. Signed: J. Adams, Proprietor."

———

EXECUTIVE: Who told you that just because I kissed you a couple of times, you could neglect your work around here? SECRETARY: My lawyer.

———

"Boss," the secretary announced one morning, "I've found a new position." "Good," said the boss, "pull down the shades."

———

"No," the new secretary said, "I can't type or take shorthand as fast as your former secretary—but what was her undressing speed?"

———

BOSS: Okay now, gang, let's take a ten-minute break for work!

"Someday," the secretary complained about her boss, "I'm going to let the old fool catch me, just to see what he'd do."

———

Advice from an executive: "There's nothing better than surrounding yourself with beautiful secretaries—but remember to keep one or two plain ones for typing."

———

A: I bet you're not working for De May anymore.
B: I should say not, not after what that rat said to me.
A: Really? What did he say?
B: You're fired.

———

SECRETARY: Mr. Brown, you're wasting your time-and-a-half.

———

She came into her office and began passing out cigars. Proudly she displayed the ten-karat solitaire and squealed, "It's a boy—six feet tall and a hundred and ninety pounds."

———

The nicest thing about those postgraduate courses: They keep the boss's son out of the business for another couple of years.

———

The young executive stopped to say good-bye to the big boss. "I'm sorry to see you go," said the big shot. "I'll really miss you. In many ways you've been like a son to me—unappreciative, fresh, arrogant."

———

She quit because her boss kept drumming his fingers. She said it made runs in her stockings.

———

Ability is what will get you to the top—if the boss has no daughter.

———

BOSS: You have been coming in late every single day. Now what do you have to say for yourself? CLERK: It's true—but you must admit, I do leave early.

———

"What's this I hear about your going to church and praying for a raise? Don't you know I never stand for anybody going over my head?"

———

I'm afraid I'll have to fire my typist. She's always interrupting my dictation and asking me to spell the simplest words—and it just gets so embarrassing to have to keep saying, "I don't know."

———

My secretary is 42-26-35 and an expert touch typist. She has to be—she can't see the keys!

———

The boss caught his secretary and one of his executives in a bit of sex in one of the storerooms during a coffee break. "Okay," the boss growled, "what's the meaning of this?" "Well," the girl explained, "neither of us likes coffee."

———

"Okay," the executive said to the sexy brunette secretary, "You're hired. Now would you like to try for a raise?"

———

My wife never trusts any secretary over 36-23-36.

## Old Maids

Comedian Jan Murray tells of two old maids who ran a country drugstore. One afternoon, a farmer dropped in and said, "I need a pill to calm me down. Every time I see a girl, I want to make love to her. What can you give me?" Chorused the sisters: "Seven hundred dollars and the drugstore!"

———

An old maid is a lady who has been good for nothing.

———

It's not too late. Instead of giving up, give in.

———

Politicians know how to run other people's business, and old maids know how to run other people's children.

Chinese say: "Old maid she do not have mush experience."

———

An old maid knows all the answers—but nobody ever asked her the questions.

———

Author Edna Ferber: Being an old maid is like death by drowning—a really delightful sensation after you cease to struggle.

———

Old Maid (calling fire department): "A man is trying to get into my room." "You don't want the fire department. What you want is the police department." Old Maid: "I don't want the police, I want the fire department. A man is trying to get into my room, and we're on the second floor and he needs a ladder."

———

Imagine my embarrassment when, according to my usual habit, I looked under the bed before retiring—and I had forgotten that I was in an upper berth.

———

An old maid rang the fire alarm and twenty firemen responded. When they arrived, she said: "There's no fire, so nineteen of you can go back."

———

Tillie and Millie met for lunch and were discussing what had occurred in their lives since their last meeting.

Millie asked, "You say, Tillie, you were engaged to a promising young lawyer?" "Yes, but he didn't keep his promise."

---

The old maid was asked which she liked most in a man—brains, money or appearance—and she answered, "Appearance—and the sooner the better."

---

The old maid found a thief under her bed. She held a gun on him and called the police. "Please send a cop over—in the morning."

---

An old maid is a girl whose father never owned a shotgun.

---

An old maid was attending a wrestling match when one of the wrestlers was thrown in her lap. She refused to give him up and kept yelling, "Finders keepers!"

---

Did you hear about the mean ventriloquist who went around throwing his voice under the beds of old maids?

---

Two old maids were sitting in the insane asylum. One said, "Y' know, I feel like having a man hug me and kiss me and make love to me!" To which the other replied, "Oh, now you're talking sense. You'll be outta here soon!"

# Opera
*(see also Ballet, Critics)*

A father takes his little boy for culture to the Metropolitan Opera. Out comes the conductor with his baton, and out comes the big diva, and she starts to sing an aria. As the conductor is waving his baton, the kid says, "Papa, why is that man hitting that woman?" The father says, "He isn't hitting her. That's the conductor." "Well, if he ain't hitting her, why is she hollering?"

---

I go to the opera whether I need the sleep or not.

---

"Tell me, how do you remember all the words in the opera?" "I just tie a little string around my finger."

---

"We'll have to go over to the Opera House and rehearse for *Carmen*." "I'm ready for her if she's ready for me."

---

"Can you hear the music?" "No. These are good seats." "I had better seats last year. They were behind a post."

---

"In the opera I stab him and then put a candle at his feet." "It's not bad enough that you stab him—you've got to give him a hot foot?"

---

"I was at the opera last night." "Grand opera?" "Oh, I should say, splendid."

---

As far as the performance was concerned, it was some of the best bracelets we ever heard. We spent the first act looking at ermine and for the rest we just let our eyes slum a bit. It was truly a night at the opera, but personally we enjoyed it much better with the Marx Brothers.

---

Two film actresses went to the opera. One actress said to the other, "If you close your eyes, can't you just imagine you're at home with the radio on?"

---

"How are you getting along with your opera?" "Not so good. I don't know whether I'm *Carmen* or goin'."

---

"What is your favorite opera?" "*The Golden Goose!*" "Was it a hit?" "It laid an egg."

---

"It's a tribute to you, making a living at opera. On the side I'm a contortionist." "A contortionist?" "Yes. I have to do something to make the ends meet."

---

To me opera is Italian vaudeville. It's where a man gets stabbed and instead of bleeding, he sings.

The trouble with opera is that there is too much singing.

---

They are going to do more operas in English—then you'll understand what's boring you.

## Optimists
*(see also Pessimists)*

An optimist is a man who goes to the window in the morning and says, "Good morning, God." A pessimist goes to the window and says, "My God, it's morning!"

---

Harry Weisbaum, of Beau Brummel Ties, got me in knots with this gag: An optimist is a guy who thinks his wife quit cigarettes, because when he came home he found cigar butts all over the house.

---

An optimist is a guy who falls off the Empire State Building and on the way down he keeps thinking, *Well, I'm not hurt yet.*

---

An optimist is a college professor who sits in the last row of the gallery and winks at the chorus girls.

---

An optimist is a guy who tells you to cheer up when things are going his way.

---

An optimist is a guy who attacks a girl, she files a complaint, and he thinks she's trying to continue the relationship.

————

An optimist is a husband who goes down to the Marriage Bureau to see if his license has expired.

————

A toast to the optimist: He doesn't care what happens—as long as it happens to somebody else.

————

I'll tell you about a real optimist: He got married when he was seventy-five—and then looked for a house near a school.

————

An optimist does not believe he's unpopular—it's just that his answering machine is.

## Orchestras

*(see also Bands, Composers)*

"What are the boys in the band doing these afternoons?" "Playing poker." "Playing poker? Don't they rehearse?" "Yes, but no matter how much they rehearse, they can only win when they deal."

————

At an orchestra rehearsal the members had just finished playing "My Old Kentucky Home." The leader, seeing a gentleman weeping, inquired in a sympathetic voice, "Are you a Kentuckian?" To which the man replied, "No, sir, I'm a musician."

"Last night I listened to a sympathy orchestra." "Symphony, fool, not sympathy." "Well, doesn't sympathy mean 'Sorry for someone'?"

————

Several Broadwayites heard a certain maestro's recordings the other day. Said one, "If he's a conductor, I want a transfer."

————

"Have you seen my baton?" "It's in your right hand." "No wonder I couldn't find it. I usually carry it in my left hand."

————

"I like an orchestra that makes my hips swing, that sets my blood running fast, that makes my blood tingle." "You don't want an orchestra, you want a body massage."

————

"I used to have a band." "You did?" "Yes, it was only two pieces." "That was unique." "And we played over the TV. The only trouble with us was that while the band was playing, one of us liked to go into the control room and listen to how the band sounded. The whole thing broke up when I met the other member of the band coming out of the control room while I was going in."

————

"Pardon me, fellers, but there is a gentleman in the house who requests 'I'm Alabama Bound.'" "Okay," he replied. "It's an old number, but we can arrange to play it for a customer." He turned to his men. "A customer wants 'I'm Alabama Bound,' boys," he asserted. "Let's give it to him, train whistle and all." The drummer started off with the train whistle and the band went into the chorus. Suddenly, the waiter rushed over and grabbed the orchestra leader's arm. "Leave out those train whistles," he panted. The leader swung around. "What are you talking about?" he snapped. "'Alabama Bound' starts off with a train whistle." "You've got it all wrong," he howled. "This customer is going by bus!"

———

"What's the idea of all the noise at this hour of the night?" "I need practice on my trombone. I've been letting it slide too much lately."

———

"You know, I heard you on a phonograph record last night."

"Oh, so that's where I was last night? I wondered what made me so dizzy!"

## Pessimists

*(see also Optimists)*

A pessimist nowadays is a man who really knows what's going on. An optimist is a man who hasn't yet read the morning papers.

———

Always borrow money from a pessimist: He never expects to be paid back.

———

A pessimist is a man who feels all women are bad. An optimist hopes so.

———

Love is responsible for most of the optimists and marriage is responsible for most of the pessimists.

———

A real pessimist is never happy unless he's miserable.

———

An optimist is a guy who expects his wife to help him with the dishes. A pessimist won't let his wife do the dishes because he's afraid she'll drop them and he'll have to buy new ones.

———

A pessimist is a guy who has a choice between two evils—and takes both.

———

An optimist is a person who thinks he can borrow money from the bank. A pessimist is one who has tried.

———

A pessimist says there are thirteen men running for president and that none of them is any good. An optimist agrees but says, "Look at it this way: At least only one of them can win."

———

My neighbor carries a little card in his wallet. It says: "I am a pessimist. In case of an accident—I'm not surprised."

———

"I believe," said the happy one, "that for every single thing you give away, two come back to you." The sad soul said, "That's been my experience. Last January I gave away my daughter and she and her husband came back in March."

## Politics and Politicians

*(see also Democrats, Elections, Presidents)*

The only reason we have elections is to find out if the polls are right. Not that it matters, but if a guy is leading in the polls, you know he is the one taking the poll.

———

If you fool people to get their money, it's fraud. If you fool people to get their votes, it's politics.

———

I'll never understand polls. A new one released this month shows that 85 percent of the Americans polled are completely confused about U.S. foreign policy. Now that's a pretty alarming figure—especially when you consider that the poll was taken at the State Department.

———

Said the politician: "If you go to the polls and elect me, all your troubles may not be over—but mine will."

———

A good candidate is one who runs his campaign deeply into debt in the hopes that he'll have a chance to do the same for the entire country.

———

The senator says, "To err is human; to blame it on the other guy is politics."

———

A good man nowadays is hard to find. That's why we have to settle for politicians.

One candidate was presenting his argument before the party's finance committee: "I want ten million dollars for my campaign," he said. "But your campaign won't cost that much," the chairman protested. The candidate said, "I know that—but in case I lose, I want to be able to live comfortably."

———

Some candidates lose because nobody knows what they've done. Others win for the same reason.

———

A magician and a politician are the same: They both fool the public. But when a magician does it taxes don't go up.

———

I like politicians. They're like heroes to me: lots of dough and full of baloney.

———

On the tax form, where it says dependents, can I check off for my senators and congressman?

———

The guys at the club were discussing their man running for Congress: All agreed that he was born poor and honest but he managed to overcome both difficulties.

———

With all the troubles in the world today, if Moses came down now, the tablets he would carry would be Anacin.

I know a big-shot politico who's about to retire and will be honored with a testimonial probe.

---

In Washington, D.C., the waitress at one restaurant told me, "Of course congressmen are poor tippers. Do you think they're as careless with their money as they are with ours?"

---

No wonder the politicians want to fix up our jails: Look how many are winding up there.

---

There are so many candidates this year, there may not be enough promises to go around.

---

Politicians used to kiss babies to get elected. Now some politicians wait till the babies are grown.

---

During a severe winter, millions of homeless people will travel to Washington, D.C., to find warmth in congressional hot air.

---

Under the recently enacted amnesty program, millions of aliens are becoming American citizens. Now they can stop hiding from immigration agents and behave like other Americans. They can start hiding from the IRS agents.

You rarely see a thin politician. It's because of all those words they have to eat.

---

On U.S. foreign policy, our dealings are an open book—a checkbook.

---

What's the difference between Congress and the Boy Scouts? The Boy Scouts have adult leaders.

---

The trouble with Congress fighting today's inflation is it's a lot like the Mafia fighting crime.

---

The U.S. Congress is an institution—which is a proper place for some of its members.

---

Congressional junkets could save us a lot of money. If only they were one-way tickets.

---

Congress can be so unpredictable. . . . You never know what urgent problem they're not going to do anything about.

---

A little girl asked her mother whether all fairy tales began with "Once upon a time." "No," replied the mother. "Today most of them begin with 'If I am elected.'"

The teacher told the student, "You'll never grow up to be president, but with your absentee record, you might make it to the Congress."

---

It's ridiculous for the Russians to accuse us of spying on them to find out what's going on in Moscow. We're too busy trying to find out what's going on in Washington.

---

These days, more and more politicians are doing something for some of their former colleagues: They're becoming "pen pals."

# Post Office

I can't believe the price of stamps nowadays. . . . I don't know anybody I want to get in touch with that much.

---

We pay so much to mail a letter or a postcard because it costs a lot to lose our mail.

---

Postage is now so high, just mailing a get-well card can make you sick.

---

They say air mail is expensive. I say you don't have to send it first class—tourist is enough. And you don't even have to show it movies.

There is nothing wrong with paying what we pay to have a letter delivered from New York to New Jersey: It works out to just a penny a day.

---

My brother is always defending the post office: "The postman always rings twice—especially if there's postage due."

---

The post office express service now guarantees same-day service: That means they promise to lose your package the same day you mail it.

---

Myron says: "With stamps going up, you should see what my girlfriend charges to play post office—and she's not even first class."

---

Talk about highway robbery. The next time the post office issues a new stamp with a higher rate, they should put Jesse James's picture on it.

---

I don't mind taking a licking, but for that kind of increase in price, they could at least flavor the backs of the stamps with chocolate, vanilla, or strawberry. If the price of stamps goes even higher, they'll have to flavor them with Valium.

---

You know how you go to the post office on your lunch hour, and they have only two clerks on duty, even though it's the busiest time of the day? And there's so many waiting in line, you can't even fit into the lobby? Well, with the increase in postal rates, they will soon be able to do something about all this: They're going to enlarge the lobbies at every post office.

---

If postal rates don't stop going up, it will be cheaper to go yourself.

---

The postmaster says the postal service is losing money and may have to raise its rates again. I can't understand why the post office should have a deficit. Look at the way volume has increased—on complaints alone.

---

I don't want to criticize the P.O., but when was the last time you got a get-well card while you were still sick?

---

If the world is getting smaller and smaller, how come it costs more and more to mail a letter?

---

They tell me the post office is going to have to eliminate some of its less essential services—like mailbox delivery. They plan to have a large mail truck just dump all the mail in the middle of the street, and you can come and get it.

---

Sooner or later, everybody gets what's coming to them, unless it's coming by mail.

---

Doesn't it seem like the mail service is against us? Rebate checks take weeks to travel through the mail, but bills always show up the day after they're posted.

---

Special delivery assures that your mail will have a nice, leisurely journey.

---

I won't say the mails are late, but the flower seeds I ordered arrived as a bouquet.

Our local postmaster is mad at me because I turned in the name of our mailman to the Missing Persons Bureau.

---

The post office is annoyed at that TV ad claiming the service is slow. The postmaster general sent a letter of complaint to the TV station three weeks ago, and as soon as it arrives, all hell will break loose.

---

One actor in Hollywood was complaining about the inefficient postal system in Los Angeles: "I'm not saying the mail in Hollywood is slow, but I just got my invitation to Elizabeth Taylor's first wedding."

The U.S. Postal Service is nothing to write home about, but I finally found a way to get back at my postman for slow service: I mailed him his Christmas gift.

———

A female letter carrier was fired for having sex with males on her postal route. It's nice to know that at least someone in the post office delivers.

———

The post office mail service was even mentioned in the Bible: "The Lord made every creeping thing."

———

Old postmen never die—they just lose their zip.

———

This gorgeous girl invited me to come and play post office—but I forgot her ZIP code.

———

The post office has a new method for sorting mail: It's called hit and miss.

———

Priority Mail: The first to get lost. First Class Mail: Guaranteed to be delivered within one week—but not necessarily to the right address.

———

My cousin was retiring after thirty years in the post office. The boss asked, "Have you learned anything after thirty years with us?" My cousin said, "Don't mail my last paycheck."

———

I really like air mail. It gives me a chance to travel around the world vicariously. For instance, I once sent a letter to a friend in Canada. She never got it, but when it was returned to me six months later it was postmarked in England, France, Italy, Australia, and Japan.

———

The post office is having big problems with deliveries. I know a letter carrier whose wife is in her twelfth month.

———

I don't want to say the mail is slow, but if Paul Revere had been a letter carrier, we'd now be known as the fifty *colonies.*

———

My grandfather wrote to the White House to complain and he just got back a reply—signed by Franklin Delano Roosevelt.

———

The post office says all problems will be solved with the nine-digit ZIP code, which will pinpoint exactly where we are now. Now all we need is a ZIP code that pinpoints exactly where our mail is.

———

Remember the mailman's creed: Neither rain, nor snow, nor sleet shall prevent the mail from being returned to sender.

The postal service's credo, updated: Neither snow, nor rain, nor gloom of night stays these couriers from the swift completion of their appointed rounds, so there must be some other reason.

———

There's a new system where you can vote by mail. That's good, except by the time the letter is delivered, the candidate is too old to serve.

## Preppies

Preppies are born, not made. Basic requirements for preppie-ism are money, connections, position, lineage, and country home. And if you have money and connections, you can forget the position, lineage, and country home.

———

Preppies do not believe in the common man because they have never seen one.

———

I know a preppie mommy on an economy kick who washed her own diamonds.

———

How do preppie families travel? They arrive on the *Mayflower* and depart in a Rolls Corniche.

———

The only thing that saved the girl from flunking her classes was the fact that she was fluent in wealthy parents.

———

There was so much boozing at my friend's son's prep school, the only thing he passed was out—but he got an A in frozen daiquiris.

———

My neighbor told me, "I think my son is home from prep school." I asked, "How do you know?" He said, "Well, I haven't had a letter asking for money in three weeks—and my car is missing."

———

One girl wrote her mom from prep school: "There is a lot of kissing and necking going on here and I don't like to be left out of it. Is it okay to remove the braces from my teeth?"

———

Another preppie girl wrote her mom: "It's only fair to tell you that I have already done it. All I want is your consent."

———

The definition of a debutante: a girl with a million-dollar smile. She only smiles at millionaires.

———

The preppie's ambition: To marry a rich girl who is too proud to allow her husband to work.

———

It takes the wool from the sheep and the bank account from one father to clothe the average preppie.

———

How long does a preppie spend in finishing school? As soon as she finds a man, she's finished.

———

Definition of a preppie: a human gimme pig.

———

A preppie's idea of heaven is dating the nymphomaniac daughter of the owner of a chain of liquor stores.

———

Then there was the mommy who was very worried about her daughter attending Vassar, who, after reading *Everything You Always Wanted to Know About Sex but Were Afraid to Ask*, wrote to the author to suggest four new chapters.

———

A real party girl is a debutante who came out five years ago and hasn't been home since.

## Presidents

*(see also Elections, Politics, and Politicians)*

Jimmy Carter gave us plenty of laughs. In fact, he was the laughing-stock of the White House.

———

I'm not too sure about George Washington's wit. . . . He's the only chief of state who didn't blame the previous administration for his troubles.

JFK threw one-liners better than any stand-up comic: "When they call a candidate a favorite son, it's the greatest unfinished sentence in history."

———

JFK on Barry Goldwater: "He's standing on his record—so nobody can see it." On Senator Eugene McCarthy: "I like the straightforward way he dodges all those issues." On Joey Adams: "He knows a lot—he just can't think of it."

———

President Jimmy Carter was asked, "How about the powerful interests that control you?" He responded, "Leave my wife out of this."

———

Said Richard Nixon about Jimmy Carter: "The president is delivering a lot of speeches in the Rose Garden—and where he stands, it's never grown so good before."

———

Abraham Lincoln: "A woman is the only thing I am afraid of that I know will not hurt me."

———

FDR's advice to speakers: "Be sincere, be brief, be seated."

———

Ronald Reagan: "I don't want to make an issue of my age, but I did once have a pet dinosaur."

Theodore Roosevelt: "I think there is only one quality worse than hardness of heart, and that's softness of head."

———

LBJ: "If there is ever a price on your head—take it."

———

The waiter at the White House raves about his job: "I love to set a president."

———

I asked the vice president if he plays an instrument. He said, "How's second fiddle?"

# Prostitutes

*(see also Sex)*

The old saying "Never mix business with pleasure" does not apply to the business of pleasure.

———

Ever since Eve gave Adam the apple, there has been a misunderstanding between the sexes about gifts.

———

The prostitute says, "You can call me mercenary or call me madam, but as I always tell my customers, just call me anytime."

———

Everything is put so nicely in England: a call girl is known as a maid to order.

A German call girl sounds so ominous. When she calls, you listen.

———

Is an Eskimo hooker called a frostitute?

———

My friend was picked up by a prostitute. When they got to her room he was amazed by the college pennants and diplomas ornamenting the walls. "Are those yours?" he asked. She said, "Sure, I graduated from Penn State. I have a master's from UCLA. I took my Ph.D. at Princeton." He said, "But how did a girl like you ever get into a profession like this?" She said, "I don't know—just lucky, I guess."

———

One girl approached an exec and said, "Please give, sir, to take a wayward girl off the street." He asked, "How much?" She smiled and said, "It depends on how long you want to keep her off it."

———

This man-about-town was cruising in his Bentley when he stopped beside a very attractive young thing and invited her to take a ride. As she got in, she slyly informed him she was a witch and could turn him into anything she wished. "Go ahead and try," he smiled. She leaned against him and whispered in his ear—and sure enough, he turned into a motel.

———

Irving was showing his out-of-town pal around the city and pointing out the beauties: "That's Helen—twenty dollars—and that's Betty—fifty—and the redhead is Gloria—eighty dollars." His pal said, "My God, aren't there any nice, respectable girls in this town?" Irving said, "Sure, but you couldn't afford their rates."

# Proverbs and Other Sayings

*(see also Confucius or Confused?)*

A man is known by the company he thinks nobody knows he's keeping.

———

A bird in the hand is bad table manners.

———

Remember, it's always darkest before the light bill is paid.

———

The old believe everything, the middle-aged suspect everything, and the young know everything.

———

One way for husbands to get the last word—is to apologize.

———

The trouble with the rat race is that even if you win, you're still a rat.

———

A smart girl is one who knows how to play tennis, piano, and dumb.

———

No man is lonely while eating spaghetti—it takes so much attention.

———

I saw one picture that was so dirty, you get arrested just for reading the marquee.

———

I don't know if drafting women is right, but it would make induction physicals more interesting.

———

As you go through life, trust absolutely no one except yourself, and when you play solitaire, cut the deck first.

———

We should be thankful for the fools who have lived and are now living in the world. Had it not been for them, the rest of us might not have succeeded.

———

An acquaintance is a person whom we know well enough to borrow from, but not well enough to lend to.

———

If efficiency experts are so smart, how come they're always working for somebody else?

———

There's one nice thing about being a kleptomaniac: You can always take something for it.

# Psychics

Nowadays, if you are worried about your future, you can just pick up the phone and call the Psychic Network. They can tell you your future even if you don't have one.

———

A woman called a psychic and said, "I only want to know one thing. When I die, will I go to heaven and be reunited with my loved ones?" "I have good news and bad news for you," the psychic said. "What's the good news?" asked the woman. "Yes, you will be reunited with your loved ones." "Then what's the bad news?" "It's tonight," replied the psychic.

———

A first-time caller dialed the hotline and asked the psychic, "How do I know if you psychics are for real?" he asked. "We can tell you the truth about yourself," replied the psychic. "Big deal," said the man. "My wife does that every day for free!"

———

"I want to speak to my dead husband," said a female caller. "Why?" asked the psychic. "I didn't get to have the last word," the woman said.

———

Another caller was told by a psychic, "I hear the spirit of your dead wife knocking." "Who's she knocking now?" he replied.

———

Appropriate signs for Gypsy tea rooms:

MEDIUM PRICES.

WE FORETELL THE FUTURE, NOT THE WEATHER.

YOUR PROBLEM SOLVED OR YOUR MANIA CHEERFULLY REFUNDED.

———

Modern-day Gypsies have given up reading tea leaves and switched to tea bags.

———

I went with my friend Myron to a very well known Gypsy tea room. As we walked in, the psychic's assistant said, "I'm sorry, sirs, but the fortune teller is very tired from reading so many minds today." I pointed to Myron and quipped, "Don't worry. His mind will be like a vacation." "I'll have you know, my mind is very hard to read," retorted Myron. "Sure," I said. "Blank pages often are." As the fortune teller entered, Myron flushed and said, "Never mind, I don't need a fortune teller. I can tell exactly what a woman is thinking when I gaze deeply into her eyes." "That must embarrass you a lot," said the psychic. Not only was she a great fortune teller, after she read his mind she also slapped his face.

———

It's always easy to tell a true Gypsy fortune teller. You go in to have your fortune told and you come out without your fortune.

―――

A rich woman went to a fortune teller and as she sat down, the Gypsy said to her, "Madam, you have peculiar lines." The woman glared at the psychic and said, "I came here to have my fortune told, not to have my facelift criticized!"

―――

A group of gin rummy players held a séance to contact a recently dead member. His spirit knocked—but somebody at the table undercut him.

―――

A woman paid a famous medium to hold a séance to contact her dead husband, Maurice, who had been a waiter. The psychic went into a trance and contacted his spirit, but when the wife tried to talk to him, he said, "Sorry, Margaret, this isn't my table."

# Psychology and Psychiatry
(see also Crazy, Doctors)

To me, psychology is the science that tells you what you already know, in words you can't understand.

―――

A man was telling his doctor about his frenzied attempts at slumber: "Last night I dreamed I was the only man in a nudist colony." The doc asked, "How did you sleep?" "Fine," said the patient, "but I didn't get any rest."

―――

The woman entered and asked, "Are you the crazy doctor?" He said, "Well, madam, I am a psychiatrist." She said, "Good, I'm very nervous and have to see you—but first, how much do you charge?" He said, "Fifty dollars an hour." She hollered, "Fifty dollars? Good-bye! That crazy I'm not!"

―――

My aunt told me about her psychiatrist: "I'm not too sure about him," she says. "During my last visit he insisted we try nude therapy. I was fully dressed and he was nude."

―――

I'm not too sure my psychiatrist knows what he's doing. Rumor has it he won his diploma in a craps game.

―――

"Now tell me why you feel your parents rejected you," the shrink told my neighbor. "Well, for one thing, there were those times when I would come home from school, and they weren't home!" The doc said, "Did it ever occur to you that they might be out taking a walk or doing errands?" "Yeah, but nobody takes the furniture with them when they go for a walk."

―――

Comedian Henny Youngman goes to the psychiatrist. He says, "Doc, I have this terrible feeling that everybody's trying to take advantage of me!" The psychiatrist responds, "Relax, Mr. Youngman. It's a common thing. Everybody thinks people are trying to take advantage of them." Youngman sighs, "Doc, that's such a relief! How much do I owe you?" The psychiatrist answers, "How much have you got?"

———

A psychiatrist never has to worry about things, as long as other people do.

———

A shrink is a person who will listen to you as long as you don't make sense.

———

Whoever said "A penny for your thoughts" never had to pay for psychoanalysis.

———

The psychiatrist said to the Internal Revenue Service agent on the couch: "Nonsense! The whole world isn't against you. The people of the United States, perhaps, but not the whole world."

———

The man visited the doctor and told him: "You must help me. I have my entire ceiling and all the walls of my bedroom covered with pictures of Joan Collins, Cher, and Dolly Parton." The shrink said, "I'd like to help you, but I don't understand what your problem is." The patient said, "My problem is that I sleep on my stomach!"

You go to a psychiatrist when you're slightly cracked and keep going until you're completely broke.

———

Dr. Rose said to his patient, "If you think you're walking out of here cured after only three sessions, you're crazy."

———

The man said, "After six years and $30,000 worth of analysis, I finally realized what my trouble was: If I had the $30,000 in the first place I wouldn't have needed the analysis."

———

"Lie down on the couch," the woman's psychiatrist said. She answered, "I'd rather not. That's how all my trouble started!"

———

The pretty little thing told the shrink, "I've been misbehaving and my conscience is bothering me." The doc said, "And you want something to strengthen your willpower?" "No, something to weaken my conscience."

———

My neighbor paid his psychoanalyst $50 to be cured of an inferiority complex. The same day he was fined $100 for talking back to a traffic cop.

———

I told my shrink, "I'm always forgetting things. What should I do?" The doc said, "Pay me in advance."

Sign in psychiatrist's office: "If you have troubles, come in and tell us about them. If not, come in and tell us how you do it."

———

Two psychiatrists meet at a convention. One says, "Charlie, I've got to see you about my inferiority complex." The other says, "But you're a psychiatrist!" The first says, "I know, but I'm not charging enough."

———

A psychiatrist was telling his colleague about a patient who believed in voodoo and black magic. "He doesn't realize that all that mumbo-jumbo is ridiculous. Voodoo is just a lot of superstition." "You told him that, of course?" the colleague asked. "Oh, no, not I," said the doctor. "Do you think I want him to put a curse on me?"

———

The patient said to the shrink: "It's a long, long story. . . . If only I had the money to tell you."

———

The patient said to the shrink: "When you say I should forget the past, does that include the money I owe you?"

———

I went to a doctor for a ringing noise in my head and he cured me. Now I've got an unlisted head.

# Puns

One day two old ladies went for a tramp in the woods, but he got away.

———

When the principal asked the teacher how long she planned to teach school, she replied, "From here to maternity."

———

The call girl recorded her daily activities in a loose-life notebook.

———

If your daughter lived with a fellow without the benefit of clergy, would you call the guy your sin-in-law?

———

Did you hear about the Swedish wife who walked out on her husband? She left his bed and smorgasbord.

———

Old accountants never die—they just lose their balance.

———

My cousin said, "Boy, did *we* throw a big party in our basement last night!" I asked, "Was fat Uncle Charlie there?" He said, "*Was* he? He was the big party we threw in our basement!"

———

The waiter at the White House raves about his job: "I love to set a president."

———

I asked the vice president if he plays an instrument. He said, "How's second fiddle?"

---

There was a family of high-class potatoes who sent their daughter to the finest schools. She came home one day and announced to her parents that she was quitting college to get married. She proudly told them she had met and fallen in love with that nationally famous newscaster, Dan Spud. Her mother shrieked, "My God, girl. After all that we have done for you, how could you marry a common tater?"

---

The woman about to be married for the eighth time explained, "I guess I'm just a sucker for a rite."

---

Two actors met at Sardi's: It was an "I" for an "I."

---

If your nose runs and your feet smell, you know you are built upside down.

---

Did I tell you that the drunk went to China to Taiwan on?

---

Have you heard about the lady of the evening who got a taxi license and is now known as the Happy Hacker?

---

They were driving down the road, and the little boy had been looking at all the signs: "Gee," he cried, "there sure are a lot of bullboards!"

---

When some local politician walked into the club, the band played "Here Comes the Bribe."

---

Men with money to burn have started many a girl playing with fire.

---

Sign at the entrance of a nudist's colony: PLEASE BARE WITH US. The first nudist convention received little coverage.

---

This eighty-year-old woman has become quite a frivolous girl: "I'm seeing six gentlemen every day," she writes. "In the morning Will Power helps me out of bed, then I go to see John. Later Charley Horse comes by. When he leaves, Arthur Ritis shows up and stays the rest of the day, and goes from joint to joint. I enjoy a brief session with Jack Daniels at dinner, and after such a busy day, I'm glad to go to bed with Ben Gay!"

---

Rock music is frequently played by those who are stoned.

---

With traffic the way it is, it seems that the city is getting too big for its bridges.

———

Adam and Eve had their first serious spat over who wore the plants in the family.

———

Miniskirts are getting higher every day. The police say, "The thigh's the limit."

———

The governor told me that because he was once signed to play for a major league baseball team and often speaks at high school and college sports banquets, he is frequently introduced as an athletic supporter.

———

Those with money or access to same are usually loved principally for their purse-onality.

———

My flat-chested sister called to tell me she just bought a new bra: "This is the real decoy."

———

Definition of a diet: girth control.

———

A lady sent this letter to the newspaper editor: "I am lonely and have had no attention for months. Please answer by return male."

———

Safety experts say all car passengers should be belted.

———

My friend tells me about a guy who goes to see a psychiatrist: "Doctor, doctor, you've got to help me. Every night I have a horrible dream. I dream I'm an Indian teepee. Other nights I go to sleep and I have the nightmare that I'm a wigwam." The doc says, "Some nights you dream you're a teepee and other nights you dream you're a wigwam?" "That's right!" "Your problem is obvious. You're two tents."

———

A politician is a guy who makes an issue of himself.

———

The rich old guy may have married the young gal to carry on the family name, but is he heir conditioned?

———

A career girl's mind moves her ahead, while a chorus girl's mind moves her behind.

———

I understand that many chess players have love affairs in Czechoslovakia: They love Czech mates.

———

The out-of-work stripper had no acts to grind.

———

A high school paper informed its readers that their football coach was up and around again "after being laid up for a week with a bad co-ed."

My wife would make a very good soccer goalie. I haven't scored in months.

My wife says I'm bisexual. I do it twice a month.

My brother says, "When people ask a bachelor like me what my philosophy on marriage is, I just tell them it's basically an institution that separates the men from the joys."

*Fireproof* is what you are when you marry the boss's daughter.

Then there was the vacationing tabby cat who wrote to her girlfriend: "Having a wonderful Tom—wish you were here."

A harried woman bought a sheet of stamps in a small post office and began licking them to stick onto a stack of letters. "Will you help me lick these?" she asked the clerk. "Can't," he replied. "Why not?" she asked. "I don't have a licker license," he said.

A young couple approached the registration desk in a big hotel. "We've just been married," the young man explained, "but we forgot to make reservations. Could you give us a suite for the night?" "Certainly," replied the clerk. "Would you like the bridal?" "Oh, no thanks," said the young man. "Now that we're married, we're going to stop horsing around!"

In Russia, when the general secretary wants attention, he just snaps his fingers: I guess you could call him the Red Snapper.

# Rednecks

It's difficult to recognize a redneck—he usually covers it with a hood.

───

I just bought the world's thinnest book: *The History of Redneck Culture.*

───

What is smarter than a smart redneck? A dumb hillbilly.

───

Why do haircuts for rednecks cost eight dollars? The charge is two dollars per corner.

───

This announcement just came over the air: "A tornado ripped through redneck territory in West Virginia and caused $6 million in improvements."

───

A Southern gentleman is a redneck with money in the bank.

───

The old mountain man was watching the storekeeper unwrap a shipment of brightly colored men's pajamas. "What's that?" he asked. "Pajamas," replied the storekeeper. "What are they for?" "You wear them at night," the storekeeper explained. "Would you like to buy a pair?" "Nope," said the mountain man. "Don't go no place at night except to bed."

───

Two farmers' wives were discussing the problems of getting their husbands up in time for work. "How do you git Herb outta bed in the mornin'?" asked Myrtle. "Well," replied Olga, "ah jes open the bedroom door and let the cat in." Myrtle asked, "Does that git him up?" "Darn right," Olga said. "He sleeps with the dog."

───

A fire burned the Redneck Library to the ground and everything was destroyed, including both books and all the crayons.

───

What does a redneck groom call his rusty red pickup truck? A bridal suite.

───

What does a redneck call a handkerchief? His index finger.

───

Two rednecks meet at the gas station. "Hey Zeek, ain't seen yah around lately. Where yah been?" said Jake. "I been to the big city and stayed at a whorehouse," replied Zeek. "Having some fun, wuz yah?" asked Jake. "Nah," said Zeek. "Just visiting kinfolk."

Redneck saying: "There's only one thing worse than a drinking man—and that's a man who don't drink."

Some rednecks get married so young, the marriage is consummated by burping the bride.

The redneck and his wife were leaning against the pig sty when she said. "Tomorrow is our twenty-fifth anniversary. Let's kill the pig and celebrate." "Naw," replied her husband. "Why punish the pig for somethin' that happened twenty-five years ago?"

Two redneck hookers were talking as they leaned up against the bar. "Ain't it a shame about Sally losing her mind and all?" said one. "No wonder," replied the other. "She worked the same whorehouse as we did for two years, and then she found out we wuz gettin' paid!"

A redneck considers a family reunion a chance to meet women.

A redneck thinks espresso is eight items or less.

A redneck is the kind of person who doesn't have curtains in his house, but does have them on his truck.

When a redneck goes to the bathroom in the middle of the night, he needs shoes and a flashlight.

If you ask a redneck, "What's the Super Bowl?" He'll probably tell you, "It's a top-of-the-line bathroom fixture."

A redneck's family tree—does not fork.

At a redneck party, the punch bowl flushes.

You're a redneck if:
—your toothbrush has been in the family for generations.
—you order your teeth from a catalogue.
—taking out the trash means having dinner with your in-laws.
—the fifth grade was your senior year.

If you are dating someone who thinks the stock market has a fence around it—he's a redneck.

If your girlfriend thinks a turtleneck is a key ingredient in soup—she's a redneck.

If you take your dog for a walk and you both use the same tree—you're a redneck.

If having a personalized license plate means your father made it—you're a redneck.

# Religion
*(see also Church)*

"Please, God," the man prayed, "you know me. I'm always praying to you, and yet I have had nothing but misery, bad luck, and despair. Look at the butcher next door. He's never prayed in his life, and he has nothing but prosperity, health, and joy. How come a believer like me is always in trouble, and the butcher next door is doing so well?" A voice boomed from beyond, "Because the butcher doesn't bug me, that's why!"

There are a lot of things to be said in favor of religion: The priests so far have the lowest divorce rate.

I know one New Yorker who's so religious, he wears stained-glass contacts.

The priest was lecturing to his audience that Jezebel was more to be pitied than censured, and we should pray for her. One listener shouted out, "I've been praying for her for years, but I never got her!"

Here are some tasty jokes to set before the prince: God called together his writers. "Gentlemen, I have a big show coming up next week on Mount Sinai and I need some material." "How about: Thou shalt not steal!" one of them volunteered. "Thou shalt not kill!" suggested another. "Thou shalt not—" "Wait!" thundered the Lord. "How many times have I told you I can't use one-liners!"

Brown suddenly got religious and was being examined by the rabbi before being fully accepted into the faith. "You have renounced sin, I'm sure?" the rabbi asked. Brown said, "Yes, sir." The man of the cloth asked, "You'll be honest and fair to all?" Brown said, "Of course." The rabbi asked, "You understand that means paying all your debts?" Brown said, "Now, hold on, Rabbi, that's out of line—you're talking business, not religion!"

Jones swore more than any member of the congregation. The parson took him aside on Sunday and said, "Every time you swear you must give ten dollars to the nearest stranger. That will cure you." As Jones left the preacher, he stubbed his toe, swore, and silently handed ten dollars to a woman just entering the church. "Okay," she whispered, "but can you wait till after the services?"

---

Two fellows opened a butcher shop and prospered. Then a preacher came to town, and one of the butchers was saved. On Thanksgiving he tried to persuade his partner to accept salvation also, but it was to no avail. "Why not, Sam?" asked the born-again guy. "Listen, Charlie," the other butcher said. "If I get religion too, who's going to weigh the turkeys?"

---

After this deacon delivered his exciting sermon about loving your neighbor as yourself, one congregant asked him privately, "Do you love your neighbor?" The deacon replied, "I try to, but she won't let me."

---

The priest explained, "There's a time and place for everything. For instance, saying 'But enough about me. Let's talk about you!' is fine at a cocktail party. But in a confession box, not so good!"

---

Most people have some sort of religion. At least they know what church they're staying away from.

---

No matter how many new translations of the Bible come out, people still sin the same way.

---

"He may preach against gambling and cheating," one parishioner admitted, "yet I have nothing but praise for our new minister." His neighbor agreed: "I noticed that when the collection plate was passed."

---

After the services, Myron remarked to his friend, "Did you hear Roberts snoring in church this morning?" "Yes I did. He woke me up."

---

The rich old couple was sitting in church when the collection plate came around. "Don't put in more than a dollar," advised the lady. "Look, Prunella," said her husband, "Andrew Carnegie gave over half a million for his seat in heaven; John D. Rockefeller gave over a million. Where the hell do you think I'll sit for a dollar?"

---

The Italian kid stayed out of school on Chanukah. The next day the teacher said, "Why did you stay out of school on the holiday? You're not Jewish." The boy replied, "Yes, teacher, but I'm in sympathy with the movement."

---

The youngster was praying: "Please, God, I don't want to go to heaven if my piano teacher is going to be there—and please put vitamins in candy instead of spinach."

The minister was explaining the facts of life to his daughter. The youngster listened attentively as her father told her about the birds and bees, then asked, "Does God know about this?"

The Sunday school girl asked her friend, "Do you really think there's a devil?" The other said, "It'll probably turn out like Santa Claus. It'll probably be my father."

Two churches were on either side of a street. The marquee on one, a liberal church, announced: THERE AIN'T NO HELL. The other one retorted: THE HELL THERE AIN'T.

A church marquee had this legend: YOU THINK IT'S HOT HERE!

One minister I know has on his calling card: "Let me knock the hell out of you!"

In a small village church, a poor widow put one dollar in the collection plate, twice her usual offering. The pastor noticed and asked why. She said, "I'm thankful that my grandchildren are visiting." Two weeks later she put a five-dollar bill in the plate and explained, "They just left."

If the cost of medicine and doctors keeps going up, we'll all have to become Christian Scientists.

My mother-in-law is a good Christian Scientist who says her prayers first thing every morning and has been doing so for many years. Lately I noticed that she has been reading the newspapers first. "Are prayers less important now?" I asked. "Not at all," she explained. "I'm just looking to see what I have to pray about."

The rabbi told me he has very strict morals: He would rather not perform a wedding ceremony. I asked, "Why? What has that got to do with morals?" He explained, "My conscience will not let me take part in a game of chance."

Too many people who occasionally go to church expect a million-dollar answer to a one-dollar contribution.

I believe in the Bible all the way: I sure respect Noah for building the Ark to preserve the species and to put two of everything on board, but why did he have to include mosquitoes, roaches, fleas, and Communists?

There's a definite return to religion in this country. A recent poll showed that 60 percent of all Americans believe in miracles: Half of them are churchgoers, and the others put their faith in the lottery.

———

The Three Wise Men were on their way to Bethlehem. Suddenly, one of them ground his camel to a halt: "Now listen, fellows," he said to the other two. "Remember, no mentioning how much we paid for the gifts."

———

Las Vegas is the most religious city in the world: At any hour you can walk into a casino and hear someone say, "Oh, my God!"

———

I've got a friend who's Catholic and whose mother is an atheist: When he goes to confession he brings his lawyer along.

———

Humor is a divine quality, and God has the greatest sense of humor of all. He must have, otherwise he wouldn't have made so many politicians.

———

The minister was discussing with some politicians what it must be like in heaven: "One thing you can be sure of, we will have a good rest. No graft, bribes, fraud, lying." One pol interrupted, "Of course not. That's not where our politicians have gone."

———

God heals—and the doctors takes the fees.

———

Union officials have only one thing against God: He worked a six-day week.

———

If Moses had been a committee, we would have had eighty-nine commandments instead of ten.

———

The first thing today's motorist prays for when he gets to church on Sunday morning is a place to park the car.

———

A Baptist church got rid of unwanted cars in their parking lot after they erected this sign: "No parking violators will be baptized."

———

The preacher was telling his flock about a biblical character who had a thousand wives and concubines and fed them all ambrosia. "Never mind what he fed them," a guy yelled from the back of the congregation. "What did *he* eat?"

———

"Jane," the Sunday school Bible teacher asked, "tell the class, who was the first man?" She cried, "Oh, please, not even my mother knows!"

Father Bob was having dinner with Rabbi Mann: "Come on," said Father Bob, "when are you going to let yourself have some ham?" The rabbi said, "At your wedding!"

---

Most people hate to think they're missing out on anything. A recent bulletin from the Bible Society mentioned that there are now 143 officially recognized sins. Since then, thousands of letters from all over the world have poured in, asking for a copy of the complete list.

---

The minister asked, "Do you know where little boys and girls go when they do bad things?" The bad boy answered, "Sure—in the back of the churchyard."

---

I've got news for you: I read the last page of the Bible, and it's all going to turn out okay.

---

I think those TV evangelists are getting a bad rap. Their ministries do bring joy and prosperity into lives— their lives. Obviously the main concern of these evangelists is the hereafter: They're here after our money.

---

The TV minister arrived in New York and was given a beautiful suite at a class hotel. When he walked in the bedroom, he saw this gorgeous red-head sitting on the bed. He called the desk and screamed, "What's the meaning of this outrage? How dare you embarrass me this way? I'm a most distinguished evangelist, and you have the audacity to humiliate me? I'm going to sue this hotel for every cent it has!" At this point, the girl got off the bed and started to leave. The minister turned to her and said, "Just a moment, miss, nobody's talking to you!"

---

One listener called the TV evangelist and asked, "How do you really feel about the ladies?" He said, "Every man should have a girl for love, companionship, and sympathy—preferably at three different addresses."

---

There are those times in life when it's useless to try to hold a man to anything he says: when he's madly in love, drunk, or a TV evangelist.

---

"Actually, there's a lot to be said for sin, you know," one clergyman said to another. "After all, if it didn't exist, we'd be out of a job."

---

My wife is so Catholic, we can't get fire insurance—too many candles in our house.

---

Hollywood Catholics are different: They're the only Catholics who give up matzoh balls for Lent.

---

# Rich People

*(see also Money, Society People)*

I know a guy so rich that when he flies, his wallet is classified as carry-on luggage. Would you believe this guy is so wealthy, he has a sleep-in banker?

___

My rich uncle says, "One of the advantages of being rich is that all of your faults are called eccentricities."

___

The millionaire had to buy another yacht—his first one got wet.

___

As a youngster, my rich cousin was so loaded, he was the only kid in town with a Rolls-Royce tricycle. . . . Who else do you know who had a Gucci Christmas tree? . . . Not only does he have a friend at Chase Manhattan, his friend *is* Chase Manhattan: When the bank needs a loan, they bypass the treasury and phone my cousin direct.

___

Don't knock the rich: When was the last time you were hired by somebody poor?

___

My neighbor is a man of untold wealth because he never reports it on his income tax return.

___

With my neighbor, money is no object. The other day he went for a drive. His gas station attendant said, "Regular or high test?" He hollered, "What regular or high test? Gimme the best—homogenized!"

___

You can't talk rich without mentioning Texas: One Texas teenager told his father he needed some oil for his hair, so his father bought him Oklahoma. I also know this magnate from Houston who bought an oil well because he was always running out of fluid for his cigarette lighter.

___

The billionaire was trying to impress his old friend, who wouldn't play along: "I got a stretch limousine with a chauffeur." "So what, quite a few people got limos with chauffeurs." The billionaire continued: "You should see my house: It's got fifty rooms in it." "I've heard of fifty-room houses before." The billionaire kept trying: "I got an eighteen-hole golf course, too." His friend asked, "Inside the house?"

___

Sure a lot of people have money to burn. Why not? It's cheaper than gas!

___

I've got news for you: There are a lot of rich people around. One Long Island neighborhood I know is so rich, the high school mascot is a mink.

___

There is one rich school I know that is now called Our Lady of the Dow Jones Average.

Money brings everything to you, especially relatives and girls. "Darling," my uncle said to the pretty little thing, "I don't know how to tell it to you, but I lost all my money. I haven't a cent in the world." She said, "That won't make any difference to me, sweetheart. I'll love you just as much even if I never see you again."

---

One businessman, already rated a millionaire by his associates, continued slaving sixty hours a week, including weekends, without a vacation. His doctor asked him, "Why do you work so hard just to make more and more money?" He said, "I'm curious to see if there's some income my wife can't live beyond."

---

An amorous old millionaire asked Cynthia to marry him. She told him, "I just happen to have the combination that opens your safe: 38-24-36." The old boy asked her, "How do I know you're not marrying me for my money?" She said, "We're both taking a risk. How do I know you won't go broke in a year or so?"

---

The self-made millionaire was addressing the graduating class at his business school. "All my success in life," he said, "I owe to one thing: pluck, pluck, and more pluck." One kid in the back said, "That's great, sir. But will you please tell us something about *who* to pluck and how?"

How easy it is for a man to die rich, if he will but be contented to live miserable.

## Russia

I know a Russian comedian, which is not so odd—his whole country is laughable.

---

Now that my friend is out of the USSR, he can afford to laugh.

---

In Russia, when you're asked embarrassing questions, you're being interviewed by the KGB. In America, you're being interviewed by TV reporters.

---

In the days of the cold war, in Russia, when you dial information, you'd better have some.

---

In Russia they are still struggling with the concept of producing talk shows for TV. They are still used to "don't talk shows."

---

My Russian friend is happy to be here and loves to compare societies: "In the U.S., it's 'innocent until proven guilty.' In Russia, it's 'guilty until you die.'"

---

Here you have freedom of speech. You can go up to the president of the United States and say, "I don't like the president of the United States." You can also do the same thing in Russia: You can go up to the party chief and say, "I don't like the president of the United States."

---

Disneyland is made up of fantasy and fairy tales. The Russians have the same thing: They're called elections.

---

Only in Russia do they have loose-leaf history books.

---

My Russian neighbor says, "At home I never wore tennis shoes. They're for running. If you ran in Russia, they'd shoot you."

---

The slogan for the Russian credit card is "Don't leave home."

---

The big commercial on Moscow TV is: "You asked for it, you got it—hard labor."

---

The favorite game in Siberia is hide and stay hidden.

---

My neighbor got out of Russia in a very unusual way: alive.

My aunt's husband told me, "I left the USSR thirty years ago on Thanksgiving Day. It was July, but any day you leave Russia is Thanksgiving."

---

A man is sitting in a park in Moscow studying a Hebrew book. A KGB agent comes over and asks, "What's the point of studying Hebrew? You can't go to Israel." The student says he knows that, but they speak Hebrew in heaven. The KGB man says, "Heaven? Maybe you'll go to hell!" The student answers, "Well, I already know Russian."

---

Russian comedians are from the real Borscht Belt.

---

Russian comedians must be careful what jokes they tell. If they say, "Take my wife, please," when they get home, she's gone!

---

Communism is when the state owns everything. Capitalism is when your wife does.

---

There are a few nice things about Russia: For example, there are plenty of parking places. Trouble is, they've got nothing to park.

---

*Vacation* is the word Americans use to describe going someplace for fun and to get away from it all. The English call it *holiday*. In Russia it's known as *defecting*.

———

There is an amusement park in Siberia called Dissidentland: When they take you for a ride, they don't bring you back.

———

The president asked the Soviet premier if he objected to jokes about himself. The premier said, "No, I like jokes about myself." The president asked, "Are there any such jokes?" The premier said, "Enough to fill three labor camps."

———

When you think about it, it's no wonder the Russians passed us up in some fields: They didn't have to spend all their money and time fighting Communism.

———

Did you read that *Pravda* started a letters-to-the-editor column this year? It's a little different from the *Post's* version: They publish all beefs, criticisms, and complaints, but you have to give your name, address, and next of kin.

———

The president says, "We need a man to talk back to the Russians." I know a thousand cab drivers who will do that.

———

In the Soviet Union, nobody dares throw eggs at the Red officials: If the people had eggs, they would eat them.

A Muscovite entered the police station and reported his parrot was missing. "Does your parrot talk?" the officials asked. "Yes," answered the frightened comrade. "But any political opinions he expresses are strictly his own."

———

This one official explained, "I really do feel toward the USSR the way I feel toward my wife. I don't love it, I can't change it, and I can't help dreaming of something better."

———

Russia is where you are allowed to go anywhere they please.

———

The last time I was in Moscow, I saw this sign in the synagogue: "In praying here, you keep your eyes closed at your own risk."

———

I remember when the newspaper *Pravda* was running a contest for the best political joke. First prize was twenty years.

———

The Moscow University professor told his class that interplanetary junketing was distinctly in the cards: "We will be able to travel to Mars, Pluto, and Venus." One student in the back of the lecture hall raised his hand: "When," he asked, "can we travel to America?"

———

The prisoner stood before the three judges in Uzbek. "And your punishment is ten years of hard labor in Siberia! Have you anything to say?" The prisoner said, "Comrade Judges, the United States is a terrible, decadent, capitalistic country. It savagely exploits the proletariat. Hunger, racism is everywhere in the land. Is that not right?" "Right," the three judges agreed. "So if you want to really punish me, why not send me there?" said the prisoner.

---

In the 1950s the Russians knew nothing about interior decorating. Why would anybody with good taste have preferred an iron curtain to venetian blinds?

---

Russia had a new track star—a fantastic runner. Every day he ran twenty or twenty-five miles—but they caught him and took him back to Russia.

---

A couple, both ninety years old, recently celebrated their seventieth wedding anniversary in their Communist village. A reporter asked, "How did you manage to live so long?" The man replied, "You call this living?"

---

Living in my house is like living in Russia: I can say anything I want, provided my wife okays it.

---

In Russia, two men are talking on the street: "What is your opinion of the recent party resolution?" "Same as yours." "Then I arrest you in the name of the secret police."

---

What's the difference between the United States and the Soviet Union? In the United States everybody talks and nobody listens. In the Soviet Union everybody listens and nobody talks.

---

An American official was playing cards with a Russian diplomat. The Russian lost all he had, and offered to stake his wife for 500 rubles. The American thought the price was too high. The Russian reduced it to 200. The Yankee still refused to go along with it. "What would you pay for her?" the Russian finally asked. "Nothing," the American said. "Okay," the diplomat said. "You can have her."

---

Another Russian diplomat was telling his colleague, " . . . it's a rotten government," when a KGB agent grabbed him and said, "You're under arrest." The diplomat asked, "What for?" "Because you said it's a rotten government." The diplomat protested, "But I never said *what* government." The agent replied, "No good. There is only one rotten government, and you know it!"

# Salesmen

A good salesman can handle any situation. The store owner said, "Did you ever see anything as unsettled as the weather the last few days?" The salesman answered, "Well, there's your bill here!"

---

Said one traveling salesman to another, "What's the matter, Max? You only had a sandwich for lunch. You on a diet?" "No," said Max. "On commission."

---

The traveling man and his wife arrived on a combined business and pleasure trip. Tired and hungry from the long journey, the husband ordered a large meal. The wife made some rapid calculations, then complained, "Jim, that adds up to about eight thousand calories." The husband replied, "Who cares? I'll put 'em on my expense account."

---

This salesman was trying to sell me a computer. "If you're selling these machines way under price, like you say," I told him, "how can you make a living?" The man said, "Simple. We make our money fixing them."

You think he's a good salesman? The only orders he takes are from his wife.

---

The greatest salesman was the one who sold two milking machines to a farmer with one cow and then took the cow as a down payment.

# Secretaries

*(see also Bosses, Business, Cheating, Labor, Office)*

I told my secretary, "You are the nicest. You are not only pretty but you dress well, you're patient and romantic, your manners are perfect. Everybody loves you." She said shyly, "Gee, thanks." I said, "And now we will discuss what to do about your typing, spelling, filing, shorthand, punctuation, and ignorance."

---

I asked one new secretary if she could take dictation. She said she believed in democracy.

---

I told one new girl, "Always add a column of figures at least three times before you show me the result." The next day she came in with a broad smile. "I added these figures ten times." I said, "Good. I like a girl to be thorough." She said, "And here are the ten answers."

———————

The boss's secretary makes very few mistakes. She never does anything.

———————

The secretary was visited by one of the other secretaries in the hospital. "How are things at the office?" she asked. "You don't have to worry about a thing," the visitor said. "We're all sharing your work: Mae is making coffee, Sarah is doing the crossword puzzles, I'm watching TV, and oh yes, Mary is making it with the boss."

———————

I had one secretary who worked eight hours and slept eight hours. I had to fire her because they were the same eight hours. My other secretary spent so much time on personal calls, the phone company threatened to take away our commercial listing.

———————

Two big executives were creating an expense account at lunch. One said, "Life is unfair. I've got a business that's gone bad and a secretary that won't."

———————

One big office has a gorgeous secretary who has everything a man could ask for—so they're all asking.

———————

The head of a secretarial school was interviewing a pretty young applicant: "In our classes in shorthand and typing," he said, "we stress accuracy above everything." The girl asked, "What about speed?" He replied, "Well, out of last year's classes, fifteen girls married their employers within the first six months."

———————

This secretary was complaining to a friend, "If it weren't for the good salary, the air conditioning, the swimming pool, the free theater tickets, the four-week vacations, and the generous pension and profit-sharing plans, I swear I'd quit this miserable job."

———————

My last secretary was fired because she lacked experience: All she knew was typing and shorthand.

———————

My neighbor says, "I don't mess with secretaries: If at first I don't succeed, they're fired. That's all."

———————

My uncle says, "My secretary thinks I'm really small-minded because I believe words can be spelled only one way."

———————

At least my secretary's honest. Last week she called in lazy.

———————

The one that you don't want is a secretary who tells you what they think—because they seldom think much of you.

———

One boss was told by his secretary, "If I don't get a raise, I'm going to start wearing long skirts."

———

Another boss told his secretary, "You've been here two months now, and I'm happy to say that your typing has improved considerably. However, it hasn't gotten so good that you can stop wearing those tight sweaters yet."

———

The boss yelled at his pretty secretary, "We may have made love a few times, but who said you could be late for work?" She said, "My lawyer."

———

The secretary confessed to me the other day that she was tired of trying to build a career. "I want to get married, but the trouble is I don't want to hitch up with a mere go-getter. I want an already-got!"

———

The secretary was bragging about her beautiful all-over tan. "How did you get it?" the stenographer asked. "I did everything under the sun," she said happily.

## Sex
*(see also Bosses, Cheating, Courtship, Dating, Gold Diggers, Honeymoon, Marriage, Money, Prostitutes)*

Everybody goes to doctors, lawyers, or psychiatrists for advice. I give it to you here without reservation and without knowing what I'm talking about. I have discovered that sex is bad for one—for two, it's great. I've discovered that a normal man wants only one thing from a woman: companionship. Of course, I'm talking about a very old man. But a man is only as old as the woman he feels.

———

One fan wrote me: "I've been married to the same woman for forty-five years and it's starting to go dull. I know her every move before she makes it." I answered, "Look, pal, if she moves, don't complain."

———

One character talked to me about his love life: "I feel bad. I cheated on my wife." I asked, "How many times?" He growled, "How the hell do I know? I'm a lover, not an accountant!"

———

The beautiful young thing cried to me: "What can I do? Help me. I'm pregnant." I asked, "Who is the father?" She cried, "How should I know? My mother never would let me go steady."

———

One nice lady writes to ask, "When should parents tell their children about sex?" My answer: "When they're old enough to understand—and before they're old enough to do what they already did."

The girl asked me, "Do you think a girl has to be an easy mark to be popular with men?" I said, "Well, it will sure keep her from having a lot of enemies."

One girl told me, "I'm against free love." I said, "Would you accept a Diners Club card?"

One nice girl asks, "Where do nice girls meet nice men these days?" I told her, "There are singles clubs all over town and in the Catskills. The girls go to look for husbands—and the husbands go to look for girls."

Women are a problem, but they're the kind of problem I enjoy wrestling with—with no holds barred.

A man told me, "I'm eighty and I just married a girl of twenty. My problem is, I'm afraid I won't be able to satisfy her. Any suggestions?" "Take in a boarder," I advised. Three months later he called and told me my advice worked: His wife was having a baby. I asked, "What about the boarder?" He said, "She's having a baby, too."

Advice to single girls: Never look for a husband. Look for a single man.

My friend the lover received this letter: "If good girls go to heaven, where do bad girls go?" The love sage answered, "Anywhere they want."

One sexy Hollywood beauty was giving free advice: "I owe my success to being in the right place at the right time." I said, "Right—in the producer's bedroom when he's there!"

Q: Is it true that behind every successful man there is always a woman? A: Yes, and usually she catches him.

A friend pleads: "How can I find out what my girl really thinks of me?" "Marry her!" I advised.

Another asked, "With sex so dangerous these days, what do you suggest?" I told him, "It's better to skip the sex entirely and go right to the cigarette."

Q: Why is sex so popular? A: It has no calories!

The young lady told me: "The man I marry must be bright and colorful and entertaining, yet when I'm in the mood for peace and quiet, I want him to remain silent. I want him to be up to the minute in sports and politics and the news of the day, and I insist that he stay home nights with me!" I answered, "You don't want a husband, you want a TV set."

---

The definition of petting and necking is the study of human anatomy in Braille.

---

Sex is everywhere. After three years in the Chicago office of a big insurance company, a girl was transferred to the New York headquarters. The boss called her in on arrival and said, "I hope you like it here. The work will be the same as in Chicago." She said, "Fine. Kiss me and let's get started."

---

The purest definition of fear is the first time you discover that you can't make love a second time. The purest definition of panic is the second time you discover that you can't make love the first time.

---

The spent Romeo was bemoaning the fact that after he retired in a couple of months, he would have only an old-age pension to live on. "My dear," his wife said, "I've got a surprise for you!" She led him to the window and pointed to the row of houses across the street. "Every time we made love," she said, "I put ten cents in the jar. We now own all those houses and we have

nothing to worry about." He sighed, "And to think if I had given you all my business, we would have had the pub on the corner as well."

---

The couple were on their honeymoon at a motel next to a church, where a watchman rang the bell every hour through the night. "Tell you what, darling," the ardent groom said. "Let's make love every time that bell rings." The next morning, pale and exhausted, the groom staggered from the hotel to find the watchman. "Here's some money," he said. "It's yours if you'll only ring that bell every two hours." The watchman answered, "I can't. Last evening a young lady paid me to ring it every half hour."

---

Personally, I don't think sex is that important. I much prefer a music concert. But lately I've begun to notice that if I don't get to a concert for a year and a half, I don't miss it.

---

"It's good to have sex with a mature woman," my brother suggests. "You take your clothes off, and she washes and irons them."

---

The thing that takes up the least amount of time and causes the most amount of trouble is sex.

---

A girl who says she'll go through anything for a man usually has his bankbook in mind.

————

The only difference between love and insanity is in the duration of the disease.

————

The best gift for Valentine's Day is sex: You can take it on a trip and it doesn't need batteries.

————

Adam may have had his troubles, but he never had to listen to Eve talk about the other men she could have married.

————

This blonde actress scoffs at the idea of going to a psychiatrist: "Why should I lie down on a man's couch, and then pay him?"

————

My ex-girlfriend lectures, "A girl can wait for the right man to come along, but in the meantime that still doesn't mean she can't have a wonderful time with all the wrong men."

————

A man said to his date: "Why don't we go to my apartment? Sex is good for relieving arthritis." She said, "But I don't have arthritis." He said, "What's the matter? You don't believe in preventive medicine?"

————

The seventy-year-old patient explained his predicament to his doctor. He had recently married a gorgeous twenty-year-old, but, unfortunately, every night at bedtime, when he and his bride were ready, he would fall asleep right away. The doctor wrote out a prescription. The old man said, "You mean that now I'll be able to—?" The doc said, "No, I'm afraid I can't do anything about that—but now she'll fall asleep, too."

————

My niece doesn't mind if a man loves her and leaves her—if he leaves her enough.

————

The modern girl has no difficulty keeping the wolf from the door. She invites him in.

————

Men don't meet the modern girl—she overtakes them.

————

In the old days, man's greatest fear was that a woman would take it to heart; today, his greatest fear is that a woman will take it to court.

————

What with all the sex films, adult books, and strip clubs, the best way to avoid sex is to get married.

————

The call girl said: "Who says hookers have it easy? How would you like to get dressed all the time just to go on a coffee break?"

————

The hysterical girl called her psychiatrist: "You've got to help me. I love him. He loves me. We like the same things. When we're apart we're miserable. I don't know what to do." The doctor said, "I don't get it. You sound like you're completely compatible and in love. What's the problem?" She said, "What's the problem? The problem is, what shall I tell my husband?"

————

The girl called the sex therapist and said, "Remember when you told me the way to a man's heart was through his stomach? Well, last night I found a new route. . . . Now I need some birth control pills." The doc asked, "What's his occupation?" The girl said, "Army." "Active or retired?" "If he wasn't active I wouldn't need these bloody pills, would I?"

————

The young man was making love to the model and said, "I don't have a lot of money like my millionaire friend, I can't afford a big diamond like my millionaire friend, but I love you." The doll said, "I love you, too, but tell me more about your millionaire friend."

————

The blond bombshell said to her date, "There's something I must get off my chest." "What is it?" he asked. "Your eyes."

I know a gal who is very sanitary-minded. She's trying to take some filthy rich guy to the cleaners.

————

Then there's the debutante who called up her boyfriend to advise him: "We'll have to postpone our marriage for a little while. I've just eloped with another man."

————

"Your new boyfriend is somewhat of a loafer," Barbara's dad grumbled. "What does the lad do, anyhow?" She explained, "He inherits."

————

Susan decided on a vacation in Rome. "Did you pick up any Italian?" her friend asked when she returned. "I'll say I did," she said enthusiastically. "Okay, let me hear you say some words." "I didn't learn any words."

————

The last remaining bachelor girl in the office came in grinning one morning and began to pass out cigars to everybody. "What's the idea?" they asked. She displayed a diamond ring and cried out, "It's a boy! Six feet tall and weighs 190 pounds."

————

The sexpot's advice: "You've got to take care of yourself: no fatty foods, no liquors, and only one cigarette after you make love. I'm down to two packs a day."

After a wild night, the star said to the pretty little doll, "Do you tell your mother everything you do?" She cried, "Certainly not. My mother couldn't care less. It's my husband who's so darn inquisitive."

---

Two teenagers were walking home from school and stopped to rest on a park bench. "Jane," he cooed, "I'm groping for words to express my love." She said, "Well, move your hands, John. I ain't got no dictionary there."

---

On a visit to the zoo, one kid asked his mom, "How do lions make love?" She answered, "I really don't know, dear. Most of your father's friends are Knights of Columbus."

---

"My darling dearest," sighed the young man, quoting from a picture he saw the night before, "I love you, I worship you, you are the sun and the moon to me—and the stars and all life." She said, "No, please, don't," as she tried to disengage herself. "What's wrong, my one and only?" he panted. She said, "I just don't want to get serious." He said, "But wait—who's serious?"

---

My neighbor was worried about how her little daughter would react to the new sex education program in school. One morning the kid came home and said, "Mommy, guess what? We learned how to make babies today." "What!" the mother screamed, Then calmly she asked, "Tell me, dear, how do you make babies?" The kid said, "Easy. You drop the *y* and add *ies*."

---

One father was complaining about his son: "I sent my boy to college and he spent four years going to parties, having fun, necking, making love, drinking, and carrying on. It's not that I'm sorry I sent him. I should have gone myself."

---

After a romantic evening on his couch, the young man said, "Isn't it nice here?" His girl said, "You silly jerk. It's nice anywhere."

---

The young man joined her at the bar and said, "You look so sad. What's your problem?" She said, "Everything I do is wrong." The boy's eyes lighted up. "Great," he said. "Let's go to my place."

---

The eighteen-year-old single girl had just been told by her doctor that she was going to have a baby. "If only I had gone to the movies with my parents that night," she sobbed. "Well, why didn't you?" the doctor asked. "I couldn't," the girl cried. "The film was rated X."

---

I asked my sister-in-law, "If you came home and found a strange man there, what would you do?" She snapped, "I'd scream, 'Finders keepers!'"

---

A worker in a record shop was discussing the sexy album covers. "One customer came in mad. He said he'd bought an album a month ago and just discovered there was no record in it."

---

The young man showed his date a lot of love and affection: He took her to a drive-in movie and let her peek into the other cars.

---

"Was your father very shy?" "Shy? My mother told me that if he hadn't been so shy, I'd be five years older now."

---

The problem with extramarital sex is that you have to be married to have it.

---

You can learn plenty about sex at the movies—that is, if you don't let the picture disturb you.

---

Help keep prostitutes off the streets: Take them to your apartment.

---

There will be sex after death—we just won't be able to feel it.

---

"Did you get a nice Valentine from your fella?" I asked one secretary. She confided, "I've broken up with him. He keeps begging me to make love to him—pleading—and I keep refusing, explaining that I'm saving myself until I get married." I said, "But you just said you've broken up with him." She said, "Yes, I did that last month, but the sex-crazy nut has phoned me every week since, asking 'Are you married yet?'"

---

Sex over fifty-five can be dangerous: Always pull over to the side of the freeway.

---

The girl at the singles bar said to the handsome man sitting next to her: "They say that people with opposite characteristics make the best marriages." He said, "That's why I'm looking for a girl with money."

---

A maid in a wealthy home, an unmarried girl of nineteen, tearfully told her mistress that she was pregnant. Anxious to keep the girl and to help her through her distress, the couple agreed to adopt the illegitimate infant. Next year, same situation, same solution. A couple of years later, ditto. Finally, the maid quit. "I'm sorry," she explained, "but I can't work in a home where there are so many children."

---

I respond to most appeals, but my favorite charity is still the sex drive.

---

A woman's best beauty aid is a nearsighted man.

———

A thing of beauty keeps you broke forever.

———

It's good to be a woman. You don't have to worry about getting men pregnant.

———

Too much of a good thing is wonderful. The ends justify the jeans.

———

I lived through the sexual revolution and never even got wounded.

———

Chaste makes waste.

———

A fox is a wolf who sends flowers.

———

I know a woman so loose:
At school she was voted the girl most likely to concede.
She could hardly wait until she got married. In fact, she didn't.
She's the kind of pushover you can make—even if you play your cards wrong.
She has a slight impediment in her speech: She can't say no.
That fur coat does a lot for her—but then, she did a lot for it.

———

You know why the Garden of Eden was called Paradise? It's because Adam was a man, Eve was a woman, and the headache hadn't been invented yet.

———

This guy asked his wife if she'd like to go to a nudist camp. She said: "I'd like to go, but I have nothing to wear."

———

You know the hardest thing to do in a nudist camp? To keep looking in a person's face while talking to them!

———

My niece told me, "I once went steady with an undertaker's son, until I found out he just wanted me for my body."

———

Whoever put Bibles in hotel rooms missed the point. When a man's alone with a woman in a hotel room, whatever he's praying for, he's already got!

———

My friend told me, "What a date I had last night! Wow! I took this great-looking broad up to my apartment to see my etchings and it worked! She bought three of them."

———

Worrying about the past is like trying to make birth control pills retroactive.

———

My doctor told my wife and I that we should enjoy sex every night. Now we'll never see each other.

———

One twin came home one morning after staying out all night and bragged to her sister, "Well, kid, we're not identical twins anymore."

———

Just think what a drive-in would be called if there were nothing on the screen.

———

When a guy asks a gal if she has a parking space he could use, he's not talking about his car: He's talking about his shoes.

———

I've about had it with women undressing me with their eyes. What's wrong with their hands?

———

Nobody knows what to give her as a gift: What do you give to the girl who's had everybody?

———

My sister believes, "Some women think men are animals, and maybe they're right. A man can be meek as a lamb, brave as a tiger, and courageous as a lion. But the minute he meets a pretty girl, he becomes a jackass."

———

A friend of mine married one of those flat-chested girls for her brains. When he gets horny he hollers, "Quick, honey, say something smart."

———

My neighbor confides: "On the subject of birth control, my husband and I believe the simpler the better. Our idea of birth control is to just turn the lights on."

———

The big executive painted pictures for diversion. He asked a young lady of his acquaintance to pose for him in the nude, insisting, "Everybody is doing it." She said, "Sorry, I'm not a model." He said, "That's okay, I'm not an artist."

———

In this country, you're allowed to buy almost anything. If you need a shirt, you have a right to buy it, but if you need sex, you don't. What's more important, sex or a shirt?

———

One thing that never went over big at the nudist camp was the masquerade ball, because even though the guys wore masks, somehow the gals were still able to identify them.

———

Some girls are music lovers—others love without it.

———

When the young sheik was bar mitzvahed, he inherited his father's harem.

"I know what to do," he announced. "But where the hell do I begin?"

---

Harry ran into his old friend Joe, who said, "It's been a long time. I hear you got married." Harry replied, "Yes, I did. I have two children: Practice, the oldest boy, and Jimmy, who is two years younger." Joe said, "That's great, but I never heard of the name Practice. Who is he named after?" Harry replied, "Nobody, actually. You see, he was born a year before we got married."

---

It is better to have loved and lost, than to have paid for it and liked it.

---

If pornography relieves sexual frustration, why aren't cookbooks given to the hungry?

---

My girlfriend has got sex on the brain: I only love her for her mind.

---

One man said to another: "I hear your wife had a mirror installed over your bed because she likes to watch herself laugh."

---

With the peek-a-boo dresses, the see-through blouses, and the mini-skirts, there is no longer any such thing as a blind date.

---

Two little girls were talking about religious knowledge. "I'm past Original Sin," boasted the first one. "That's nothing," answered the other. "I'm beyond Redemption."

---

He said to his girl, "Come a little closer, my love. I'm going to make you melt in my arms." She answered, "No, thanks. I'm not that soft and you're not that hot."

---

The eighty-year-old was vacationing with another octogenarian. During their stay they both met some ladies younger than themselves and decided to get married in a double ceremony. Following the wedding night, they were both sitting in their rocking chairs. One said, "You know, I'd better see a doctor." The other asked, "Why?" "Well," the first says, "I couldn't consummate the marriage." "Oh," said the second, "I'd better see a psychiatrist." "Why?" says the first. "I didn't give it a thought," explained the second.

---

One fella told me he dated a pair of Siamese twins. I asked if he had a good time. He said, "Yes and no."

---

A man went to see the doctor complaining that he could think of nothing but girls. "You have to stop that," the doctor said, "or you'll lose your hearing." "Is that so?" asked the patient. "What did you say?" asked the doctor.

---

The battle of the sexes will never be won by either side: There is too much fraternizing with the enemy.

---

I never go to pornographic films. I object to seeing someone have more fun in an hour than I had in a lifetime.

---

Kissing a girl is like opening a bottle of olives: If you get one, the rest come easy.

# Signs

*(see also Advertising, Bloopers and Typographical Errors)*

At a fire hydrant: PARK NOW—PAY LATER.

---

In the window of an auto store: COME IN AND HAVE FUN WITH OUR PARTS.

---

Behind the bar at "Fortune Gardens": NOT RESPONSIBLE IF OUR BARTENDER'S OPINIONS CONFLICT WITH YOUR ANALYST'S.

---

Sign on the gate of a new factory on Long Island: MEN WANTED TO WORK ON NUCLEAR-FISSIONABLE ISOTOPE COUNTERS AND THREE-PHASE PHOTOSYNTHESIZERS. *NO EXPERIENCE NECESSARY.*

Sign in a brassiere shop: WE FIX FLATS.

---

Sign in bar: IF YOU ARE OVER 80 AND ACCOMPANIED BY YOUR PARENTS, WE WILL CASH YOUR CHECK.

---

Bumper stickers:
HONK IF YOU LOVE QUIET.

DRIVE CAREFULLY. WE NEED EVERY TAXPAYER WE CAN GET.

PUTTING YOUR SHOULDER TO THE WHEEL IS A DANGEROUS WAY TO DRIVE.

TWO HEADS ARE BETTER THAN ONE—EXCEPT IN A HEAD-ON COLLISION.

KEEP AMERICA BEAUTIFUL—EAT A BEER CAN!

WIFE SWAPPING IS THE SUBURBS' ANSWER TO BINGO.

---

Sign in IRS office: IN GOD WE TRUST—EVERYONE ELSE WE AUDIT.

---

One reducing salon advertises: REAR TODAY—GONE TOMORROW.

---

Sign on a diner: DON'T MAKE FUN OF OUR COFFEE—YOU TOO MIGHT BE OLD AND WEAK SOMEDAY.

---

Sign on one of our sanitation-removal trucks: OUR GUARANTEE! IF YOU ARE NOT SATISFIED WITH OUR METHODS, YOU WILL RECEIVE DOUBLE YOUR GARBAGE BACK.

Sign on one road upstate: MAIN HIGHWAY OPEN FOR TRAFFIC WHILE DETOUR IS BEING REPAVED.

———

Outside the town of Comfort, Texas, which happens to be between the villages of Alice and Louise, a motel has this invitation: SLEEP IN COMFORT BETWEEN ALICE AND LOUISE.

———

On the wall of a large business office: THOSE WHO ARE UNDERPAID WILL BE THE LAST TO BE FIRED.

———

One union official posted this sign: IT WOULD BE A CINCH TO LIVE TO A RIPE OLD AGE—IF WE DIDN'T HAVE TO WORK SO HARD PROVIDING FOR IT.

———

In the window of a Washington, D.C., laundry: WE DO NOT TEAR YOUR CLOTHES WITH MACHINERY—WE DO IT CAREFULLY BY HAND.

———

One man had this card on his windshield: NOTICE TO THIEVES: THIS CAR HAS ALREADY BEEN STOLEN.

———

Sign on store window: OUR GOING-OUT-OF-BUSINESS SALE WAS SUCH A SUCCESS, WE'RE HAVING ANOTHER ONE NEXT WEEK.

———

A beauty shop proclaims: WE CAN GIVE YOU THE NEW LOOK IF YOU STILL HAVE THE OLD PARTS.

———

A sign in a slenderizing palace: LET US TAKE YOU IN SO THE BOYS WILL TAKE YOU OUT.

———

Sign in a singles bar: MEN: NO SHIRTS, NO SERVE; WOMEN: NO SHIRTS, NO CHECK.

———

Sign in a Hollywood jewelry store: WEDDING RINGS FOR RENT.

———

Sign in a women's shop: SEE-THROUGH BLOUSES FOR THE GIRL WHO HAS EVERYTHING.

———

Pawnshop: PLEASE SEE ME AT YOUR EARLIEST INCONVENIENCE.

———

In the window of a restaurant: WE HONOR DINERS CLUB, CARTE BLANCHE, AMERICAN EXPRESS, AND MONEY.

———

A cafeteria has this notice on the wall: EFFICIENT, COURTEOUS, FRIENDLY, PROMPT SELF-SERVICE.

———

This sign on a church: REMEMBER THAT DETROIT IS NOT THE ONLY PLACE WHERE THE MAKER CAN RECALL HIS PRODUCT.

An advertisement for donkey rides in Thailand: WOULD YOU LIKE TO RIDE ON YOUR OWN ASS?

———

Notice in a Parisian cocktail lounge: LADIES ARE REQUESTED NOT TO HAVE CHILDREN IN THE BAR.

———

In Dublin, Ireland, this sign was displayed prominently in Murphy's restaurant: MURPHY'S LAW: DON'T MESS WITH MRS. MURPHY.

———

This poor soul saw a sign on an escalator at the railroad station: DOGS MUST BE CARRIED ON THE ESCALATOR. He started looking around desperately, mumbling, "Now, where the hell am I going to find a dog at this hour of the night?"

———

For Sale sign on a posh condo: ANY REASONABLE OFFER WILL BE REFUSED.

———

There is this sign displayed in the show window of a shop on Broadway: DO NOT BE FOOLED BY IMITATORS—WE HAVE BEEN GOING OUT OF BUSINESS IN THIS LOCATION SINCE 1950.

———

Big sign in the office of a Wall Street brokerage house: IT WOULD BE A WELCOME CHANGE TO SEE A HORSE'S HEAD AROUND HERE ON OCCASION.

Sign at farm: EGGS LAID WHILE YOU WAIT.

———

Sign in the No Smoking section of a midtown restaurant: IF YOU SIT HERE WITH OTHER PATRONS, PLEASE BUTT OUT.

———

Sign in supermarket: NOBODY UNDER $21 ADMITTED.

———

This sign on the wall at a German circus: NEVER PLAY LEAPFROG WITH A UNICORN.

———

The traffic court judge canceled the fifty-dollar ticket against the man who said he completely misunderstood the sign where he left his car. It read, FINE FOR PARKING.

———

The sign in the back of the diner said: SO YOU LIKE HOMEMADE BREAD? SO YOU LIKE HOMEMADE BISCUITS? SO YOU LIKE HOMEMADE PIES? THEN GO HOME!

———

There's a sign in a small town: 30 DAYS HATH SEPTEMBER, APRIL, JUNE, AND NOVEMBER—AND ANYONE EXCEEDING OUR SPEED LIMIT.

———

Sign on a church bulletin board: ON THURSDAY THERE WILL BE A MEETING OF THE LITTLE MOTHERS CLUB. ALL WISHING TO BECOME LITTLE MOTHERS WILL MEET THE MINISTER IN HIS STUDY.

———

Sign in the window of a ladies' shoe store: FRENCH HEELS—IDEAL FOR STREET WALKING.

Sign in the window of a vacant shop: WE UNDERSOLD EVERYBODY.

Sign in an obstetrician's office: WE DELIVER 24 HOURS A DAY.

Sign in a bar: PLEASE DON'T DRINK ON AN EMPTY WALLET.

Sign for a travel agency: DO US A FAVOR AND GO AWAY.

Notice posted in a hotel in Utica, New York: IN CASES OF ILLNESS, LIFT YOUR RECEIVER AND ASK FOR THE HOUSE PHYSICIAN. WHILE AWAITING HIS ARRIVAL, YOU MAY HAVE THE MAID ON THE FLOOR.

## Small Towns

My friend tells me the two happiest days of his life were the day he bought the house in the country—and the day he sold the house in the country.

Living in the country is great if you're one of those freaks who likes health and trees and fresh air—and yawning.

I'm a city boy. I even like pollution. . . . At least you can't see the insects.

The biggest change when you move to a small town is the banks. In New York they have gigantic financial institutions. Do you know what the name of the bank in Dullsville is? Chuck's Savings and Loan. And they all have tellers who are sixteen-year-old girls with names like Wendy and Fifi and Cookie. Tell me, are you going to entrust your life savings to a girl named Cookie? I was driving through the town and stopped at the bank and asked the girl to change a twenty. She said, "Do you have anything smaller?"

People in small towns think differently. One woman came home after three years in New York and told her mom, "My boyfriend and I have been living together for two years." Mom sniffed. "Hmmm. I wouldn't even think of *driving* without a license."

I placed a call from Utah to an aunt who lives in a small town in Iowa. After I gave my aunt's number to the Utah operator, the local Iowa operator came on the line. "I'll ring now," she said, "but I don't think they're home. Their car is gone."

Small towns are okay with me. It's just that once you've seen the cannon in the park, there's nothing to do. I was in this one town that was so small, the local hooker was the community chest. And dull? If it weren't for mouth-to-mouth resuscitation, there wouldn't be any romance at all. Dull? The mayor went to a Gypsy fortune teller, who read his lifeline and in the middle got bored and turned on the TV.

---

One good thing about small towns: They don't have crime in the streets. . . . Well, let me clarify that. They got crime; what they don't have is streets.

---

I will not knock the little villages. Some of the greatest men of all time have come out of there. Abe Lincoln wasn't exactly born in a log condominium.

---

That little town of Bethlehem will always be proud of the great star it gave birth to.

---

I know a town so dull, they print the newspaper there three weeks in advance.

---

I know a town so small, the fire department uses a water pistol.

---

That town is so small, they have only one fire hydrant—and they didn't get that until the mayor bought a dog.

Having fun there means going downtown and watching the parking meter expire.

---

They just named my uncle fire chief. They had to. They're using his garden hose.

---

You know some towns have a Godfather? Well, my uncle's town couldn't afford a Godfather, so they had a second cousin.

---

Some of our presidential candidates come from small towns. How small? So small that not only did they never have a presidential candidate, but they never even had a voter.

---

This one town is so small, the milkman is a cow, and the mayor is an Elk—a real elk.

---

Another town I know is so small:

The dentist's office is the public library.

The local theater is a couple who hate each other and keep the windows open.

They had to close the zoo because the cat died.

The only protection the bank has is one guy standing at the door with bad breath.

They had a dust storm and nobody knew it because there was nothing to blow away.

The town spinster and the local hooker are the same person.

The main street goes through a car wash.

———

Small? The twenty-four-hour diner closes at noon.

———

My uncle lives in an even smaller place: They don't exactly have a taxi service; instead, they have a guy with a large skateboard. And you know how big cities have professional call girls? This town has to get along with volunteers. The town clock is a wristwatch. And they couldn't teach the parrot to say, "Polly want a cracker," because there was no one to give it to her. A stranger visited and asked my uncle, "Does this town have any nightlife?" My uncle said, "Yes, but she's ill today."

———

My cousin's another one for small towns. In his town, Howard Johnson's has only one flavor. . . . The tallest building is a Fotomat. . . . The mayor's kid has a piggy bank—it's a real pig. . . . They had to fire the dogcatcher—they caught the dog. . . . Their idea of a traffic jam is three people in one car. . . . Formal wear is a T-shirt.

———

There's a town so small that they don't have gossip, because it would either have to be about the person who was telling it or the one who was listening. Small? There was nobody to watch the Fourth of July parade, because everybody in town was in the parade.

———

The hillbilly woman told me: "I come from farm country, real farm country, where a woman is considered liberated if she stops after eight kids."

———

Some kind of record was set in marital affairs when a rich hillbilly died last month and left his estate in trust for his wife: She can't touch any of it until she's fourteen.

## Smoking
*(see also Cigarettes)*

Cigarettes Anonymous is a new organization: When you feel like smoking, you dial a number and hear a minute of coughing.

———

People who give up smoking have the same problem as the newcomers in the nudist camp: They don't know what to do with their hands.

———

The best way to stop smoking is to use wet matches.

———

Talk about a progressive society. I know one public school that has a smoking and nonsmoking section for first graders.

My father never knew from Surgeons General or Surgeons Corporal. He never said much about it being good for us or bad for us. All he ever said was if he ever caught us smoking, he would be hazardous to our health.

———

The young graduate cornered his girl in the backseat of the car and was amorously trying his hand at her. She kept resisting and finally shrieked, "Myron, I don't know what's come over you! You've always been so restrained and gentlemanly." He said, "Yes, I know, but I just can't help it. I'm trying to give up smoking!"

———

The government puts health warnings on cigarettes. Why don't they put them on bombs?

———

In some areas smoking is a felony. Mugging is okay, but cigarettes and cigars are out.

———

There's a filling station that displays a big sign saying: "No Smoking. Your life may not be worth much—but gasoline is."

———

Psychiatrists are great to help you stop the smoking habit: The sessions cost so much, you can't afford to buy cigarettes anymore.

———

The romantic young man said to the pretty little girl at the singles bar, "Do you mind if I kiss your hand?" She said, "Not at all, but don't burn your nose on my cigarette."

———

The sign in the motel said, "Do not smoke in bed without umbrella—extra-sensitive sprinkler system."

———

What's the big deal about giving up smoking? I've done it a thousand times.

———

I don't like the idea of the government telling you what's no good for you: First it's smoking. What if sex is next?

———

Doctors tell you if you quit smoking you'll be able to taste food. I know one guy who took the advice and quit smoking completely: "Now," he said, "I can really taste food—and I find I've been eating a lot of things I don't like."

———

"You and your diets," the patient gasped to his doctor. "I cut out sweets, I cut out starches. That I didn't mind! But you limited me to one cigar a day. I never smoked before—and that damn cigar a day nearly killed me!"

———

A reformed smoker: "I haven't smoked in three years, eight months, and ten days—and I never miss it or think about it. "

## Society People
*(see also Money, Rich People)*

I've always been interested in society. That's because in my old neighborhood, we never had any. In my part of town:

The post office delivered warrants in the mail marked "occupant."

The most popular form of transportation was the stretcher.

There was a sign in the local hotel: WASHINGTON WOULDN'T SLEEP HERE.

When you made a reservation at the restaurant, you requested the non-shooting section.

The garbage trucks didn't pick up—they delivered.

---

I know a young socialite who wears a riding habit just to pitch horseshoes. The only thing the rich scum ever did for a living was read his father's will.

---

Another wealthy lad was boasting to me about his family tree: "My family traces its ancestry back to Charlemagne." I said, "I suppose you'll be telling me next that your ancestors were in the Ark with Noah." He said, "Indeed, no. My people had a boat of their own."

---

Most society snobs like to live in the suburbs. That's a community in which a man will lend you his wife, but not his golf clubs.

---

*Society* is not a dirty word to me. Some of those guys are pretty classy. I know one guy so rich, he even goes to a drive-in movie in a taxi. I can understand why he has a car with an unlisted number, but a glass-covered golf course is too much. He even owns a split-level Chrysler.

---

These society characters are all trying to top one another. One bought his son a bicycle with whitewall tires. Another bought his daughter an air-conditioned baby carriage. One big man is proud of his little girl, who is selling Girl Scout croissants. And how about the classy guy who has *TV Guide* in hardcover? Don't you think his four-room Cadillac is a bit ostentatious?

---

One chic snob decided to take a job for kicks—but he insisted on an unlisted Social Security number.

---

Two older society gals, poor but snobbish, were talking about a matrimonial prospect. "He's got plenty of money," one said, "but he's too old to be termed eligible." The other said, "Dahling, he's too eligible to be termed old."

---

Then there's the most fashionable lady of them all: If she were going to shoot her husband, she'd wear a hunting outfit.

———

A snob is one whose grandfather made money and who therefore refuses to associate with persons who have made it themselves.

———

A very aristocratic Boston family was shocked to hear that one of the daughters had become a call girl in New York. As they sat in council to discuss the disgrace, old Aunt Amelia broke the silence: "How terribly disgusting," she thundered, "that one of our family should have to work!"

———

A society snob is a person who craves equality—but only with his superiors.

———

The distinguished stuffed shirt was lecturing at the country club to a roomful of stuffed shorts: "Those X-rated movies are disgraceful. I saw one last night that included sexual perversion of every kind, every vulgarity. It was a disgrace to the human eye." He concluded, "And now, ladies, will there be any questions?" In unison, three women shouted, "Where is it playing?"

———

Mrs. Vanderschwartz was showing off as usual: "I have all my diamonds cleaned with caviar juice, my rubies with strictly imported wine, my emeralds with the finest brandy from Spain, and my sapphires with fresh milk from baby goats." Mrs. Snobhead interrupted: "When my jewels get dirty, I throw them away." She's such a snob, she won't ride in the same car with her chauffeur.

———

This haughty socialite died and arrived at the gates of heaven. "Welcome," said St. Peter. "Come right in." The snob sneered, "I will not! Anyplace where a perfect stranger can get in without a reservation is not my idea of heaven."

———

You can't keep a good snob down: Even when he's broke he's puttin' on the Ritz.

———

I know one character who can't afford air conditioning, but he doesn't want his friends to know. So he drives around on the hottest days with his car windows closed and sweats off ten pounds every summer.

———

Two women met at the chic restaurant. "Sylvia, what have you done to your hair?" one asked. "It looks like a wig." The other said, "It is a wig." "Isn't that marvelous," said the first. "I never would have guessed."

# Sons

He was only a traffic cop's son—but he preferred the red light district.

———

He was only a salesman's son—but he was always looking for free samples.

———

He was only a football player's son—but he made a pass at anybody.

———

He was only a TV evangelist's son—maybe that's why he believed so much in loving thy neighbor.

———

He was only a tennis player's son—but boy, did he try to score.

———

He was only a jockey's son—but he tried to get every gal in the saddle.

———

He was only a farmer's son—but could he throw the bull.

———

He was only a banker's son—but he gambled so much even his cash bounced.

———

He was only an explorer's son—but he tried to go too far with the girls.

———

He was only a baseball manager's son—but he struck out with every girl he met.

———

He was only an accountant's son—but he played with all the right figures.

———

He was only a sanitation man's son—but he tried to pick up anything that moved.

He was only a violinist's son—but he tried to pluck every G string.

———

He was only a chambermaid's son—but he was a devil between the sheets.

———

He was only a lawyer's son—but he tried to break every girl's will.

———

He was only a stockbroker's son—but he tried to sell every girl short.

———

He was only a comedian's son—but only his lovemaking was laughable.

———

He was only an actor's son—but every time he looked in the mirror, he took a bow.

———

He was only an obstetrician's son—but with a girl he couldn't deliver.

———

He was only a union leader's son—but he put plenty of girls in labor.

———

He was only a judge's son—but he could never pass a bar.

———

He was only a politician's son—but he lied, cheated, and stole on his own.

## Sports

*(see also Athletes, Baseball, Hunting, Golf)*

I'm not exactly athletic: I get winded turning on the TV set.

———

How can you tell your wife is fed up with Monday Night Football? When she strips, comes into the den, stands in front of the TV set, and announces, "Play me or trade me."

———

Did you hear about the football lineman whose coach told him to put on a clean pair of shorts every day? By the sixth day he couldn't get his pants on over them.

Why do ball players smoke marijuana? They like to spend their afternoons and evenings on grass.

———

Skiing is best when you have lots of white snow and plenty of Blue Cross.

People go to ski lodges to find romance. My cousin tells me, "I met a girl and we ended up in bed: We were both in traction."

———

My friend told me, "I met a girl at a ski lodge and it was a case of opposites being attracted to each other: My cast was on my left leg, hers was on her right leg."

———

The national pastime in Tahiti is making love. Us silly fools, we picked baseball.

———

I'd never ski. I do not participate in any sport with ambulances at the bottom of a hill.

———

My neighbor's wife was bragging, "My uncle has a gold medal for swimming, a silver cup for golfing, and a solid gold watch for high jumping." I said, "He must be a great athlete." She said, "No, he owns a hock shop."

———

Do you know what seven-foot basketball players do in their off time? They go to the movies and sit in front of you.

———

Fish may be dumb, but have you ever seen one buy $500 worth of equipment to hook a man?

———

Bob told me, "I'm thinking of giving up golf. I can't even break ninety when I cheat."

———

Bob asked his priest, "Will I sin if I play golf on Sunday?" The father answered, "The way you play, it's a sin to play any day."

———

Bob says, "I wear Arnold Palmer shirts, Arnold Palmer shoes, and Arnold Palmer clubs—and I play like Betsy Palmer."

———

Bob explains, "It's not that I cheat with golf. I play for my health, and a low score makes me feel better."

———

The elite have found a special way to fall down—it's called skiing. Skiing has to be the only sport in the world that requires you to spend an arm and a leg to break an arm and a leg.

## Subways

*(see also New York)*

With so many vigilantes riding the subways now, the transit authority is getting letters from muggers asking for safer working conditions.

———

Today a group of liberal lawyers began lobbying for a law that would require subway riders to carry at least $100, so muggers could make a decent living.

———

These days you really have to watch out for muggers on the subway. You know what a mugger is? A guy who takes your money without having to get elected.

———

The other day two muggers shot each other in a case of mistaken identity: Each mugger thought the other was a vigilante.

———

I took the subway once. It was so crowded, I couldn't even put my hand in my pocket—somebody else's hand was already there.

———

Some Hollywood stars are planning to entertain our fighting forces next Christmas. I know a subway in New York that would love to have them.

———

Not all muggers work in subways. A number of gunmen held up one of our big banks. They herded all the men into one vault and slammed the door. The girls were taken by another mugger into a private office and ordered to lie down on the floor. The girls meekly started to lie down on their backs. "Turn over!" the mugger yelled. "This is a stick-up, not a directors' meeting."

Did you know that the subways are mentioned in the Bible? "And the Lord created all manner of creeping things."

The mayor is in favor of police being stationed in subways: "It has been a big help: Up until today, not one train has been stolen."

## Taxes

The only fallacy in raising taxes to reduce the federal debt is that it increases our own.

———

Congress is worried about lowering taxes because it could establish a dangerous principle: The right of the people to keep their own money.

———

A fair tax structure is one that gives every taxpayer an equal opportunity to cheat.

———

Let's face it: Nowadays, America's favorite pastime is tax evasion.

———

A Wall Street bookshop is doing big business with the sale of a new book telling you how to save 90 percent on your income tax: It's packaged with a one-way plane ticket to Fiji.

———

I blame it all on the IRS. . . . Income tax has made more liars out of the American people than golf has.

———

Who is Congress to tell me what I can deduct for charity?

I put six of my wife's relatives down under contributions. I defy the government to prove they're *not* an organized charity.

———

Listen, my accountant can come up with so many extra deductions, you'll wind up with enough money left over to post bail.

———

I did some figuring. We can soon balance the federal budget if we close twenty-seven states.

———

A communist government won't let you make a lot of money. A democratic government will let you make all you want—but they won't let you keep it.

———

Now that the tax reform bill has gone through, we are no longer treated unfairly by the old tax laws—we're treated unfairly by the new tax laws.

———

To control the budget deficit, the Congress wants to increase taxes on cigarettes and alcohol. We might even be able to *balance* the budget if more people had bad habits.

The Congress can balance the budget, they tell me, if smokers will pay $300 a pack for cigarettes. That should drive you to drink, and then we can put a higher tax on booze.

———

The new tax laws are like a do-it-yourself mugging.

———

I've got nothing against the new tax laws: It's just that every time my ship comes in, the government unloads it.

———

I think the new tax laws deserve a lot of credit: They've brought poverty within the reach of all of us.

———

There are no atheists in the IRS waiting rooms. Let us bow our heads and pay.

———

The IRS is the nearest thing to a Chinese dinner: No matter how much you gave them, a year later they're hungry again.

———

In filing your income tax return, make sure you let an accountant instead of your conscience be your guide.

———

Taxation without representation was tyranny, but it was a lot cheaper.

———

Only in a democracy do the citizens have complete freedom in deciding how to pay their taxes—by check, cash, or money order.

———

If crime could be taxed, there would be no need for other taxes.

———

When the meek inherit the Earth, they will have very little left after paying inheritance, capital gains, and other taxes.

———

The only person who gets paid for sticking his nose in other people's business is the tax collector.

———

Some taxpayers close their eyes, some stop their ears, some shut their mouths, but all pay through the nose.

———

The way taxes are going these days, a fellow has to be unemployed to make a living.

———

My neighbor told me, "Last year I saved so much money on taxes, my wife wants us to go to Europe, I want us to go to Africa—and the government wants us to go to Leavenworth."

———

Fifty percent of Americans file their income tax; the other fifty percent chisel it.

There are dozens of books on how to make out your income taxes—but none of them has a happy ending.

---

Don't get excited about any promised tax cuts—it's like a mugger giving you back carfare.

---

Remember, before sealing your IRS envelope, be sure you've enclosed your Social Security number, all W-2 forms, and an arm and a leg.

---

The American public owes a lot to the IRS: ulcers, nausea, shingles. . . .

---

As far as we're concerned, the people of the IRS are just pickpockets with taxes.

---

My CPA has this sign on his desk: "Telling the truth will invariably confuse the IRS."

---

I asked a well-known novelist to tell me his greatest work of fiction. He said, "My 1986 income tax return."

---

I just received my tax form today. . . . Well, so much for my New Year's resolution about not swearing.

---

My uncle told me, "I love reading mysteries. I can hardly wait to get my new tax forms."

---

My uncle says, "I think the IRS ought to serve coffee and doughnuts. The Red Cross does when they take your blood."

---

My accountant was lecturing, "It's April 15, when the money supply gets out of hand: out of your hand and into the government's."

---

I just paid my taxes and now I know what IRS stands for: Internal Robbery Service. Hiring an accountant can save you a lot of money on your taxes, and you'll need it—to pay your accountant. Watching an accountant do your income taxes is always a fascinating experience. It's like putting your savings on hold. I have my taxes done by a very considerate, very compassionate fella: He's the only accountant I know with a recovery room.

---

There will always be two classes of people who don't like to pay income taxes: men and women.

---

Income taxes could be a lot worse. Suppose we had to pay on what we think we're worth.

---

You've got to admit the government's shrewd: They've got this thing called withholding taxes—a sneaky way of getting at your paycheck before your wife does.

———

I really don't mind paying taxes. The way I look at it is, if I didn't spend my money on taxes, I'd probably just squander it away on foolish luxuries like groceries, rent, electricity. . . .

———

I'm proud to be an American taxpayer, but to tell the truth, I could be just as proud for half the money.

———

No wonder newborn babies cry. They've got nothing to eat, no clothes—and they already owe the government about $2,000.

———

The businessman said, "I want my last will and testament to contain a provision that after my death, my remains are to be cremated." His lawyer asked, "And what do you want done with the ashes?" The businessman said, "I want them sent to the IRS with a notice reading, 'Now you've got it all.'"

———

Listen, the way taxes are today, you may as well marry for love.

———

I just decided. I'm sending my entire income to Washington. Who can afford taxes?

———

When I went up to the tax department, I really let them have it—every dollar I had.

———

It's very confusing to be an American. The "Star-Spangled Banner" tells us it's the land of the free. The IRS tells us, "Forget it!"

———

My neighbor tells me, "I had good news and bad news today. The good news is, I got a phone call and a deep, throbbing, sensuous voice said, 'Your place or mine?' The bad news is, it was an auditor from the IRS."

———

A fool and his money are soon parted; the rest of us wait to be taxed.

———

The way to get rich is to cover up with something that's low-priced, habit-forming, and tax-deductible.

———

My brother screamed at the tax guy, "You mean that after paying taxes all these years, I can't list the government as a dependent?"

———

I hope you have a good accountant. An accountant is a man hired to explain that you didn't make the money you did.

---

My accountant is a man who solves a problem you didn't know you had in a manner you don't understand.

---

Speaking of taxes, everybody is worried about entertainment expenses. The government wants you to keep a diary, so when I went out with some people the other night, I marked everything down: $100 for food, $40 for champagne, $20 for tips. . . . The government disallowed it. They found out I was a guest.

---

There was a time when this country didn't have an income tax. I think it was known then as the Garden of Eden.

---

I'm always worried about our marriage around tax time: My wife always lists our relationship for a depreciation allowance.

---

We always complain about the Ten Commandments like they were something new. There were internal revenue services back in biblical times. You remember Moses came down from Mount Sinai with two tablets? One was the Ten Commandments, the other was an expense account.

Listen, even the president has to file an income tax return. Can you imagine the IRS asking the president questions about his return? "Tell me, Mr. President, do you have any liabilities?" "Yes, I do. The Congress."

---

I never worry about the future. High interest rates have taught me how to live within my income, and high taxes have taught me how to live without my income. But, listen, don't get me wrong. I think it's a privilege to pay income taxes. It's just that sometimes I get the idea I'm definitely overprivileged!

---

You've got to hand it to the tax people. If you don't, they'll come and get it.

---

This guy is in trouble now: He deducted $5,000 because he had water in his basement—then they found out he lives on a houseboat.

---

I feel like writing a letter to the Income Tax Bureau and telling them I can no longer afford their service.

---

One thing about my tax man—he's the type who could swim safely through shark-infested waters. No doubt he'd be given professional courtesy.

---

If the average citizen gets robbed once in a year, it's called a crime wave. If he gets robbed every day of the year, it's called government.

It wasn't until I was called for an audit by the IRS that I learned my accountant worked his way through college performing in clubs as a juggler.

I hear talk about lowering taxes. I hope they lower them enough so we can pay them.

The working man's big problem is that his paycheck comes minus tax—and his bills come plus tax.

My Uncle Sam is beginning to cost me as much as my wife.

What an honest guy! On his 1040, he reported half his salary as unearned income.

It's hard to believe this country was founded partly to avoid paying taxes.

I lied on my income tax last year. I listed myself as head of the household.

My accountants pledge that if I'm audited, they'll stop by and feed my dog until I get paroled.

The income tax guys must love poor people—they're creating so many of them.

I know a terrific accountant: He's available twenty-four hours a day. One phone call and the warden brings him to the phone.

The capitalist system is the best in the world. Where else could you make enough to owe so much?

The IRS has a new easy payment plan: 100 percent down and nothing per month.

America should be a very clean place. Every day the average taxpayer gets taken to the cleaners.

This year the government claims the tax forms will be very simple: "Even a five-year-old can understand them"—providing he's a CPA.

## Taxis and Taxi Drivers

I think cabbies are very helpful. They'll take you anyplace *they* want to go.

I was in one taxi where the driver skillfully avoided four pedestrians in a row. "If you hit 'em," he explained, "you've got to fill out a report."

———

At school, if you couldn't find the shortest distance between two points, you became a cab driver.

———

Rain is what makes flowers appear and taxis disappear. In fact, the off-duty lights on Manhattan cabs are wired to go on whenever they are touched by a drop of rain.

———

All things come to those who wait for a taxi on a rainy day—except a taxi.

———

Taxi drivers have the uncanny knack for knowing when people are late for work: That's when they pass them by every time.

———

The pretty lady gave the cabbie an address outside of town and asked him to stop at a park. She invited him to the backseat, then said, "I'm really a prostitute and I have to charge you fifty dollars." He paid her and they made love. Later he sat motionless behind the wheel. "Aren't we leaving?" asked the hooker. He said, "Not yet. I'm really a cab driver and the fare back is fifty dollars."

I like cab drivers. I find if you do exactly what they want, you have no problems. Want to light a cigarette? The driver's allergic. Want change? He has none. Want a receipt? He just gave away his last one.

———

Cab meters go faster than the cabs. In fact, taxis are getting so expensive, it's cheaper to be mugged and wait for an ambulance.

———

I went to a Gypsy fortune teller who predicted I was going to take a long trip. An hour later I was in a taxi going across town.

———

Did you ever get in one of those traffic jams? I was in one so bad, it's the first time I was ever passed by an abandoned car.

———

My cabbie hit the car in front of him three times. I screamed at him. He said, "Sorry, my windshield is covered with safety stickers. I couldn't see a thing!"

———

Do you want to frustrate your cab driver? Tell him to take you to his garage.

———

At a New York bar, a Texan was bragging about the Dallas Cowboys. The bartender said to him, "Okay, so they're great, but here in New York

City, we have great cowboys too; they're modern, they're on wheels. We call them the New York cab drivers."

---

A pedestrian was struck down by a taxi and dragged about twenty feet. He was carried to the sidewalk and an ambulance was summoned. A police car arrived and the officer asked the victim if he had gotten the license number of the cab. The victim said he had. "Let's have it," the cop said, starting to write. The victim shook his head. "Please," he said. "Leave me out of it. I don't want to get involved!"

---

It's a shame that the people who really know how to run this country are too busy driving taxis for a living.

## Telephones

They say the breakup of the telephone company into dozens of parts has brought warmth into our homes— and I believe it. I get hot every time I see my phone bill.

---

Anybody who believes this country has free speech must not be paying his telephone bill.

---

JOE: I'm going home—I expect a phone call. JACK: From whom? JOE: I don't know. JACK: Then how do you know the phone will ring? JOE: I'm going to take a bath. JACK: That's right—the phone generally rings when I take a bath, too. JOE: Yeah, but sometimes I have to take two or three baths to make it ring.

---

They claim they cut up AT&T so things would be easier for everybody. The next time I have a full day with nothing to do, I'll have enough time to get out my phone bill and read it from beginning to end. And the rate increases are something. . . . You now pay for everything separately: the wires, the buttons, the telephone, the operator's laundry.

---

I just got an obscene phone call from AT&T. They want me to pay my bill.

---

My friend lost a quarter in a pay phone and asked the operator to refund it. "Give me your name and address," the operator said, "and we'll mail you a refund." My friend declined this logic and pushed the coin return button once more. A rush of coins came down the chute, and the operator, realizing what was going on, said, "Please put them back." My friend responded: "If you'll just give me your name and address. . . .

---

Car phones make you think the person in the car is the busiest guy in town. The truth is, if the guy was so busy, he'd be at work instead of riding around gabbing on the phone.

———

Having a car phone could be great in a crisis—like if you're in the backseat with your girl at a drive-in movie and need to place an emergency call to Dr. Ruth.

———

Telephone prices are like babies: They get changed pretty often.

———

It's true that money talks, but these days only Arabs can afford to speak on the phone.

———

It's not surprising to find that they have to raise the phone rates: Somebody has to pay for those Out of Order signs on the phone booths.

———

Those street phones are like people employed by the government: Only one in three works.

———

Progress works both ways. In the old days you could dial wrong numbers only locally. Now you can dial them all over the world—and wrong numbers will cost you twice as much.

———

When the telephone operators finish lunch, they don't call it going back to work. It's more like returning to the scene of the crime.

I still remember that blue Monday in 1929 when the holders of the gilt-edged AT&T stock were ready for the big jump. I remember putting a dime in the coin telephone slot and a voice said, "God bless you, sir."

———

I think this direct dialing is wonderful. The other day I made an overseas call. I dialed 1-0-285-369-842796-4397-1-829 and you know what I wound up with? A blister.

———

Now, for the first time, you can reach long-distance wrong numbers without operator assistance.

———

People frequently complain about the service they receive from the telephone company. One man called to find out the number of information. The operator told him he'd have to dial information.

———

Even the atheists have a number to call when they're in need. It's the same as Dial-a-Prayer. The only difference is, no one answers.

———

Alexander Graham Bell transmitted his first telephone message to his assistant in the next room: "Mr. Watson, come here, I want you!" "Who is calling?" Watson asked.

If there had been a teenager in the house, Alexander Graham Bell never would have bothered inventing the telephone.

———

We've come a long way. Those push-button phones are great time-savers. Today I got three wrong numbers in the time it usually takes me to get one.

———

I installed my own phone. It works great, except every time somebody calls, the burglar alarm goes off, and I have to ring the doorbell to get a dial tone.

———

I've got one of those long-distance services where you have to dial twenty-seven numbers. By the time you finally get through to the people you're calling, they've moved.

———

Now I save a lot of money on long-distance service: I wait for my friends to call *me*.

———

I asked the phone company to start sending my bill in Arabic. I figured, why the hell not? I don't understand what I'm paying for anyway.

———

Listen, if you were a creative TV producer, you could make your phone bill into a miniseries.

———

Did I tell you that AT&T may merge with Playboy? Now you will be able to reach out and touch something worthwhile.

———

The voice on the other end said, "I'd like to talk with your wife." I said, "She's out right now. Do you want to leave a message?" The voice said, "Yes." I waited, then said again, "Do you want to leave a message?" The voice asked, "Are you a recording?" I said, "No." The voice said, "I'm sorry. I was waiting for you to beep."

———

Now, with the breakup of the phone company, there is so much confusion, an operator called *me* for directory assistance.

———

My neighbor showed up at a party with a bandaged nose. I asked what happened. He said, "The telephone got it broken. I called a friend at three in the morning because the rates are cheaper. When he got out of bed and answered the phone, I said, 'Guess who?'" I asked, "So how did you get your nose broken?" "He guessed who," my neighbor replied.

———

The phone company had better be careful about raising the rates. There are very few conversations worth the money now.

———

One friend showed up at my party minus an appendix. I said, "I didn't know you had appendicitis." He said, "I didn't, but I had to run into my doctor's office to use his phone—and how could I leave without buying something?"

———

One company is selling a new toll-free 800 service for only a dollar a month. And it works like every other 800 number. Your customers can call it from anywhere, toll-free, seven days a week, twenty-four hours a day—and get a busy signal.

———

The man who said talk is cheap never gave his teenage daughters their own phones.

## Television

I just met the town's richest man: a television repairman who moonlights as an air conditioner repairman.

———

In my opinion the greatest spectacular of the year was my TV repairman's bill.

———

A good commercial is what makes you think you've longed all your life for a thing you've never heard of before. Let's be honest about it. What four out of five doctors really prefer, they couldn't show on television!

TV is so bad I can hardly wait for next year's political programs.

———

Cable TV is performing a great service—getting nudity off the theater screen and back into the home where it belongs.

———

I'm now enjoying television more than ever. I have a six-foot screen. It's Chinese, and I have it in front of my TV set.

———

When I was growing up, we didn't have a TV set, so we bored a hole through the wall to our neighbor's apartment and watched wrestling every night—until we found out our neighbor didn't have a TV set either.

———

I love watching old movies on TV, but some of those movies on late-night television are too old to be kept up that late.

———

People tell me they enjoy TV because it takes them away from the frustrations of real life. I enjoy real life because it takes me away from television.

———

The word is being spread about a new TV soap opera. The plot centers around an unfaithful wife, a drug addict, a student anarchist planning on bombing the White House, a dirty old man, and a corrupt public official. It will be called "Just Plain Folks."

Say, if there's a ban on bombs, how come so many of them got on TV this season?

Some of the quiz shows and game shows on TV are getting ridiculous. I know a nine-year-old kid who had to get married because he won a honeymoon vacation for two in Hawaii.

TV is education. It teaches you how much you can put up with.

Reading maketh a well-rounded person. So doth watching TV with potato chips and a six-pack of beer.

Television has gotten so bad, kids are doing their homework.

When I was a kid, you could see two pictures for a dime in any theater. Now it costs you $500 for a TV set, and what do you get? The same two pictures.

## Texas

Ever since December 29, 1845, when Texas was kind enough to annex the USA, they have refused to put *small* in their dictionaries.

*Big* is a little word in Texas. They start with *tremendous, fantabulous, expansive, gigantic*—and then they get larger.

Did you hear about the loaded Dallas farmer who was so rich, he bought his dog a little boy?

One banker from Houston chided his son, "I heard you asking a man just now what state he was from. If a man is from Texas, he'll tell you; if he's not, there's no use embarrassing him."

A friend was admiring a Texan's new sports car. "And is it air conditioned?" he asked. "No," replied the oil man, "but I always keep a couple of cold ones in the refrigerator."

I know a Texan who has two Cadillacs: one for red lights and the other for green.

And how about the Dallas Cowboy who hated wearing glasses, so all his cars have prescription windshields?

This Dallas oilman had a bankroll so big, he had to have it put on microfilm before he could stuff it in his pocket. A Houston playgirl seated herself next to him in the bar. Soon they were talking business. In the middle of it all, she asked the chap, "Pardon me, how much did you say your name was?"

# Traffic

*(see also Accidents, Automobiles, Cars, Driving)*

The warning sign on upper Broadway says: "Beware of children going to and from school—especially if they are driving cars."

———

The new laws warn you to drive carefully: "The life you save may belong to a pedestrian on his way to remove his car from the parking place you're looking for."

———

The main trouble with the straight and narrow path is, there's no place to park.

———

This guy was stopped so often by traffic cops, they finally gave him a season ticket.

———

The police are really cracking down on bad drivers. I know one guy who got fifty traffic tickets. He used to drive one of those fancy foreign sports cars, but the cops finally caught up with him. Not only did they take away his driver's license, they even deported his car.

———

Listen, the judgment of a traffic cop is not always right, but his customers are always wrong.

———

I was out driving one afternoon when a traffic policeman pulled me over to the side. "Hey," the cop yelled. "Do you know you were doing sixty miles an hour?" I answered, "That's ridiculous, officer. I'm not even on the road an hour."

———

I'm such a lousy driver, would you believe I got two tickets on my written exam?

———

One way to solve the traffic problem in New York would be to keep all the cars that are not paid for off the streets.

———

When a New Yorker is in a hurry, he doesn't take a taxi, he walks.

———

A cab driver picked up a passenger who wore a hearing aid. The cabbie said, "I guess just about all of us have something the matter. Take me, for instance. I can hardly see!"

# UFOs

Suddenly we have lots of new reports of UFO sightings. "What's new about it?" my brother asks. "All I have to do is come home loaded one night. You never saw so many unidentified flying objects thrown at me—and my wife never misses."

———

A Martian landed in New York and found he had broken one of the little wheels on his spaceship. That night, while passing the deli, he noticed some bagels in the window. "I'd like to buy some of those wheels," he told the manager. "Those aren't wheels," he was told. "They're bagels. You eat them." The manager sliced a bagel in half and offered it to him. After taking a bite, the Martian beamed, "Hey, this is great. It should be good with cream cheese and lox."

———

Two UFOniks come to Brooklyn and land on an apartment house in Flatbush. They see all the TV antennae, and one says, "Hey, dig the beautiful broads!"

———

A spaceship from Mars tried to land in New York City but couldn't find a parking place, so the ship moved to New Jersey.

———

A spaceman brought his contraption down in Atlantic City just as a slot machine player hit the jackpot. As the shower of silver dollars poured out noisily, the Martian patted the machine and said, "Buddy, you'd better do something about that cold."

———

The visitor from outer space was kissing and hugging a traffic signal when it quickly changed from GO to STOP. The visitor snickered, "I should have known. Earth women are all teases."

———

If you think the space program is expensive now, just wait till the astronauts' union is formed and they start charging by the mile.

———

"Your mission on Earth," said the moon boss to the explorers, "will be to capture two earthlings and bring them back alive." The moon men zipped down to Earth and brought back two gasoline pumps. "Great," said the moon boss. "You accomplished your mission. We'll breed them and soon there will be slaves for all." The captain of the spaceship interrupted, "You're all nuts. Can't you see they brought back two male pumps?"

An Earthnik landed on Mars and saw a large crowd gathered around one store. There was a machine in the window that was delivering babies. Every time this Martian pressed a button, a newborn baby arrived. "What kind of thing is this?" he asked one onlooker. "That's our baby machine. Don't you make babies like that on Earth?" replied the alien. The Earthnik said, "Are you kidding? On Earth we use a completely different method: A couple gets married, goes on a honeymoon, and nine months later they have a baby." The alien said, "Up here, that's how we make trucks."

## Ugly People
*(see also Faces)*

I asked my friend why he picked the ugliest girl in town for his wife. "The beauty of marrying a homely girl," he explained, "is that in twenty years, you know she'll be pretty as ever."

My neighbor asked her older sister, "How come you're marrying this man? He's so old and wrinkled!" My sister said, "Yeah, but so's his money."

If you're not pretty, cultivate your voice; at least you'll look better on the telephone.

Like I said to my neighbor, "You have beautiful children. Thank God your wife cheats."

Two men met at a cocktail party, and as they stood talking, one glanced across the room and remarked, "Get a load of that ugly broad—a nose like a pomegranate, walks like a cow, and a backside to match." The other guy said, "Hey, that's my wife." The first guy said, "Oh, I'm sorry!" The husband said, "*You're* sorry!"

After one week of marital bliss, a wife asked her husband, "Will you love me when I'm old and wrinkled?" He said, "Of course I do!"

The shorties use their height to their advantage: They walk under turnstiles. If they're superstitious, they walk under black cats.

The baldies have it made: They don't need barbers. They comb their head with a twirl, and they are proud that they have a beautiful head of skin.

I'm tired of all those beauty pageants like Miss Universe, Miss America, Miss Bagel . . . How about a Miss Ugly contest? Like my neighbor: She has Early American features—she looks like a buffalo. The only person who ever asked her to get married was her mother. . . . A Peeping Tom reached into her window and pulled *down* the shade.

———

A sure winner in the men's division is the guy who sent his picture to the lonely hearts club. They not only sent it back, they touched it up first. They returned it with the explanation that they were lonely, not desperate. . . . When his girl kisses him, she closes her eyes—she *has* to! . . . He was an ugly baby. He used to go to parties and play Spin the Bottle, where if you didn't want to kiss anybody, you had to give that person a quarter. Would you believe by the time this guy was twelve, he owned his own home?

———

The contestants for the Miss Ugly contest are coming in by the thousands. . . . I like the very religious one: People look at her and say, "Oh, God!" . . . Men look at her and dress her with their eyes. . . . She got her nose from her father—he's a plastic surgeon. . . . At one time this girl was considered an ugly duckling. Now she's not considered at all. . . . I'll tell you one thing: This girl makes a fortune by renting herself out for Halloween parties.

———

Another girl is so ugly:

She's proud of the fact that the police put her picture in all the jails in the country to discourage sex offenders.

The only man who thinks she's a ten is her shoe salesman.

When she walks into a bank they turn off the camera.

She spends hours at the beauty parlor just for estimates.

Her passport pictures come out nice.

———

My doctor made me a deal. He'll take out my appendix if I'll take out his daughter.

———

My uncle is not too pretty. Customs made him put somebody else's picture on his passport. He's got the kind of face that grows on you—if you're an ape.

———

First prize goes to my friend Charlie: If you really believe man is made in the image of God, one look at him would make you an atheist. His photographs do him an injustice—they look like him.

———

My sister laments, "You've heard of body language? I have nothing to say."

———

A man told his drinking buddy, who had been badly beaten: "I think you were pretty stupid to call that guy's girlfriend ugly, Ralph." "I didn't call her ugly," Ralph said. "I just asked if she was allowed on the furniture."

# United Nations

*(see also Diplomats)*

Every time there's trouble in the world, somebody calls the U.N., and the U.N. is finally doing something about it. They're getting an unlisted number.

---

We have to be careful cutting back on foreign aid to Third World nations. They need our aid to buy Soviet weapons.

---

The delegates at the U.N. read an eye chart looking for a hidden meaning.

---

Diplomacy is the art of saying "Nice doggie" until you have time to pick up a rock.

---

The art of diplomacy is to say nothing, especially when you're speaking.

---

I asked the diplomat, "What's your favorite color?" He said, "Plaid."

---

A diplomat is one who thinks twice before saying nothing.

---

I have come to the conclusion that one useless man is called a disgrace, two are called a law firm, and three or more are called the U.N.

---

Diplomacy is the ability to take something and act as though you are giving it away.

---

A real diplomat is one who can cut his neighbor's throat without having his neighbor notice it.

---

I asked one U.S. diplomat how he felt working in the U.N. He said, "It's okay, except that there are too many foreigners."

---

The secretary of the U.N. said to the American ambassador one morning: "I have checked all the cables, newspapers, and TV. There is no trouble in the world. What will we do?" The American ambassador consoled him: "Don't worry, something will happen. I have faith in human nature."

---

Someone who saw a camel for the first time exclaimed: This must be a horse designed by a U.N. committee!

---

Four U.N. diplomats meet a gorgeous blonde at a reception at the U.N. The Frenchman kisses her hand. The Englishman shakes her hand. The American puts his arms around her.

The Russian cables home for instructions.

The U.N. was started after World War II to make everybody act like friends. So far they're all acting like relatives.

The U.N. says it wants all the countries in the world to live as one big family. If you want to take my family as an example, they've succeeded.

The best way to describe the U.N. is to compare it to an ex-girlfriend of mine: All the parts are there, but they just can't get together.

Diplomatic language has a hundred ways of saying nothing but no way of saying something.

The U.N. keeps the peace all right. In all the years of its existence, there has never been a war in the U.N. building.

A true diplomat is always ready to lay down your life for *his* country.

A typical American is somebody who feuds with his neighbors, argues with his employees, disagrees with minority groups, yells at his family—and can't understand why the people at the U.N. can't get along with each other.

A diplomat is a person who can tell you to go to hell in such a way that you actually look forward to the trip.

The best definition of a diplomat is the story about two men talking in a bar when the subject of Green Bay, Wisconsin, came up. The first guy said, "It's a real nice place." The other said, "What's nice about it? Only things ever come out of Green Bay are the Packers and ugly prostitutes." The first said, "Hold it, you punk. My wife comes from Green Bay." The other replied, "Oh, does she? What position does she play?"

A diplomat must learn to yawn without opening his mouth.

Diplomacy is the art of letting someone have your way.

A good diplomat never stands between a dog and a hydrant.

One thing about those foreign delegates: They are all sincere—whether they mean it or not.

An optimist believes that at the U.N. every man is as honest as the next guy. A pessimist believes the same thing.

———

The U.N. had an art exhibition. I admired one abstract painting. I looked at it from all angles, and I must admit it's the best picture of the U.N. I ever saw: No matter which way you look at it, it doesn't make sense.

———

The credo of the U.N.: "I regret that I have but one lie to give for my country."

———

A lot of diplomats will do anything to help their country—except shut up.

———

The trouble is, the world is getting smaller. The Near East is too near, and the Far East isn't far enough.

———

The U.N. is a strange world. A man gets up, speaks for an hour, and nobody listens to him, but as soon as he sits down, everybody disagrees with him.

## Vacations and Travel

Let's face it: Vacations aren't any fun unless you can go someplace you can't afford.

———

A European vacation is a great equalizer. People come back from them just as broke as their neighbors who couldn't afford to go.

———

A well-organized vacation is having your two weeks run out before your traveler's checks do.

———

Vacation is a time when you get away from being cooped up with your wife and kids in a tiny apartment, and spend two weeks with them cooped up in a tiny motel room.

———

My wife and I are making vacation plans. She decides where to go and I decide how to pay for it. We're saving a fortune on our trip to China this year—we're not going.

———

Over 30 million Americans will go camping this summer. They'll also go camping this winter—they can't afford to pay rent.

———

Two women were meowing at lunch: "I was talking to Sylvia the other day about vacation plans, and she tells me that you aren't going to Paris this summer." The other lady said, "No, that was last year. This year we're not going to Rome."

———

Two of my friends just got back from a wild cruise. The highest ranking officer aboard ship was the wine steward.

———

One thing I've learned about vacationing by car: The clean restrooms are all locked. . . . . It's always great to get back home. At my age real security is knowing that the bathroom is in the same place every night.

———

One motel on the road was murder. Nothing was free. I even had to rent a pen to sign the register.

———

My neighbor told me, "I was looking for a place to board the dog while I'm on vacation, and one kennel offers air conditioning, gourmet food, and lots of petting and affection. I was so impressed, I'm sending the dog on vacation and I'm staying at the kennel."

Vacation: That's a system whereby people who are merely tired become exhausted!

What I like about a vacation is it fills your year. If you take your vacation in August, you get your pictures back in September, your bills back in October, your health back in November, and your luggage back in December.

If you look like your passport photo, you aren't well enough to travel.

There's a book that tells you where to go on your vacation: It's called a checkbook.

What most Americans would like is a dollar that will go a long way—but won't go very fast.

My neighbor told me: "We just got back from Europe. We spent most of our time studying ruins—our budget."

It's summer vacation time: Everybody goes to the beach for the same reason: hoping to see a body in worse shape than theirs. That's why I like to go to the beach: It makes everybody else so happy.

There may not be anything new under the sun, but there's a lot more of it showing on the beach.

I get sunburned easily. Whenever I lie in the sun, I can just hear the excited voices of hundreds of mosquitoes exclaiming: "Oh, boy, a barbecue!"

My neighbor told me he's having a great vacation this year. He bought a new car and put all his kids in the backseat—and he's taking a cruise.

My nephew told me, "Money is pretty tight this year. About all we can afford for a vacation is a roll of film, some suntan lotion, and maybe a couple of nights in the Laundromat."

They say if you take a European vacation it shows you've got money. Wrong—it shows you had money.

Summertime is the greatest for the nice long weekend motor trips—one day driving and two days folding the road maps.

---

Please make this a safe summer. Riding on the parkway is like Russian roulette: You never know which driver is loaded.

---

I was lucky on my trip last summer: They had the highway open while the detour was being fixed.

---

One nice thing about going on a summer trip: After it's over, you're still reminded of your memories for years to come—usually right around the first of each month.

---

On our last trip we stopped at the Hilton, the Intercontinental, and a lot more hotels whose names I'd like to tell you, but at the moment those towels are still in the laundry.

---

My wife likes to take home a souvenir whenever we vacation. Other people invite friends over to see the slides of their trip. We invite them over to see our ashtrays!

---

When you visit a relative, it's because you want family ties. When relatives spend their vacations at your house, it's because they're freeloading bums.

Two ladies were relaxing at the pool. "How about a cocktail before dinner?" one suggested. "It's vacation time." The other said, "No, thanks, I never drink." "Why not?" "Well, in front of my children, I don't think it's right, and when I'm away from my children—who needs it?"

---

While visiting Alaska, this girl met a man, and married him after a very brief acquaintance. I asked her how come their courtship was so short. She explained, "When it was dark enough to park, it was too cold. And when it was warm enough, it was too light."

---

My neighbor told me he's going to the usual place for his summer vacation: to a bank for a loan.

---

The husband said, "I can hardly wait for our vacation." The wife agreed, "It will be good to get away." He said, "Yeah! Forget about rising utility bills and house payments." She said, "Forget about the way food prices are going up." He: "Forget about Social Security rates and property taxes." She: "Forget about gas prices and airfare." He: "Forget about the vacation!"

---

Two expectant fathers were nervously pacing the floor of the maternity ward waiting room. "What tough luck," one grumbled. "This had to happen on my vacation." The other groaned, "What the hell are you complaining about? I'm on my honeymoon!"

———

My friend spent two weeks fishing at an expensive resort and didn't get a bite, but on the last day of his vacation, he caught one fish. "See that fish?" he said to a bystander. "It cost me a thousand dollars." The man said, "Ain't you lucky that you didn't catch two."

———

A couple I know decided to spend their vacation at a nudist camp. "What are you going to do there?" I asked. She said, "Oh, I guess it's a good way to air our differences."

———

It's hard to settle down when you return from vacation. It's even harder to settle up.

———

There's an increasing need for three-week vacations: That would give your postcards time to reach home before you do.

———

The person who said you can't take it with you never saw a camper truck packed for a vacation.

———

My neighbor told me, "We're thinking about separate vacations this year. My wife could go to Canada, the kids could go to Disneyland, and I could go bankrupt."

Nobody remembers exactly when we lost control of the economy, but it might have been when we discovered that fifty weeks of work couldn't pay for a two-week vacation.

———

There are certain basic rules of travel you should be aware of. Like, when they say you should travel light, they mean your suitcase, not your wallet.

———

Husbands are like traveler's checks: You can't leave home without them.

———

Last year we discovered a vacation spot that was convenient, comfortable, relaxing, informal, and priced right. It's called the living room.

———

A husband and wife walked into a hotel in Vermont and asked the desk clerk, "Do you take children?" The clerk replied, "No, we take only cash and credit cards."

———

My vacation plans are very simple: My boss tells me when I can go, and my wife tells me where.

———

All the trouble in the Garden of Eden started when Eve bit into a piece of fruit. I had the same problem in Mexico.

# Wall Street

*(see also Money)*

Wall Street is on the up side. They've even relaxed security and taken the locks off the upper floor windows.

———

The stock market is jumping all around. I've been poor before and I've been rich before, but never in the same day.

———

You've got to look at the positive side of Wall Street: The sound, secure investments of today are the tax losses of tomorrow.

———

Stocks no longer provide for your old age, but they do hasten its arrival.

———

My stockbroker is a golf nut. One day he called me and said, "Guess what? I just broke eighty!" I replied, "I know. I'm one of them."

———

I don't want to criticize my broker's recommendations, but Wall Street just voted him Man of the Year—1929!

———

The stock market has its own unique system of checks and balances: For every nut selling, there's another nut buying.

———

I had a big talk with my broker yesterday and I feel much better about the market. We set up a calculated, all-encompassing program designed to reach certain investment goals during the next five years—like getting even.

———

Do you think this means anything? My broker has stopped wearing his crash helmet!

———

My neighbor was reading the stock market report and said to his wife: "Remember that stock I was going to retire on at fifty-five? Well, my retirement age is now 350!"

———

Then there's the sad story of the Wall Street broker whose migraine just split two for one.

———

I know you can't take it with you, but the way things are going, I think my stocks will get there before I do.

———

My broker has been wrong so many times, he's been offered a job as a government economist.

———

One guy buys a hundred shares at ten; the stock goes up to twenty and he wants to sell. The broker says, "This stock is now a better buy at twenty than it was at ten." The guy says, "Gee, if I had only waited."

———

My stocks aren't listed on the business pages anymore. I now find them in the obituary column.

———

My broker is a professional consultant. That's a guy who knows fifty ways to make love, but can't get a girl.

———

I don't want to say my brokerage firm has a closed mind but the company suggestion box is a garbage disposal.

———

The minister was counseling a young stockbroker: "You know, the Lord works in mysterious ways." The broker said, "I know that, Reverend, but when he plays the market, is there some method he uses?"

You can always tell when prosperity has come back to Wall Street: You look on a window ledge and see more pigeons than brokers.

———

I saw a very disturbing sign at the financial center: It said, THE BUCK DROPS HERE.

———

They sure make a lot of money on Wall Street. Down there, if your income isn't six figures, you qualify for food stamps.

———

I asked my uncle, "If your broker keeps losing your money, why do you stay with him?" He said, "I never have to worry about taxes."

———

A stock market investor is someone who is alert, informed, attuned to the economic heartbeat of America—and cries a lot.

———

Wall Street is the only place you can take a bath without water. Forget about prayer in school—what we need is a prayer in the stock market.

———

The stock market has made everybody money-mad: I'm mad because they took my money away.

———

What's the difference between a rich man and a poor man? A rich man has a wallet crammed with bills. A poor man has a wallet crammed with bills, too—unpaid ones.

———

The stock market has really caused inflation. Even barbers have to charge more now—the faces are longer.

———

My neighbor cried to me: "My financial situation is now fluid. Everything's going down the drain!"

———

Frankly, I've stopped accepting calls from my broker. I kept getting obscene prices.

———

After ten years in the business, my broker has learned to do one thing very well: apologize.

———

Actually, I'm not sure what's going on in the market today, but my broker just moved his office to a crap table in Atlantic City.

———

I don't know if it's true, but I hear they're moving the Wailing Wall from Israel to Wall Street.

———

Life has become much more sophisticated. Years ago it was ghosts and goblins and monsters and witches that scared you. Now it's the Dow Jones Average.

———

They say the institutions are getting back in the market. What bothers me is that Bellevue is an institution—and so is Leavenworth.

———

Because of oil, the Arabs have most of their wealth in the ground. Because of the stock market, so do we.

———

Two New York Stock Exchange officers were comparing notes one morning. "Boy, I wish I had a secretary like Klein's got," said one. "Why?" asked his friend. "Do you think she fools around?" The first said, "Are you serious? Last week she made the NYSE's most active list."

———

I take a philosophical view of things. Like, if God had intended us to be rich, he never would have given us the stock market.

———

My mother taught me never to get mixed up with bad company. So did the stock market.

———

The only difference between the current stock market and the *Titanic* is that the *Titanic* had a band.

———

My broker called me and said, "I think you should buy a thousand shares of this company." I asked, "Why should I buy them?" He said, "Because it's the only way I can sell mine."

———

The ninety-five-year-old multimillionaire was still looking to make more. He met with his financial adviser, who told him excitedly, "I just found out about an investment I can make for you that will double your money in five years!" The old man screamed, "Five years? Are you kidding? At my age I don't even buy green bananas!"

———

What a country! Where else can you see somebody invest in the stock market with a welfare check?

———

Even now my broker called with a hot tip. He's not worried. He got out of the market a month ago—and they are still looking for him.

———

I have an incompetent broker. He jumped out of a basement window.

———

The more you visit your stockbroker today, the more you'll visit your pawnbroker tomorrow.

———

# Women and Women's Lib

Would you believe women still want equal rights? What do they mean, equal? Women who want to be equal to men lack ambition.

———

A group of women's libbers was demonstrating outside the White House as the president was about to leave. One woman cried out, "Free women!" The prez hollered back, "Marvelous! Do you deliver?"

———

A career woman is one who would rather go out and take orders than stay home and be boss.

———

Marriage is a lot like the U.S. Constitution: A man begins by laying down the law to his wife—and ends up accepting all her amendments.

———

My neighbor's wife cries: "If you do housework for $200 a week, that's domestic service. If you do it for nothing, that's matrimony."

———

Listen, anyone who believes a woman's place is in the kitchen hasn't tasted my wife's cooking.

———

When my mother married my father, a promise was made to love, honor, and obey. And my mother did her very best to make sure my dad kept that promise.

———

Women's lib came up with a very interesting argument: If God was satisfied with Adam, how come he made Eve so different?

———

My aunt says, "When it comes to taxes, women are equal."

———

If it's true that men are such beasts, this must account for the fact that most women are animal lovers.

———

To a smart girl, men are no problem—they're the answer.

———

Sex appeal is fifty percent what you've got and fifty percent what people think you've got.

———

Women are a problem, but they're the kind of problem I enjoy wrestling with.

———

That no two women are exactly alike is proven by the fact that when two members of the gentle sex feel sorry for each other, the chances are one has a baby and the other one hasn't.

My niece tells me, "What's the hang-up about whether we're supposed to dress for men or women? With me, it's simple: I dress for women and undress for men."

———

My aunt claims: "A woman is like a tea bag: You never know her strength until you drop her in hot water."

———

They caution pregnant women not to drink alcohol. It may harm the baby. I think it's ironic: If it weren't for alcohol, most women wouldn't be that way.

———

I'm always attracted to older women. They don't slap as hard.

———

My sister said about her stockbroker: "If it weren't for his money, he wouldn't have any personality at all."

———

My sister again: "Love is more important than money. I intend to wait until the right millionaire comes along. I'll wear my long, low-cut gown—that'll show them a thing or two."

———

A woman's age is like the speedometer on a used car: You know it's been set back, but you don't know how much.

———

If there hadn't been women, we'd still be squatting in a cave eating raw meat. We made civilization in order to impress our girlfriends.

———————

My neighbor: "Women's lib sure has changed our way of thinking. I used to believe that old maxim, Never send a boy to do a man's job. Today you'd better send a woman!"

———————

I won't say some of today's women dress scantily, but I know a doctor who went crazy trying to vaccinate one woman in a place where it wouldn't show.

———————

The lady pressed a gun in the doctor's ribs. "Crime doesn't pay," he lectured her. She answered, "Well, neither does housework, buster, so hand over your wallet."

———————

My aunt claims: "Nowadays, if a woman says she sits around all day talking to her plants, it could mean her electronic plant in Pennsylvania and her textile plant in New York."

———————

My niece says her husband gave her a household hint on what to do with her old clothes: Wear them.

———————

My sister cried to me: "With my facelift, my only shock was finding that the one underneath looked even worse."

One mother I know has a real problem. She has two daughters: One is mad at her because she won't let her wear a bra yet, and the other is mad because she won't let her throw hers away.

———————

Women's lib means opening the door for a lady and standing aside so she can rush in and take the job you're after.

———————

Generally speaking, I think a woman's mind is cleaner than a man's. It has to be—she changes it more often.

———————

My aunt: "I'm a firm believer in loyalty. I think when a woman reaches an age she likes, she should stick with it."

———————

Frankly, I think no woman will ever be elected president. They never reach the legally required age!

———————

"I'm joining the women's lib movement," my aunt told me. "I want to get married and not have to work anymore."

———————

I think women are better at math. Only a woman will divide her age by two, double the price of her dress, triple her husband's salary, and add five years to the age of her best friend.

The first girl asked, "Wouldn't you like to be liberated?" The second girl said, "No, I'd much rather be captured."

___

My aunt claims: "There are two kinds of male chauvinists: those who think men are superior to women, and those who think women are inferior to men."

___

My sister reminds us: "Just desserts—that's a man marrying a woman because he wants someone to cook and keep house, and then discovering she married him for the same reason."

___

My sister-in-law has a one-sided opinion: "It has been said that women are more irritable than men. Maybe so, but the reason is probably that men are more irritating."

___

Listen to my sister: "The reason that few females play golf is that we women have more important things to lie about."

## Worst Jokes

SHE: The baby has swallowed the matches. HE: Here, use my lighter.

___

The day after the bank robbery, the teller phoned the man and said, "Your pictures are ready."

___

"I'm glad I wasn't born in France," my friend said. "Why?" I asked. "I can't speak French."

___

The doctor opened the window wide and said, "Stick your tongue out the window." I said, "What for?" He said, "I'm mad at my neighbors!"

___

Last night I ordered a whole meal in French, and even the waiter was surprised. It was a Chinese restaurant.

___

They showed real old movies on the plane. Even the pilot wouldn't get on— he had already seen the picture.

___

A duck, a frog, and a skunk wanted to go to the movies. The admission was one dollar. Which one of the three couldn't afford it? The skunk. Why? The duck had a bill, the frog had a greenback, but the skunk had only a scent.

___

The nice lady said to the young man, "Are you the brave little boy who jumped into the icy river and saved my boy from going over that horrible waterfall?" "Yes, I am, ma'am, I sure am." "What did you do with his mittens?"

___

My neighbor told me, "My pioneer great-grandfather went west in a covered wagon. He was a rugged man, but he died after having his ears pierced." I asked, "How could he die from having his ears pierced?" My neighbor explained, "They were pierced by an Indian's arrow!"

———————

Another neighbor told me, "My brother just opened a shop." I asked, "How's he getting on?" He said, "Not very well. It wasn't his shop."

———————

The penalty for bigamy is two mothers-in-law.

———————

My uncle's cat committed suicide: shot herself in the head nine times.

———————

What would you do if you were alone in a jungle and an elephant charged you? Pay him!

———————

Who knows if it's true: Benjamin Franklin's wife was responsible for his famous discovery. When he told her he was going to try to harness the electricity of lightning, she cried: "Go fly a kite!"